INTRODUCING
PSYCHOLOGICAL RESEARCH

Also by Philip Banyard

PSYCHOLOGY: THEORY AND APPLICATIONS (*with Nicky Hayes*)

APPLYING PSYCHOLOGY TO HEALTH

INTRODUCING PSYCHOLOGICAL RESEARCH

Sixty Studies that Shape Psychology

Philip Banyard and Andrew Grayson

NEW YORK UNIVERSITY PRESS
Washington Square, New York

First published in the U.S.A. in 1996 by
NEW YORK UNIVERSITY PRESS
Washington Square
New York, N.Y. 10003

Library of Congress Cataloging-in-Publication Data
Introducing psychological research : sixty studies that shape
psychology / edited by Philip Banyard and Andrew Grayson.
p.   cm.
Includes bibliographical references and index.
ISBN 0–8147–1275–4
1. Psychology—Research.   2. Psychology, Experimental.
3. Psychology—History.   I. Banyard, Philip, 1953–   .
II. Grayson, Andrew, 1963–   .
BF76.5.I58   1996
150'.72—dc20   95–42254
                                                      CIP

Printed in Great Britain

CONTENTS

List of Figures   xiv

List of Tables   xvii

Preface   xx

Acknowledgements   xxii

PART I: SOCIAL PSYCHOLOGY   1

1   Social Pressure   3

EIGHT OUT OF TEN OWNERS SAID THEIR CATS PREFERRED IT   5
■ ASCH, S.E. (1955). Opinions and social pressure.
Scientific American, 193, 31–35.

HELPING BEHAVIOUR   11
■ PILIAVIN, I.M., RODIN, J.A. & PILIAVIN, J. (1969).
Good samaritanism: An underground phenomenon?
Journal of Personality and Social Psychology, 13, 289–99.

BE A GOOD BOY AND DO AS YOU ARE TOLD   17
■ MILGRAM, S. (1963). Behavioral study of obedience.
Journal of Abnormal and Social Psychology, 67, 371–78.

2   Social Cognition   24

IS SHE REALLY GOING OUT WITH HIM?   25
■ NISBETT, R.E., CAPUTO, C., LEGANT, P. & MARECEK, J.
(1973). Behaviour as seen by the actor and as seen by
the observer.
Journal of Personality and Social Psychology, 27, 154–64.

I'M NOT PREJUDICED, BUT...   33
■ LAPIERE, R.T. (1934). Attitudes vs. actions.
Social Forces, 13, 230–37.

CHANGING OUR MINDS   37
■ FESTINGER, L. & CARLSMITH, J. M.(1959).
Cognitive consequences of forced compliance.
Journal of Abnormal and Social Psychology, 58, 203–10.

3 **Social Roles**   44

THE PRISON SIMULATION   45
■ HANEY, C., BANKS, W.C. & ZIMBARDO, P.G. (1973).
A study of prisoners and guards in a simulated prison.
Naval Research Review, 30, 4–17.

BEHAVIOUR IN GROUPS   51
■ BALES, R.F. (1955). How people interact in conferences.
Scientific American, 192, 31–35.

4 **Prejudice**   57

THE ROBBER'S CAVE   59
■ SHERIF, M. (1956). Experiments in group conflict.
Scientific American, 195, 54–58.

THE JIGSAW TECHNIQUE   65
■ ARONSON, E. & BRIDGEMAN, D. (1979). Jigsaw groups and
the desegregated classroom: In pursuit of common goals.
In E.Aronson (ed.), *Readings about the Social Animal*, 6th edn,
pp. 329–40; originally in *Personality and Social Psychology Bulletin, 5*,
438–66.

THE MINIMAL GROUP STUDIES   69
■ TAJFEL, H. (1970).
Experiments in intergroup discrimination.
Scientific American, 223, 96–102.

PART II: COMPARATIVE AND PHYSIOLOGICAL PSYCHOLOGY   75

5 **Learning**   77

THE FLIGHT OF THE KILLER PIGEONS   79
■ SKINNER, B.F. (1960). Pigeons in a pelican.
American Psychologist 15, 28–37.

LEARNING TO BE HELPLESS   84
■ SELIGMAN, M.E.P. & MAIER, S.F. (1967).
Failure to escape traumatic shock
Journal of Experimental Psychology, 74, 1–9.

TALKING TO THE ANIMALS   89
■ GARDNER, R.A. & GARDNER, B.T. (1969).
Teaching sign language to a chimpanzee.
Science, 165, 664–72.

6   Bio-psychology   94

A BRAIN OF TWO HALVES   96
■ SPERRY, R.W. (1968). Hemisphere deconnection and
unity in conscious awareness.
American Psychologist, 23, 723–33.

HOW DO YOU FEEL?   103
■ SCHACHTER, S. & SINGER, J.E. (1962). Cognitive, social
and physiological determinants of emotional state.
Psychological Review, 69, 379–99.

TO SLEEP, PERCHANCE TO DREAM   110
■ DEMENT, W. AND KLEITMAN, N. (1957). The relation of
eye movements during sleep to dream activity:
An objective method for the study of dreaming.
Journal of Experimental Psychology, 53, 339–46.

7   Ethology   116

THE COLONY OF MONKEYS   118
■ RAWLINS, R. (1979). Forty years of rhesus research.
New Scientist, (12 April 1979), 108–10.

A FISHY TALE   123
■ TINBERGEN, N. (1952). The curious behaviour of
the stickleback.
Scientific American, 187, 22–26.

RAT CITY: THE BEHAVIOURAL SINK   129
■ CALHOUN, J.B. (1962). Population density and
social pathology.
Scientific American, 206, 139–48.

PART III: HUMAN DIVERSITY   135

8   Gender   137

GIRLS JUST WANT TO HAVE FUN   139
■ KITTO, J. (1989). Gender reference terms: Separating
the women from the girls.
British Journal of Social Psychology, 28, 185–87.

LEARNING TO FAIL   143
■ DWECK, C.S., DAVIDSON, W., NELSON, S. & ENNA, B.
(1978). Sex differences in learned helplessness:
II. The contingencies of evaluative feedback in the
classroom and III. An experimental analysis.
Developmental Psychology, 14, 268–76.

RITES OF PASSAGE   150
■ KOFF, E. (1983). Through the looking glass of menarche:
What the adolescent girl sees.
In S. Golub (ed.), *Menarche*, pp. 77–86. Lexington, Mass: D.C. Heath.

9   Measuring Personality   156

MEASURING MASCULINITY AND FEMININITY   157
■ BEM, S. (1974). The measurement of psychological
androgyny.
Journal of Consulting and Clinical Psychology, 42, 155–62.

HOW GULLIBLE ARE YOU?   164
■ FORER, B.R. (1949). The fallacy of personal validation:
A classroom demonstration of gullibility.
Journal of Abnormal and Social Psychology, 44, 118–21.

10 Cultural Diversity   170

MIS-MEASURING INTELLIGENCE   171
■ GOULD, S.J. (1982). A nation of morons.
New Scientist (6 May 1982), 349–52.

BLACK DOLLS AND WHITE DOLLS   178
■ HRABA, J. & GRANT, G. (1970). Black is beautiful:
A re-examination of racial preference and identification.
Journal of Personality and Social Psychology, 16, 398–402.

BLACK IDENTITY   183
■ NOBLES, W. W. (1976). Extended self: Rethinking the
so-called Negro self-concept.
Journal of Black Psychology, 2.

11 Abnormality   189

YOU DON'T HAVE TO BE MAD TO WORK HERE. YOU DON'T EVEN   191
HAVE TO BE MAD TO BE IN HERE . . .
■ ROSENHAN, D.L. (1973). On being sane in insane places.
Science, 179, 250–58.

SHRINK WRAPPED: THE CHOICE OF THERAPIST 197
■ SMITH, M.L. & GLASS, G.V. (1977). Meta-analysis of
psychotherapy outcome studies.
American Psychologist, 32, 752–60.

THE THREE FACES OF EVE 202
■ THIGPEN, C.H. & CLECKLEY, H. (1954). A case of multiple
personality.
Journal of Abnormal and Social Psychology, 49, 135–51.

FEAR TODAY, GONE TOMORROW 208
■ LANG, P.J. & LAZOVIK, A.D. (1963). Experimental
desensitization of a phobia.
Journal of Abnormal and Social Psychology, 66, 519–25.

PART IV: DEVELOPMENTAL PSYCHOLOGY 215

12 Attachment 217

CAN YOU HEAR ME MOTHER? 219
■ HARLOW, H.F. (1959). Love in infant monkeys.
Scientific American, 200, 68–74.

FAMILY LIFE 223
■ HODGES, J. & TIZARD, B. (1989b). Social and family
relationships of ex-institutional adolescents.
Journal of Child Psychology and Psychiatry, 30, 77–97.

EMOTIONAL DEPRIVATION 229
■ KOLUCHOVÁ, J. (1972). Severe deprivation in twins:
A case study.
Journal of Child Psychology and Psychiatry, 13, 107–14.

13 Moral Development 233

THE MORAL PRINCIPLE OF JUSTICE 235
■ KOHLBERG, L. (1968). The child as a moral philosopher.
Psychology Today, 2, 25–30.

THE MORAL PRINCIPLE OF CARE 240
■ GILLIGAN, C. & ATTANUCCI, J. (1988). Two moral
orientations: Gender differences and similarities.
Merrill-Palmer Quarterly, 34, 223–37.

BASHING BOBO   246
■ BANDURA, A., ROSS, D. & ROSS, S.A. (1961).
Transmission of aggression through imitation of
aggressive models.
Journal of Abnormal and Social Psychology, 63, 575–82.

14 The Classic Approaches   253

I WANT A GIRL, JUST LIKE THE GIRL, THAT MARRIED DEAR
OLD DAD   254
■ FREUD, S. (1909). Analysis of a phobia of a
five-year-old boy.
In *The Pelican Freud Library* (1977), *Vol 8, Case Histories 1,* pp. 169–306.

PIAGET'S COGNITIVE APPROACH   261
■ SAMUEL, J. & BRYANT, P. (1984). Asking only one
question in the conservation experiment.
Journal of Child Psychology and Psychiatry, 25, 315–18.

THE TALE OF LITTLE ALBERT   268
■ WATSON, J.B. & RAYNER, R. (1920).
Conditioned emotional reactions.
Journal of Experimental Psychology, 3, 1–14.

15 Communication   275

THE DANCE OF THE NEONATES   277
■ CONDON, W.S. & SANDER, L.W. (1974). Neonate movement
is synchronized with adult speech: Interactional
participation and language acquisition.
Science, 183, 99–101.

LISTEN WITH MOTHER   284
■ FERNALD, A. (1985). Four-month-old infants prefer to
listen to motherese.
Infant Behavior and Development, 8, 181–95.

TALKING PROPER   289
■ LABOV, W. (1969). The logic of nonstandard English.
In P.P. Giglioli (ed.), *Languages and Social Context,* pp. 179–215.
Harmondsworth, England: Penguin; originally in *Georgetown
Monographs on Language and Linguistics, 22,* 1–31.

PART V: COGNITIVE PSYCHOLOGY   295

16 Memory   297

REMEMBERING PICTURES   299
■ BARTLETT, F.C. (1932). *Remembering: A Study in Experimental and Social Psychology*, pp. 177–85.

EYEWITNESS TESTIMONY   305
■ LOFTUS, E.F. & PALMER, J.C. (1974). Reconstruction of automobile destruction: An example of the interaction between language and memory.
Journal of Verbal Learning and Verbal Behavior, 13, 585–89.

MODELS OF MEMORY   310
■ CRAIK, F.I.M. & LOCKHART, R.S. (1972). Levels of processing: A framework for memory research.
Journal of Verbal Learning and Verbal Behavior, 11, 671–84.

17 Perception   317

WALKING OFF A CLIFF   319
■ GIBSON, E.J. & WALK, R.D. (1960). The 'visual cliff'.
Scientific American, 202, 64–71.

WHY DID THE ANTELOPE CROSS THE ROAD?   324
■ DEREGOWSKI, J.B. (1972). Pictorial perception and culture.
Scientific American, 227, 82–88.

WILL THE REAL RALPH RICHARDSON PLEASE STAND UP   331
■ YOUNG, A.W., HAY, D.C. & ELLIS, A.W. (1985). The faces that launched a thousand slips: Everyday difficulties and errors in recognizing people.
British Journal of Psychology, 76, 495–523.

18 Mind   338

AUTISM AND THEORIES OF MIND   340
■ BARON-COHEN, S., LESLIE, A.M. & FRITH, U. (1985). Does the autistic child have a 'theory of mind'?
Cognition, 21, 37–46.

I'M SORRY DAVE, I CAN'T DO THAT   345
■ Searle, J.R. (1980). Minds, brains, and programs.
The Behavioral and Brain Sciences, 3, 417–57.

PART VI: HEALTH PSYCHOLOGY   351

19 Stress and Coping   353

LIFE IS STRESS   355
■ HOLMES, T.H. & RAHE, R.H. (1967). The social
re-adjustment rating scale.
Journal of Psychosomatic Research, 11, 213–18.

STRESS? I CAN HANDLE IT!   360
■ BILLINGS, A.G. & MOOS, R.H. (1981). The role of
coping responses and social resources in attenuating
the stress of life events.
Journal of Behavioral Medicine, 4, 139–57.

AIDS AND UNCERTAINTY   367
■ WEITZ, R. (1989). Uncertainty and the lives of persons
with AIDS,
Journal of Health and Social Behavior, 30, 270–81.

20 Health Behaviour   373

TYPE A OR NOT TYPE A   375
■ FRIEDMAN, M. & ROSENMAN, R.H. (1959). Association of
specific overt behavior pattern with blood and
cardiovascular findings.
Journal of American Medical Association, 169, 1286–96.

IN CONTROL   381
■ LANGER, E.J. & RODIN, J. (1976). The effects of choice and
enhanced personal responsibility for the aged:
A field experiment in an institutional setting.
Journal of Personality and Social Psychology, 34, 191–98.

WHERE DOES IT HURT?   387
■ MELZACK, R. (1992). Phantom limbs.
Scientific American, April, 90–96

PART VII: METHODOLOGY   393

21 Frameworks and Approaches   395

DEMAND CHARACTERISTICS   395
■ ORNE, M.T. (1962). On the social psychology of the
psychological experiment: With particular reference to
demand characteristics and their implications.
American Psychologist, 17, 776–83.

DULL RATS AND BRIGHT RATS   402
■ ROSENTHAL, R. & FODE, K.L. (1963). The effect of experimenter bias on the performance of the albino rat.
Behavioral Science, 8, 183–89.

TEACHERS' BLOOMERS   408
■ ROSENTHAL, R. & JACOBSON, L. (1966). Teachers' expectancies: Determinants of pupils' I.Q. gains.
Psychological Reports, 19, 115–18.

WHO ARE PSYCHOLOGY'S SUBJECTS?   413
■ SEARS, D.O. (1986). College sophomores in the laboratory: Influences of a narrow data base on psychology's view of human nature.
Journal of Personality and Social Psychology, 51, 513–30

DISCOURSE ANALYSIS   419
■ POTTER, J. & EDWARDS, D. (1990). Nigel Lawson's tent: Discourse analysis, attribution theory and the social psychology of fact.
European Journal of Social Psychology, 20, 405–24.

A REPERTORY GRID STUDY OF MANAGERS   426
■ BROWN, C.A. & DETOY, C.J. (1988). A comparison of the personal constructs of management in new and experienced managers.
In F. Fransella & L. Thomas (eds), *Experimenting with Personal Construct Psychology.* London: Routledge and Kegan Paul.

Suggested Answers   433

Glossary   470

References   489

Index   498

LIST OF FIGURES

1.1	The percentage of correct answers for each critical trial	6
1.2	Percentage of errors made compared with the number of confederates	7
1.3	Layout of adjacent and critical areas of subway car	12
1.4	What the 'learner' said while he was being 'shocked'	19
1.5	The number of people who continued to obey the experimenter as the voltage increased	21
2.1	Number of situational and dispositional explanations given by subjects for their own and their best friend's choice of girlfriend	29
2.2	Cognitive dissonance: balancing a lie with a bribe	39
2.3	How enjoyable were the tasks?	41
3.1	The 'prisoners' in the prison simulation study	47
3.2	Average proportion of acts in the main areas of Bales' taxonomy	54
4.1	Sociograms of group structure	62
6.1	Visual pathways in the brain	98
6.2	Self reports of emotion in the various conditions of the Schachter and Singer experiment	107
6.3	The recall of dreams after REM and non-REM sleep	112
7.1	A summary history of all the social groups	120
7.2	The stages of mating in the stickleback	124
7.3	Effect of population density on behaviour	130
8.1	The selection of girls or women for high and low-status jobs	141
8.2	Feedback on correctness of work	145
8.3	Percentage of the total positive feedback and total negative feedback	146
8.4	Percentage of positive work-related feedback and negative work-related feedback	147

8.5	Drawing of a premenarcheal girl, time 1	151
8.6	Drawing of a premenarcheal girl, time 2	151
8.7	Drawing of a postmenarcheal girl, time 1	152
8.8	Drawing of a postmenarcheal girl, time 2	152
8.9	Drawing of a girl whose menarcheal status changed over course of study – premenarcheal, time 1	153
8.10	Drawing of a girl whose menarcheal status changed over course of study – postmenarcheal, time 2	153
9.1	Distribution of ratings	167
9.2	Acceptance of sketch items	168
10.1	Part six of examination Beta for testing innate intelligence	173
10.2	Choices of doll 'they want to play with' and 'nice doll'	180
11.1	Responses of medical staff to a simple request from pseudopatients	194
11.2	Letter from Eve	204
11.3	Snake avoidance scores for experimental and control groups	212
12.1	Number of adolescents with special same-sex friend	226
14.1	Average number of errors made by the children	265
14.2	Classical conditioning	269
15.1	Frame by frame microanalysis of sound and movement	281
16.1	Example of successive reproductions	300
16.2	Example of successive reproductions	302
16.3	Speed estimates for the different verbs used in the witness question	306
16.4	Response to the question 'Did you see any broken glass?'	307
16.5	Traditional multi-store model of short-term and long-term memory	311
17.1	The effect of context on the perception of a simple shape	318
17.2	The visual cliff	320
17.3	Pictorial depth perception	325
17.4	Ambiguous trident	326
17.5	Elephant drawing: split-view and top-view perspective	327
17.6	Some faces in a crowd often look a bit familiar even when they are not	333
18.1	Experimental scenario	342
18.2	Examples of Chinese characters	347
19.1	The experience of stress	361
20.1	Change in self-reports of the residents	385
20.2	Phantom limbs	388

21.1   Example of a T-maze   403
21.2   Average number of correct responses per rat per day   405
21.3   Subject populations and research sites in social
       psychology articles 1980   414
21.4   Nigel Lawson looking for a conspiracy   422
21.5   The structure of a repertory grid   427

LIST OF TABLES

1.1 Distribution of age and occupational types in the
Milgram study   18
2.1 Actors' and observers' estimates of the probability that
the actor would volunteer for a similar task, as a function
of whether or not the actor volunteered to entertain
the 'important visitors'   27
2.2 Number of entity (situational) reasons and dispositional
reasons given by subjects as explanations of their own
and their best friend's choices of girlfriend   29
2.3 Mean number of traits (out of possible 20) that were
ascribed to each stimulus person   30
2.4 Replies to the question, 'Will you accept members of the
Chinese race as guests in your establishment?'   35
2.5 Average ratings on interview questions for each condition   41
3.1 Average proportion of acts in each category of Bales'
taxonomy   54
6.1 Which hemisphere deals with sources of information   97
6.2 The conditions in the Schachter and Singer experiment   106
6.3 The self-report rating scale used by Schachter and Singer 106
6.4 The recall of dreams after REM and non-REM sleep   112
6.5 Results of dream-duration estimates after 5 or 15
minutes of rapid eye movements   113
8.1 Contingency table showing subjects' selections of
candidates for high and low-status jobs   141
9.1 Distribution of ratings   167
9.2 Distribution of 'true' responses   167
9.3 Group acceptance of sketch items   168
10.1 Percentage responses to the doll questions   180
10.2 Similarities between political and scientific colonialism 185
10.3 Differences between African and European world views   186

11.1   Judgement of all admission patients as to the likelihood
       that they are pseudopatients   192
11.2   Self-initiated contact by pseudopatients with
       psychiatrists, nurses and attendants   194
11.3   Rank ordering of ten types of therapy   199
11.4   The snake avoidance test: experimental design   211
11.5   Number of subjects who held or touched the snake
       during the avoidance test   211
11.6   Mean snake avoidance scale scores at Tests 2 and 3, mean
       change scores, and the Mann–Whitney U-test   212
12.1   Teachers' assessment of popularity with peers   225
13.1   Contingency table showing moral orientation by gender   243
13.2   Bandura's eight experimental groups   247
13.3   Mean aggression scores for experimental and control
       subjects   250
14.1   Mean errors of judgement for all the tests   265
14.2   Mean errors of judgement for all ages   266
15.1   Correspondence of infant movements with live speech   279
15.2   Correspondence of infant movements with recorded
       speech and non-speech sounds   280
16.1   Speed estimates for the verbs used in the estimation
       of speed question   306
16.2   Response to the question 'Did you see any broken glass?'   307
18.1   The percentage of correct responses to each of the four
       'Sally-Anne' questions   343
19.1   Characteristics of the sample   355
19.2   Social re-adjustment rating scale   357
19.3   Composition of method and focus of coping measures   362
19.4   Mean percentage of coping responses for each type of
       stressful event   364
19.5   AIDS   367
20.1   Type A and Type B behaviour patterns   374
20.2   A comparison of the subjects who displayed Pattern A
       and Pattern B behaviours   377
20.3   A comparison of blood and illness for Group A and
       Group B   378
20.4   Locus of control   382
20.5   Average scores for self-report, interviewer ratings and
       nurse ratings   384
21.1   Number of correct responses per rat per day   405

21.2 Mean time in minutes required to make correct response   406
21.3 Percentages of experimental and control Ss gaining 10, 20
      or 30 IQ points   410
21.4 Subject populations and research sites in social
      psychology articles in 1980 and 1985   414
21.5 Examples of the construct labels from new and
      experienced managers   430

PREFACE

Psychology is based on evidence from research studies. The main conclusions from these studies are often gathered together and put into a text book of psychology, but the details of the studies are usually left out. In this book we are presenting the details of sixty-four research studies that we think reflect the discipline of psychology. Our aim is to provide clear and accurate summaries of these important pieces of work in psychology so that you can weigh up the evidence for yourself and come to your own conclusions about what it means.

Students often do not have the opportunity to read original research articles. There are a number of reasons for this including the major problem that many of the important articles are not readily available. Even if you have access to a good library, then it takes a long time to search out the material you are looking for, and when you find the original research study it is often written in an impenetrable style.

We have tried to address these problems in this book. We are presenting the studies in a clear style (we hope), with enough details for you to be able to get a good idea of the research, and all in one volume so you do not have to trail round the local university library. The summaries are written with a brief introduction to provide some background for the research. Then we describe how the work was carried out and what was found, and we add some comments at the end to suggest one or two possible criticisms or further developments. Questions are included after each summary (with suggested answers at the back of the book) to help consolidate and develop what you have learnt.

Having read the summaries you should find the original papers relatively easy to follow, and we would encourage you to track down any that you find particularly interesting. Our feeling is that reading journal articles is a skill that needs to be developed, rather than something we can all just (magically) do. Indeed, one intention of this book is to provide an intermediate stage between standard textbooks and the original articles upon which those textbooks (and the entire discipline of psychology) are based.

In the limited space of one book we can only present a small number of studies. We have been incredibly selective, especially when you consider that thousands of pieces of research are published every year. We have chosen our studies to illustrate how psychology has developed over the years, and we have tried to present a range of studies that illustrate the breadth of psychological research covering the areas of biological psychology, comparative psychology, social psychology, human diversity, developmental psychology, cognitive psychology and health psychology. We have also taken care to include studies that reflect the wide range of methods used by psychologists in their research, from hard-nosed experimentation to in-depth interviewing and literature searches.

Psychological evidence is still mainly presented in the form of research papers, and the studies we have chosen reflect the way that psychology is being conducted and reported. The summaries are presented in parts that are based on the traditional research areas of the subject. It is worth noting, however, that the divisions between the different areas are sometimes quite arbitrary and most of the studies have relevance in more than one area.

We hope that this book encourages you to read further in the subject and to dig out some of the original papers if you can. We also hope that you enjoy reading the material and find it as provocative and interesting as we do. Most importantly, though, we hope that you develop your own opinions about psychology drawing on the evidence presented in this text.

We would like to acknowledge the support of our colleagues in the Psychology Division at The Nottingham Trent University who provide a positive and friendly working environment.

Phil Banyard
Andy Grayson

ACKNOWLEDGEMENTS

The authors and publishers wish to thank the following for permission to use copyright material.

Academic Press, Inc. for material from E.F. Loftus & J.C. Palmer, 'Reconstruction of auto-mobile destruction', *Journal of Verbal Learning and Verbal Behavior, 13*, 1974, Tables 1, 2 (pp. 306, 307). American Association for the Advancement of Science for material from W.S. Condon & L.W. Sander, 'Neonate movement is synchronized with adult speech: Interactional participation and language acquisition', *Science, 183*, 1974, Tables 1, 2, adapted, pp. 99–100, Figure 1, p. 100 (pp. 279–81). Copyright © 1974 American Association for the Advancement of Science; and D. L. Rosenhan, 'On being sane in insane places', *Science, 179*, 1973, Table 1. Copyright © 1973 American Association for the Advancement of Science (pp. 192, 194). American Medical Association for material from M. Friedman & R.H. Rosenman, 'Association of specific overt behaviour pattern with blood cardiovascular findings', *Journal of American Medical Association, 169*, 1959, Tables 1, 2. Copyright © 1959 American Medical Association (p. 377). American Psychological Association for material from P.J. Lang & A.D. Lazovik, 'Experimental desensitisation of a phobia', *Journal of Abnormal and Social Psychology, 66*, 1963, Tables 1, 2, 3, pp. 522, 523 (pp. 211–12); E.J. Langer & J. Rodin, 'The effects of choice and enhanced personal responsibility for the aged: A field experiment in an institutional setting', *Journal of Personality and Social Psychology, 34*, 1976, Table 1, p. 195 (p. 384); J. Hraba & G. Grant, 'Black is beautiful: A re-examination of racial preference and identification', *Journal of Personality and Social Psychology, 16*, 1970, Table 1, adapted, p. 399 (p. 180); an illustration from I. Piliavin, J. Rodin & J. Piliavin, 'Good samaritanism: An underground phenomenon?' *Journal of Personality and Social Psychology, 13*, 1969 (p. 12); Tables 2.1, 2.2, 2.3 from R.E. Nisbett, C. Caputo, P. Legant & J. Marecek, 'Behaviour as seen by the actor and as seen by the observer', *Journal of Personality and Social Psychology, 27*, 1973, Table 1, p. 157, adapted, Table 2, p. 159, adapted, and Table 5, p. 161. Copyright © 1963, 1976, 1970, 1969, 1973 by the American Psychological Association (pp. 27, 29, 30); and adapted tables from C.S. Dweck, W. Davidson, S. Nelson & B. Enna, 'Sex differences in learned helplessness', *Developmental Psychology, 14*, 1978, pp. 268–76 (pp. 145–47); Association for Child Psychology & Psychiatry for material from J. Hodges & B. Tizard, 'Social and family relationships of ex-institutional adolescents', *Journal of Child Psychology and Psychiatry, 30*, 1989, Elsevier, Table 11, p. 88, Figure 2, p. 89 (pp. 225–26); and J. Samuel & P. Bryant, 'Asking only one question in the conservation experiment', *Journal of Child Psychology and Psychiatry, 25*, 1984, Elsevier, Table 2, p. 317 (pp. 265–66). Behavioral Science for material from R. Rosenthal & K.L. Fode, 'The effect of experimenter bias on the performance of the albino rat', *Behavioral Science, 8*, 1963, Tables 1, 2, pp. 185, 186 (pp. 405–6). Cambridge University Press for illustrations from F.C. Bartlett, *Remembering: A Study in Experimental and Social Psychology*, 1932, pp. 178–80 (p. 302). Chapman & Hall for an illustration from P. Banyard & N. Hayes, *Psychology: Theory and Application*, 1994, p. 446 (p. 19). Elsevier Science Ltd for material from T.H. Holmes & R.H. Rahe, 'The social re-adjustment rating scale', *Journal of Psychosomatic Research, 11*, 1967, Table 3, p. 216 (p. 357); and S. Baron-Cohen, A.M. Leslie & U. Frith, 'Does the autistic child have a "theory of mind"?' *Cognition, 21*, 1985, Figure 1, p. 41 (p. 342). Sharon Golub for material from E. Koff, 'Through the looking glass of menarche: What the adolescent girl sees' from *Menarche*, ed. S. Golub, 1983, Figures 5.1a–c, 5.2a–c, pp. 80–4 (p. 151–53). Alexandra Milgram for material from S. Milgram, 'Behavioural study of obedience', *Journal of Abnormal and Social Psychology, 67*, 1963, Table 1 (p. 18). New Scientist for graphic from R. Rawlins, 'Forty years of rhesus research', *New Scientist, 82*, 1979, pp. 110 (p. 120). W.W. Norton & Company, Inc. for material from Stephen Jay Gould, *The Mismeasure of Man*, Figure 5.5, p. 211. Copyright © 1981 by Stephen Jay Gould (p. 173). Plenum Publishing Corporation for material from A.G. Billings & R.H. Moos, 'The role of coping responses and social resources in attenuating the stress of life events', *Journal of Behavioral Medicine, 4*, 1981, Tables 1, 3, pp. 146, 149 (pp. 362, 364). Psychological Reports and R. Rosenthal for material from R. Rosethal & L. Jacobson, 'Teachers' expectancies: Determinants of pupils' IQ gains', *Psychological Reports, 19*, 1966, Table 2, p. 117 (p. 410). Scientific American, Inc. for illustrations by Eric Mose, from N. Tinbergen, 'The curious behaviour of the stickleback', *Scientific American, 187*,

Dec. 1952, pp. 24, 25 (pp. 124, 125); by Carol Woike Donner from J.B. Deregowski, 'Pictorial perception and culture', *Scientific American*, *227*, Nov. 1972, pp. 83, 86 (pp. 325, 326, 327); by Sarah Love from Robert F. Bales, 'How people interact in conferences', *Scientific American*, *192*, March 1955, p. 35 (p. 54) and Muzafer Sherif, 'Experiments in group conflict', *Scientific American*, *195*, Nov. 1956, p. 57 (p. 62); and by Bunji Tagawa from John B. Calhoun, 'Population density and social pathology', *Scientific American*, *206*, Feb. 1962, pp. 140–1 (p. 130). Camera Press London for the photograph on p. 333; Popperfoto for the photograph on p. 422; and Philip Zimbardo for the photograph on p. 47.

Every effort has been made to trace all the copyright holders, but if any have been inadvertently overlooked the publishers will be pleased to make the necessary arrangement at the first opportunity.

PART I

SOCIAL PSYCHOLOGY

Social Psychology, as the label suggests, is concerned with the social side of human life. Social psychologists look at the numerous complex issues which surround human interaction and human relationships. They look at how the *individual* behaves rather than how groups behave because this is psychology, not social anthropology or sociology. However, the individual is studied against the background of the *social contexts* which both frame and direct their actions and experiences.

When we study social psychology it is important to bear in mind that we are at one and the same time the producers of, *and* the products of, the relationships, groups, cultures and societies we belong to. Society moulds us, but we also mould society. Indeed, one of the ongoing tensions in social psychology is how much importance to give to the individual or to the society in our explanations of social behaviour. In other words, when we are trying to understand why someone has done or said something (for example), do we look to that person or do we look to the society for the causes of that action? When someone does or says something, do their actions and words 'belong' to that person, or to the culture of which they are a part?

Intuitively we tend to say that it is the person that is really behind actions and words. We may acknowledge social constraints and influences, but in the end we believe that individuals are responsible for what gets done and what gets said. We see that their actions and words belong to them. Who or what else could they belong to?

However, this intuition may be a culturally specified thing. For a start, when we used the word 'we' in the previous paragraph we were probably talking about people in US and British cultures who place great

1

emphasis on the individual; not all cultures have this same emphasis. This perspective (we would argue) is very strong and ingrained within us, such that answering the 'who or what else could they belong to?' question is actually a very difficult thing to do.

So, let us just think more deeply for a minute about this idea of who owns what gets done and said. Take for example the actions of a police officer or of a judge. Many of the things that these people do are specifically set down for them by society. When a police officer says, '*I arrest you. Anything you say might be taken down in evidence . . .*' (or whatever it is that they say; both authors claim no direct personal experience of this situation), they are not really doing or saying their own thing. The same goes for a judge who says, '*I sentence you to five years in prison . . .*'. These people are fulfilling the requirements of roles, and doing and saying things that in a sense belong to all of us.

When you read the summaries of studies that are included in this part we would like you to bear these issues in mind. The topics that are covered (social pressure, social cognition, social roles, and prejudice) represent four cornerstones of traditional social psychology, and provide a good starting point for your own explorations of these sorts of questions.

1 SOCIAL PRESSURE

Social pressure is about how our actions can be influenced by others. It is an important area of social psychology because the findings from many studies on social pressure challenge some of our most deep-seated beliefs about our own autonomy. We like to think that we are true to ourselves in what we do and say, and that we only follow everyone else when we want to. But a number of social psychological investigations have suggested that we may be more susceptible to social pressure than we think, and two of these are summarised in this section. Asch (1955), for example, observed a proportion of his subjects going along with a strong majority decision about something even though that decision was blatantly wrong. And Milgram (1963) showed the extent to which ordinary people are susceptible to following the demands of an authority figure, even when those demands require them to do something which is morally indefensible.

There are many things that you might note about the studies in this chapter, but two things are particularly important. First, the studies are all concerned with *behaviour*. That is, they are direct studies of what subjects actually did in real situations. This is important because if you were to ask people how they would behave in situations like those set up by Milgram and Asch (Milgram actually did ask people this question), most people would give answers in line with their *beliefs* about their own autonomy; most people would predict that they would be unmoved by the social pressures that were exerted. For example, many people will say that advertisements have no effect on them, but advertisers know that this is not the case because an advertising campaign can dramatically increase the sales of a product. By studying behaviour, rather than opinion, Milgram and Asch were able to show that most people's predictions in this respect would be wrong!

Secondly we should note that although Milgram and Asch both studied actual behaviour in real situations, they were not studying

3

actual behaviour in *realistic* situations. By this we mean that the 'real situations' that were set-up were rather artificial, and somewhat removed from everyday experience. One thing which separates their situations from everyday life situations, is that in everyday life we are usually with other people who we know. We rarely find ourselves having to make decisions (for example) in the disorienting context of having no-one else around except complete strangers. Yet this is exactly what Asch's and Milgram's subjects had to do.

The study by Piliavin, Rodin & Piliavin (1969) has been included partly as a methodological contrast to the other two studies. This naturalistic experiment examined the way in which people behaved in a real-life setting (on a subway train in New York). It constitutes part of the tradition of work on *bystander apathy* which is most closely associated with Latané & Darley (1970), and which set out to understand the role of social influences on the decision we make to help people in trouble.

EIGHT OUT OF TEN OWNERS SAID THEIR CATS PREFERRED IT

■ ASCH, S.E. (1955). Opinions and social pressure.
Scientific American, 193, 31–35.

INTRODUCTION

How conformist are you? Do you say, and do, and think what you like, or are you influenced by the behaviour of people around you? The obvious answer is that we are all influenced to some extent by the people around us. If we were not, then we would not be a member of any social group. To belong to a group means to adjust to other people and to conform to at least some of the social norms of the group. But how, and to what extent we are influenced by others are important questions.

These questions about social conformity are important for many reasons, one of which is that some people try to manipulate our sociability for their own ends. These ends can be political or personal or commercial. Attempts are made to influence us to do and believe things because *'the electorate feels that...'*, or because *'everyone else I know is doing this...'* or because *'eight out of ten owners said their cats preferred it'*.

Asch was interested in the circumstances in which people would be most likely to conform. In his paper he refers to hypnosis as an extreme form of *suggestibility,* and suggests we should view everyday social behaviour as being susceptible to this suggestibility. Early studies conducted by, among others, Edward Thorndike had demonstrated that the opinions of students could be changed by giving an account of the (fictitious) opinions of a majority of their peers. Asch chose to look at the process more systematically.

THE STUDY

In the basic design of the Asch study, a group of seven to nine male college students were assembled in a classroom for a 'psychological experiment in visual judgement'. The experimenter told them that they would be comparing the lengths of lines. He showed them two white cards. On one was a vertical dark line, the standard which was to be judged. On the other card were three vertical lines of various lengths.

The subjects were asked to choose the one that was the same length as the standard. One of the three lines was actually the same length as the standard, and the other two were substantially different. The subjects were asked to give their judgements out loud and they did so in the order in which they were seated.

There was, in fact, only one subject in each group. The rest of the people giving judgements were *confederates* of the experimenter. The real subject would sit one from the end of the row, so all but one of the confederates gave their answers before them. On certain pre-arranged trials the confederates were instructed to give unanimous incorrect answers. The experimenters then looked to see the response of the one subject to this majority opinion. Each series of line judgements had 18 trials, and on 12 of these the majority gave unanimous incorrect answers.

RESULTS

The trials that were of interest, of course, were the 12 on which incorrect answers had been set up. On these, around 75 per cent of the 123 subjects went along with the majority at least once. Under the pressure

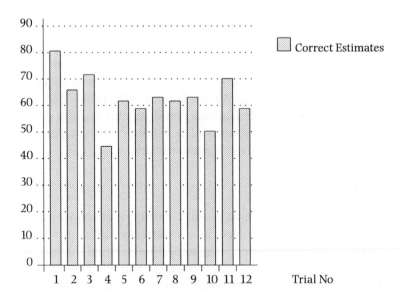

Figure 1.1 *The percentage of correct answers for each critical trial*

of the group, the subjects accepted the judgement of the majority on 37 per cent of the trials. Figure 1.1 shows the percentage of correct responses for each of the 12 test trials.

There were considerable individual differences with about 25 per cent of the subjects never agreeing with the majority, while some other subjects agreed with the majority most of the time. The subjects were interviewed after the study and their reasons for their behaviour were recorded. Among the *independent* individuals (Asch's description of the non-conformers), many had staunch confidence in their own judgement and a capacity to recover from doubt. Also, some believed that the majority was correct but continued to dissent because it was their obligation to 'call it as they saw it'. Among the *yielding* individuals (Asch's description of the people who conformed), some took the line '*I am wrong, they are right*', some suspected that the others were sheep following the first person to answer, but still yielded, and some saw it as a general sign of deficiency in themselves and tried to merge with the majority to cover up.

A number of variations of the study were carried out including adjusting the size of the majority group. The results of these studies are shown in Figure 1.2. It would appear that the conforming pressure peaks with three or four experimenter confederates. Another variation

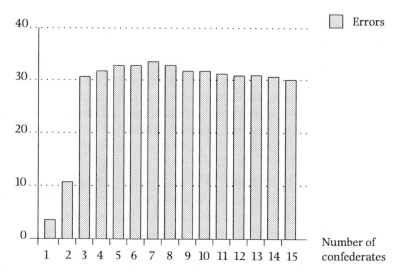

Figure 1.2 *Percentage of errors made compared with the number of confederates*

looked at the effect of a dissenting partner. In this case one of the confederates also disagreed with the majority, though half way through the trials the support of this other dissenter was removed. In half of the cases the support was removed by the person leaving the room, after which the conformity rate rose a little. In the other half, the dissenter 'went over' to the other side and started to agree with the majority. This *desertion* induced high levels of conformity in the subjects.

DISCUSSION

Some studies which give a further insight into Asch's work are the replications of the original study carried out by Perrin and Spencer. In the first replication (Perrin & Spencer, 1980), they used engineering undergraduates as the experimental confederates who had been instructed to give incorrect answers. The experimental participants were also engineering undergraduates. This replication produced no conformity, and the researchers initially concluded that the Asch study was 'a child of its time' (p. 405), a product of the pressures towards social conformity in the 1950s.

This finding, however, was challenged by Doms & Avermaet (1981), who pointed out that engineering students were particularly inclined to value accurate measurement, and so to use them as the participants in a study of conformity based on judgements of line length was to introduce a bias against conformity which did not show in replications performed with other students.

Following this, Perrin & Spencer (1981) performed two further replications which did not involve students. In one, the experimental confederates were probation officers, and the experimental research participants were young men on probation. The participants had an average age of 19, and so were very different from the majority group on the basis of three factors: age, professional status and power. In this case, Perrin and Spencer achieved conformity levels which were similar to those achieved by Asch. In the third replication, the experimental confederates were unemployed young men from inner London of Afro-Caribbean backgrounds, again with an average age of 19. The experimental participants were also Afro-Caribbean youths, and the experimenter was White. In this case, too, the researchers obtained conformity levels similar to those obtained by Asch.

In each of these cases, the level of conformity which was being displayed by the research participants made extremely good social sense, given the situation and context. Perrin and Spencer argued that conformity is actually a socially adaptive strategy, rather than a social problem. They concluded that those social problems which are associated with conformity arise from people exploiting the social responsibility of their fellow citizens, not from a personal weakness in the general population.

Returning to Asch's comments about hypnosis, it is worth noting that some psychologists (see for example Orne, 1966) believe that the behaviour of people in the presence of hypnotists is more a sign of social conformity and a desire to please the hypnotist than an indication of an altered state of consciousness (see also Orne, 1962, Chapter 21 of this volume).

Some general criticisms of the conformity research include:

(a) The research concentrates on the individual rather the situation they are in.
(b) The research invariably deals with very trivial tasks or judgements. For example 'how long is a line?'. Well who cares?
(c) The research does not distinguish between independent action (doing what you think is right) and anti-conformity (awkward for the sake of it).
(d) There is an underlying assumption that conformity is 'bad' and independence is 'good'.
(e) The research is usually conducted on students.

QUESTIONS

1   What features of the Asch study made the research participants more likely to conform?

2   What requests do you conform to and what requests do you resist? Make two lists and compare the differences.

3   List some positive aspects of conformity and some negative aspects of conformity.

4   What criticisms can you make of the method used by Asch to investigate conformity?

Suggested Answers start at p. 433

KEY WORDS

ecological validity	hypnosis
group	social conformity

HELPING BEHAVIOUR

■ PILIAVIN, I.M., RODIN, J.A. & PILIAVIN, J. (1969).
Good samaritanism: An underground phenomenon?
Journal of Personality and Social Psychology, 13, 289–99.

INTRODUCTION

The spark for research into the behaviour of bystanders was the brutal murder of a young woman in a New York street in 1964. The assault and murder took place over a period of half an hour, and more than 40 people heard the screams of the young woman. Not one person tried to help or make contact with the police. Social psychologists at the time viewed the most important aspect of this event as the behaviour of the inactive witnesses and set up a range of studies to investigate this. Many of these studies were conducted in the laboratory and looked at how people would respond to an emergency situation either when alone or in the presence of others. The emergency situations included hearing someone fall off a ladder, or being in a waiting-room and finding that smoke was coming under the door (for example, Latané & Darley, 1970). The studies suffered from a certain inauthenticity (in other words they lacked *ecological validity*), and the subjects often realised that the emergency was bogus. However, the researchers were able to introduce two new concepts into our understanding of social behaviour; *pluralistic ignorance* and *diffusion of responsibility*.

Diffusion of responsibility is the idea that people are less likely to intervene to help someone who seems to need it if there are others present, because they perceive responsibility as being shared between all present, and therefore see themselves as being less responsible personally.

Pluralistic ignorance is the tendency for people in a group to mislead each other about a situation; for example, an individual might define an emergency as a non-emergency because others are remaining calm and not taking action. If, say, I am walking down a road and I see smoke (or could it be steam?) coming from a building, do I shout 'Fire!' straight away? It is more likely that I proceed coolly and look at the behaviour of other observers. They are proceeding coolly so therefore it must be steam and not smoke. I go home comforted and only feel concerned when I hear on the radio that the building has burnt down.

The Study

A series of incidents were staged on the New York subway between the hours of 11 a.m. and 3 p.m. over a period of two months in 1968. About 4450 travellers on the trains witnessed the incidents. The train travelled through a range of areas in the city and the average racial mix of the passengers on the trains was 45 per cent Black and 55 per cent White. The average number of people in the train carriage was 43, and the average number of people in the *critical area* where the incident was staged was 8.5. Figure 1.3 shows a diagram of the carriage and the designated critical area.

Two particular trains were selected for the study because they did not make any stops (between 59th Street and 125th Street) for about seven or eight minutes. On each trial, a team of four students (two males and two females) got on the train using different doors. There were four different teams of four, and overall they conducted 103 trials. The females were observers and they took up seats outside the critical area and recorded the events as unobtrusively as possible.

As the train passed through the first station (70 seconds after the journey started) the 'victim', who was standing in the critical area, staggered forward and collapsed. Until he received help, the victim stayed on the floor looking up at the ceiling. If no one offered any help the victim stayed on the floor until the other male experimenter (the 'model') helped him to his feet and then off the train at the first stop. The observers would also leave the train, and they would all get on the next train going back the other way and repeat the procedure. About six to eight trials were run in any one day.

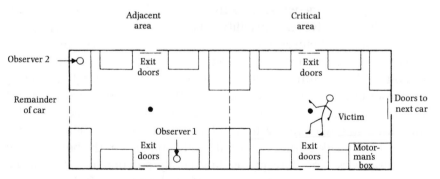

Figure 1.3   *Layout of adjacent and critical areas of subway car*
Source: Piliavin, Rodin & Piliavin (1969)

The victims were male, aged between 26 and 35, and three were White and one was Black. On 38 trials the victim smelled of alcohol and carried a bottle wrapped in a brown paper bag (drunk condition), and in the other 65 trials he appeared sober and carried a cane (cane condition). The reason for the different numbers of trials in the two conditions was the reluctance of the students to carry out the drunk condition.

The models were all male, aged between 24 and 29 and all White. For some of the trials the model was instructed to offer some help to the victim and a note was made on whether the model helped early (approx 70 seconds after the collapse), or late (approx 150 seconds after the collapse), and also whether he had been standing in the critical area or the adjacent area.

The observers recorded the race, age, sex and location of every passenger in the critical area of the carriage who helped, and how many helped. They also recorded the same information on the people in the adjacent area, and the time it took before someone started to offer help.

RESULTS

The passengers were far more helpful than predicted by the experimenters, so that it was not possible to look at the effects of the model's help because the victims had already been helped before the model was supposed to act. The cane victim received spontaneous help on 62 out of 65 trials, and the drunk victim received spontaneous help on 19 out of 38 trials. And on 60 per cent of the 81 trials on which the victim received spontaneous help, he received it from two or more helpers. Once one person had started to help, there were no differences for different victim conditions (Black/White, cane/ drunk) on the number of extra helpers that appeared. When the characteristics of the first helpers were analysed it showed that males were more likely to help than females, and there was a slight tendency towards 'same-race helping' (p. 293), though only in the drunk condition.

The other passengers were observed and although nobody left the carriage during the incident (mainly because the train was moving), on 21 of the 103 trials a total of 34 people left the critical area. They were more likely to leave in the drunk condition than the cane condition. Among the comments recorded, the following came from the women passengers:

'It's for men to help him';
'I wish I could help him – I'm not strong enough';
'I never saw this kind of thing before – I don't know where to look'.
(p. 295)

The diffusion of responsibility hypothesis predicts that as the number of bystanders increases, then the likelihood that any individual will help decreases. From the data gathered by the researchers they were able to compare the speed of the response of the helpers with the number of potential helpers in the critical area. The fastest response, in fact, came from the largest groups which at first glance refutes the diffusion of responsibility hypothesis. (However, unlike the laboratory experiments where there was only one subject in each group and the rest were confederates of the experimenter, in this case, the more people there were in the group, the more potential helpers there were).

DISCUSSION

Piliavin *et al.*, conclude their paper by outlining a model of response to emergency situations. The model includes the following assumptions: observation of an emergency creates an emotional arousal state in the bystander; this state will be interpreted in different situations (see the study by Schachter & Singer, 1962, Chapter 6 of this volume) as fear, disgust, sympathy, and so forth.

The state of arousal is heightened by:

(a) *empathy* with the victim;
(b) being *close* to the emergency;
(c) the *length of time* the emergency continues for.

The arousal can be reduced by:

(a) helping;
(b) going to get help;
(c) leaving the scene;
(d) believing the victim does not deserve help.

The response depends on a *cost–reward analysis* by the individual which includes the costs associated with helping (for example, embarrassment), the costs associated with not-helping (for example, self-blame), rewards associated with helping (for example, praise), and the rewards associated with not-helping. The *motivation* for helping according to this model is not based on altruism but on a desire to remove a negative emotional state.

The study highlights the problems of conducting research in an everyday setting, and also shows the inadequacy of data derived from laboratory studies. In addition, it shows the negative way that social psychology viewed people at that time, by denying that they can show any altruistic behaviour or act according to their values.

If we go back to the stimulus for the studies, it is interesting to note that not all psychologists believe that the behaviour of bystanders is the most important issue to look at in the murder of the young woman. Piliavin *et al.*, and a number of other psychologists chose to investigate the inactivity of the bystanders, but not why women are violently and sexually attacked by men regardless of the presence or absence of bystanders. They seem to have gone to the theatre and described the audience without ever looking at the play.

The murderer in this case, Winston Moseley, had murdered three other women, raped at least four more, and attempted rape on other women. He had a 'taste' for raping dying women, hence the nature of the attack that caught the attention of the psychologists. Surely the central problem that needs to be addressed is not the behaviour of the bystanders, but the behaviour of the murderer, and the construction of male sexuality that encourages grotesque acts of violence against women. Why, then, did the psychologists choose to study the behaviour of bystanders? We have to conclude that rape was not regarded as a significant social problem at that time. Howitt (1991) suggests that the general view at the time of the murder and the development of the psychological theories was that rape was carried out by deviant men, and that certain women (usually of questionable morality) were more prone to attack. Ironically, the psychologists became passive bystanders themselves to the crime, looking the other way and avoiding the reality of male violence.

QUESTIONS

1 What are the problems of conducting this study in the everyday world?

2 What are the advantages of conducting an investigation like this in the everyday world?

3 Why did they recruit students to conduct the study, and why did the authors not do it themselves?

4 What ethical evaluation can you make of this study?

5 What other aspects of social life in the city could be investigated by psychologists?

Suggested Answers start at p. 433

KEY WORDS

altruism
bystander apathy
cost-reward analysis
diffusion of responsibility

ecological validity
emotional arousal
helping behaviour
pluralistic ignorance

BE A GOOD BOY AND DO AS YOU ARE TOLD

■ MILGRAM, S. (1963). Behavioral study of obedience.
Journal of Abnormal and Social Psychology, 67, 371–78.

INTRODUCTION

'Why won't you do as you're told?', says the teacher or parent to the truculent child. But the question that has concentrated the mind of social psychologists has been quite the reverse: why *do* we do what we are told, even when we do not want to do it? Stanley Milgram wanted some explanation for the horrors of the Second World War when six million Jews, Slavs, gypsies and homosexuals were slaughtered by the Nazis who ruled Germany at that time. He wanted to design an experiment that could measure obedience and find out why the Germans were particularly obedient. In fact, he did not follow through with this line of thought because he discovered that obedience to authority was not a feature of German culture but a seemingly universal feature of human behaviour.

Milgram was a student of Solomon Asch (who's study on conformity is described earlier in this chapter), and he wanted to extend this work in a more realistic setting. Interestingly, he was also a classmate of Philip Zimbardo (see the prison simulation study) in their working-class secondary school in New York. The study Milgram developed is probably the most provocative and controversial piece of research in modern psychology. It continues to amaze students, and challenges us all to consider our own behaviour.

THE ORIGINAL STUDY

The basic design of the study was to order a subject to administer an electric shock to another person and to see how far they would go with this procedure. Milgram created an impressive 'shock generator' with 30 switches marked clearly in 15 volt increments from 15 to 450 volts. Under the switches were some verbal labels, from 'Slight Shock' to 'Danger: Severe Shock'. The phoney generator had buzzers, lights that flashed and dials that moved, all designed to make it appear authentic.

The subjects were obtained via a newspaper advertisement and direct mailing – their age and work profile is given in Table 1.1. The subjects believed they were taking part in a study of memory and learning at Yale University. They were paid for their participation but told that the payment was simply for coming, and they could keep it no matter what happened after they arrived.

The experiment was carried out in the psychology laboratories at Yale. The role of 'experimenter' was played by a 31-year-old school biology teacher, and the role of the 'victim' was played by a 47-year-old accountant who was mild mannered and likeable.

The subjects went to the university and were led to believe that the 'victim' was another subject like themselves. They were told about the relationship between learning and punishment, and how this experiment was designed to investigate the effect of punishment on learning. They were told that one of them would be the 'teacher', and one of them would be the 'learner'. They drew slips of paper to select their role, and the subject always drew the slip marked 'teacher'. The subject was then shown the learner being strapped into a chair, and heard the experimenter tell the learner 'Although the shocks can be extremely painful, they cause no permanent tissue damage' (p. 373). The subject was given a sample shock of 45 volts to enhance the authenticity of the study.

The teacher was then seated in another room in front of the shock generator and asked to read a series of word pairs to the learner. The learner was asked to memorise these pairs as they would form the basis of the learning task. The teacher then read the first word of one of the pairs plus four possible responses for the learner. The learner gave his response by pressing one of four switches which illuminated a light

Table 1.1   Distribution of age and occupational types in the Milgram study

Occupation	20–29 years	30–39 years	40–50 years	% of total (occupations)
Workers, skilled and unskilled	4	5	6	37.5
Sales, business and white-collar	3	6	7	40.0
Professional	1	5	3	22.5
% of total (age)	20	40	40	100

Source: Milgram (1963)

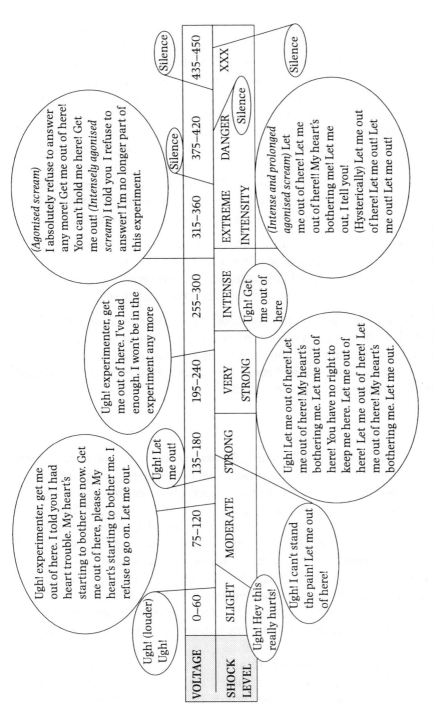

Figure 1.4 *What the 'learner' said while he was shocked'*
Source: Banyard & Hayes (1994)

on top of the shock generator. If the answer was correct the teacher had to move on to the next word on the list, if the answer was wrong the teacher had to tell the learner the correct answer and then the level of punishment they were going to give them. They would then press the first lever on the shock generator. For every subsequent incorrect answer the teacher was required to move one lever up the scale of shocks.

The teacher was able to hear the learner and as the shocks increased in intensity, the learner started to protest and shout out his discomfort. Unknown to the teacher, no shocks were actually given, and the cries of the learner were taped. A summary of the learner's responses is shown in Figure 1.4. If the teacher asked advice from the experimenter he would be given encouragement to continue with a sequence of 'prods':

Prod 1   'Please continue', or 'Please go on';
Prod 2   'The experiment requires that you continue';
Prod 3   'It is absolutely essential that you continue';
Prod 4   'You have no other choice, you must go on'.   (p. 374)

The sessions were filmed and notes were taken by observers looking through an observation mirror. After the study, the subjects were interviewed and various psychometric measures taken to check they were alright. A friendly reconciliation was also arranged with the victim whom they thought they had shocked.

RESULTS

During the study, many of the subjects showed signs of nervousness and tension. For example, a number had laughing fits. Milgram writes, 'Full-blown, uncontrollable seizures were observed for 3 subjects. On one occasion we observed a seizure so violently convulsive that it was necessary to call a halt to the experiment' (p. 375). Of the 40 subjects, all obeyed up to 300 volts (the 20th switch) at which point five refused to continue. Four gave one more shock before breaking off, but 26 continued to the end of the scale (see Figure 1.5). After the maximum shock had been given, the teacher was asked to continue at this level until the experimenter eventually called a halt to the proceedings, at which point many of the obedient subjects heaved sighs of relief or shook their heads in apparent regret.

The level of obedience was totally unexpected, and was greeted with disbelief by the observers. Another unexpected feature of the study was the extraordinary tension created by the procedures. So why did

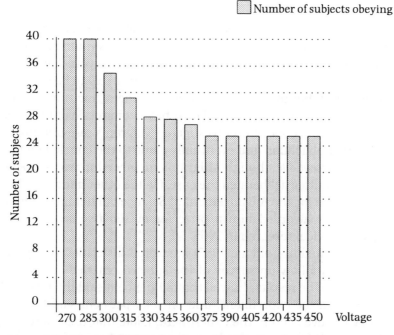

Figure 1.5   *The number of people who continued to obey the experimenter as the voltage increased*

the subjects continue rather than declining to take part? Milgram suggested that the following features of the study contributed to the obedience rate:

(a) The location of the study in the prestigious Yale University.
(b) The apparent worthy purpose of the study.
(c) The subject believed that the victim (learner) had volunteered and consented to the study.
(d) The subject had made a commitment (the Magnus Magnusson Effect: 'I've started so I'll finish').
(e) Obligation was strengthened by the payment.
(f) The subject's role of 'teacher' was a chance selection (or so he believed), and he could have been the 'learner'.
(g) The situation was novel for the subjects and they could not use past precedents for behaviour, nor could they discuss it with anyone.
(h) The subjects were told the shocks were not harmful.
(i) Up until the 20th shock the 'learner' provided answers so was still taking part in the study.

DISCUSSION

The study created enormous debate and there were two main themes of criticism. The first concerned ethics. Even this summary contains details of the subjects' responses that might shock you. The subjects were not screened in any way to see if they were likely to be affected by the stress, and Baumrind (1964), among others, mounted a fierce assault on the ethics of the study. The ethical committee of the American Psychological Association investigated Milgram's research not long after the first publication and eventually came to the conclusion that it was *ethically acceptable*, though Milgram's membership was suspended while the committee deliberated the case. On the other hand, the American Association for the Advancement of Science did not have the same misgivings, and awarded him a prize for *outstanding contribution* to social psychological research in 1965.

Milgram (cited in Colman, 1987) answered his critics by reporting the results of a follow-up survey of the subjects, carried out one year after the study. The results showed that 84 per cent said they were 'glad to have been in the experiment', and only 1.3 per cent said they were very sorry to have been in the experiment. (Note that this survey must have been carried out on the subjects from several of his follow-up studies otherwise it would not have been possible to get a value of 1.3 per cent from the original 40 subjects.) Milgram also described how the subjects had been examined by a psychiatrist one year after the study who was unable to find one subject who showed signs of long-term harm.

The other main criticism concerned the *ecological validity* of the study. Orne, among others, suggested that the subjects were not really deceived, but were responding to the demands of the social psychology experiment (see Orne, 1963, Chapter 21 of this volume). Evidence in support of Milgram's findings in this respect comes from subsequent work, most famously by Hofling *et al.* (1966), where nurses were asked to give potentially lethal injections to patients, and 21 out of 22 appeared prepared to do it; and by Sheridan & King (1972), where people were asked to give real electric shocks to a real puppy. This request met with no disobedience despite the very obvious distress of the animal.

Milgram went on to carry out around 20 variations of the study in which he changed the procedure slightly to investigate factors that would enhance or diminish obedience. The book 'Obedience to Authority' published in 1974 indicates that over a thousand people acted as subjects in this work, despite the severe distress of many of the people taking part. In some ways it is worth thinking about how trapped Milgram became in the experimental procedure, to continue it for so long.

QUESTIONS

1   Why did people obey the authority?

2   What are the advantages of obedience to the individual and to society?

3   What are the disadvantages of obedience to the individual and to society?

4   What ethical guidelines did Milgram break?

5   Was it right to carry out the study?

Suggested Answers start at p. 434

KEY WORDS

ecological validity   obedience
ethics   stress

2 Social Cognition

When we talk to people we usually have an opinion about anything and everything. We can pass judgement on types of music, political ideas, styles of fashion, the behaviour of our friends, and so on. We can speculate on who is doing what to whom and how often, and why they are doing it. These things are the subjects of everyday conversation and gossip. But how do we make these judgements?

Social cognition is the area of social psychology which deals with how we make sense of our social worlds. In particular it focuses on our social perceptions of people, our social judgements about their behaviour, and our attitudes. The study by Nisbett *et al.* (1973), for example, looked at how we explain our actions. They were working within the influential tradition known as *attribution theory* (see for example Kelley, 1967), which holds that people attempt to understand their social world by searching for the causes of their own and other people's actions.

The studies by LaPiere (1934) and Festinger and Carlsmith (1959) look at *attitudes*, and in particular the relationship between what we *think* and what we *do*. LaPiere set out to discover to what extent people behave in accordance with their professed beliefs. He was able to show a rather shaky relationship between *attitudes* and *social behaviour*; his subjects did not seem to do the things they said they believed in. Festinger and Carlsmith's investigation flipped this issue on its head, and addressed the question of how much, and under what circumstances, our social behaviour can affect our beliefs. They were able to show that under certain circumstances, being required to express an opinion that contradicts your actual beliefs can actually cause your beliefs to move towards the opinion that you were required to express. In other words, instead of doing what we believe in, we tend to believe in the things we find ourselves doing.

Is She Really Going Out With Him?

■ Nisbett, R.E., Caputo, C., Legant, P. & Marecek, J. (1973).
Behaviour as seen by the actor and as seen by the observer.
Journal of Personality and Social Psychology, 27, 154–64.

INTRODUCTION

Nisbett *et al.* (1973) set out to demonstrate the differing explanations that *actors* and *observers* have concerning the perceived causes of people's behaviour. They suggested that when we explain our own behaviour we make different attributions than when we explain the behaviour of someone else. In this context the term 'actor' refers to the person 'doing' the behaviour in question, and the term 'observer' refers to someone who is trying to explain the behaviour of the actor. Nisbett *et al.* argued that we tend to see our own behaviour as being caused more by the situation which we are in than by ourselves (the actor's perspective). Conversely we see the behaviour of other people as being caused more by them themselves than by the situation that they are in (the observer's perspective).

An example may clarify this argument. Let us say that a person fails an examination. The person themselves (according to Nisbett *et al.*) will tend to explain their failure as being caused by the difficulty of the examination, or by the uncomfortable environment of the examination hall, or by the fact that their neighbours had been playing loud music throughout the night before. These are all *situational* factors. An observer, on the other hand, will be more likely to attribute the failure to the person themselves, suspecting, for example, that that person is not clever enough to pass the examination, or that they had not prepared themselves adequately for it, or that they are lazy. These are *dispositional* factors.

The three studies that Nisbett *et al.* report in this paper are simplified in the summaries given below.

THE FIRST STUDY

Subjects

Data were reported from 28 pairs of female students from Yale University. Some were paid $1.50 for their participation, and others received credits on an introductory psychology course.

Design

This experiment used an independent measures design with two independent variables (a 2×2 factorial design). The first independent variable was manipulated by random assignment of subjects either to the 'actor' condition or to the 'observer' condition. The actors then either 'volunteered' to undertake a particular task, or 'did not volunteer', giving the two values of the second independent variable.

Procedure and rationale

Subjects were paired up, and in each pair one subject was allocated to the 'actor' condition, the other to the 'observer' condition. The allocations were made randomly. Subjects in the actor condition were taken to a room in which one of the experimenters was sitting along with the observer with whom they were paired, and two confederates of the experimenter (the role of the confederates need not concern us here). The actor was spun a story and asked to make a decision about whether they would volunteer (in return for an hourly payment) to entertain a group of important visitors who were financing work at Yale concerned with 'learning among the underprivileged and in minority groups' (p. 156). Since the observer was in the same room at the time, they saw what decision the actor made. The actor's decision was recorded.

The actors were subsequently asked to estimate, on a nine-point Likert scale, how likely they would be to volunteer to perform a similar sort of task (namely to help canvass for the 'United Fund'). Each observer also estimated the likelihood of the actor with whom they had been paired volunteering to canvass for the United Fund. On the Likert scale a score of eight denoted 'very likely' to volunteer, a score of zero meant 'not at all likely'.

The hypothesis was that there would be an interaction between the actor–observer variable and the variable of whether or not the actor actually volunteered for the original task. They specifically predicted that the observers' estimates would be influenced more by the actors' actual decisions than would be the actors' estimates. This is because the observers would be likely to attribute the actor's original decision to a stable trait or disposition which would presumably cause the same person to make the same sort of decision in the future (for example, 'he is the sort of person who helps others'). The actor, on the other hand, would put their own original decision down to some feature of the situation they were in at the time (for example, 'it was a worthy cause'). Consequently, the actors' own estimates of how likely they would be to volunteer for the United Fund task should not be influenced to a very great extent by whether they had volunteered or not for the original task.

Results

Table 2.1 shows how the estimates given by the actors themselves, regarding the likelihood of volunteering for the United Fund task, were relatively unaffected by whether they actually volunteered or not for the first task. In fact, those that did not volunteer for the first task rated themselves as slightly *more* likely to volunteer for the United Fund task. In contrast, the observers' estimates seem to have been more substantially influenced by the actors' actual decisions. Those that had volunteered for the original task were rated as being much more likely to volunteer again (reported as a statistically significant difference at the level of $p < .05$). The interaction effect is reported as reaching a significance level of $p < .07$.

Table 2.1 Actors' and observers' estimates of the probability that the actor would volunteer for a similar task, as a function of whether or not the actor volunteered to entertain the 'important visitors'

Rater	Actors' behaviour	
	Volunteered	Did not volunteer
Actor	3.31	3.92
n	16	12
Observer	4.27	2.78
n	15	18

Source: Adapted from Nisbett, Caputo, Legant & Marecek (1973)

THE SECOND STUDY

Subjects

Male undergraduates from Yale University made up the subjects for studies two and three. In study two, data were collected from 23 of these subjects; in study three data were collected from 24 subjects. They were paid $1.50 to participate.

Design

Study two employed a two-condition repeated measures experimental design. In one condition subjects were asked to write about their own behaviour; in the other condition they were to write about their best friend's behaviour.

Procedure and rationale

Subjects were asked to write four short paragraphs, one on each of the following topics: why they liked the 'girl they had dated most frequently in the past year' (p. 158); why they had chosen to study what they were studying at university; why their best friend liked the girl he had dated most frequently in the past year; why their best friend had chosen his university course.

The paragraphs were coded by one of the experimenters, and scored according to how many 'dispositional' and 'situational' reasons each one contained. Situational reasons were those which focused on the characteristics of the girlfriends and of the university courses. Dispositional reasons were those which focused on the person whose behaviour they were trying to explain (either themselves or their best friend). An independent coder, who had no knowledge of the experimental hypothesis, also coded the paragraphs. The experimenter's codings were used in reporting the results, but the authors claim that 'almost identical' (p. 158) results emerged from the independent coder's version of the data.

The paragraphs which subjects wrote about their own choices were, in effect, actors' descriptions of their own behaviour, whereas the paragraphs about best friends were written from the perspective of an observer. The authors expected that the subjects would use more situational attributions to describe their own behaviour, and more dispositional attributions when describing the behaviour of their friends.

Results

Table 2.2 shows that on average the paragraphs written about the actors' own reasons for liking their girlfriend contained more than twice the number of situational reasons compared to dispositional

Table 2.2 Number of entity (situational) reasons and dispositional reasons given by subjects as explanations of their own and their best friend's choices of girlfriend

Explanation	Reasons for liking girlfriend	
	Entity ('situational')	Dispositional
Own behaviour	4.61	2.04
Friend's behaviour	2.70	2.57

Source: Adapted from Nisbett, Caputo, Legant & Marecek (1973)

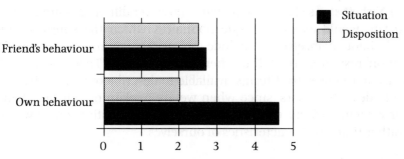

Figure 2.1 *Number of situational and dispositional explanations given by subjects for their own and their best friend's choice of girlfriend*

reasons (significant at the level of $p < .02$). The same results are shown in graphical form in Figure 2.1.

THE THIRD STUDY

Subjects

The subjects were the same as for study two.

Design

Study three was based on a questionnaire in which subjects had to decide which trait adjectives to use to describe themselves, their best friend, their father, an acquaintance, and a famous television commentator.

Procedure and rationale

Subjects completed five questionnaires, one on each of five people: themselves, their best friend, their father, an acquaintance, and a famous television commentator (Walter Cronkite). Each questionnaire consisted of the same 20 items. The items consisted of a trait term (for example, 'bold'), its opposite ('cautious'), or the phrase 'depends on the situation'. The subjects had to choose the most apt description of the 'stimulus person'. The order in which subjects completed the questionnaires was counterbalanced; in other words the order in which the subjects thought about each stimulus person was systematically varied from subject to subject.

If Nisbett *et al.*'s claims about actor–observer differences are correct, then you would expect the questionnaires which the subjects completed about themselves to include, on average, more 'depends on the situation' responses than the other questionnaires. Their ideas imply that we have fewer trait terms available to describe ourselves than we have to describe others, since when we are explaining our own behaviour we tend to focus on characteristics of the situation which we are in, rather than on characteristics of ourselves.

Results

Table 2.3 shows how, on average, fewer trait descriptions were ascribed to the self than to all other stimulus persons. In other words people selected 'depends on the situation' more frequently on the questionnaires about themselves than on the questionnaires about others. The differences between the average self ratings and the ratings on the other four questionnaires were all significant at the level of at least $p < .05$.

Table 2.3 Mean number of traits (out of possible 20) that were ascribed to each stimulus person

Item	Stimulus person				
	Self	Best friend	Father	Acquaintance	Cronkite
Actor	11.92[a]	14.21[bc]	13.42[b]	13.42[b]	15.08[c]

Note: Means not sharing a superscript differ from each other at the .05 level or more: $N = 24$
Source: Nisbett, Caputo, Legant & Marecek (1973)

Discussion

All three studies lend support to Nisbett *et al*'s claims regarding the different perspectives of actor and observer when it comes to explaining behaviour. The observers in study one seemed to attribute the actors' original decision to some stable personal disposition, which would make them likely to make the same sorts of decision in the future. In study two, actors used more situational than dispositional reasons to account for their liking for their girlfriend; observers used more dispositional than situational reasons to account for their best friend's choice of university course. Study three suggested that people have fewer trait terms available to describe themselves than they have available to describe others.

To the extent that the studies suggest people have 'a tendency to hold a different implicit personality theory for the self than for others' (p. 162), the results are interesting. But the authors acknowledge other explanations for the patterns within the data. For example, in study one, the *only* information the observers had to go on in making their estimate of the actor's likelihood to volunteer for the United Fund task was the decision they had seen the actor make, since the actor–observer pairs were strangers to one another. No wonder the observers were more influenced by this one decision than the actors themselves, since the actors presumably knew themselves considerably better, and had much more information to go on in making their estimate. In other words, the results of study one may be an *artefact* of the experimental procedures.

But the authors treat their data sensibly and put a lot of effort into arguing against alternative explanations. It is not possible in this short summary to explore in detail the authors' efforts to stand up for their hypothesis of actor–observer differences in explaining behaviour. But it is worth noting that in the end they do not claim too much for the studies they have carried out:

> ...the studies cannot be said to indicate that the hypothesis generally holds true. The studies should be regarded merely as demonstrations of some interest in their own right, which are consistent with a proposition that is too widely applicable to be either proved or disproved by anything short of a very large and extremely variegated research program.
> (p. 163)

This level of modesty may be one of the secrets of good research.

QUESTIONS

1   Why did the experimenters get an independent person to code the paragraphs of text in study two? And why was this person unaware of the experimental hypothesis?

2   Write down a list of things that you have done in the past year. Then write an explanation of each item in your list. Are the explanations situational or dispositional?

Suggested Answers start on p. 435

KEY WORDS

actor
attribution
attribution theory
disposition
factorial design
interaction effect

inter-observer reliability
Likert Scale
observer
situation
trait (trait adjectives)

I'M NOT PREJUDICED, BUT . . .

■ LaPiere, R.T. (1934). Attitudes vs. actions.
Social Forces, 13, 230–37.

Introduction

Common sense would suggest that we have a set of values, beliefs and attitudes that shape our behaviour. Consequently, psychologists have expended considerable effort in attempts to measure and to change our attitudes in the belief that this would bring about changes in our behaviour. This connection between *attitudes* and *behaviour* was challenged as early as 1934 in this classic piece of work by LaPiere.

Although the study does not have the rigorous control of more modern studies, it raises a number of issues about attitudes and research in social psychology that are relevant today.

The Study

LaPiere suggests that attitudes are acquired from social experience, and provide the individual with some degree of preparation to adjust in a well defined way to certain social situations if they arise. However, these attitudes are usually measured by asking people to make a verbal response to a hypothetical situation. The use of questionnaires and interviews is controlled, cheap and creates massive data bases, but questions remain about their effectiveness in measuring attitudes.

Questionnaires on controversial or embarrassing topics are particularly suspect. For example, on surveys of prejudice or racism it is difficult to find out what people's attitudes and behaviour really are because they have learnt the appropriate social responses. So, in this study, LaPiere investigated the behavioural responses of people and then attempted to obtain a measure of their reported attitudes.

Starting in 1930, and continuing for two years, LaPiere travelled extensively in the United States with a young Chinese student and his wife. According to LaPiere, 'both were personable, and charming, and quick to win the admiration and respect of those they had the opportunity to become intimate with' (p. 231). They were born in China and they were easily identified as 'not-American'. (At this time, there was considerable hostility towards Chinese people down the western coast of the USA). LaPiere describes how he entered a hotel in a small, and famously narrow-minded town with some concern about whether his Chinese companions would be accommodated. The concern was misplaced and they obtained rooms with ease, but when LaPiere telephoned the hotel two months later to ask whether they could accommodate 'an important Chinese gentleman' (p. 232), the response was a definite 'No'. This event stimulated the study.

During their travels they investigated this contradiction between what people say and what people do. In their ten thousand mile motor journey, twice across the United States and up and down the western coast, they received the following responses: received at 66 hotels, auto-camps and 'tourist homes' and rejected only once; served in 184 restaurants and cafés, receiving very good service in 72 of them.

Wherever possible, the Chinese people made the reservations or the orders, but LaPiere had not told them about the study (to prevent them becoming self-conscious) and so he had to invent a number of ruses to be absent or distracted when they went into the various establishments. LaPiere came to believe that the main factors affecting behaviour towards the travellers were not race, but other features such as appearance, cleanliness, an air of self-confidence, and smiling. LaPiere also noted that when some tension did develop with the Chinese people, then it would evaporate when they spoke in unaccented English.

From this survey it would appear reasonable to conclude that the attitudes of US citizens in 1930 were relatively positive towards Chinese people. However, negative attitudes towards Chinese people *did* exist and were commonly shown in attitude surveys.

Six months after the initial visit, LaPiere sent a questionnaire with an accompanying letter to every place they had visited. The questionnaires all asked the same question, 'Will you accept members of the Chinese race as guests in your establishment' In half the questionnaires, this question was presented alone, and in the other half it was embedded in similar questions about Germans, Jews, Japanese, Italians and so forth. There was very little difference between the results from the two sets of questionnaires so the data are combined in Table 2.4. Of the 251 establishments, 128 replied. The replies showed that 92 per cent of the visited establishments, and also 92 per cent of a further group of unvisited establishments answered 'No' to the question.

LaPiere notes the contradictory results of his two alternate methods of measuring attitudes towards Chinese people. The *attitudes* expressed

Table 2.4 Replies to the question, 'Will you accept members of the Chinese race as guests in your establishment?'

	Hotels etc. visited	Hotels etc. not-visited	Restaurants etc. visited	Restaurants etc. not-visited
No	43	30	75	88
Undecided: depend on circumstances	3	2	6	7
Yes	1	0	0	1
Total	47	32	81	96

Source: LaPiere (1934)

by representatives of the visited hotels did not match up with the *behaviour* of the people at those hotels. He suggests that conventional attitude surveys have limited applications. For example, a political survey might be a good predictor of voter behaviour at an election, but it will not predict how particular voters will behave when they meet the candidate on the street. The questionnaire, says LaPiere, is limited because it asks for a verbal reaction to an entirely symbolic situation, and it will not indicate what a person will actually do in a real situation. He concludes by writing:

> The questionnaire is cheap, easy and mechanical. The study of human behaviour is time consuming, intellectually fatiguing, and depends for its success upon the ability of the investigator. The former method gives quantitative results, the latter mainly qualitative. Quantitative measurements are quantitatively accurate; qualitative measures are always subject to errors of human judgement. Yet it would seem far more worthwhile to make a shrewd guess regarding that which is essential than to accurately measure that which is likely to prove quite irrelevant.
> (p. 237)

DISCUSSION

There are a number of factors in the study that influence the low relationship between the two measures. First, the request for service was made to the desk clerk or the waiter or waitress, but the questionnaire probably went to the proprietor or manager. Secondly, the request for service was a specific act that did not allow time for reflection before the person responded. The questionnaire, on the other hand, asked for a general statement that could be thought about at leisure.

The poor relationship between attitudes and behaviour has been demonstrated in other studies, and most recently in studies on health behaviour. Although many of us hold attitudes that value healthy living and heathy eating, at least one of the authors is inclined to relax with a beer and a bag of chips in front of the television. This lack of relationship between health attitudes and health behaviour undermines many attempts to promote health. In particular, the early health education literature on HIV and AIDS was remarkably unsuccessful in changing the sexual behaviour of people, despite changing some of their attitudes towards sexual behaviour (for example, see Sarafino, 1994). It is clear that the relationship between attitudes and behaviour is a complex one, and is affected by a range of social, personal and environmental factors.

QUESTIONS

1   What attitudes do you have that you do not act on? (If you're stuck, think of all the things you do that you know are unhealthy).

2   Why do you not act in accordance with these attitudes?

3   What methodological problems are there with this study?

Suggested Answers start at p. 435

KEY WORDS

attitudes	qualitative measures
behaviour	quantitative measures
prejudice	questionnaires

Changing Our Minds

■ Festinger, L. & Carlsmith, J.M. (1959).
Cognitive consequences of forced compliance.
Journal of Abnormal and Social Psychology, 58, 203–10.

Introduction

'What happens to a person's private opinion if he is forced to do or say something contrary to that opinion?' (p. 203). This is the starting point for Festinger and Carlsmith's study. They cite some previous work by Janis & King (1954) which showed that, in certain circumstances, when people are required to argue a point of view with which they do not agree, their private opinions can end up shifting towards that point of view. Janis and King had put this effect down to the person's search for, and rehearsal of, new arguments in favour of that point of view.

What factors contribute to these shifts in opinion? Clearly one such factor must be the person's reason for saying something that they do not believe, since without good reason people would usually say what they *do* believe. Obvious reasons would be threats and rewards. And it would appear sensible, on the face of it, to expect that the bigger the threat, or the more attractive the reward, the greater the shift in opinion would be. However, Festinger and Carlsmith pointed out that this expectation was not borne out by the evidence. They cite a study by Kelman (1953) which showed that, counter to our intuitions, large rewards for publicly contravening a private belief seemed to produce *smaller* changes in those private beliefs than did small rewards.

This finding which seems to go against common sense can be explained by the theory of *cognitive dissonance* which was proposed by Festinger (1957). The theory is based on four basic propositions:

(1) Inconsistencies between cognitions in an individual generate a feeling of dissonance.
(2) Dissonance is unpleasant and the individual is motivated to remove it.
(3) In addition to trying to remove dissonance, the individual will actively avoid situations and information that may increase it.
(4) The motivation increases with the increase in dissonance which depends, in turn, on the differentness of the cognitions.

So how does this theory explain the findings of Kelman's study mentioned above? An example will help to show the reasoning. Say, for example, that you were forced at gun point to say 'I believe X' when in fact you believe 'Y'. You will experience *dissonance* between your cognitions 'I believe Y' and 'I said I believed X'. But you will experience a high level of *consonance* between your cognition 'I said I believed X' and your cognition concerning the *reasons* for saying 'X'. After all, you had a very good reason for saying 'X'. This high level of consonance goes someway to counterbalancing the related dissonance. So the overall levels of dissonance are relatively low, and the shift in opinion should be small.

Now imagine instead that that person had simply threatened to call you a coward if you did not say 'I believe X', and so you did, even though you believe 'Y'. Just as in the example above you experience dissonance between the cognitions 'I believe Y' and 'I said I believe X'. But this time you will experience much less consonance between the cognition 'I said I believed X' and your cognition concerning the reasons for saying 'X'. This time you would probably feel that you did not have quite such a good reason for saying 'X', because the threat was not nearly as serious. In this case overall dissonance will be relatively high, and so to reduce the dissonance you must change your opinion. The dissonance is reduced because your cognitions are now something like 'I said I believed X' and 'perhaps I really *do* believe X'.

The Study

In the above examples the same rationale would hold for rewards. According to the theory of cognitive dissonance, the larger the reward that a person is offered for publicly voicing a point of view with which they privately do not agree, the smaller will be any subsequent change in their privately held point of view; the larger the reward, the better the reason for the public statement. The study undertaken by Festinger and Carlsmith set out to test this prediction empirically by offering one group of students $20 each, and one group of students $1 each, to go against their privately held views. Their hypothesis was that the subjects in the $1 condition would show a greater change in their privately held views than the subjects in the $20 condition (see Figure 2.2).

Subjects

The subjects were 71 male students studying an undergraduate psychology course at Stanford University.

1.   BALANCE: the bribe is big enough to justify the lie and maintain cognitive balance

$$\frac{\text{LIE} \qquad \$20}{\triangle}$$

2.   DISSONANCE: the bribe is *not* big enough to justify the lie, so the only way to restore cognitive balance is for the lie to become smaller

3.   BALANCE: the lie is smaller because the person rationalises that the experiment wasn't so boring after all

$$\frac{\text{lie} \qquad \$1}{\triangle}$$

Figure 2.2   *Cognitive dissonance: balancing a lie with a bribe*

Design

This was a three-condition experiment, with different subjects in each condition (an independent measures design). The three conditions were a control condition, a $1 condition, and a $20 condition. The independent variable was the amount paid to the subject. The dependent variable was the subject's private opinion about some tasks that they were asked to complete during the course of the experiment.

Procedure

Festinger and Carlsmith's paper has one of the longest procedural sections that this author has ever seen in a psychology study, stretching from page 204 to page 207. The reason for this is that the experiment rested on a highly scripted and intricate deception. Subjects were required to perform two extremely boring tasks, each of which took one half-hour. One of the tasks involved a tray with 48 square pegs. With one hand the subject had to 'turn each peg a quarter turn clockwise, then another quarter turn, and so on' (p. 204) for 30 minutes. The other task was also mind-numbingly dull. The subjects in the $1 and the $20 conditions were then spun a story about how the experimenter would like them to tell the next subject (actually a confederate) how 'enjoyable', 'fun', 'interesting', 'intriguing' and 'exciting' the experiment had been. In return they would receive either $1 or $20 depending upon which condition they were in.

In order that this request made sense, the subjects were led to believe that there were two conditions in this study: one in which subjects did the tasks with no introduction (as they had done), and one in which subjects did the tasks having been given an enthusiastic introduction. The next 'subject' was supposedly in the 'enthusiastic introduction' condition, hence the need to tell them how much fun the tasks had been. The success of the study depended to a large extent on the subjects believing (wrongly) that the real experiment was testing differences in performance between the group with no introduction to the tasks, and the group with the enthusiastic introduction. The control subjects were not subjected to this deception and were not asked to talk to the next subject.

The subjects then took part in what was ostensibly a survey of all experimental work in their department. This was apparently to evaluate the usefulness of the studies that were being undertaken, and was presented as though it was administered as a matter of course after every psychology experiment. In this survey, the subjects had to respond on Likert scales to the following questions about the tasks they had just performed:

(1) Were the tasks interesting and enjoyable?
(2) Did the experiment give you an opportunity to learn about your ability to perform these tasks?
(3) From what you know about the experiment and the tasks involved in it, would you say the experiment was measuring anything important?
(4) Would you have any desire to participate in a similar experiment? (p. 206)

For questions one, three and four the expectation was that the $1 group would give much more favourable ratings than the subjects in the control and $20 groups. Question two was included as a neutral question. There was no theoretical reason to expect differences in scores across the groups in question two, so if the same sorts of differences were observed as in the other three questions, the validity of the experiment would be called into question.

Eleven subjects were excluded from the final analysis for various reasons, one of which was that some of them guessed the real experimental hypothesis, and indicated as such. This left the data from 20 subjects in each condition.

To summarise, the subjects in the $1 and the $20 conditions were encouraged to make public statements (to a bogus subject) about the nature of the tasks. These statements presumably contradicted their private feelings about the tasks which were undeniably tedious. The so-called 'independent' survey was used to gauge the extent of any shift in attitude after the public statements, measured against the baseline provided by a group of control subjects who made no such public statements.

RESULTS

Differences among the three groups on questions one, three and four were in the predicted direction (see Table 2.5). Question one was regarded as the most important, in that it was most directly related to cognitive dissonance. For this question there were significant differences ($p < .02$) between the ratings from the $1 condition and the

Table 2.5 Average ratings on interview questions for each condition

Question on interview	Experimental condition		
	Control	One dollar	Twenty dollars
How enjoyable tasks were (rated from −5 to +5)	−0.45	+1.35	−0.05
How much they learned (rated from 0 to 10)	3.08	2.80	3.15
Scientific importance (rated from 0 to 10)	5.60	6.45	5.18
Participate in similar exp. (likelihood rated from −5 to +5)	−0.62	+1.20	−0.25

Source: Festinger & Carlsmith (1959)

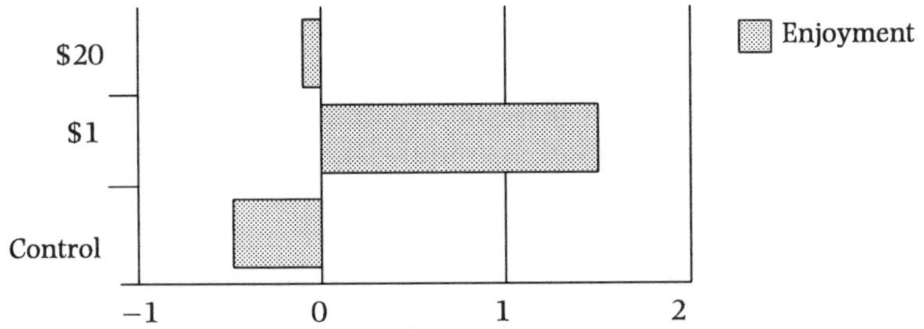

Figure 2.3 *How enjoyable were the tasks?*

ratings from the control condition, and between ratings from the $1 condition and ratings from the $20 condition ($p < .03$). Figure 2.3 shows the same data in graphical form.

DISCUSSION

The answers to question one are interpreted by the authors of the study in the following way. The answers of the control subjects provide a base-line. They were not asked to make any public statement so their responses to the question should not have been subject to the effects of dissonance. The answers of the $20 subjects are slightly, but not significantly, more positive than the answers of the control subjects, indicating no real shift in private opinions about the tasks. The answers of the $1 subjects are significantly more positive than the answers from both other groups of subjects, indicating that their private feelings about the tasks had shifted since making their public statement to the bogus subject. Thus, the results support the prediction from cognitive dissonance theory; the *higher* the reward offered for contradicting a private belief, the *lower* the subsequent shift in that belief.

The theory of cognitive dissonance has been used in wider contexts, as well. For example, it offers an explanation of how harsh initiation rites foster group cohesion. The dissonance is created by the submission to the humiliation or hardship of initiation, and reduced by the increased value put onto the group that the individual has been initiated into. The dissonant cognitions are 'I am suffering', 'I don't like this', and the cognition that can reduce the dissonance is 'Yes, but this group is very important'. So, for example, having to work 120 hours a week for a couple of years or more used to act as a mechanism which cemented doctors' identification with the British medical profession, and convinced them that those who had not been through it were 'outsiders'. Fortunately, this seems to be an attitude which is dying away, although not very quickly.

The effects of cognitive dissonance can also be seen in the ways that people evaluate their level of personal risk. For example, McMasters & Lee (1991) investigated the knowledge and beliefs of smokers. They compared smokers, non-smokers and ex-smokers and found that all of the groups had a similar amount of factual knowledge about the effects of smoking. According to the theory of cognitive dissonance, the smokers should have dissonant cognitions about smoking; 'I am a smoker',

'Smoking will damage my health'. How will they reduce this dissonance? McMasters and Lee found that when the smokers were asked to estimate their personal risk, they rated it as lower than it would be for the average smoker, and they were much more likely to support rationalisations and distortions of logic regarding smoking than the non-smokers or ex-smokers.

QUESTIONS

1   Why would the validity of the experiment have been called into question if the same sorts of differences across the groups had been observed for question two as for the other three questions?

2   Why is it so important for reports of empirical work to give a detailed description of the research procedures that were used?

Suggested Answers start on p. 435

KEY WORDS

attitude change	consistency
cognitions	Likert Scale
cognitive dissonance	opinions

3 SOCIAL ROLES

We all play a variety of different *roles* in our lives, much like an actor on the stage. Any given person might be, say, a woman, a student, a mother, a daughter, a wife, a colleague, a friend, a squash partner, a neighbour and so forth. All of these roles are played in relation to other people: to play the role of student there has to be a teacher, to be a mother there must be a child, to be a squash partner there must be another squash partner, to be a hero there must be a villain. So roles do not exist in isolation but are constructed within a large social network.

Each role carries with it certain *rules* about how we must behave to fulfill the requirements of that role. Squash partners, for example, have to turn up at an agreed time on an agreed day. They have to play squash according to the rules of the game, and then go to the bar afterwards to mull over the game and the week's events. They then have to arrange the next match before leaving for home. So a person's behaviour, whilst playing the role of squash partner, is constrained by the rules which govern how that role must be played. Sometimes when we are trying to play two or more roles at once, the requirements of each role conflict with each other and cause problems. For example some people have to balance the demands that are made on them by virtue of being a mother, a wife, and a student.

The studies which are included in this chapter simply look at the nature of certain social roles. Haney, Banks & Zimbardo (1973) showed the powerful affect that roles can have on people's behaviour. In this case, the roles were given to the subjects and they were asked to play them. In contrast, the other study in this chapter by Bales (1955), looks at how people create roles within a social group.

THE PRISON SIMULATION

■ HANEY, C., BANKS, W.C. & ZIMBARDO, P.G. (1973).
A study of prisoners and guards in a simulated prison.
Naval Research Review, 30, 4–17.

INTRODUCTION

Some psychological studies produce very surprising results for the researchers and the participants. Sometimes the results are so striking that they challenge our explanations of human behaviour and human motivation. One example is the Milgram study described earlier in this book. Another one is the work of Zimbardo and his associates.

The central question in this study concerns how much of our behaviour is structured by the social roles that we occupy. One of the famous 'soundbites' from Shakespeare is, 'All the world's a stage, And all the men and women merely players' (*As You Like It*). The 'life is drama' metaphor is developed in role theory and the work of, among others, Erving Goffman. This approach to human behaviour and experience suggests that *we are what we play*, and a limited sense of selfhood and identity is shaped by the demands of the situation we are in.

THE STUDY

Twenty-four subjects were selected from an initial pool of 75 respondents to a newspaper advertisement which had asked for male volunteers to participate in a psychological study of prison life. The volunteers completed a questionnaire and interview designed to screen subjects, and the selected people were described as 'normal', healthy, male college students who were predominantly middle class and White.

The simulated prison was created in the basement of the Psychology Department at Stanford University. It was made up of three cells (each 6 ft × 9 ft) with three prisoners to a cell. A broom cupboard (2 ft × 2 ft × 7 ft) was converted into a 'solitary confinement room'. Several rooms in an adjacent wing of the building were used as guards' rooms, interview rooms and a bedroom for the 'warden' (Zimbardo).

There was also a small enclosed room used as a 'prison yard' in which there was an observation window behind which was video equipment, and room for several observers.

The subjects were randomly assigned their roles of either 'prisoner' or 'guard', and signed contracts on that basis. The contract offered $15 a day and guaranteed basic living needs, though it was made explicit to the prisoners that some basic civil rights (for example, privacy) would be suspended. The prisoners were given no information about what to expect and no instructions on how to behave. The guards were told to 'maintain the reasonable degree of order within the prison necessary for its effective functioning' (p.6), though they were explicitly prohibited from using physical aggression.

The prisoner subjects remained in the mock prison 24 hours a day for the duration of the study. Nine were arbitrarily assigned three to each cell, and the remaining three were on stand-by at home. The 'guard' subjects worked on three-man eight-hour shifts, and went home after their shifts.

Both sets of subjects were given uniforms to promote feelings of anonymity. The guards' uniform (plain khaki shirt and trousers, whistle, baton, and reflecting sun glasses) was intended to convey a military attitude and to give symbols of power. The prisoners' uniform (loose fitting smock, number on front and back, no underwear, light chain and lock around ankle, rubber sandals and a cap made from nylon stocking) was intended to be uncomfortable, humiliating and to create symbols of subservience and dependence (Figure 3.1).

Zimbardo obtained the help of the local police department to unexpectedly 'arrest' the prisoner subjects. A police officer charged them with suspicion of burglary or armed robbery, advised them of their rights, handcuffed them, thoroughly searched them (often in full view of the neighbours!) and drove them to the police station. Here they had their fingerprints and picture taken and were put in a detention cell. They were then blindfolded and driven to the mock prison. During the induction period the arresting officers did not tell the subjects that this was part of the study. When they arrived at the mock prison, the prisoner-subjects were stripped, deloused, made to stand alone and naked in the 'yard' and then given their uniform and cell and told to remain silent.

The prisoners were then greeted by the warden who read them the rules which had to be memorised. After this they were referred to only by their number. The prisoners were to be given three meals a day,

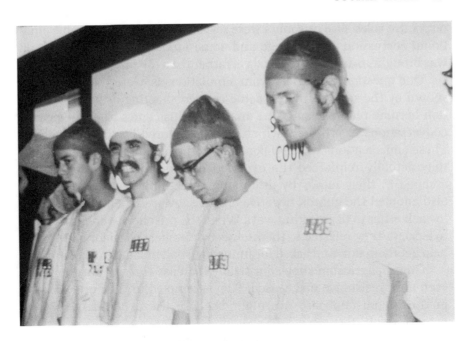

Figure 3.1 *The 'prisoners' in the prison simulation study*
Source: Philip Zimbardo

allowed three supervised toilet visits, two hours privilege time for reading and letter writing, two visiting periods a week, exercise periods and film rights. They were also required to conduct work assignments and line up for a 'count' on each new guard shift. The initial purpose of the count was to check that all the prisoners were present, and to test their knowledge of the rules and their I.D. numbers. The first counts took around ten minutes but as conditions in the prison deteriorated, they increased in length until some lasted for several hours.

RESULTS

The prison had a much more dramatic effect on all the players in the drama than had been anticipated. The mood of the prisoners and guards became increasingly negative. The prison was *internalised* by prisoners and guards (in other words, they started to believe in it) and they adopted very contrasting behaviours, which were appropriate for their respective roles. Five prisoners were released early due to extreme emotional depression, crying, rage and acute anxiety, and the simulation was brought to an end after six days rather than the projected 14 days.

One question that arises from simulations is 'were the behaviours shown by the subjects merely some very good acting or had the situation become real to them?' One answer to this comes from the private conversations of prisoners which were monitored by the researchers. These conversations were 90 per cent on the prison, which shows that they actually reinforced the experience even when they could have escaped in their minds by discussing something else. The prisoners also adopted the guards' negative attitude towards them, and referred to each other in deprecating ways. When the prisoners were introduced to a priest, they referred to themselves by number, asked for a lawyer to help get them out, and asked for immediate bail and a parole board.

Guard aggression showed a steady increase throughout the study, even after resistance had ceased. They attempted to 'hide' one prisoner in the broom cupboard overnight because the experimenters were being 'too soft'.

The most dramatic demonstration of the reality of the prison came with the mock parole board. The five remaining prisoners were asked by Zimbardo in turn whether they would forfeit the money they had earned as a prisoner if they could be paroled (released from the study). Three of the five said 'yes', which meant they were effectively terminating their contract to take part in the study. Yet, when they were told to return to their cells while it was considered, they did so rather than just walk out.

DISCUSSION

Zimbardo suggested that the reason for the deterioration in guard behaviour was *power*. The guards were able to exert control over the lives of other human beings and they did not have to justify their displays of power as they would have to in their daily lives. After day one, all prisoner rights became redefined as privileges, and all privileges were cancelled.

Zimbardo describes the social deterioration of the prisoners as the *pathological prisoner syndrome*. To start with, the prisoners rebelled against their conditions, but every attempt was undermined by the guards, and social cohesion collapsed among the prisoners. Half of the prisoners responded by becoming sick, and eventually had to be released before the study was finally brought to a conclusion. For those who remained, the model prisoner reaction that developed was passivity, dependence and flattened affect (emotions). Zimbardo suggested that there were a number of processes that contributed to the deterioration of the prisoners including:

(a) The loss of personal identity.
(b) The arbitrary control exerted by the guards. This made the prisoners' lives increasingly unpredictable and their treatment increasingly unfair. Their behaviour showed signs of *learned helplessness* (see the study by Seligman & Maier, 1967, Chapter 5 of this volume).
(c) Dependency and emasculation. The guards created a *dependency* in the prisoners which *emasculated* them to the extent that when the prisoners were debriefed they suggested that they had been assigned to be prisoners because they were smaller than the guards. In fact, there was no difference in average height between the prisoners and the guards, and the perceived difference was a response to the prisoners' perceptions of themselves and their lack of power.

What does all this mean? Zimbardo describes it as a simulation of prison life, but that is not quite the case. None of the subjects had any experience of prison life before the study, and their roles were played from the social perceptions of how prison life should be. It is, in fact, a simulation of what we *expect* prison life to be, rather than what it is. However, the study still gives a powerful demonstration of the effect of social roles, and also the power of the social psychological experiment to make us behave in ways we did not think possible (see Orne, 1963, Chapter 21 of this volume).

Not altogether surprisingly, there were numerous ethical objections to the study, though like Milgram, Zimbardo made a robust defence (Zimbardo, 1973, and MacDermott, 1993). He argued that the studies provide a special insight into human behaviour and experience, and illuminate 'a dark side'. His personal criticism of the study concerns his own role as both researcher and warden. He became as trapped in his warden role as the other players in the simulation, and that prevented him responding appropriately as the lead researcher. It is also important to note that the study received the approval of the American Navy (who sponsored the research), the Psychology Department at Stanford, and also the University Committee of Human Experimentation before it was carried out. None had predicted the outcome, but then why should they? If researchers already knew what was going to happen in their research then there would not be much point in carrying it out.

QUESTIONS

1 What were the main features of the prisoners' behaviour?

2 What ethical objections can be made to this study?

3 Was the study justified even if it was unethical?

4 Why do you think the researchers chose the subjects they did? And what would be the differences in the outcome of the study if the subjects had not been predominantly young students?

Suggested Answers start at p. 436

KEY WORDS

dependency	power
emasculation	role
learned helplessness	simulation
personal identity	

BEHAVIOUR IN GROUPS

■ BALES, R.F. (1955). How people interact in conferences. *Scientific American, 192*, 31–35.

INTRODUCTION

Many of the most famous and influential studies in social psychology have focused on, or at least been set within the context of, 'people in groups'. For example, Sherif (1956) and Tajfel (1970) (both in this volume) examined the issue of inter-group conflict; Asch (1955) (also in this volume) studied the effects that a group can have on the behaviour of its individual members; Moscovici, Lage & Naffrechoux (1969) investigated the phenomenon of 'minority influence'; and Lewin *et al.* (1939) and Fiedler (1967) analysed group leadership. The emphasis within social psychology on groups is welcome, because being in groups is such a fundamental feature of our social lives.

Bales' concern with groups arose out of his early fieldwork on the effectiveness of Alcoholics Anonymous in helping hardened alcoholics to reform. He became particularly interested in the characteristics of communication within groups. Having become somewhat uncomfortable about observing real-life groups with real-life problems, he left the field and returned to the laboratory so that he could work under more controlled conditions. The studies which he describes in this paper were undertaken in his laboratory at Harvard University in 1947.

THE STUDY

Although Bales had given up fieldwork, he was still clearly interested in questions which bore directly on everyday life. In this paper he examines in detail the dynamics of communication which operate within decision-making groups. Since many important things are decided for us by people in decision-making groups (just think about the influence of government select committees, boards of directors, management groups and so forth) it is very important that we understand clearly how such groups operate. Perhaps such an understanding could lead to decision-making groups making better decisions.

Having said this, it is important to bear in mind that the first stage of 'understanding' in any scientific discipline involves careful description of the thing which we are trying to understand. In this paper, Bales is not concerned with improving the performance of decision-making groups; he simply sets out to examine and document some of the characteristics of such groups. The specific questions which guided his study were: what proportion of communications within a decision-making group are directly concerned with solving the problem at hand?; what stages does a typical decision-making group go through in pursuit of its goal?; and what roles do the different group members play?.

Subjects

Each group that Bales studied was comprised of between two and seven people. No details are given in this paper about who the subjects were. Each group followed the procedure outlined below.

Design

This is a study based on techniques of structured observation. There is no manipulation of variables. The observations were carried out in a laboratory under controlled conditions in order that sensible comparisons could be made across different groups of subjects. Despite taking place in the laboratory, the task was designed to be as true to life as possible.

Procedure

Each group of subjects met four times for up to 40 minutes each time. Their task was to discuss 'a complex human relations problem of the sort typically faced by an administrator' (p. 32), and make recommendations about how the problem should be addressed. All subjects in each group had been briefed about the problem before the first meeting. They did not know one another and were unsure about whether they had received the same information about the problem as the other group members.

The subjects performed this series of joint decision-making tasks in a laboratory, where they were observed by a team of researchers sitting in an adjoining room behind a one-way mirror. Audio-tape recordings of the discussions were made. The observers were watching for, and recording, the occurrence of communicative acts. Each observer used a type of *event recorder* which produced a continuously moving paper tape on which every communicative act was written. The codes that were used to identify acts included a way of identifying who performed the act, and to whom the communication was directed. The 12 category taxonomy which Bales developed in order to classify communicative acts is shown in the results section below. The 12 acts shown in the middle column of Table 3.1 are grouped into four types of acts, shown in the left-hand column.

The subjects were aware that they were being observed and that their communicative behaviour was being recorded. All subjects completed questionnaires after each session, which among other things asked for each person's opinion of who had the best ideas in the group, and which group member was the best liked.

RESULTS

Table 3.1 shows that 56 per cent of the acts in the 'average' group session were classified as 'problem-solving attempts'. Bales suggests that these directly task-related acts were balanced by questions and reactions (positive and negative) which made up the remaining 44 per cent.

The paper also shows that the rate of information-giving within a group decreased across the first, middle and last stages of an average meeting, whilst the rates of suggestions, positive reactions and negative reactions increased. The giving of opinions seemed to occur most frequently in the middle phase of the meeting.

Bales identifies two particular types of role within the groups: the 'ideas' role, which was filled by the person who took a lead in terms of the problem-solving task at hand, and the 'most-liked' role, filled (of course) by the most popular group member. In some groups there was a high level of agreement in response to the questionnaire items about who had the best ideas, and who was best liked in the group. Bales also asserts that the subjects' subjective ratings usually matched up with the more objective measures taken by the observers. In other words, those who were identified by group members as having had the best ideas, also tended to talk the most, and to give the most suggestions. Those identified by the group as being the most-liked person also tended to score more highly than average in the 'shows tension release'

Table 3.1   The average proportion of acts in each category of Bales' taxonomy, over 96 group sessions

Area	Act	Per cent
Positive reactions	Show solidarity	3.4
	Shows tension release	6.0
	Shows agreement	16.5
Problem-solving attempts	Gives suggestion	8.0
	Gives opinion	30.1
	Gives information	17.9
Questions	Asks for information	3.5
	Asks for opinion	2.4
	Asks for suggestion	1.1
Negative reactions	Shows disagreement	7.8
	Shows tension	2.7
	Shows antagonism	0.7

Source: Bales (1955)

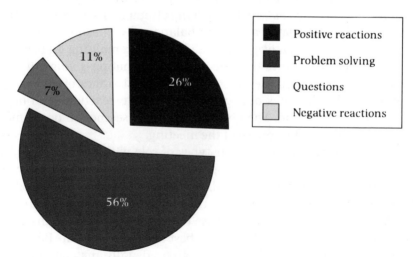

Figure 3.2   *Average proportion of acts in the main areas of Bales' taxonomy, over 96 group sessions*

category (laughing and smiling are examples of this kind of act). By the end of four discussion sessions it was unlikely that the person with the best ideas was also seen as the most-liked person. Bales does not cite raw data in support of these assertions concerning the different roles of the group members.

DISCUSSION

Perhaps the most interesting feature of this piece of work is the emphasis on how group interactions develop over the course of time. He likens the processes engaged in by his laboratory groups to the processes involved in 'a large-scale communication and control system such as an air-defense network' (p. 32), and outlines a complex seven-stage structure for problem-solving which is grounded in this analogy. The seven stages take the group from the starting point of 'making an observation' to the finishing point of proposing a 'specific action'. His data appear to support the stages he proposes. For example, information giving ('making an observation') is most prevalent at the beginning of the process at the stage when the group is gathering together the knowledge of all its individual members. As time wears on, progressively more of the communications within the group are geared towards making suggestions (proposing 'specific actions').

The changes in task-oriented communications are counterbalanced by changes in the more social and emotional communications. At the outset, negative reactions are relatively infrequent since information-giving is less controversial than the expression of opinions and the suggestion of strategies and ideas. Needless to say, as the number of suggestions increases, so too do the number of negative reactions from group members who do not agree with these suggestions. But note that positive reactions, which from the beginning occur at a much higher rate, increase in parallel with the negative reactions. It is as if groups need to maintain a surplus of positive acts in order to move forward in pursuit of their goal. The intricate interweaving of all these different acts, and the way that changes in the frequency of one act are related to changes in the frequency of other types of acts, indicates that the group operates as a kind of self-regulating *system*. Indeed, Bales' analysis of group dynamics is often referred to as a 'systemic' analysis.

Bales went on to become an influential researcher and writer in the field of group dynamics, and his 12-category taxonomy for studying verbal communication within decision-making groups is still used today.

QUESTIONS

1 What information is captured by recording acts on a moving paper tape which is harder to capture on a standard observation checklist?

2 Why are there several observers? Give at least two possible reasons.

3 Why is it important that we know that the group members knew they were being observed?

4 Bales' work was carried out on 'decision-making groups'. How do these groups differ from the everyday groups to which you belong or just find yourself in?

Suggested Answers start at p. 436

KEY WORDS

decision-making groups	reactivity
event recorder	sequences
fieldwork	structured observation
group dynamics	system
inter-observer reliability	taxonomy

4 Prejudice

Prejudice is defined by Allport (1958) as '... an antipathy based on a faulty and inflexible generalisation. It may be felt or expressed. It may be directed toward a group as a whole, or toward an individual because he is a member of that group.' (p. 10)

Alternatively, prejudice can be seen as part of the general process of *ethnocentrism*, which can be described as the following *syndrome of behaviours*:

(1) the tendency to under-value the products of the *outgroup* (any group that we do *not* belong to);
(2) increased hostility and rejection to outgroup members;
(3) the tendency to over evaluate the products of the *ingroup* (any group that we *do* belong to);
(4) increased liking for ingroup members, along with a pressure for conformity and group cohesion.

Psychological theories of prejudice have tended to concentrate on two approaches; the *psychoanalytic* and the *interactions of groups*. The most prominent psychoanalytic theory was 'The Authoritarian Personality' proposed by Adorno *et al.* (1950), which described prejudice as being the result of unresolved childhood conflicts. The approach suggests that prejudice is confined to a few 'sick people', and that the majority of people are alright. The approach is unable to explain the widespread prejudiced attitudes and behaviours that exist in our society.

The other approach sees prejudice developing from interactions between groups and within groups. The work of Sherif (1956) described in this chapter suggests that competition between groups is the key to understanding prejudice. The paper by Aronson and Bridgeman (1979) builds on Sherif's approach to evaluate a method for reducing prejudice. And the influential work of Tajfel (1970) suggests that *competition*

57

is not necessary for ethnocentrism to develop; the mere existence of *categorisation* into groups is enough.

Psychology itself does not have a good record on prejudice on a number of counts. First, it has provided a platform for distasteful statements about 'racial superiority' that have been dressed up in the clothes of bogus science; for example, see Rushton (1990) in the principle journal of the British Psychological Society. Secondly, much of the research that is used to make generalisations about all people is, in fact, based on a very narrow sample of people from Europe and the USA, who are predominantly middle class and White. Thirdly, the study of prejudice itself tends to look at the behaviour and experience of people who are prejudiced, rather than those who experience it. In the study of racism we have the perspective of the *racists* but not the *victims of racism*. This is a strange omission if we want to explore the phenomenon of prejudice.

The Robber's Cave

■ Sherif, M. (1956). Experiments in group conflict.
Scientific American, 195, 54–58.

Introduction

Psychology has offered two basic approaches to describe the phenomenon of prejudice. One line of argument sees it as an individual problem; a sick person model of prejudice. The major influence here is
psycho-analysis and the work of Freud, with the root of prejudice being
seen to be in childhood experiences that create a damaged adult personality. Adorno *et al.* (1950) presented the picture of the authoritarian personality who projects his or her unresolved childhood conflicts onto
minority groups. The authoritarian personality is narrow minded, a
stickler for rules, inhibited about sex, unquestioningly submissive to
authority, intolerant of ambiguity, and politically conservative. The
basic flaw in this approach to prejudice is the insistence that prejudice
is a sign of a sick personality, and that, by implication, most people are
not prejudiced.

The other major line of argument sees prejudice as a result of group
membership and group interaction. An example of this approach is the
work of Sherif and his associates who proposed a *conflict* model of prejudice. Their model suggests that when groups interact with one another
they inevitably generate attitudes towards each other. If the groups are
'positively independent', and working towards common goals, then
good inter-group relations develop and the inter-group attitudes are
positive (see also Aronson & Bridgeman, 1979, in this chapter). On the
other hand, if the groups are 'negatively independent', in competition
for scarce resources perhaps, then group conflict develops and *ethnocentric* attitudes appear. Sherif and his associates tested this theory in a
number of field studies.

The basic question under investigation was, could they take a
group of people without any hostile attitudes towards each other,
divide them into groups, create conflict in the groups through introducing competition, and thereby create ethnocentric attitudes and
behaviour?

THE STUDY

The field experiments were conducted in 1949, 1953 and 1954, and this article gives composite findings. Sherif wanted to study informal groups so that he could observe the natural and spontaneous development of group organisation and attitudes. To do this the researchers created an isolated summer camp as an experimental setting.

The subjects were boys aged 11 to 12. According to Sherif they were picked by a 'long and thorough procedure' involving interviews with family, teachers and school officials, and also by the use of school and medical records, scores on personality tests, and observations of them in class and at play. The boys were unknown to each other and 'all were healthy, socially well adjusted, somewhat above average in intelligence and from stable, White, Protestant, middle-class homes' (p. 54). The sample was deliberately homogeneous to reduce the chances of bringing in established social conflicts (such as class or race prejudice) to the study.

The boys were unaware that they were part of an experiment on group relations. The investigators appeared as regular camp staff, and the boys met the staff and each other for the first time in the buses on the way to camp. To maintain *ecological validity*, the experiments were conducted within the framework of regular camp activities and games. The researchers made unobtrusive records of behaviour, and, on occasions, used cameras and microphones.

In the first phase of the study, Sherif and his associates observed the development of group structure. To start with the boys were housed in one large bunkhouse where they were able to choose their own 'buddies' (Sherif's term). After a few days they divided the boys into two groups and took care to separate 'best friends' into different groups.

The boys were given a range of challenging activities including hikes and campouts, and athletics and sports. In each group, the boys divided up the tasks and organised duties. Leaders and lieutenants emerged, and each group developed its own jargon, special jokes, secrets and special ways of performing tasks. They maintained social control through ridicule, threats and ostracism; for example, insulting any boy who did not pull his weight at a particular task. Each group selected a symbol and a name which was put on their baseball caps and T-shirts (fashion point: it is interesting to note that in 1954 the style for boys was very close to the style of 1996). The 1954 study was carried out near to a famous hideaway of Jesse James called the Robber's Cave (the study is often referred to as the Robber's Cave Experiment), and the groups called themselves 'The Eagles' and 'The Rattlers'.

To test the social evaluations of the boys, the researchers invented a game of target practice. There were no marks on the target board, and a judgement of accuracy was made by the watching peers. However, the board was also secretly wired to give an objective measure of accuracy. The boys consistently overestimated efforts of highly regarded boys and underestimated efforts of the lowly regarded. The researchers also made diagrammatic records of group structure, one of which is shown in Figure 4.1. They asked each boy to name his friends in the group. The boy who was chosen most times was regarded as having the highest status, and the boy who was chosen the least was chosen as having the lowest status.

The two groups shown in the figure have very different structures; the group on the right is very hierarchical with one clear leader and lieutenant along with seven low-status boys. The group on the left has a clear leader but also a number of other boys of intermediate status. This latter group was reportedly better at a range of tasks.

OBSERVATIONS

Sherif's prediction had been that '. . . when two groups have conflicting aims, their members will become hostile to each other even though the groups are composed of normal well adjusted individuals' (p. 57). In the second phase of the study the researchers introduced conflict through games. The tournament started in good spirit but the boys soon started to call their rivals 'stinkers', 'sneaks' and 'cheaters' (fashion point 2: clothes style might not have changed but language certainly has!). The boys refused contact with the opposing group, and turned against their previous buddies. When they were asked to give ratings to the other boys in the camp, they gave negative ratings to boys in the other group. During this period *solidarity* increased *within* each group. Name calling, scuffles and 'raids' (for example, stealing the other group's flag and setting fire to it) became the pattern of behaviour.

The hypothesis was supported alarmingly easily and this created a problem of how to reduce the conflict. The initial attempts involved bringing the groups together for an activity, but these occasions ended

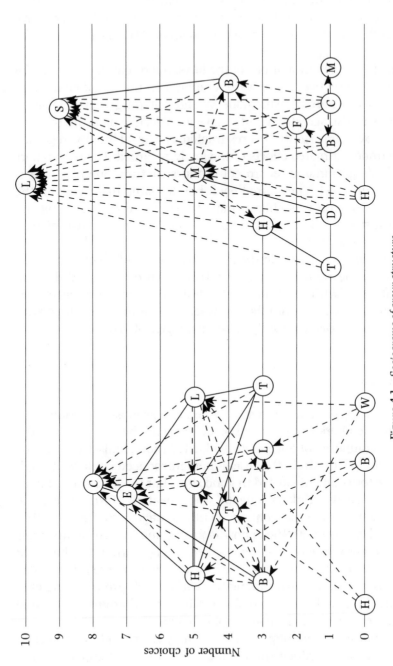

Figure 4.1 *Sociograms of group structure*

Sociograms represent patterns of friendship choices within the fully developed groups. One-way friendships are indicated by broken arrows; reciprocated friendships, by solid lines. Leaders were among those highest in the popularity scale. Bulldogs (*left*) had a close-knit organisation with good group spirit. Low-ranking members participated less in the life of the group but were not rejected. Red Devils (*right*) lost the tournament of games between the groups. They had less group unity and were sharply stratified.

Source: Sherif (1956)

in fights and abuse. So a further hypothesis developed: '. . . working in a common endeavour should promote harmony' (p. 57).

In the third and final phase, the researchers had to establish *superordinate goals* for the two groups. They created a series of urgent and natural situations, for example by interrupting the water supply, and making the camp truck break down on an outing. This latter 'crisis' had to be resolved by the boys pulling the truck. The boys developed new friendships in the opposing groups as they worked through these crises, and, according to Sherif, by the end of the camp the groups were 'actively seeking opportunities to mingle, to entertain and to "treat" each other' (p. 57). The boys made far less negative ratings of the opposing group, and the hostility seemed to have disappeared.

DISCUSSION

This is a remarkable piece of research on a number of counts. The methods are very inventive, with a number of measures of social behaviour being seamlessly introduced into everyday situations. The study also has considerable ecological validity which was a feature of social psychology conducted before 1960 (see Sears, 1986, Chapter 21 of this volume). The study lacks a certain amount of control, but the trade off with relevance seems a good one. You cannot help but wonder whether the level of hostility alarmed the researchers, and whether they were able to reduce this hostility quite as successfully as they claim.

The study tells us one of the ways of creating inter-group hostility and, therefore, ethnocentric attitudes and behaviour. This suggests that we should see, for example, racial prejudice as a consequence of competition for resources between different ethnic groups. In this case, we would predict that prejudice would rise when economic hardship increased, and to a certain extent this is supported by observation. However, the model does not explain why some groups should be singled out for racism and not others. For example, in Nottingham, where the authors live, there are a number of large ethnic groups which include Irish, Ukrainian and Polish, as well as a number of Black and Asian groups. All these groups are in the same competition for a limited number of jobs, houses and welfare resources, but the Black and Asian groups are subject to more racism than the Europeans. Clearly the conflict model does not tell us the whole story.

QUESTIONS

1   What is the conflict model of prejudice?

2   What measures of social behaviour and social judgement did the researchers take?

3   List some of the (numerous) ethical concerns with this study.

4   What groups in everyday life are in conflict with each other?

5   What are the advantages of carrying this study out in 'the field'?

Suggested Answers start at p. 437

KEY WORDS

conflict model   prejudice
ecological validity   racism
ethnocentrism   superordinate goals
field experiment

THE JIGSAW TECHNIQUE

■ ARONSON, E. & BRIDGEMAN, D. (1979). Jigsaw groups and the desegregated classroom: In pursuit of common goals.
In E. Aronson (ed.), *Readings about the Social Animal*, 6th edn, pp. 329–40; originally in *Personality and Social Psychology Bulletin*, 5, 438–66.

INTRODUCTION

In the USA in 1954, the Supreme Court put a stop to school segregation as a result of the historic *Brown versus Board of Education* case. This meant that from then on it was illegal to bar pupils from schools on the grounds of their race. During the course of the court case, the expert evidence of psychologists was accepted in the form of oral testimony and in the form of what has come to be known as the 'Social Science Statement'. This was written by Clark, Chein and Cook, and was signed by 32 social scientists. It argued the case for desegregation on the grounds that segregation of schools sustained inter-racial prejudice, and had negative effects on the 'segregated against' minority groups, particularly in terms of self-esteem.

Twenty-five years later it was evident in the school system of the United States that desegregation had not been a magic cure for prejudice. Gerard & Miller (1975, cited by Aronson and Bridgeman) found that children from different racial groups still tended to spend their time with members of their own groups. In addition, a review of relevant studies by Stephan (1978, cited by Aronson and Bridgeman) found that not one of these studies showed any significant increase in self-esteem among children from minority groups since desegregation, and around a quarter of the studies actually showed significant *decreases* in self-esteem among children from minority groups.

'What went wrong?' (p. 330) is the question that forms the background to Aronson and Bridgeman's paper. The answer appears to be that the desegregated classroom is not, in itself, enough to reduce prejudice and to increase the self-esteem of minority children in schools. More active strategies are needed to achieve these ends. Aronson and Bridgeman's paper describes and evaluates just such a strategy, known as the 'jigsaw' group. It is a review article that examines the evidence from several studies (by a variety of authors) relating to the effectiveness of jigsaw groups.

THE JIGSAW GROUP TECHNIQUE

The jigsaw technique involves children working in groups of six. Each child has one-sixth of the material about the subject which is being taught. The task requires children to share all their bits of information with one another in order to understand the whole lesson; in other words they have to fit the information together like a jigsaw. In working through this task each child spends a certain amount of time as an 'expert' (whilst they are teaching the others about the information which they have), and a certain amount of time listening to their peers. They are, in short, interdependent upon one another and 'in pursuit of common goals' (p. 332). Aronson and Bridgeman argue that this spirit of interdependency is not characteristic of the average United States classroom which is governed more by competition than cooperation.

The central idea of reducing prejudice by creating situations in which groups of children have to collaborate to achieve a common superordinate goal is reminiscent of Sherif's work in the 'Robber's Cave' study (Sherif, 1956, the previous summary in this chapter). This showed that simple contact between rival groups of children was not sufficient to break down the intergroup hostility which had been created. It was only after the different groups faced a common set of challenges, and were forced to work together, that prejudices began to break down.

The jigsaw procedure as described in this paper constitutes a form of *action research*. This term refers to research procedures which are not simply intended to provide data. They are also meant to benefit the subjects directly in their real lives. Action research projects are particularly common in the field of education where they are used to evaluate the effectiveness of teaching programmes and strategies in the classroom.

A typical research design involves allocating children to one or more 'treatment' groups and to one or more control groups. In the case of jigsaw evaluation studies the treatment groups contain all the children who are to use the jigsaw group technique. The children in the control group(s) are matched with the experimental children on a number of relevant criteria (age, educational attainment and so forth). They are also from classes that are using some other teaching programme which is equivalent to the jigsaw programme in terms of variables such as teacher motivation, additional tuition time, level of interest and novelty, and so on.

RESULTS

Since Aronson and Bridgeman's paper is a review article about jigsaw group research, the results they report are in the form of general patterns of outcomes from a variety of investigations. All references in the following three paragraphs are taken from Aronson and Bridgeman's account.

They begin by stating that 'Systematic research in the classroom has produced consistently positive results' (p. 333), and go on to summarise the findings of three separate projects. Blaney *et al.* (1977) showed significant increases in self-esteem for children who had been in a six-week jigsaw group programme over children who had been taught for the same period by highly rated teachers. Equally, the jigsaw children 'showed significant increases in their liking for their groupmates both within and across ethnic boundaries' (p. 334).

Blaney *et al.'s* results were replicated by Geffner (1978) in a study in California. This investigation showed, in addition, that negative stereotypes of ethnic groups decreased among the experimental jigsaw children.

Lucker *et al.* (1977) demonstrated gains in academic performance among ethnic minority children who had been taught in ethnically mixed jigsaw groups for two weeks compared with children taught in conventional ways. Significantly, they also showed no decrease in performance for the majority ethnic group children. In other words the gap in attainment between the majority and minority children was closed by the jigsaw group, but not by pulling down children's performances.

DISCUSSION

Having cited the generally favourable evidence, Aronson and Bridgeman go on to discuss why jigsaw groups increase self-esteem, attainment, and liking for members of other ethnic groups. They argue that increased active participation in lessons is one important factor. It is well known that active learning is effective learning. They also argue that an ethic of interdependency encourages genuinely 'equal status contact' (p. 331) among members of different ethnic groups. For example all children in the group have to act as an expert at some stage in the learning process, and teach the other members of the group about their particular bit of the lesson. This should contribute to raising each child's status in the eyes of all the others.

Aronson and Bridgeman's most insightful comments are, perhaps, about 'empathic role taking'. This is the ability to put yourself in another person's shoes, to see and understand things from that other person's perspective. The authors cite evidence from Bridgeman (1977) that jigsaw groups increase children's ability for empathic role taking. Perhaps this is because jigsaw groups force children to listen to each other, and encourage them to frame their own contributions in a way that fits with the needs of the rest of the group. The idea of empathic role taking is strongly related to notions of 'theories of mind' which have taken off as a core feature of developmental psychology in the 1980s and 1990s (see Baron-Cohen, Leslie & Frith, 1985, Chapter 18 of this volume).

QUESTIONS

1   Why would the children in the control groups come from classes in which they were undertaking programmes that were arguably equivalent to the jigsaw groups?

2   How did Sherif set up the 'superordinate goals' which reduced conflict among the Robber's Cave children?

Suggested Answers start at p. 438

Key Words

action research	prejudice
desegregation	self-esteem
empathic role taking	superordinate goal
equal status contact	theories of mind
jigsaw groups	

THE MINIMAL GROUP STUDIES

■ TAJFEL, H. (1970). Experiments in intergroup discrimination. *Scientific American*, *223*, 96–102.

INTRODUCTION

What does it take to make you believe you are a member of a group? The tradition of the British pantomime usually has one piece where the audience is asked to sing, divided into two groups, and encouraged to compete against each other to see who sings the loudest. The members of the audience invariably oblige by singing their hearts out. Each person believes they are a member of a team and acts to support that team. The studies by Sherif (summarised earlier in this chapter) suggested that groups only develop strong intergroup feelings when there is conflict, and this conflict is the crucial precursor of *ethno-centrism*. However, conflict is not present in all interactions between groups, but ethnocentrism can still develop.

One curious observation from Sherif's summer-camp studies suggests that just being in a group is enough to create ethnocentrism, and the conflict is not necessary. In one of Sherif's studies, the boys were initially separated into two groups and did not know of each other's existence. However, when they became aware that another group was in the vicinity, they showed signs of competitiveness towards the other group before the intergroup competitions were announced by the experimenters. Just being in one group and becoming aware of a second group was enough to trigger feelings of rivalry. Henri Tajfel took this one step further and showed, in his *minimal group studies*, that merely being *categorised* is enough to create intergroup rivalry.

THE STUDY

Tajfel begins his article with a brief review of psychological approaches to prejudice. He observes that much of the research was concerned with attitudes rather than behaviour, with prejudice rather than discrimination. This approach has certain drawbacks because of the weak links between attitudes and behaviour (see LaPiere, Chapter 2 of this volume). Tajfel suggests that the most important feature of our attempts to make sense of the social world we live in, is our classification of groups as 'we' and 'they'. To put this in psychological terms, we talk about *ingroups* (which are groups we belong to) and *outgroups* (which are groups we do not belong to). Tajfel goes on to suggest that we experience so many ingroups and outgroups that we develop norms of behaviour towards them. We learn how to behave towards 'one of us' or 'one of them' regardless of how that distinction is defined.

Tajfel and his colleagues carried out two experiments to investigate the factors that will enhance discrimination in groups.

Experiment one

The subjects were 64 boys aged between 14 and 15 years who all came from a state school in Bristol (UK). They went to the psychology laboratory in separate groups of eight, and all of the boys in each of the groups knew each other well before the experiment. The first part of the experiment was designed to create *group categorisation*, and the second part of the experiment investigated the effects of this.

In the first part, the boys were told that the psychologists were interested in the study of visual judgements. Forty clusters of varying numbers of dots were flashed onto a screen. The boys were asked to estimate the number of dots in each cluster. The experimenters then pretended to assess the judgements of the boys, and told them what kind of judgements they had made. Some of the groups were categorised on the basis of accuracy, and some were categorised on the basis of over or underestimation. The boys were assigned to groups at random and were told they were either an 'overestimator' or 'underestimator' in one condition, or highly accurate or poorly accurate in the other condition.

The boys were then asked to give rewards of real money (though not very much) to the other boys in the experiment. They did not know the identity of the boys they were giving the money to, but they did know which group they were in (for example, whether or not they were an overestimator). Each boy was given an eighteen page booklet with sets of numbers. They were asked to choose a pair of numbers that would allocate money to two other boys. The numbers were arranged in a style similar to that shown below:

Choice number	1	2	3	4	5
Boy Number 1	9	11	12	14	16
Boy number 2	5	9	11	15	19

They were required to make three types of choice:

(a) Ingroup choices: where both top and bottom row referred to members of the same group as the boy.
(b) Outgroup choices: where both top and bottom row referred to members of the different group from the boy.
(c) Intergroup choices: where one row referred to the boys' own group and one row referred to the other group.

Results of experiment one

The important choice for Tajfel is the intergroup choice, and he found that a large majority of the boys gave more money to members of their own group than to members of the other group. Bear in mind that the boys came into the psychology laboratory as a group of eight, were *arbitrarily* divided into two sub-groups of four by the psychologists, and were not aware of who else was in their sub-group. Tajfel investigated this phenomenon further in a second experiment.

Experiment two

Three new groups of 16 boys were tested, and this time they were divided on the basis of their supposed artistic preferences. The boys were shown 12 paintings by the abstract expressionist painters Paul Klee and Wassily Kandinsky. The boys were then randomly told that they had preferred either Klee or Kandinsky. Tajfel then asked the boys to fill out similar sets of reward booklets to the first experiment. However, in this experiment he was interested in which of three variables would have the greatest effect on the boys' choices. The three variables were:

(a) *maximum joint profit* – where the boys could give the largest reward to members of both groups;
(b) *largest possible reward to ingroup* – where the boys could choose the largest reward for the member of their own group regardless of the reward to the boy from the other group;
(c) *maximum difference* – where the boys could choose the largest possible difference in reward between members of the different groups (in favour of the ingroup).

If we look again at our example choices (shown below) then we can see how these three variables can be examined.

Choice of number	1	2	3	4	5
Boy Number 1 (in-group)	9	11	12	14	16
Boy number 2 (out-group)	5	9	11	15	19

Maximum joint profit and giving the *largest reward to the ingroup* would both be achieved by choosing the last pair in the row, giving 16 to a member of your own group, and 19 to a member of the other group. However, to maximise your own rewards while also *maximising the difference*, you might well choose one of the middle boxes and give 12 to a member of your own group and only 11 to a member of the other group.

Results of experiment two

When Tajfel examined the boys' choices he found that maximum joint profit had very little effect at all, and the most important factor in their choices was maximising the difference between the two groups. This is a relatively surprising result because it meant that the boys left the study with less money than if they had all given each other the most amount of money available.

Tajfel concludes that outgroup discrimination is extraordinarily easy to trigger off. Once it has been triggered off, then we have norms of behaviour for outgroups which include discriminating against them.

DISCUSSION

There are a number of criticisms of Tajfel's studies including his interpretation of the results. Brown (1988), for example, suggests that the behaviour of the boys can be seen in terms of fairness as much as discrimination. Although the boys showed bias towards their own group, this bias was not very extreme and seemed to be moderated by a sense of fairness. Another criticism concerns the artificial nature of the studies, and the suggestion that the design is so unlike a real life situation that the results might well be just a product of the experiment itself. In other words, the boys just conformed to the *demand characteristics* of the experimental design (for a further discussion of this see the study by Orne, Chapter 21 of this volume).

If we try and explain why the boys behaved as they did, then we have to consider another question. Is this outgroup discrimination just a feature of Western cultures? Brown (1988) observes that research suggests the effect does occur in other cultures but to a much lesser extent. It could be, then, that the design of the study reminded the boys of competitive games at school and so they chose to compete because that's what boys do in Western societies.

QUESTIONS

1   The study was carried out on teenage boys. What effect do you think this had on the results?

2   What groups do you belong to? And what groups do you *not* belong to?

Suggested Answers start at p. 438

KEY WORDS

categorisation	ethnocentrism
conflict	ingroup
demand characteristics	minimal group
discrimination	outgroup

PART II

COMPARATIVE AND PHYSIOLOGICAL PSYCHOLOGY

Comparative psychology explores human behaviour and experience by comparing people with other species. The basic argument is that it is not just our bodies that have evolved over the centuries, but also our behaviour. The *evolution of behaviour* can be seen, for example, in species of birds who are often far easier to spot by what they do (for example the way they build a nest) rather than by what they look like. Evolutionary studies have shown how the three factors of *behaviour*, *biology* and *environment*, interact to develop a species. Animals adapt behaviourally (for example, feeding and mating patterns) and biologically (for example, size and digestive system) over a number of generations, to fit with their changing environment.

Animal psychologists have come up with some remarkable insights into animal behaviour and experience, but the question to be answered is how much these insights can be applied to people. Are there some major differences between humans and the animals, or are we just another animal with a little more dress sense? Depending on your point of view you can concentrate on the similarities or the differences. The danger of the human–animal metaphor is that we see human behaviour as *just* being due to evolutionary forces. In this argument we view acts of kindness or altruism as being simple animal displays and accept bad behaviour as natural (like, for example, male aggression) – *'I'm sorry I invaded Poland, I was just responding to my animal instinct'*. That reference to Nazi aggression during the 1939–45 war is not without some relevance since, according to Rose, Kamin & Lewontin (1984), the famous Austrian animal psychologist, Konrad Lorenz, wrote a paper during the war giving an evolutionary argument in favour of the Final Solution (the Nazi policy of killing people they regarded as inferior – Jews, Slavs, homosexuals, gypsies, the mentally ill, and so forth.)

During this century there have been two major strands of animal psychology. *Comparative psychology* has largely been associated with laboratory work and, in particular, studies on rats and pigeons. These animals have been chosen for study not for their evolutionary significance, but because of their size and docility. One of the major concerns of the comparative psychologists is how we learn, and in this part we include three papers on this topic. The other major strand of animal work has been *ethology*, which attempts to study animals in as natural a habitat as possible. We include three studies that illustrate some of the important themes of this work.

Physiological psychology explores human behaviour and experience by looking at people *as if* they are biological machines. This idea has some value because it is clear that our biology affects our behaviour and experience. On a simple level we (the authors!) know that six pints of Shufflebottom's Old Disgusting beer on a Friday night will have alarming affects on the way we see the world and the way we behave. Also, it has been observed for a long time that damage to the brain and nervous system can have an effect on behaviour and experience. So the structure of the nervous system and the action of chemicals are the two main themes of physiological psychology. However, the question that arises is very similar to the one we have to answer for comparative psychology – how much does our biology affect us and what other factors intervene to affect the response? In this selection we include three studies that show some of the concerns of physiological psychology, and highlight the interaction between biological and psychological variables. Some issues of physiological psychology are also considered in Part VI, especially the paper on phantom limbs by Melzack (1992). The studies in Part VI also explore the interaction between physiological and social factors in our behaviour and experience.

5 LEARNING

Learning can be defined as '... a relatively permanent change in behavioural potential which accompanies experience but which is not the result of simple growth factors or of reversible influences such as fatigue or hunger' (Kimble 1961, cited in Gross, 1992). This definition takes in the following points:

(a) *Relatively permanent* – change in behaviour is a sign of learning, but our behaviour often just fluctuates without learning, so psychologists include the phrase 'relatively permanent' to distinguish learning from the everyday fluctuations in performance.

(b) *Behavioural potential* – when we have learnt something we do not always act on it; for example, the fact that I sometimes drink too much alcohol does not mean that I have not learnt what the consequences will be. It just means that I am too stupid to respond to what I've learnt.

(c) *Growth factors* – some behaviour and experience develops through maturation (a biological unfolding) and this is usually distinguished from learning. However, this distinction is far from simple and there is an interaction between maturation and learning.

The psychological study of learning has been dominated by behaviourism – the movement founded by John B. Watson in the early part of this century, which concentrated on behaviour (what someone does) rather than experience (what someone thinks or feels). A paper by Watson is included in Part IV of this book, on Developmental Psychology. The behaviourists suggested that we learn by the simple process of associating one event with another. The work of Pavlov in developing the concept of *classical conditioning* is an important part of this argument. Pavlov showed that dogs will learn to associate simple reflex behaviours, such as salivating, with a previously neutral stimulus, such as a bell. In this way they were taught to salivate at the sound of a bell. They learnt a new reflex action which Pavlov called a *conditioned reflex*. This type of learning can only explain a limited range of behaviour, but the work of Thorndike and Skinner provided an explanation for much more of our learning.

Thorndike made some ingenious puzzle boxes from which cats had to learn to escape. He showed that they were able to learn how to escape without ever showing any sign of understanding how they managed to do it. He proposed the *Law of Effect* which says that the result of a successful behaviour is that it will be repeated in similar circumstances. Skinner elaborated on this work and developed the concept of *operant conditioning* which showed how animals (and people) can learn a whole range of behaviours through reinforcements and punishment. One of the strengths of this work is the experimental rigour which the behaviourists employed, but this is also one of the weaknesses. The controlled nature of the studies meant that the animals were observed in very restricted situations with a very limited range of behaviours to show, so the relevance of this work to learning in everyday life is seriously questioned.

The three papers chosen for this chapter all show how the basic concepts of behaviourism have been applied to wider concerns. The first paper is a delightful report by Skinner on his attempts to encourage the American military to let his pigeons pilot their missiles. Strangely, they declined the offer, but Skinner provided a powerful case for his suggestion. The paper by Seligman starts with a simple learning experience in dogs and looks at how this might be applied to a range of human experience including depression. The final study by the Gardners looks at the attempts to teach language to a chimpanzee, and the criticisms of this study focus on the differences between the way animals learn to communicate and the way children learn language.

THE FLIGHT OF THE KILLER PIGEONS

■ SKINNER, B.F. (1960). Pigeons in a pelican.
American Psychologist, 15, 28–37.

INTRODUCTION

Around the turn of the twentieth century, American psychologist Edward Lee Thorndike investigated how animals learn. In one series of observations he placed a cat in a 'puzzle box' and measured the time it took to escape. Over a number of trials the time taken to escape decreased, yet the animal showed no sign of *insight* into the problem. It got out but it did not understand how it did it. From his observations he developed the Law of Effect, which states that the consequence of a successful behaviour is that it is more likely to recur in similar circumstances. This provided a description of animal behaviour that did not require notions such as consciousness or thought.

This work was developed by the behaviourists including B.F. Skinner. They argued that all behaviour in human or non-human animals is caused, shaped and maintained by its consequences. This can happen in a number of ways including:

- *Positive Reinforcement* – when a pleasant stimulus follows a particular response it strengthens that response; for example, giving your pet a doggo-choc when it sits on command will make it more likely to sit next time you tell it to.
- *Negative Reinforcement* – when an aversive stimulus is removed following a response it is also likely to strengthen that response. This is sometimes referred to as escape conditioning.
- *Punishment* – when an aversive stimulus follows a behavioural response it weakens that response and makes it less likely to recur.

The above procedures can be used to *shape* new behaviours into an animal by reinforcing *successive approximations* to the required response. For example, if you wanted your pet to learn to jump through a hoop of fire you would not start by showing it a lighted hoop and saying 'Jump!'. Instead, you would reward the animal for walking through an unlit hoop on the ground, and then gradually raise the hoop and reward the animal for every new height achieved. Finally, when the animal will jump through the hoop, you can try it with a lighted one. In this way, the animal learns the behaviour step by step until the whole complex action has been shaped by the careful use of rewards.

Skinner used the above procedures to explain an array of complex behaviours in humans believing that it was unnecessary to look for underlying causes beyond the reinforcement contingencies that could be used to change that behaviour. We recommend that you try and read some of Skinner's own writings (for example, Skinner, 1973 and 1974) because his work has been so influential in psychology.

THE STUDY

Skinner describes in this paper how, during the Second World War (1939–45), he developed a programme to train pigeons to guide missiles. With startling originality, but admirable directness, the programme was called 'Project Pigeon'. This was not the first time, nor the last, that the potential of animals has been exploited in warfare. Skinner reports that the British Navy used seagulls to detect submarines in the First World War (1914–18). The Navy would send its own submarines into the English Channel to release food. This would attract flocks of seagulls who would then learn to associate the sight of an underwater vessel with the appearance of food. They would then follow any submarine whether it was British or German. Therefore, a flock of seagulls in the Channel would be the sign of an approaching German submarine. Dogs and dolphins are among the other animals that have been used for military purposes, and the consequences for these animals was often not a good meal, but an early death as the explosives which were attached to them were detonated.

The original studies by Skinner tested the ability of a pigeon to steer towards a target by using a moving hoist. The pigeon was held in a jacket and harnessed to a block, and was immobilised except for its neck. It could eat grain from a dish and move its head in appropriate directions. Movement of the head operated the motors of the hoist. The bird could make the apparatus move upwards by lifting its head, downwards by lowering it, and travel from side to side by moving its head to the side it wanted to travel to. The whole apparatus was mounted on wheels and pushed across a room towards a bulls-eye. The task of the pigeon was to adjust the position of the hoist while it was being pushed across the room so that it would end up at the bulls-eye where the bowl of grain could be found. The pigeons were remarkably successful and could direct the apparatus to the bulls-eye regardless of the starting position and also during rapid approaches.

The American military were initially unimpressed by the work and it took support from a private company to develop it further. This work found that a guiding system that was dependent on the movements of the pigeon would respond too late to accurately direct the missile to its target. Skinner and his associates then developed a screen that showed the target to the pigeon. The screen was arranged so that when the pigeon pecked the screen it activated the guidance system, and the position of the pecks would alter the orientation of the visual display. The visual display was constantly in motion and the target would go out of view unless the pigeon continued to control it with its pecks.

Once again the perceptual skills of the pigeons were remarkable and they were able to direct the guidance system towards particular object shapes such as ships, to ignore other objects and concentrate on just one, and to guide the system towards a particular road junction on a city map. They studied ways of enhancing the performance of the pigeons though changes in reinforcement schedules and the use of energising drugs. They also investigated the effects of changes in temperature, pressure, sound, acceleration, oxygen levels and centrifugal force.

The argument for the pigeon controlled missiles was strong. They had better *perceptual acuity* than humans, they were lighter, cost less and were regarded as expendable. At this stage of the project in 1943, the military became interested and provided Skinner and his associates with details of the missile (The Pelican) which might be flown by the pigeons. They were able to use the specifications to design a pigeon-controlled version of the missile. The mechanism was relatively simple and, according to Skinner, foolproof. They also designed the apparatus to work with three pigeon pilots rather than one, so that the majority vote would help to avoid embarrassing mistakes.

Despite some excellent results from the laboratory, the team of scientists who examined the data and the project were unable to recommend its progress, probably because they were uneasy at the thought of large quantities of explosives being controlled by pigeons. The project was cancelled.

DISCUSSION

Skinner refers to the idea behind 'Project Pigeon' as 'crackpot', yet he showed how the birds could be trained using simple operant techniques to carry out a seemingly very complex function. In the world of 1990s warfare, we are asked to marvel at cruise missiles, yet they are probably less accurate than the pigeons would have proved to be. Behaviourists see the success of 'Project Pigeon' (and its peacetime follow-up 'Project Orcon' – for ORganic CONtrol) as evidence that apparently complex tasks such as guidance can be brought under the control of very simple learning contingencies.

Many readers will be appalled at the callous disregard for the pigeons. If the project had been brought into operation, Skinner would have trained pigeons who would then unwittingly be the agents of their own destruction as they guided themselves, and their missiles, towards detonation on an enemy ship. However, ethics must always be seen in the context of the times, and during the Second World War it appeared to many that it was right to go to war against Nazism, and that this war should be concluded as soon as possible to avoid defeat and further loss of life. In the paper Skinner writes: 'The ethical question of our right to convert a lower creature into an unwitting hero is a peace-time luxury'. You might still not accept this as a justification for the use of animals in warfare, but it does highlight that the issue of ethics is not a simple one and that people sometimes choose to act by criteria that conflict with their normal ethical standards. As Spock suggested in Star Trek II 'The needs of the many outweigh the needs of the few'.

QUESTIONS

1   Summarise how the pigeons were trained.

2   What are the advantages of using pigeons rather than people in spotter tasks?

3   Do you think the use of animals in warfare is ever justified? Try and give an example where it might be justified and where it would not be justified.

4   What other tasks would the perceptual skills of pigeons be useful for?

Suggested Answers start at p. 439

KEY WORDS

behaviourism
consciousness
ethics
Law of Effect
negative reinforcement
operant conditioning

perceptual acuity
positive reinforcement
punishment
shaping
successive approximations

LEARNING TO BE HELPLESS

■ SELIGMAN, M.E.P. & MAIER, S.F. (1967). Failure to escape
traumatic shock.
Journal of Experimental Psychology, 74, 1–9.

INTRODUCTION

We have all experienced feelings of helplessness at one time or other in
our lives. The feelings are not pleasant. They are experienced when we
are unable to control what happens to us, when whatever we do seems
to have no effect on events. For most people this is a temporary state of
affairs, associated perhaps with a mild bout of depression. But for some
people feelings of helplessness persist, even when events are, in fact,
potentially within their control.

Sometimes we clearly are unable to control events. In such cases our
feelings of helplessness are grounded in some kind of reality. But at
other times our feelings of helplessness may be misguided. We may
have the potential to exercise more control than we realise, but for one
reason or another we fail to realise that potential.

One cause of this problem could be the phenomenon of *learned helplessness.* Consider the following scenario. You continuously find yourself in situations where whatever you do seems to have no effect on
what happens to you. Gradually your coping and problem-solving
actions become extinguished, because if you learn that your actions
have no important consequences for you, then you will stop bothering
to act. So when you now encounter a situation in which you do have
the potential to control events, you have long since lost the capabilities
to exercise that control. You have learnt to be helpless.

THE STUDY

That is the theory which Seligman and his colleague Maier set out to
investigate in the simplified arena of the psychology laboratory. They
wanted to see whether learnt helplessness could be experimentally
induced in laboratory dogs. The experiment had three conditions and
involved two phases. In the first phase, some of the dogs (the 'escape'
group and the 'yoked control' group) were placed, one at a time, in an

apparatus which delivered electric shocks to them through their feet. Some of the animals (the escape group) were able to stop the shock by pressing a panel with their heads, but the others (the yoked control group) were unable to do anything to escape the shock. The dogs in the escape group successfully learnt to terminate the shocks.

In phase two, all the dogs were placed in shuttle boxes. The shuttle boxes were divided into two by a barrier set at shoulder height to each dog. Electric shocks were delivered through the floor of the boxes, but if the dog jumped over the barrier into the other half of the box, it would break a photocell beam and the shock would be terminated. In other words, dogs in all the conditions could escape from the shock. Seligman and Maier predicted that the dogs in the yoked control condition would be less likely to learn to jump the barrier than dogs in the other conditions, because the dogs in the yoked control condition had learnt helplessness in phase one.

Seligman and Maier's paper is a report of two experiments. This summary deals only with the first.

Subjects

Twenty-four 'experimentally naïve' mongrel dogs were used, eight in each condition.

Design

A standard independent measures (between subjects) experimental design was used, with one experimental condition and two control conditions. The three conditions were labelled 'escape', 'normal control' and 'yoked control'. The comparison of most interest was between the 'escape' and 'yoked control' conditions.

Procedure

Escape Condition: Phase One Each dog in the escape condition was suspended in a hammock with four holes for its legs. Attached to its two hind legs were electrodes through which the electric shocks were delivered. The dog's head was held in position by panels on either side. If the dog pressed either panel with its head the shock was terminated. Each dog received 64 shocks of a 6.0 mA magnitude. The shocks were delivered at random time intervals which varied between 60 seconds and

120 seconds (the mean interval was 90 seconds). If the dog failed to press a panel during any given shock, that shock would be terminated after 30 seconds. Each shock counted as one trial.

Escape Condition: Phase Two   After 24 hours the escape condition dogs were subjected to ten trials in the shuttle box. Each trial began with the lights in the box being switched off (the neutral stimulus). After ten seconds a shock was delivered through the floor of the box (the unconditioned stimulus). The shock could be terminated if the dog jumped the barrier which divided the box into two parts. If the dog jumped the barrier after the neutral stimulus had occurred and before onset of the shock, the shock was not delivered. Through the process of classical conditioning the neutral stimulus was to become a conditioned stimulus which signalled the onset of a shock. The time taken to escape was measured from onset of the neutral/conditioned stimulus. If the dog failed to escape after 60 seconds the shock was terminated and the next trial was begun. Trials were separated by a mean interval of 90 seconds.

Yoked Control Condition: Phase One   The dogs in this condition were placed in the same hammock apparatus as the escape dogs. They were treated in exactly the same way except that they were unable to terminate any of the 64 electric shocks. Each shock was of the same duration as the mean length of shock for the equivalent trial in the escape condition. Since the dogs in the escape condition learnt to terminate the shocks more and more rapidly as the trials progressed, the duration of each successive shock in the yoked control condition gradually diminished.

Yoked Control Condition: Phase Two   After 24 hours the dogs in this condition were subjected to ten trials in the shuttle box. The procedure was exactly the same as for phase two of the escape condition. After seven days those dogs in this condition which failed to learn to escape were tested again in the shuttle box, once more following the same procedure.

Normal Control Condition: Phase One   The dogs in this condition did not take part in phase one. They just relaxed and prepared for the onset of phase two.

Normal Control Condition: Phase Two   The dogs in the normal control condition were subjected to ten trials in the shuttle box, following the same procedure as in the other two conditions.

RESULTS

Seligman and Maier present various measures of the dependent variable. Dogs in the yoked control condition (those who had been unable to terminate the shock in phase one of the experiment) took 48.22 seconds on average to escape from the shocks, whereas the dogs in the other two conditions took less than 27 seconds on average to escape. These differences in escape times were statistically significant ($p < .05$, Duncan's multiple-range test). In addition, three-quarters of the dogs in the yoked control condition failed to escape on nine out of the ten trials, whereas only 12.5 per cent of dogs in the normal control condition, and no dogs in the escape condition failed this number of times. Overall, the dogs in the yoked control condition were more likely to fail to escape than the dogs in the other conditions ($p < .05$, Duncan's multiple-range test).

DISCUSSION

The failure of the dogs in the yoked control condition to exercise their potential control over the electric shock suggests that the notion of learned helplessness has some validity. The experience of these dogs in the first phase when they had no control over what happened to them seemed to interfere with their ability to learn what was evidently a fairly straightforward escape response. Even dogs from this condition which did happen to jump the barrier during a trial 'reverted to "passively" accepting shock' (p. 4) on subsequent trials.

Animal experiments are a very controversial feature of psychological research. Quite apart from the idea of delivering electric shocks to animals, the reader of the original paper may be shocked to discover that one dog in the yoked control condition died 'during treatment'. And the language of the paper does not convey especially warm feelings for the animals ('Three dogs were *discarded* from the Escape group...' (p. 2, emphasis added).

Having said this, the ethics of psychological and animal research is no straightforward matter. Learned helplessness can be argued to be an important feature of human experience, especially for those who are socially, economically and politically disadvantaged. It may be, for example, that learning to be helpless is related to the phenomenon of institutionalisation, whereby people who have been in long-stay hospitals and residential units appear to lose their individuality and capacity for self-direction. The phenomenon might occur because people in institutions have a very limited ability to control their own lives. Whatever they do, however they are, their life is still pretty much determined by the routines and demands of the institution. Seligman and Maier's work (which of course extends beyond just one simple study reported here) may provide valuable insights into the nature of institutionalisation which could contribute to our knowledge of how to combat and reverse the process. Among the applications of the concept are Seligman's (1975) work on depression and Dweck *et al's* (1978) work on classroom performance (see Chapter 8 of this volume).

QUESTIONS

1   In phase one, the trials in the yoked control condition were carried out after the trials in the escape condition. Why?

2   What do you feel about the use of animals in the psychology laboratory?

3   Give some examples of situations in which people might learn to be helpless?

Suggested Answers start at p. 439

KEY WORDS

conditioned stimulus
extinction (extinguished)
helplessness
learned helplessness

neutral stimulus
shuttle box
unconditioned stimulus
yoked control

TALKING TO THE ANIMALS

■ GARDNER, R.A. & GARDNER, B.T. (1969). Teaching sign language to a chimpanzee.
Science, 165, 664–72.

INTRODUCTION

Can we talk to the animals? This is a delightful possibility and a number of researchers have attempted to go beyond simple commands like 'sit' and 'die for the Queen', and tried to create a dialogue with another species. The most likely animals for success are the primates, and in particular the chimpanzee. The early attempts, however, by Kellogg & Kellogg (1933), and by Hayes (1950) to teach chimps to talk failed to show any language ability in the animals. It appeared that apes do not have the equipment to speak, so further attempts were made to teach other sorts of language to them.

The results of these later studies have fascinated the scientific community and the public, but there has not been much agreement on what they tell us. According to Gardner and Gardner, 'the results of project Washoe presented the first serious challenge to the doctrine that only human beings have language'. Eric Lenneberg (1967), on the other hand, writes, 'there is no evidence that any non-human form has the capacity to acquire even the most primitive stages of language development'.

Before we look at the study, it is important to distinguish between language and communication.

Language   A small number of signals (sounds, letters, gestures) that by themselves are meaningless, but can be put together according to certain rules to make an infinite number of messages.

Communication   The way in which one animal or person transmits information to another and influences them.

Everyone agrees that animals can communicate with each other, the disagreement is over whether they can use something similar to human language to do this.

THE STUDY

The failure of the early studies to encourage chimpanzees to use speech sounds led the Gardners to look for a different mode of communication. The expressive qualities of a chimpanzee's gestures suggested that sign language might be effective. They chose to use American Sign Language (ASL) which has its own rules of use, and, like other foreign languages, does not directly translate into English. Some of the signs are iconic (look like the concept) and some of the signs are arbitrary (look nothing like the concept). In this study, they did not use the additional 'finger spelling' of human signers to deal with uncommon or technical terms, so they had to use the signs that were available (for example, they translated psychologist as 'think-doctor'). ASL is in common use, and the Gardners reasoned that they could compare the progress of their chimp with the progress of a deaf child born to deaf parents.

For practical reasons, it was not possible to take a chimp from birth, and it was estimated that Washoe (named after the home county of the University of Nevada) was between 8 and 14 months old when she arrived. Chimps are usually totally dependent until the age of two years, partially dependent until four, reach sexual maturity at eight and full adult maturity between 12 and 16 years. The young age of Washoe meant that little progress could be made for the first few months. The environment for Washoe was designed to provide the minimum of restriction and the maximum of social stimulation. A human helper was with Washoe throughout her waking hours, and all the helpers were fluent in ASL.

Chimpanzees are remarkable *imitators*, and in the early interaction, Washoe was encouraged to imitate the gestures of the humans. She would be rewarded for her efforts with tickles! Later in the programme, when Washoe made an incorrect sign or a badly formed sign, then she would be encouraged to imitate the correct one. However, if she was pressed too hard for the right sign, Washoe sometimes became diverted from the original task, or ran away, or went into a tantrum, or even bit the tutor.

An example of *delayed imitation* is described by the Gardners. For some time they had been insisting that Washoe use a toothbrush to clean her teeth after meals (what for, goodness only knows!). They would sign the command to brush her teeth, and although she clearly did not like the procedure, she would submit to it. Later, on a visit to the Gardners' home, Washoe explored the bathroom, climbed on the

sink, looked at the toothbrushes and signed 'toothbrush'. The importance of this was that it was the first time she had made this sign, and
there was no obvious motivation for making the sign other than to just
identify the object. It is unlikely that she wanted the toothbrush or that
she wanted to brush her teeth.

One of the striking features of human language acquisition is the *babbling stage*, when the baby makes many of the sounds of its language, but
in no meaningful way. In the early stages of 'Project Washoe', the chimp
did not appear to babble but as the project went on she made more and
more sign-like gestures without any real meaning (the Gardners called
this 'manual babbling'). They encouraged this babbling with smiles
and claps.

The researchers used *operant techniques* like shaping (see the study
by Skinner earlier in this chapter) to introduce new signs into Washoe's
vocabulary, though it is fair to say that operant training is not a part of
language acquisition in children. After learning a new sign like 'open'
in one particular context, Washoe was able to *generalise* the sign to new
contexts.

To start with, the researchers kept full records of Washoe's signs, but
this recording became difficult as her vocabulary increased. After 16
months they introduced a recording system where they recorded a
new sign only after three different observers had observed Washoe
make it spontaneously (with no prompts other than 'what is it?') and
in an appropriate context. This sign was accepted as being in the
vocabulary if it appeared at least once each day for 15 consecutive days.
At the end of the 22nd month of the project, Washoe used 30 signs that
met these stringent criteria.

The researchers describe how Washoe came to differentiate new
signs. For example, when she first learnt the sign for 'flower' she would
use it in a number of contexts (like when she found a tobacco pouch) to
indicate 'smell'. She was *shaped* to use the new sign of 'smell' for the
appropriate context though the Gardners note that she still made a
number of errors with these two signs.

The most important, and controversial, observations centred
around the combinations of signs. Naming objects and actions is one
thing, but human language puts words together in certain structures
that create complex meanings. Could Washoe combine her signs to
create a simple grammar? In this paper, the Gardners report that
Washoe was just starting to combine signs into simple two-sign combinations.

DISCUSSION

The Gardners established that signs are the appropriate medium for two-way communication with a chimpanzee. However, it is clear that there are very real differences between Washoe's communications and the language of children. Aitchison (1983) suggests there are ten criteria that distinguish communication from language including:

(1) arbitrariness of the symbols (the symbol is not like the object or the action it is describing);
(2) semanticity (the use of symbols to mean objects or actions);
(3) displacement (refers to things that are distant in time and space);
(4) it is used spontaneously;
(5) it involves turn-taking;
(6) it is structure dependent (the symbols can be combined according to the rules of grammar).

Although Washoe used arbitrary symbols, and showed semanticity, the other features were far less evident in her signs.

Another study, of a similar nature, was carried out by Terrace (1979) on a chimpanzee called Nim Chimpsky (named after the US linguistics expert, Noam Chomsky, who was very unimpressed by Washoe's performance). Terrace recorded, on tape, over 20 000 communications from Nim during a two year period. When the data were analysed, a disappointed Terrace found some striking differences between Nim's communication and child language. First, there was no increase in the length of Nim's communications, whereas children show a steady increase in sentence length with age. Secondly, only 12 per cent of Nim's communications were spontaneous (the rest were prompted by the teacher), whereas children initiate more communications than they respond to. Thirdly, the amount of imitation increased with Nim, whereas with children it declines as language develops. Fourthly, and perhaps most importantly, Nim made frequent interruptions and did not seem to learn to take turns in communication in stark contrast to the turn-taking skills of children.

The overall conclusion seems to be that it is possible to initiate simple communication with chimpanzees and to encourage them to use a number of signs to communicate a range of concepts. They do not, however, learn language in the same way that children do, and it seems unlikely that they ever will. As Noam Chomsky wrote 'It is about as likely that an ape will prove to have language ability as that there is an island somewhere with a species of flightless birds waiting for human beings to teach them how to fly' (cited in Terrace, 1979).

QUESTIONS

1 Describe some examples of animal communication. How do these communications differ from human language?

2 Describe some forms of human communication that do not use language.

3 What are the strengths and weaknesses of the Gardners' case-study method to collect information.

4 What do you think are the main difficulties in recording sign language in a chimp?

5 People usually do not interrupt each other in conversation. How do they know when to speak and when to be silent?

6 Try to invent an appropriate sign for 'psychologist'.

Suggested Answers to start at p. 440

KEY WORDS

babbling stage	language
case-study	operant conditioning
communication	semanticity
displacement	structure dependent
iconic	turn-taking
imitation	

6 Bio-Psychology

How much is our behaviour and experience influenced, or controlled, by our biology? It is this question which physiological psychologists explore when they investigate how the brain works. Their studies are concentrated on the structure and function of the nervous system, and, in particular, they look at how the brain is made up and how messages pass through the nervous system.

The brain consists of three major layers which reflect our evolutionary development. At the top of the spinal cord is the *brain stem* which appears to control the basic life support functions of the body. When someone is declared as being 'brain dead', then it is this part of the brain that is showing no signs of activity. On top of the brain stem is a large structure known as the *cerebral cortex* which appears to control the cognitive functions like thought and memory and also action (movement). In between the cortex and the brain stem is a collection of structures known as the *limbic system* whose function is much less clearly known. However, they are thought to have some effect on emotions as well as on some cognitive processes.

Psychology text books often give a diagrammatic map of the brain which gives a summary of the findings from physiological psychologists. These diagrams present a 'car engine' model of the brain with different parts doing different jobs. For example, it has been possible to identify an area of the cortex that affects vision (the visual cortex) and an area that affects movement of the body (the motor cortex). There are, however, a number of problems with this naming of parts of the brain. First, there are large areas of the brain whose function is relatively unknown. Secondly, it is difficult to distinguish one area from another because some are no more than just a slight thickening of the tissue. Thirdly, it is clear that the areas interact with each other, so a simple wiring diagram does not do justice to the complexity of the brain.

Another issue to consider is *reductionism*. Reductionism is the attempt to explain complex behaviour in terms of simple causes. In the case of physiological psychology, it is the attempt to explain what we do and think and feel in terms of brain structure and brain chemicals. So a person in love may poetically think 'My heart goes ping when I think of you', but according to physiological psychologists it is just their love-neurones (made-up name) firing. With this analysis, we seem to lose something of a very special human experience by reducing it to a series of chemical changes. On the other hand, however, the reduction-ist explanations are very plausible and this is shown by how often people are given chemicals (such as tranquillisers) to change their mood or their behaviour.

Physiological psychology suggests some answers to the big question for psychologists – what is a person? The hard-line reductionist answer is that we are merely the sum of our chemicals and nerves. Any other answer begs further questions. If you argue that you have free will, then where does this free will come from, and where does it reside? So, physiological psychology can give us a number of fascinat-ing insights, and can describe phenomena of the brain, but it is open to question what this all means.

The studies chosen for this book look at a range of issues in physio-logical psychology but all of them highlight the interaction between physiological variables and psychological variables. This interaction is also explored in Part VI on Health Psychology. In this chapter, the paper by Sperry (1968) looks at the phenomenon of people with a brain split in two. This challenges our notion of what a person is – should a person with two brains have two people inside their head? Do they? The study by Schachter & Singer (1962) explores what emotions are, and how we experience them. Their two-factor theory suggests an interaction between physiological and psychological variables. The study by Dement & Kleitman (1957) puts a scientific focus on a phenom-enon that has puzzled philosophers for centuries – why do we sleep, and what is the purpose of dreams?

A BRAIN OF TWO HALVES

■ SPERRY, R.W. (1968). Hemisphere deconnection and unity in conscious awareness.
American Psychologist, 23, 723–33.

INTRODUCTION

'Your left hand doesn't know what your right hand is doing' is a saying used to convey the idea of disorganisation. Strangely, some people experience exactly that feeling because the part of their brain that knows what one hand is doing really does not know what the other hand is doing. How could this be? The brain is divided into two relatively symmetrical halves; they are only relatively symmetrical because although they look the same they have very different functions. The split occurs from nose to back so the two halves are known as the right hemisphere and the left hemisphere. They are joined at the base of the hemispheres by *commissural* fibres which are bundled into structures called 'commissures' (the *corpus callosum,* the *massa intermedia,* and the *anterior commissure* are the most important of these structures). If these fibres are cut, the two hemispheres of the brain become disconnected and have no internal means of communicating with each other.

The reason the fibres are sometimes cut by surgeons is to reduce the effects of epilepsy. When someone has a *grand mal* (major epileptic seizure) their brain cells fire excessively, and they start having uncontrollable movements and often lose consciousness. If these attacks are uncontrolled they can be life threatening because of the strain on the heart and the damage done to the person when they are unconscious. In some extreme cases the brain is 'cut in half' to contain the attack within one half of the brain.

The two halves of the brain do not carry out the same tasks and so communicate with each other through the commissural fibres. In right-handed people the major functions of language are carried out in the left hemisphere. This division of tasks between the two sides is referred to as *lateralisation of function.* It is very easy to get confused over right and left because many of the nerve fibres swap sides in the nervous system, so Table 6.1 gives a brief summary of the important functions described in this study.

Table 6.1 Which hemisphere deals with sources of information?

Function or stimulus	Part of brain
the RIGHT visual field	LEFT hemisphere
the LEFT visual field	RIGHT hemisphere
language	LEFT hemisphere
information from the LEFT hand	RIGHT hemisphere
information from the RIGHT hand	LEFT hemisphere
information from the LEFT ear	90% RIGHT hemisphere
information from the RIGHT ear	90% LEFT hemisphere
information from the LEFT nostril	LEFT hemisphere
information from the RIGHT nostril	RIGHT hemisphere

THE STUDIES

The following sections provide an overview of a whole variety of controlled laboratory studies which have been carried out with people with *hemisphere deconnection*.

Subjects

The subjects in the studies summarised in Sperry's paper were 11 patients who had undergone 'the most radical disconnection of the cerebral hemispheres attempted thus far in human surgery' (p. 723). All had had a history of advanced epilepsy, and the surgery was seen as a 'last-resort' (p. 723). Sperry reports excellent therapeutic outcomes for two of the patients with regard to their epilepsy, and holds judgement on the success of the intervention in the remaining nine cases since they had only relatively recently undergone the surgery.

Design

There are a variety of designs used in the studies which are reported here, but overall the work carried out appears to have been a mixture of quasi-experiments and case studies. The quasi-experiments involved comparing the performance of the 11 subjects on various tasks with the performance of people with no inter-hemispheric deconnection. The case studies were extensive investigations of the 11 subjects themselves which aimed to pin down the effects of hemisphere deconnection, and thereby to address the question of how the hemispheres work in a 'normal' brain. Clinical case studies of people who have either accidentally, or for some therapeutic reason, experienced damage to specific areas of the brain are an important research method of the brain and behavioural sciences. They can be thought of as a kind of 'opportunistic' experimentation.

Procedure

Sperry used standard procedures for investigating lateralisation of brain function. The requirements for such investigations are controlled laboratory conditions and specialised equipment which allow tasks to be set separately to the two hemispheres of the subject's brain via sight, sound, smell and touch.

The two hemispheres receive different visual information. However, it is not as simple as the left eye sending information to the left brain and so on. It is best described in the following way. Imagine looking straight ahead. Then the view to the right of your nose is the 'right

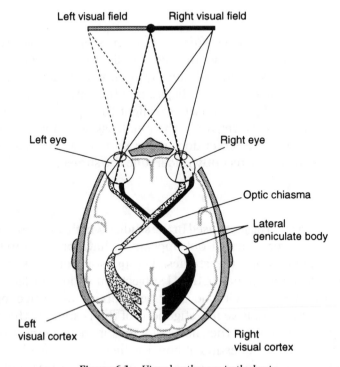

Figure 6.1   *Visual pathways in the brain*

visual field' and the view to the left of your nose is the 'left visual field'. The nerves of the visual system are arranged in such a way that the view of the left visual field goes to the right hemisphere of the brain and the view from the right visual field goes to the left hemisphere of the brain (see Figure 6.1).

An example of a standard task for investigating lateralisation involves subjects responding to visual information that is sent to just one half of the brain. This is achieved by blindfolding one of the subject's eyes, instructing them to fixate with the seeing eye on a designated point in the middle of a screen, and then projecting the stimuli on either the left or right hand side of the fixation point for less than 1/10 of a second.

Another example would be a tactile task in which the subject's hands are hidden from their own view. Again, information from stimuli that are presented to the left hand goes to the right hemisphere. Auditory and olfactory stimuli can also be presented to one side of the brain using various methods of blocking the unused ear or nostril. Note that in the case of sound about ten per cent of the information goes to the same side of brain, the remaining 90 per cent going to the opposite hemisphere; and in the case of smell all the information goes to the same side of the brain (information from the left nostril is processed by the left hemisphere).

RESULTS

Needless to say in a paper which summarises a series of research studies there are a lot of results reported. This section will briefly describe a number of the findings.

Subjects who were presented with an image in one half of their visual field were only able to recognise the image as one they had already seen if it was presented again within the same half of the visual field. If the same image was re-shown to the other side of the brain the person would respond as if they had never seen the image before.

Right-handed subjects were able to give good descriptions of any image that was presented to the right-hand side of the visual field, but reported that images displayed on the left-hand side were either not noticed or appeared as just a flash. However, the subjects were able to respond non-verbally to images presented on the left of the visual field, perhaps by pointing with their left hand to a related object. Remember that for right-handers language is controlled by the left hemisphere.

This language-related effect could also be seen when two symbols were presented simultaneously, one on either side of the visual field. If the person was asked to draw with their left-hand (shielded from their own view) what they had seen, they would draw the left-hand symbol. But when asked to say what they had just drawn the subject would say the name of the right-hand symbol!

The same effects were evident when the subjects were responding to tactile information from either hand. The left hand would seem to be unable to respond to any stimulus presented to the right hand. In addition, objects put in the subject's right hand could be named and described in words, whereas only appropriate non-verbal responses could be made to objects presented to the left hand.

The separation of function between the two hemispheres could be very clearly seen in tasks which involved parallel responses by both hands to two different stimuli presented simultaneously to the two sides of the visual field. The performance of 'normal' subjects would be slowed down by the competing demands of the tasks, yet the people with hemisphere deconnection could actually perform these double tasks in parallel as quickly as they were able to perform one of the tasks on its own. Sperry is quick to point out, however, that although the patients did not appear to be particularly worse off mentally than people with intact inter-hemispherical connections, they were certainly not better off. Enhanced performances of the sort just described were only noted on very specific and highly unusual laboratory tasks.

DISCUSSION

The numerous effects which Sperry reports add up to a convincing account of 'an apparent doubling in most of the realms of conscious awareness' (p. 724) for the 'deconnected' patients. In many of the tasks that were set, it was evident that 'the second hemisphere does not know what the first hemisphere has been doing' (p. 726). Indeed, Sperry argues that the effects are easier to understand if one thinks 'of the mental faculties and performance capacities of the left and right hemispheres separately' (p. 727), rather than looking at the behaviour of each subject as a single individual. The different hemispheres seemed to have their own perceptions, their own memories and their own phenomenology.

In intact brains, lateralisation of brain function is complemented by lines of communication across the hemispheres. For the patients described in this series of studies it appeared that the lack of communication across the hemispheres was, under normal conditions, compensated for by other information-disseminating strategies. For example, the patients could use speech as a means of telling the right hemisphere what was going on in the world of the left hemisphere. In the laboratory, subjects had to be prevented from talking as they performed tasks in order that this line of communication was also disconnected. So to the informal observer, and probably to the patients themselves, the dual lines of consciousness were most likely not noticeable and could only be isolated by Sperry and his colleagues under highly controlled, laboratory conditions. Indeed, Sperry argues that in general the deconnection of the hemispheres did not appear to affect the patients' intelligence or personality. The effects of the surgery did however show themselves in short-term memory difficulties, limited concentration spans and orientation problems.

Sperry ends by warning the reader that the results that he summarises are imperfect generalisations:

> Although the general picture has continued to hold up in the main as described, it is important to note that, with respect to many of the deconnection symptoms mentioned, striking modifications and even outright exceptions can be found among the small group of patients examined to date.
> (p. 733)

QUESTIONS

1 Why does the presentation of the visual stimuli need to be so brief (less than 1/10 of a second)?

2 In the tactile tasks in which objects are presented to one hand, why is it important that the subject cannot see their own hand?

3. Why are people who have specific localised damage to areas of their brain so popular with researchers in the brain and behavioural sciences?

Suggested Answers start at p. 441

KEY WORDS

auditory   lateralisation of function
case study   olfactory
commissural tissue   phenomenology
epilepsy   quasi-experiment
hemisphere   visual field

How do you Feel?

■ SCHACHTER, S. & SINGER, J.E. (1962). Cognitive, social and physiological determinants of emotional state. *Psychological Review, 69,* 379–99.

INTRODUCTION

How do you feel? It's a question that we are often asked, but always find difficult to answer. If you try to describe how you feel when you are angry or afraid or happy, you will probably use descriptions of bodily changes, for example, 'my legs turned to jelly' or 'I felt warm' or 'I had butterflies in my stomach' or 'my heart went ping'. We experience various bodily changes when we experience emotion, and there is clearly a strong connection between the reactions of our body and our feelings.

In 1890 William James proposed that these changes occur as a response to some stimulating event, and our experience of these changes is what we call emotion. The Danish psychologist Carl Lange suggested a similar idea around the same time, and so the theory is referred to as the James–Lange theory. The theory suggests, counter-intuitively, that we are afraid *because* we run, and we are angry *because* we strike. This seems to be the wrong way round, but it is easy to think of instances where the recognition of emotion does come after the bodily responses. If you trip on the stairs you automatically make a grab for the bannister before you have a chance to recognise a state of fear. After the crisis is over, the emotion you feel includes the perception of a pounding heart, rapid breathing, and a feeling of weakness or trembling in your arms and legs.

In 1929 Walter Cannon produced a critique of the James–Lange theory that was, until recently, considered devastating. His objections included the observations that:

(1) The same changes in the internal organs occur in a range of emotional responses, so how can we tell anger from fear.
(2) Artificial changes in the state of the internal organs brought about by, for example, injections of adrenalin, do not produce the experience of emotion.

Subsequent studies found some slight differences between the bodily responses to different emotions, but these differences were not enough to explain the very different experiences we have in different emotions. So psychologists started to look at the role of cognitive factors in the experiences of emotion.

THE STUDY

Schachter and Singer describe the work of Marañon (1924), who carried out an experiment to see whether stimulation of body changes by injections of adrenalin would produce feelings of emotion. About 70 per cent of subjects experienced physical symptoms such as a dry mouth or a pounding heart, but no emotion. The remainder reported experiences of emotion, but qualified their statements by saying that they felt 'as if' they were undergoing an emotional experience. Marañon also found that if he questioned his subjects about a painful event before the injection they were unlikely to respond emotionally, but after the injection they often became upset. This suggests that the physiological arousal brought on by the injection was not enough to produce emotion unless the person was provided with an appropriate cognition such as an upsetting memory.

Schachter and Singer brought the available evidence together in their two-factor theory of emotion. The two-factor theory suggests that emotion comes from a combination of a state of *arousal* and a *cognition* that makes best sense of the situation the person is in. There are three propositions:

(a) If a person experiences a state of arousal for which they have no immediate explanation, they will label this state and describe their feelings in terms of the cognitions available to them. The same state of arousal could be labelled as 'joy' or 'fury' or 'jealousy' and so forth, depending on the situation the person is in.

(b) If a person experiences a state of arousal for which they have an appropriate explanation, then they will be unlikely to label their feelings in terms of the alternative cognitions available.

(c) In similar situations, a person will react emotionally or experience emotions only if they are in a state of arousal.

The procedure

The experimental test of the propositions required (a) the experimental manipulation of a state of physiological arousal, and (b) the manipulation of the explanation that an individual will give to this arousal.

The subjects were told that the aim of the experiment was to look at the effects of vitamin injections on visual skills, and were asked if they would mind having an injection of suproxin (made up name). If they agreed (and 184 out of 185 did), they were given an injection of either adrenalin (epinephrine) or a placebo. The effects of adrenalin are very similar to the effects of arousal of the sympathetic division of the autonomic nervous system (as in the *fight or flight* syndrome) – increases in blood pressure, heart rate, blood sugar level, respiration rate, and blood flow to the muscles and brain, with an accompanying decrease in blood flow to the skin. This is often experienced as palpitations, tremors, flushing and faster breathing. The effects begin after three minutes and last from ten minutes to an hour. Note that all the subjects *thought* they had received an injection of vitamins.

The subjects were then put into one of the four experimental conditions:

(a) *ignorant* – subjects were given an adrenalin injection and not told of the effects of the drug;

(b) *informed* – subjects were given an adrenalin injection and warned of the 'side effects' of the drug (hand shake, heart pounding, dry mouth etc.). These subjects were therefore prepared for the effects of the adrenalin (although they thought these were to do with the suproxin);

(c) *misinformed* – subjects were given an adrenalin injection and told to expect side effects but were told these would be numb feet and headache. These subjects would, therefore, not be expecting the effects of the adrenalin;

(d) *placebo* – subjects were given an injection that would have no effect and were given no instructions of what to expect.

In the *ignorant condition* the subjects experience arousal without any obvious reason for it. The theory predicts that they will describe this arousal in terms of the situation they are in. The subjects in the *informed condition* on the other hand, will experience the same arousal but will have an obvious explanation for it (the adrenalin). Their experience, then, will not be affected by the situation they find themselves in. To test this out, the subjects were either put in a situation designed to produce euphoria or a situation designed to produce anger:

In the *euphoria situation*, the subject was left in a room for 20 minutes with a stooge 'to let the drug be absorbed before the vision test'. The stooge started to fool around in the untidy waiting room, playing

Table 6.2   The conditions in the Schachter and Singer experiment

Euphoria	Anger
Informed	Informed
Ignorant	Ignorant
Misinformed	
Placebo	Placebo

'paper basketball', airplanes, catapults, hoola-hoop and generally behaving as if they were on a 'Club 18 to 30' holiday.

In the *anger situation*, the subject was left with the stooge for 20 minutes and asked to fill in a questionnaire. The stooge expressed displeasure at the injection and increasing displeasure at the questionnaire which asked increasingly personal questions. The first few questions were inoffensive but later it asked; 'Do you hear bells?', 'Do you bathe and wash regularly?', and later 'How many times a week do you have sexual intercourse' (remember this was 1962 and sex hadn't been invented yet), and finally 'With how many men, other than your father, has your mother had extra-marital relationships – 4 and under, 5 to 9, or 10 and over?'

The study ran seven conditions as shown in Table 6.2.

Table 6.3   The self-report rating scale used by Schachter and Singer

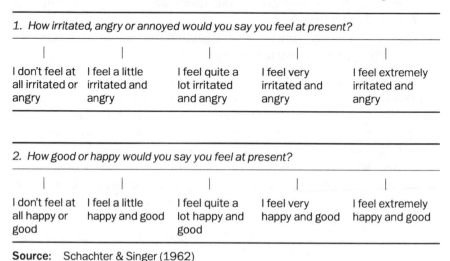

1. *How irritated, angry or annoyed would you say you feel at present?*

I don't feel at all irritated or angry	I feel a little irritated and angry	I feel quite a lot irritated and angry	I feel very irritated and angry	I feel extremely irritated and angry

2. *How good or happy would you say you feel at present?*

I don't feel at all happy or good	I feel a little happy and good	I feel quite a lot happy and good	I feel very happy and good	I feel extremely happy and good

Source: Schachter & Singer (1962)

Measurement

The researchers made *observational measures* of emotional response through a one-way mirror, and also took *self-report measures* from the subjects. The self-report questionnaire contained a number of mock questions but the crucial ones are shown in Table 6.3.

The subjects were all psychology students, and their health records were checked to make sure that the adrenalin would not have an adverse effect.

RESULTS

The subjects who received the injections of adrenalin reported clear feelings of arousal in comparison to the placebo subjects. For the score of self-reported emotion, the irritation/anger score was subtracted from the happiness score to produce the data shown in Figure 6.2.

The scale is a measure of happiness minus anger, so in the euphoria situation the ignorant and the misinformed groups appear to experience the greatest happiness and least anger (as predicted) and in the anger situation the ignorant group experiences the least happiness and greatest anger (also as predicted).

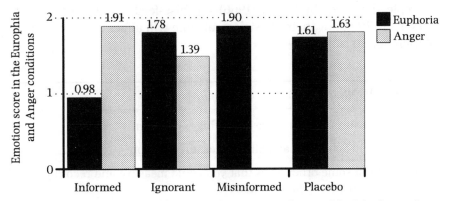

Figure 6.2 *Self reports of emotion in the various conditions of the Schachter and Singer experiment*
Source: Schachter & Singer (1962)

DISCUSSION

Perhaps because people wanted to believe the theory, and perhaps because of the complexity of the experiment, no attempt at replication was made until 1979 when Marshall and Zimbardo failed to obtain the same results as the original study.

A closer inspection of the original study reveals a few problems:

(a) the differences between the groups of subjects were small and only became significant after a number of the subjects were discarded;

(b) some of the subjects in the misinformed and the ignorant groups attributed their arousal state to the injection saying, for example, 'the shot gave me the shivers'. This is a problem because these subjects were meant to have experienced arousal without an obvious cause;

(c) the results were presented as a measure of relative emotion – happiness minus anger, when in fact the self reports of all the experimental subjects in both the euphoria and the anger situations were on the happy side of neutral. This shows that Schachter and Singer were unsuccessful in their attempt to induce anger;

(d) there was no measure of the subject's mood before the experiment;

(e) the misinformed condition was not reported in the anger situation.

The two-factor theory is a fascinating idea, and it seems clear that physiological changes and cognitive evaluations form part of our experience of emotion. Subsequent work has shown that the relationship is more complex than the two-factor theory predicts, and, for example the work by Valins (1966) on false-feedback showed that a person's *belief* about their physiological state will affect them regardless of their actual state.

QUESTIONS

1   Briefly summarise the design of this experiment.

2   How did Schachter and Singer measure emotion?

3.   Suggest some other ways that you could measure and record your own and other people's emotions.

4   What are the ethical concerns with this study?

5   Do you think the results would have been different if they had not used students in their study?

Suggested Answers start at p. 441

KEY WORDS

adrenalin	happiness
arousal	observation
cognition	placebo
emotion	self-report
false-feedback	two-factor theory

To Sleep, Perchance to Dream

■ Dement, W. & Kleitman, N. (1957). The relation of eye movements during sleep to dream activity: An objective method for the study of dreaming.
Journal of Experimental Psychology, 53, 339–46.

Introduction

We are both fascinated and frightened by our dreams. Why do we have these strange images and stories during our sleep, and what do they mean? In this culture we are reluctant to discuss the content of our dreams in case they are seen to be a sign of a disturbed mind, so we often keep the products of our sleeping activity to ourselves. However, the topic remains fascinating for everyday conversation and also for scientific enquiry.

Empson (1989) draws together some information that shows how important dreams have been in other cultures and in the past of our own culture. A number of ancient texts, including the Bible, make repeated references to revelations that occur during dreams. The plays of Shakespeare have many references to dreams, some of which are prophetic, for example the dream of Julius Caesar's wife which predicts his death. This tells us something about the beliefs that Elizabethan audiences held about the nature and interpretation of dreams.

A more modern influence on our view of dreams was provided by Freud, who suggested that they are the product of our *unconscious mind.* We have certain unconscious wishes, and these wishes are expressed in our dreams. Often the nature of the wish is heavily disguised in the dream so that it does not alarm us. This view is probably most representative of the popular view of dreams today.

Until the work by Dement and Kleitman, very little was known about the frequency of dreaming, the length of dreams and the value of dreams for healthy sleep.

The Study

Dement and Kleitman note that an earlier observation had shown that people have periods of prolonged *rapid eye movements* (REM) during sleep, and there seemed to be some connection with the occurrence of these periods and the experience of dreaming. It is possible to see the eyes of a sleeping person, or animal, move during these periods without the use of sophisticated equipment. The study set out to look at three questions:

(1) Does dream recall correlate with periods of REM?
(2) Is there a correlation between the estimate of dream length and the time in REM?
(3) Is the type of eye movement related to the content of the dream?

Subjects

Seven adult males and two adult females were studied. Five were studied intensively, while minimal data was gathered from the other four just to confirm the findings of the main five.

Procedure

In a typical study, the subject reported to the laboratory just before their usual bedtime. They had been asked to eat normally but to avoid caffeine or alcohol on the day of the study. Two or more electrodes were attached near to the eyes to record electrical changes, and hence movement of the eyes. Two or three further electrodes were attached to the scalp to record brain activity during the night. The electrodes were connected to an *electroencephalograph* (EEG) which amplified and recorded the signals.

At various times during the night they were woken up to test their dream recall. The return to sleep usually took less than five minutes. The nine subjects were studied over a total of 61 nights, with a total of 351 awakenings which averaged out at 5.7 awakenings per night.

RESULTS

All the subjects showed periods of REM every night. These periods occurred at regular intervals during the night, though each subject had their own pattern. The average period between each REM period was 90 minutes with individual norms varying between 70 minutes and 104 minutes. The length of the REM periods varied between 3 minutes and 50 minutes, and they tended to increase in length as the night progressed. The REM periods were accompanied by a particular pattern on the EEG of brain wave activity. The REM EEG was characterised by a low voltage, relatively fast pattern.

The subjects were woken up by a door bell ringing close to the bed. The subject then had to speak into a tape recorder near the bed, and to say whether they had been dreaming, and what was the content of the dream. In an attempt to eliminate the possibility of experimenter effects, the experimenter did not communicate with the subjects during the night. The subjects were only recorded as having dreamed if they were able to relate a coherent and relatively detailed description of

Table 6.4   The recall of dreams after REM and non-REM sleep

Subject	Rapid Eye Movements (REM)		Non-Rapid Eye Movements (N-REM)	
	Dream recall	No recall	Dream recall	No recall
DN	17	9	3	21
IR	26	8	2	29
KC	36	4	3	31
WD	37	5	1	34
PM	24	6	2	23
KK	4	1	0	5
SM	2	2	0	2
DM	2	1	0	1
MG	4	3	0	3
Total	152	39	11	149

Source: Dement & Kleitman (1957)

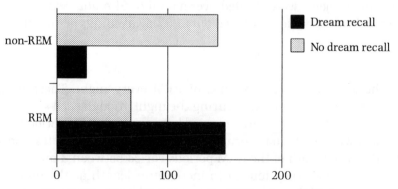

Figure 6.3   *The recall of dreams after REM and non-REM sleep*

the dream content. Table 6.4 shows the results of these awakenings, and the results are shown graphically in Figure 6.3. The results show that REM sleep is predominantly, though not exclusively, associated with dreaming, and N-REM (non-REM) sleep is associated with periods of non-dreaming sleep.

Sometimes the subjects were awakened during periods of deep sleep (which is shown by a particular pattern of brain waves with no REM). On these awakenings the subjects were often bewildered and sometimes said they had been dreaming without being able to state the content of the dream. They also described a great variety of feelings, such as pleasantness, or anxiety, but these feelings could not be related to any dream content.

A series of awakenings were carried out to see if the subjects could accurately estimate the length of their dreams. They were woken up either 5 minutes or 15 minutes into a REM period, and asked to say whether they thought the dream had been going on for 5 or 15 minutes. Table 6.5 shows that these estimates were fairly accurate.

It was also hypothesised that the REM represented the scanning of visual images and so a connection should be possible between the measurement of the REM and the content of the dream. The subjects were woken up to test this idea after some particular patterns of REM. The patterns were:

(a) mainly vertical eye movements;
(b) mainly horizontal eye movements;
(c) both vertical and horizontal eye movements;
(d) very little or no eye movement.

Table 6.5   Results of dream-duration estimates after 5 or 15 minutes of rapid eye movements

Subject	5 Minutes		15 Minutes	
	Right	Wrong	Right	Wrong
DN	8	2	5	5
IR	11	1	7	3
KC	7	0	12	1
WD	13	1	15	1
PM	6	2	8	3
Total	45	6	47	13

Source: Dement & Kleitman (1957)

The recall of the dreams showed some relationship to the type of eye movements. For example, a person who was woken up after a series of vertical movements reported standing at the bottom of a cliff and operating a hoist, whereas a person woken up after some horizontal movements reported dreaming of watching two people throw tomatoes at each other.

DISCUSSION

The study gives us a clear indication of a connection between REM and dreaming, though that relationship is far from being fully understood. The study formed the basis of much subsequent research which has been able to use more sophisticated equipment to build up a picture of the different patterns of brain waves that occur through a normal night's sleep.

A similar study by Goodenough *et al.* (1959) raises some questions about the connection between REM and dreaming. They questioned 60 people about the frequency of their dreams and then persuaded the eight most frequent dreamers ('dreamed every night'), along with the eight least frequent dreamers to take part in laboratory recordings of their sleep patterns. When they woke the high dreamers from their REM sleep they reported dreams on 44 out of 49 occasions. They also reported dreams on half the awakenings during non-REM sleep. On the other hand, the self-reported low dreamers only reported dreams when woken during 19 out of 42 REM sleeps, and only seven out of 43 non-REM sleeps. So there would appear to be some large differences between individuals in the reports of dreaming during REM.

Dement and Wolpert (1958) tried to affect the content of dreams by providing some stimulation to the dreamers. They did this by playing a tone, or flashing a light or spraying them with cold water. A number of subjects incorporated the stimulation into their dreams and one, for example, dreamt about spilling a glass of water on himself.

The matching of eye movements to the dream content has not received support in subsequent research and it appears that people who were blind from birth, and new born babies, both show REM even though they may have poor, or non existent, imaging skills.

QUESTIONS

1   What do the results tell us about REM sleep?

2   What observations would you make about the subject sample?

3   What are the controls in the study?

4   What other controls can you suggest?

5   What are the main differences between sleeping in a laboratory and sleeping in your own bed?

6   Get someone to wake you up after you've been in REM sleep for five minutes. Record what you call them.

Suggested Answers start at p. 442

KEY WORDS

dreams   sleep
electroencephalograph   unconscious mind
REM

7 ETHOLOGY

Ethology is the study of animal behaviour in its natural habitat. The modern discipline of ethology dates from the early 1920s, and the concerns of that time still set the agenda for modern studies. The key questions of ethology are:

(a) What is the immediate cause of a behaviour?
(b) How has that behaviour developed in the lifetime of the animal?
(c) What is the function of behaviour (how does it enhance the survival of the animal)?
(d) Why is the function dealt with in this way?

So, ethologists look at behaviour from an evolutionary perspective which sees animals being designed by their ability to survive. Some body adjustments and some behaviour will make the individual more adapted to the local environment, and therefore more likely to mate and pass on their genes. Everything has a cause, and that cause is survival.

Ethologists have looked at a range of species and developed a number of concepts, some of which have drifted into everyday speech. One of the early concepts to develop centred around the stereotyped behaviour of animals in certain situations. The idea of the *Fixed Action Pattern* (FAP) describes the relatively fixed way that an animal will approach a particular task. For example, Tinbergen (1952) describes the FAP of the stickleback when mating. Studies like this have been able to describe the FAPs of various animals and the simple signs or signals (sign stimuli) that precede these behaviours. Another concern of the ethologists has been *dominance hierarchies* or pecking orders. Some animals show a social structure where some members of a group have prior access to resources. Sometimes it is food, sometimes it is mating. The hierarchy helps to maintain order in the group by reducing the number of conflict situations, and also helps to share out the available resources in such a way that the survival of the group is protected at the expense of the weaker (or unluckier) individuals.

Ethologists have also observed aggression in animals and described the uses of aggressive behaviour for a species and an individual. Like many of the animal concepts, this work has been popularised to offer explanations for anti-social human behaviour. For example, it is not uncommon to see the behaviour of crowds compared with the behaviour of animals that live in groups, so you see a herd of wildebeest sweeping across some plains in Africa and then cut to a scene of Chelsea supporters sweeping across Fulham Bridge in London. This is a nonsense on two counts. First it is well known that wildebeest support Arsenal (bad joke), and secondly the behaviour of the wildebeest is a characteristic of the species. All wildebeest behave in that way, whereas the behaviour of the football fans represents a choice rather than an expression of their biological nature.

In this chapter, the study by Rawlins (1979) looks at the development of social behaviour in a monkey troop over a number of years. Although the environment is artificially constructed, it still provides one of the clearest accounts of monkey behaviour 'in the wild'. The study by Tinbergen (1952) provides a classic account of his work with sticklebacks and illustrates his imaginative use of methods to investigate FAPs and sign stimuli. The last study by Calhoun (1962) is not strictly ethological since it describes the behaviour of rats in a laboratory environment. However, it also looks at the development of social behaviour, and has been extensively quoted in discussion on the dangers of high-density living.

One last issue to consider before looking at the studies is *anthropomorphism*. This term describes the tendency to see human characteristics in the behaviour of animals. So some people might describe a dog as being 'brave' or a lemming as 'committing suicide'. The problem with the use of these human terms is that in people they imply a choice behaviour. Behaviour is brave when a person knows the possible dangerous consequences of their behaviour but continues with it regardless. Does a dog make this evaluation? Suicide is a choice to finish your own life, yet no one could suggest that lemmings wake up one morning and consider their possible alternatives before ending it all. Anthropomorphism is a danger when studying animals, and some of the studies in this book are guilty of attributing some human characteristics to their animal subjects.

THE COLONY OF MONKEYS

■ RAWLINS, R. (1979). Forty years of rhesus research.
New Scientist, 82, 108–10.

INTRODUCTION

Ethology is the study of animals in their natural habitat. This would seem to be the most obvious place to investigate animal behaviour, but much of the early work on animals was carried out in laboratories. In fact, a lot of psychological research was conducted using specially bred strains of animals, usually rats, who would not be able to survive in their natural habitat. This study of artificially created animals in artificial environments gained a strange prominence in psychology for a number of years. The advantages of this sort of work are the high levels of control that are possible, and the ease and cost of the work. The disadvantages are more obvious.

The study of animals in their natural habitat, on the other hand, is difficult, costly and time consuming. Look at it this way, would you find it easier to work in a laboratory all day and go home in the evening, or spend six months in the middle of a rain forest trying to catch up with a troop of primates who hide from you and throw fruit at you?

It is only in the last 40 years that ethological studies have been able to provide us with much detailed information about the behaviour of animals. Remarkably, our knowledge about the behaviour of primates is still relatively light, though the article by Rawlins presents the evidence from a fascinating longitudinal study.

THE STUDY

The small island of Cayo Santiago lies one mile off the coast of Puerto Rico in the Caribbean. A number of US academic institutions wanted a supply of primates for research, so it was decided to create a primate colony on Cayo Santiago. At the start of 1939, 450 rhesus monkeys (captured in India) and 14 gibbons (captured in South East Asia) were released onto the island, having first been screened for tuberculosis, and marked with an identifying tattoo.

The first 18 months marked a period of adjustment. After a lot of fighting in which many of the monkeys died, a social organisation developed and six social groups emerged. The gibbons did not fare so well. They competed with the rhesus monkeys for food and living space, and attacked people and monkeys. Eventually they were recaptured and sold. Once the gibbons had been removed, the researchers decided to concentrate on the rhesus monkeys and no further animals were added.

Two scientists, Carpenter and Tomlin, studied the monkeys and noted who made up the groups, how they behaved, what kind of *hierarchies* existed in the groups, and how they moved around the island. Other scientists studied mating, menstrual cycles and haematology.

During the Second World War (1939–45) this research was seen as non-essential and so supplies were difficult to obtain. Over 450 animals were removed from the island for research on disease and by 1944 only 200 monkeys were left. For the next ten years the island was mainly used as a resource of animals for medical research, but in 1956 a regular census was reintroduced, and a good record exists of the social organisation of the monkeys from that time up to the present day. However the haphazard selection of monkeys for research continued and this made the study of social organisation difficult since the social order of the troops was constantly being disrupted.

This changed in 1970 when the new scientist in charge ensured that the four main remaining social groups were left intact, and the research monkeys were taken from the rest of the population. This facilitated the start of long-term studies into social development in monkey troops. The island was attractive to researchers because of the ease of access from the major research institutions, the ease of getting around the island and the high visibility of the monkeys. However, the environment was not entirely natural to the monkeys and they had to be provided with food.

The social organisation in 1979

In 1956, when the census was reintroduced, there were 150 animals in two groups, and in 1979 (when the paper was written) there were 610 monkeys living on the now re-forested island.

The animals were divided into six social groups ranging in size from 53 to 139 animals. A further six males were living a solitary existence. The monkeys were trapped once every year to tattoo new animals and take blood samples. The maternal line (who is the mother to each monkey) was known, though the paternal line could not even be guessed at because of the multiple matings of the females.

The daily activity of the animals has a clear rhythm. In the cool of the day, at first light, the animals look for food. During the heat they rest and groom each other, and as the heat subsides in the afternoon they feed and play before going up the trees to sleep at sunset. The grooming appears to have both a health function and a social function, and the observation of this activity, particularly who is grooming whom, gives some insight into the social structure of the troop.

Each group is made up of a number of adult males and between two and four *matrilines*. The matrilines consist of an adult female, her adult daughters and all their juvenile offspring. Males leave the troop they were born in when they mature at around three to four years, but the females remain. The adult males sometimes move on to another troop, but they never return to the troop they were born into. The movement of the males reduces the chances of inbreeding.

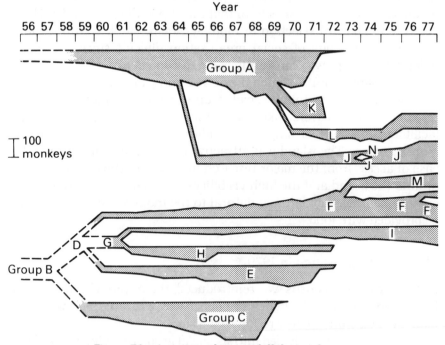

Figure 7.1   *A summary history of all the social groups*
The thickness of the lines represents the number of animals in the groups, which split when they become too large.
Source: Rawlins (1979)

In each troop the males and females have separate hierarchies. The hierarchies affect the access to food and grooming partners, and also limit the aggression in the troop. The animals have a developed system of *signals* for dominance, threat, defeat and subordinance, and these signals are part of the system for controlling aggression. The position of each individual in the hierarchies is established by fighting, but after the fight the position remains fixed for a considerable period of time. In general, the older males hold the highest positions in the hierarchy. Each matriline has a group rank, and all members of the top matriline appear to outrank all members of the other matrilines. Within the matriline the dominant individual is the mother. As the juvenile females reach puberty they immediately rise in status above their older sisters. This means that the mother is at the top of the hierarchy, followed by the youngest mature daughters. Young males take the rank of their mother until they leave the troop, when they have to establish themselves from scratch in the new troop (see Figure 7.1 for an outline of how the troops developed).

The same general social structure can be observed in all six troops on the island, but there are considerable differences in the amount of friendship and fighting within each troop.

DISCUSSION

The study of animal behaviour is valuable in its own right. There is always a pressure, however, to consider what parts of the study can be applied to human behaviour. In this case it must be noted that rhesus monkey are not our closest 'relatives'. The primates that have the greatest biological similarity to people are chimps and gorillas, and these animals have very contrasting patterns of social organisation. It is dangerous, then, to attempt any extrapolation to the social organisation of people.

Whenever we consider animals there is always some bias towards *anthropomorphism*. It is, however, very difficult to write about animal behaviour without making some reference to human behaviour and experience. The problem is not to allow the inadequacies of language to obscure the differences between people and animals. In this study, the struggle for dominance and the development of hierarchies seems to have a similarity to the behaviour of some people. However, the main difference is that people can choose their life style (up to a point), and have created a wide range of different types of social organisation. The connection of these social organisations to the behaviour of the monkeys on Cayo Santiago is, therefore, very limited.

QUESTIONS

1 Identify some advantages and disadvantages of the longitudinal approach used in this study.

2 How could the researchers assess the dominance of a particular monkey?

3 In the original article, Rawlins writes 'it is the males who stir the genetic pot' – what does this mean? And how do they do it?

4 What do you think are the important differences between Cayo Santiago and the natural environment of the rhesus monkeys?

5 What effects do you think these differences have on the behaviour of the rhesus monkeys?

Suggested Answers start at p. 442

KEY WORDS

anthropomorphism	hierarchy
dominance	longitudinal study
ethology	matriline
grooming	social organisation

A FISHY TALE

■ Tinbergen, N. (1952). The curious behaviour of
the stickleback.
Scientific American, 187, 22–26.

INTRODUCTION

Before the emergence of the theory of evolution, people believed that
there was a clear distinction between human beings and animals. It
was believed that the wonders of animal behaviour were due to
instinct, and that it was the gift of *reason* that made human beings
unique. The theory of evolution challenged this distinction and forced
people to review their studies of both human beings and animals. It
was no longer enough just to describe animal behaviour as instinctive,
and a need developed to explore how animals behave in the way they
do and why.

The careful observation of different species led to the discovery of
various social processes. For example, the Norwegian psychologist
Schjelderuppe-Ebbe (1992, cited in Hayes, 1994, p. 897), described the
pecking behaviour of chickens, and was able to demonstrate that they
have a rigid hierarchy that was indicated by who pecked whom, and
how often. The most dominant bird pecked all other birds. The next
most dominant bird pecked all birds except the most dominant bird
and, in turn, was pecked only by the most dominant bird. This *pecking
order* has been observed in a number of other species, and various
attempts have been made to apply the concept to human social
behaviour.

There are a number of problems with the observation of animals,
including practical ones of access. Tinbergen made the unlikely choice of
the stickleback for study because it is small, relatively tame and does not
react adversely to handling, probably because it depends on its spines for
protection. It also displays some dramatic and intriguing behaviours.

THE STUDY

This study concentrates on the courtship and reproductive behaviour of
the stickleback. In their natural habitat, the fish mate early in spring in

IN FIRST STAGE of courtship the male stickleback (*left*) zigzags toward the female (*right*). The female then swims toward him with her head up. The abdomen of the female bulges with from 50 to 100 eggs.

IN SECOND STAGE, seen from above, the male stickleback swims toward the nest he has built and makes a series of thrusts into it with his snout. He also turns on his side and raises his dorsal spines toward the female.

Figure 7.2   *The stages of mating in the stickleback*

shallow fresh waters. The *mating cycle* has a particular ritual which can be observed in the tank as well as the natural habitat:

- the male leaves the school and creates a *territory* for itself from which it will drive any intruder, either male or female;
- the male builds a nest – digging a small pit in the sand, filling it with weeds, and boring a tunnel through it;

IN THIRD STAGE, also seen from above, the female swims into the nest. The male then prods the base of her tail and causes her to lay her eggs. When the female leaves the nest, the male enters and fertilizes the eggs.

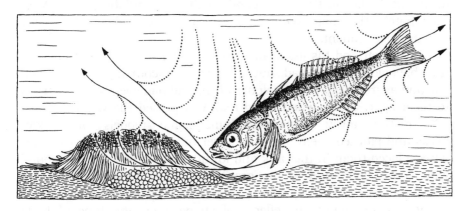

IN FOURTH STAGE the male "fans" water over the eggs to enrich their oxygen supply. The dotted lines show the movement of a colored solution placed in the tank: the solid lines, the direction of the water currents.

Figure 7.2 *(Continued)*
Source: Tinbergen (1952)

- the male then changes colour – from grey, to a bright red underside and a blueish white top;
- the females have, meanwhile, changed shape and become bulky with 50 to 100 eggs;
- the male courts any approaching female with a zig-zag motion –the 'dance' continues until the female responds and swims towards the male with a 'head-up' posture;

- the male then swims towards the nest and the female follows;
- at the nest he makes a series of rapid thrust with his snout into the entrance;
- the female enters the nest – nose out one end, and tail out of the other;
- the male prods her tail with rhythmic thrusts and she lays her eggs;
- she then leaves the nest and the male swims in to fertilise the eggs;
- the whole ritual takes about one minute (see Figure 7.2).

The male may escort as many as five females through the nest and fertilise their eggs. Then his colour reverts to normal (as the mating drive declines) and he starts to drive away all other sticklebacks including the females. The male guards the nest from predators and 'fans' the water over the nest to enrich the supply of oxygen to the eggs. The more developed the eggs become, the more oxygen they need and the longer the male spends each day ventilating them. After they hatch, the male keeps them together for a day before they become independent.

Tinbergen and his associates carried out a number of studies on this behaviour. They had noticed that the courting male would respond aggressively to red coloured fish, and had even been observed to react aggressively when a red mail-van passed the window some 100 metres away. Tinbergen built some models of stickle-backs and painted them red, pale silver or green. They put them on wires, placed them in the tank and found that the fish would respond with some aggression to the green and silver models, but would respond most aggressively to the red models. They carried out similar studies to investigate the effects of shape, size, and type of body movement on the rituals of the stickleback behaviour. Among the observations was that a female stickleback will follow a red model wherever it goes, and will attempt to enter a non-existent nest if the model is poked into the sand. Tinbergen concluded that the stickleback responds to *sign stimuli* – a few characteristics of an object rather than to the object as a whole. However, they would only respond when they were in the breeding season, and the sign stimuli had no effect at other times.

The researchers carried out a series of manipulations including filling the sand pit of the male repeatedly, and castrating the male. In the case of the sand pit, the male kept re-digging the pit for a while but then continued with the nest building regardless of the missing pit.

With castration, the first phase of courtship was left out of the ritual, but if the eunuch male was given a nest of eggs then it would vigorously fan it. This suggests a complex relationship between the *internal* drives to mate, and *external* sign stimuli.

When the male becomes territorial it becomes hostile to other sticklebacks, though very little fighting is observed. When two males meet at the border of their territories, they begin a series of attacks and retreats. Each takes the offensive in their own territory and the conflict see-saws back and forth. Neither fish touches the other, but they dart back and forth 'as though attached by an invisible thread' (p. 24). If the fighting becomes more intense, the fish become vertical and make jerky movements.

Tinbergen observed that when the fish were in a crowded tank where the territories were small and the fighting intense, then both fish began to dig in the sand. This behaviour appears to be irrelevant to the fight and seems to challenge the connection between sign stimuli and behaviour. However, other species display incongruous behaviour, and it may be that the animal is showing *displacement activity* – finding an outlet in irrelevant action to release its tension.

The theory of displacement was tested in a further experiment. A red model was placed in the male's territory, and when the male attacked it, the model was moved to hit the male. The fish retreated to the weeds, and when it returned it approached the model, and then adopted the vertical position. Tinbergen suggested that the escape drive and the attack drive are balanced so the fish needs some displacement activity to resolve the conflict.

DISCUSSION

Tinbergen asks the question about the usefulness of studying one animal in such detail. He points out some of the dangers but suggests that 'the many years of work on sticklebacks, tedious as much of it has been, has been highly rewarding' (p. 26). The rewards include the observation of the sign stimuli, the discovery of the displacement activity and the observations of the interaction between internal drives and external signs. Tinbergen goes on to suggest that this interaction is likely to be a feature of mammal, and even human behaviour.

The strength of the work is in the detail of the observations and the identification of the various signs that stimulate ritualised behaviour. It is clear that the development of ritualised behaviour has survival value for species. What is less clear, is how far we can extrapolate the ideas of sign stimuli, displacement activity, courtship, and territory to human behaviour.

QUESTIONS

1   What methods does Tinbergen combine in this series of studies?

2   What sign stimuli does he identify in this study?

3   Suggest some examples of sign stimuli for people – simple signs that provoke stereotyped behaviour.

4   What are the differences between territorial behaviour in the stickleback and territorial behaviour in people.

5   Suggest some examples of displacement activity in people.

Suggested Answers start at p. 443

KEY WORDS

courtship   pecking order
displacement activity   sign stimuli
evolution   territorial
instinct

Rat City: The Behavioural Sink

■ Calhoun, J.B. (1962). Population density and social pathology. *Scientific American, 206,* 139–48.

Introduction

If rabbits 'breed like rabbits', why isn't the world overrun with rabbits? It seems that, when left undisturbed by human interference, animals manage to balance the size of their population to fit the environment they are living in. But what would happen to the behaviour of animals if the population increased in a restricted space?

The study of animal behaviour shows that most species have developed structures of social behaviour that enhance the survival value of the species. In some species which are fiercely *territorial*, such as the robin, there are rituals of behaviour that space out the territories of the birds to allow each territory an adequate food supply, and also prevent serious conflict between the individuals. In other species that are more social, there are social structures that limit the size of each group.

Calhoun was interested to investigate what would happen if the environment was structured so that the animals could not disperse in their usual way.

The Study

Six populations of laboratory rats (the domesticated white albino Norway rat) were studied in two series of three populations each. In the first series, each population began with 32 rats, and in the second series each population began with 56 rats. In all cases the rats were just past weaning and were equally divided between males and females. By the 12th month, all the populations had multiplied to the size of 80 adults, and after this the researchers removed the infants that survived birth and weaning in order to keep the populations steady.

The rats were placed in groups of equal size in each of the four pens that made up the apparatus. As shown in Figure 7.3, the apparatus was in the form of a square, but the separation of the pens by an electric fence, and the use of small bridges to move between them, effectively turned the environment into a row of four pens, with two end pens

Figure 7.3   *Effect of population density on behaviour*
See description opposite
Source: Calhoun (1962)

(with only one entrance) and two middle pens. The whole apparatus was 10 foot by 14 foot. The pens were complete living units and each one contained a drinking fountain, a food hopper, and an elevated artificial burrow reached by a winding staircase. Calhoun estimated that each pen could comfortably hold 12 rats, which is the size of groups in which they are usually found. When the population reached 80 in the apparatus, then each pen would be likely to have 20 rats if they spread themselves out evenly (see Figure 7.3).

Results

Calhoun expected that sleeping groups would develop with around 13 to 27 in each. In fact, during the 10th to 12th months, when they looked at 100 sleeping groups, only 37 fell in this range. Thirty-three groups had fewer than 13 rats and 30 had more than 27. Only in the groups of expected size was the sex ratio equal. The smaller groups were most commonly made up of six females and two males, and the larger groups tended to be male dominated. The females distributed themselves equally over the four pens but the males were concentrated in the two middle pens.

The major cause of this concentration of males was the *dominance fighting* that created *social hierarchies*. These fights took place in all four pens, but in the two end pens it was possible for one male to take over

---

Figure 7.3 Description   EFFECT OF POPULATION DENSITY on the behavior and social organization of rats was studied by confining groups of 80 animals in a 10-by-14-foot room divided into four pens by an electrified fence. All pens (numbered 1, 2, 3 and 4 clockwise from the door) were complete dwelling units. Conical objects are food hoppers; trays with three bottles are drinking troughs. Elevated burrows, reached by winding staircases, each had five nest boxes, seen in pen 1, where top of burrow has been removed. Ramps connected all pens but 1 and 4. Rats therefore tended to concentrate in pens 2 and 3. Development of a "behavioral sink," which further increased population in one pen, is reflected in pen 2, where three rats are eating simultaneously. Rat approaching ramp in pen 3 is an estrous female pursued by a pack of males. In pens 2 and 3, where population density was highest, males outnumbered females. In pens 1 and 4, a dominant male was usually able to expel all other males and posses a harem of females. Dominant males are sleeping at the base of the ramps in pens 1 and 4. They wake when other males approach, preventing incursions into their territories. The three rats peering down from a ramp are probers, one of the deviant behavioral types produced by the pressures of a high population density.

the whole pen as his territory. Once dominance had been established, the male slept at the bottom of the ladder of the one entrance to the end pen. From this position he was able to keep all other males out, while allowing free access to females.

The account by Calhoun is very *anthropomorphic* in parts; for example, writing about the male rats in the end pens he says:

> ... he would sleep calmly through all the comings and goings of his *harem*; seemingly he did not even hear their *clatterings* up and down the wire ramp. His conduct during his waking hours reflected his dominant status. He would move about in a *casual and deliberate* fashion, occasionally inspecting the burrow and nest of his *harem*.
>
> (p. 143, emphasis added)

There were some other males in the end pens, but they were subordinate, remained hidden in the burrows most of the time and never attempted sexual activity with the females. Interestingly, when they did come out, they attempted to mount the dominant male who did not reject the advances.

In the end pens, the population was lowest and the mortality rate among the females and the infants was also low. The females built nests for the young and nursed them effectively. Half the infants born in these pens survived. On the other hand, the young in the middle pens did not fare so well. In the first series, 96 per cent died before weaning, and in the second series 80 per cent died before weaning. Females in the middle pens became progressively less effective at building nests and nursing their young, eventually failing to even attempt nest building. Infants were abandoned on the floor of the pen, where they died and were eaten by the adults. Females who lived in the middle pens received excessive attention from the males when they came into oestrus.

The social organisation in the middle pens showed some large changes from the behaviour that is normally observed. Some distinct patterns emerged in the male behaviour, and Calhoun described how four types of male emerged.

(1) *Aggressive Dominant Males*   In every group of 12 or more males, one was the most aggressive and the most common victor in fights. However, this rat was periodically ousted from his position, and a new rat emerged as the dominant animal. These rats were 'the most normal in

our population' (p. 145), though even these were occasionally prone to bursts of attacking females and the young.

(2) *Homosexual Males* Calhoun calls this group homosexual, though in fact they were just very sexually active, and would try and mount males, females not in oestrus, juveniles, and anything on four legs that squeaked. These animals rarely battled for status.

(3) *Passive* These animals 'moved through the community like *somnambulists* [sleep walkers]' (p. 145). They ignored all the other rats of both sexes and all the rats ignored them. They did not even make advances to female rats in oestrus. They looked the healthiest because they were fat, sleek and did not have any scars or missing fur from fighting, 'but their social disorientation was nearly complete' (p. 145).

(4) *Probers* These rats were hyperactive and hypersexual, though much more discriminating than the 'homosexual' rats. In time, many of them became *cannibalistic*.

DISCUSSION

This is one of those studies in psychology that is commonly misreported. It is often claimed that the animals were left to breed at will (when in fact after the size reached 80 the young were removed), and that all the populations died out (when in fact they did not). In the study Calhoun claims that 'the evidence indicates that in time failures of reproductive function would have caused the colonies to die out' (p. 139), but it is not clear what he bases this on, since as the size of the population decreased the pressure on space would have declined and the social organisation might have returned to normal. Also, in his original observation of wild rats restricted in an enclosure of a quarter of an acre, the population grew to 150 and then remained stable.

It is very tempting to make connections between the breakdown in social organisation of the rats in this environment, and the social problems of life in the city. However, there are some very real distinctions to be drawn. For example, human beings do not have species-specific patterns of 'nest-building' and child-rearing. Different cultures live in different domestic arrangements, some in fixed homes, others are nomadic. Child care practices are varied and affected by changing fashions.

QUESTIONS

1   What are the controls of the study?

2   What are the problems with the design of the study?

3   What is the problem with referring to one group of rats as homosexual? Why do you think Calhoun chose to use this term?

4   If you were writing an article for a newspaper about the problems of inner city life, how could you use the findings of this study?

5   Give some examples of anthropomorphism from the text.

Suggested Answers start at p. 443

KEY WORDS

aggression	harem
anthropomorphism	hypersexual
dominance	somnambulist
oestrus	territory

PART III

HUMAN DIVERSITY

Psychology often makes *generalisations* about people. How people behave, how people think, and how people feel. Although some of these general statements are quite useful, they ignore the *differences* between groups of people, and between individual people. For example, if we wanted to talk about human aggression we might be able to say something about how all people show their aggression, but we would have to acknowledge the differences that exist. Some groups of people are much more aggressive than others; for example men are, on the whole, more aggressive than women, and army commandos are, on the whole, more aggressive than Buddhists. These are examples of groups that have different levels and styles of aggression. Also, within those groups there will be some individual differences. You might know some women who are very aggressive, and some men who are non-aggressive. The problem for psychology is to identify the features that we *share* with other people and still acknowledge the *differences* between individuals.

The studies in this part have been selected to show how psychology has approached the issues surrounding diversity. One such issue which has stimulated a considerable amount of research concerns the differences that exist between men and women. We have included four studies (Kitto, 1989; Koff, 1983; Dweck *et al.*, 1978; and Bem, 1974) that look at a range of issues to do with sex and gender. Another concern of psychology has been to *measure* the differences between people, and considerable effort has been put into developing reliable measuring instruments for a range of psychological variables. We have included five studies (Bem, 1974; Forer, 1949; Gould, 1982; Hraba & Grant, 1970;

and Smith & Glass, 1977) which look at some of the attempts that there have been to measure psychological qualities, and the problems that have arisen as a result of this enterprise.

Much of the psychology that is taught in British and US universities and colleges is fairly insensitive to cultural differences. However, the different cultures that exist within our societies, and around the world, do not share the same behaviours and social structures. We have included three studies to give a flavour of the issues surrounding cultural diversity.

Finally in this part, we look at what psychologists refer to as abnormality. Some people have very unusual thoughts and feelings, or display some unusual behaviour patterns. Sometimes we regard this as *eccentricity* and sometimes we regard this as a sign of mental ill-health. The judgement to make is whether someone is just being different, or whether they are being odd. The way we make this distinction is influenced by a range of factors including our culture, class, religion and general outlook on life. We have included four studies that look at the issues of defining abnormality and the treatment of people with a variety of mental health problems.

8 GENDER

When the birth of a new baby is announced, the first question on everyone's lips is 'Is it a boy or a girl?' This is a very important question for people, and you will find that out if you refuse to give the questioner the answer. If you say, 'Well, there is not a lot of difference between boys and girls at birth so in order to stop you behaving towards the child in accordance with your gender stereotypes, I am not going to tell you, and the child's name is Chris', then you will create a surprising amount of resentment (believe me, I've done it!). The category of boy or girl is perhaps the most important categorisation of your life.

Psychologists often make a distinction between sex and gender. *Sex* is seen as the biological differences between male and female whereas *gender* is defined as the 'psychological attributes, characteristics, and behaviours that are acquired within a social context and are related to the social meanings of sexual categories in a given society' (Williams, 1987, p. 135). The concepts of sex and gender can not be completely separated because they interact with each other. Your biology will affect your behaviour and your behaviour will also affect your biology. For example, in men the level of testosterone will affect the level of aggression, and the display of aggressive behaviour will affect the level of testosterone.

Psychology has tended to concentrate on the *differences* between men and women rather than the *similarities*. This has been for a number of reasons, not least the preference for statistically significant results in published articles. If a study finds 'no difference' then it attracts less interest and is less likely to be published. Also, as Williams (1987) points out, the differences that are recorded *between* men and women in, for example, reading or mathematics are often very slight and are far outweighed by the differences *within* the two gender groups.

One difference between men and women that is very clear is the power and status they have in our society. The study by Kitto (1989) shows how an apparently inconsequential bit of everyday language can affect our perception of people, and, in particular, diminish opportunities and respect for women. The paper by Dweck *et al.* (1978) looks at the subtle differences in behaviour shown towards boys and girls by teachers, and shows how this can have an effect on their classroom performance. Koff (1983) uses an interesting *projective technique* to explore the experience of the important female life event of menarche. This study also relates to the power and status differential since issues which are specifically of concern to women have characteristically been under-researched in psychology.

GIRLS JUST WANT TO HAVE FUN

- KITTO, J. (1989). Gender reference terms: Separating the women from the girls. *British Journal of Social Psychology, 28,* 185–87.

INTRODUCTION

Does it matter what words we use to describe and label people? Feminist writers have argued that it *does* matter (see for example Lakoff, 1975). Their argument is that words do not just reflect our beliefs and attitudes, but actually play a part in forming and reinforcing those beliefs and attitudes. The use of the pronouns 'he', 'him' and 'his', for example, to refer to people (both women and men) is more than just a neutral, unimportant grammatical convention. It has the effect of putting men implicitly at the centre of anything that is spoken about, whilst 'backgrounding' women. The effect is subtle, but pervasive and powerful. Nowadays most social scientific publications require writers to use non-gender specific pronouns when referring to people.

The experiment summarised here was designed to investigate whether or not these kinds of subtle effects of language could be demonstrated empirically. Specifically, it set out to examine whether people's attitudes to an adult female could be affected by her being described either as a 'girl' or as a 'woman'. Should the tendency to describe adult women as 'girls' be seen as endearing and harmless? Or is there something more important and problematic going on when people do this?

THE STUDY

The study involved subjects choosing which of two candidates was the more suitable for a hypothetical job. Each candidate was presented to the subjects by means of a reference which had apparently been written by their previous employer. One of the references referred to the candidate as a 'girl' and the other referred to her as a 'woman'. The subjects actually performed this task twice; once for a low-status job, and once for a high-status job. Kitto's hypothesis was that the candidates referred to as girls would be more likely to be thought suitable for the low-status job, and the candidates referred to as women would be more likely to be nominated as suitable for the high-status job.

Subjects

Sixty-four subjects participated, 32 women and 32 men. No further details of subjects are given.

Design

This experiment used a two-condition repeated measures design. The independent variable was the term used to describe the candidate ('girl' or 'woman'); the dependent variable was measured by means of the subjects' judgements of the candidates' suitability for the particular jobs.

Procedure

Each subject received two job advertisements. One was for a high-status job ('personal assistant for top executive'), the other for a low-status job ('helper/server in a café'). With each advertisement were references, ostensibly written by a former employer, for two candidates. For each job, one of the candidates was referred to as a 'girl', the other was referred to as a 'woman'. All four references were matched in terms of the personal qualities and abilities that were described for each candidate, the extent and relevance of the candidates' previous experience, and their age (all were 25). Each reference appeared an equal number of times in each of the two conditions; that is, for half the subjects reference 'A' referred to the candidate as a girl, and for the other half of the subjects reference 'A' referred to the candidate as a woman.

Each subject was required to choose, for each of the two jobs, which of the two candidates they thought was more suitable. The order in which the subjects made these decisions was randomised, so that some saw the high-status job advertisement and references first, and some saw the low-status job advertisement and references first. Subjects were also asked to give reasons for their decisions.

RESULTS

Note that the measures in Table 8.1 are 'dependent'. In effect each subject appears in two cells in the table, so the chi-square test of homogeneity is not a suitable inferential statistic in this instance. Kitto reports using a McNemar matched samples test (a chi-square test for dependent samples) to show a statistically significant difference in subjects' choices in the high-status job condition, in favour of 'woman' ($p < .001$).

Table 8.1   Contingency table showing subjects'
selections of candidates for high and low-status jobs

	Low status	High status
Girl	40	18
Woman	24	46

Source: Kitto (1989)

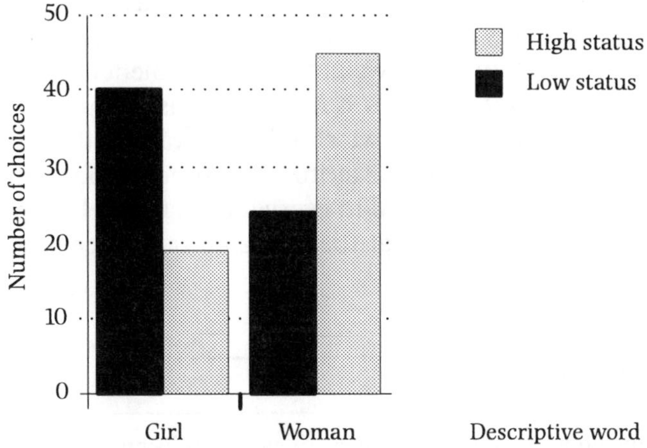

Figure 8.1   *The selection of girls or women for high and low-status jobs*

About 40 per cent of the subjects reported having been aware of the usage of the embedded terms in the different references that they saw. Kitto labelled these subjects the 'aware' group and compared their pattern of responses with the 60 per cent of unaware subjects. Both groups showed the same preference for the girl for the low-status job and the woman for the high-status job. 'Thus the results cannot be explained as an artifact caused by a small number of subjects self-consciously making selections they thought the experimenter wanted' (p. 186).

DISCUSSION

The results seem to support Kitto's hypothesis. The candidates referred to as girls were more likely to be thought suitable for the low-status job, whilst candidates referred to as women were more likely to be thought suitable for the high-status job.

The reasons that subjects gave for their decisions suggested that the inferences they made about the candidates were affected by the embedded terms 'girl' and 'woman'. For example, the subjects for whom the candidate was described as a 'woman' were more likely to give their reasons for choosing her in terms of her maturity, reliability and trustworthiness. On the other hand, the subjects for whom the candidate was described as a 'girl' were more likely to give their reasons for choosing her in terms of her youthfulness, vivaciousness and liveliness. The inferences tended to be positive for both embedded terms, but appeared to work against the person labelled as a girl when it came down to assessing suitability for a responsible, high-status position.

The results certainly lend weight to the argument that the tendency to refer to adult women as 'girls' is more than just a harmless linguistic convention. Kitto argues that we should be aware of the subtle effects that language can have on our attitudes to others. The terms 'girl' and 'woman' are so frequently used in everyday life to label people, that we may not notice the effects that they have on our perceptions of those people.

QUESTIONS

1   Why did each reference appear in each condition an equal number of times? That is, why did the same reference refer to the candidate as a girl for some subjects, and as a woman for other subjects?

2   It is very common in the English language to use 'he' to mean 'all people'. What other gender specific terms can you think of that are used to describe people of both sexes?

3   Most of the inferences attached to the term 'girl' were positive ones. This seems to be a particularly interesting observation. Why?

Suggested Answers start at p. 445

KEY WORDS

backgrounding   inequality
chi-square test   inference
feminist   labels
gender

Learning to Fail

■ Dweck, C.S., Davidson, W., Nelson, S. & Enna, B. (1978).
Sex differences in learned helplessness:
II. The contingencies of evaluative feedback in the classroom
and III. An experimental analysis.
Developmental Psychology, 14, 268–76.

Introduction

The concept of *learned helplessness* was developed by Seligman (see Seligman & Maier, 1967, Chapter 5 of this volume) to describe the behaviour of animals in an inescapable unpleasant situation. Dweck takes the idea a step further and applies it to human experience suggesting that learned helplessness exists when failure is perceived as insurmountable. She suggests that when we have this perception we are likely to attribute our failure at a task to stable and uncontrollable factors like lack of ability. In this circumstance, the failure is often followed by a deterioration in performance. On the other hand, people who explain their failure in terms of modifiable and unstable factors, like the amount of effort they put in, or the difficulty of the particular task they failed on, will often show improved performance following the failure.

Dweck and other researchers found in previous studies that girls are more likely to show the helpless pattern of attributions than boys. They are also more likely to give up sooner or show decreased performance after failure or threat of failure. One explanation for this effect suggested by psychologists was the different socialisation of boys and girls. Boys are encouraged to be more independent and so develop their own standards which makes them less susceptible to the judgements of others. However, some studies (for example Dweck & Bush, 1976) found that the helplessness of the girls was not a generalised trait. In fact, it did not occur when the judgements of failure came from peers rather than adults. They found, perhaps surprisingly, that girls respond with the greatest helplessness to the evaluations of female adults.

The issue to consider is why do girls learn to be helpless with adults despite performing better in schools, and receiving less negative classroom feedback than boys? The research of Dweck *et al.*, looks at patterns of classroom feedback and attempts to identify the differences in these patterns for girls and boys that might explain the helplessness effect. The basic suggestion they tested was that the widespread use of negative comments to boys in all manner of circumstances reduces the impact of negative comments about academic performance. Whereas the less frequent use of negative comments for girls makes the negative evaluations about their work seem to be a comment on their ability rather than their conduct. Therefore, the more criticism the teacher delivers to boys relative to praise, the more feedback about academic failure will be attributed to a characteristic of the teacher ('you're just saying that because you don't like me') rather than of the child. And the more positive the teacher is to girls, the more likely feedback about academic success will be attributed to her favourable attitude ('you're just saying that because you like me'). Conversely, if the teacher praises the boys or criticises the girls about their schoolwork, this will have more effect because it does not fall into the usual pattern.

The paper reports two studies. The first is an observational study of feedback given by teachers to girls and boys in a classroom. It was predicted that, compared to girls, boys will receive:

(a) more negative feedback;
(b) a greater proportion of their feedback for conduct and non-intellectual aspects of the work;
(c) more attributions of their failure to their motivation.

It was also predicted that teachers would use *positive* feedback more specifically to refer to the academic performance of the boys, but more generally for girls to refer to conduct and the non-intellectual aspects of their work.

The second study used the patterns of behaviour observed in the first study to see whether it was possible to induce helplessness attributions in children.

The First Study

The subjects were 79 children in the 4th and 5th grades of a predominantly White, lower middle class, US school. The observations were carried out over a period of five weeks for two full days each week. All evaluative feedback from the teachers was coded and analysed according to the sex of the child. The observations included whether the evaluation was:

- positive or negative;
- conduct or work-related;
- intellectual (e.g. competence and correctness) or non-intellectual (e.g. neatness, speaking clearly).

They also noted the type of attributions the teacher gave for success or failure of the child.

The observers were five undergraduates who were unaware of the hypotheses. They were given 14 hours training until they obtained 90 per cent agreement on videotaped observations. Of the classroom observations, 25 per cent were conducted with two observers to provide a reliability check. The average *inter-observer* agreement was 91.5 per cent.

Results

Figure 8.2 shows there is no sex difference in the amount of feedback given on the intellectual quality of the work. However, Figure 8.3 shows a sex difference in the feedback given for intellectual aspects of the work as a percentage of the total feedback (including non-intellectual aspects and conduct aspects, as well as the intellectual quality of the

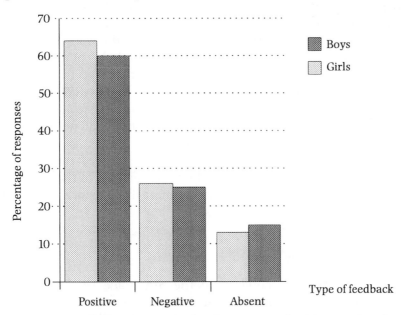

Figure 8.2 *Feedback on correctness of work: percentage of positive, negative, absent*
Source: Adapted from Dweck, Davidson, Nelson & Enna (1978)

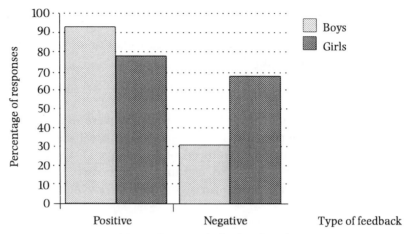

Figure 8.3   *Percentage of the total positive feedback and total negative feedback that was given for the intellectual quality of the work*
Source: Adapted from Dweck, Davidson, Nelson & Enna (1978)

work). For boys, more than 90 per cent of all the positive feedback they received concerned the quality of their work, whereas for girls it was under 80 per cent. Even when the comments about conduct ('you naughty boy') were left out of the analysis there was still a sex difference showing that the positive comments about the work were largely about intellectual quality for the boys but contained comments about neatness and so forth for the girls (non-intellectual aspects).

The difference is even more marked for the negative comments (see Figure 8.4). For boys, only 54 per cent of the work-related criticism referred to intellectual inadequacy, whereas for girls 88 per cent of the criticisms referred to intellectual performance.

In summary, despite the fact that girls received more positive and less negative evaluations than boys, the pattern of the comments and attributions made by teachers were more likely to increase feelings of helplessness in girls than in boys.

THE SECOND STUDY

The subjects were 60 children in the 5th grade (30 boys and 30 girls), who were randomly assigned to each of three experimental conditions. Parental permission was obtained for all the children who participated.

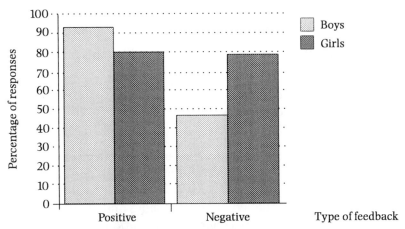

Figure 8.4 *Percentage of positive work-related feedback and negative work-related feedback given for the intellectual quality of the work*
Source: Adapted from Dweck, Davidson, Nelson & Enna (1978)

The children were taken individually from their classroom to the testing room with the male experimenter. (The experimenter was male because past research had shown greater sex differences in helplessness responses with female adults). The child was given some 'word puzzles' which consisted of 20 four-letter anagrams. The child was given four cardboard squares with a letter on each and asked to make a word from them in 15 seconds. After some practice trials the children were given 20 experimental trials which consisted of 10 soluble anagrams (for example, EAMG) and ten insoluble anagrams (for example, FTOE).

The experimental conditions varied in the type of failure-feedback that the experimenter gave the child. In one condition (the 'teacher–boy condition') the experimenter gave the sort of feedback that the boys received in the classroom observation: a mixture of failure feedback about the correctness of the task, and also the non-intellectual aspects such as neatness. There were two further conditions where the experimenter gave the sort of feedback that girls received in the classroom observation: the failure-feedback was addressed specifically to the correctness of the solution.

After the anagram tests, the children were all given another set of problems to solve. They were told to hurry in the tasks, but were all stopped before they had completed each task and told they had not done very well. After three failures to complete the task, each child was asked to answer a simple question on a piece of paper to find out what they attributed their failure on this new task to. The question read:

If the man told you that you did not do very well on this puzzle, why do you think that was?

(a) I did not try hard enough.
(b) The man was too fussy.
(c) I am not very good at it (p. 273).

After the experiences of failure, the children were given some other tasks to do which they were successful at and given copious praise to cheer them up.

The results showed that children (both boys and girls) who were in the 'teacher–boy condition' made far less attributions to their own ability when asked to explain their failure on the second task. They were more likely to explain it in terms of effort ('I did not try hard enough'), or the fussiness of the experimenter. On the other had, the children in the 'teacher–girl conditions' were more likely to explain their failure in terms of their lack of ability ('I am not very good at it').

DISCUSSION

The study supports the initial hypotheses about the different styles of praise and criticism for boys and girls, and their effects on the child's judgement of his or her ability. The general praise given to 'good girls' dilutes the impact of praise for good work, whereas the general criticism given to 'naughty boys' dilutes the impact of criticism for poor work.

The first study is more convincing than the second because of the rather contrived nature of the experiment. This highlights the difficulties of carrying out controlled experiments on complex social and personal experiences.

The study takes us one step on from the rather general, and not very helpful, explanations of sex differences that suggest they are due to 'socialisation'. The study looks in detail at some specific exchanges between adults and children. The study makes clear predictions based on theory and is able to test these through *structured observation*. The structured observation inevitably simplifies the complex interactions between the children and their teachers, and does not include the rich social world of the school classroom. However, despite its limitations, it still provides some useful data for our analysis of the different social worlds of boys and girls.

QUESTIONS

1   What did the observers record in the classroom?

2   What else might they have examined which would have been relevant to this study?

3   What other situations might create a sense of helplessness in people?

4   In what ways was the experiment unlike the usual experience of children in school?

Suggested Answers start at p. 445

KEY WORDS

attribution
classroom performance
experiment
feedback
inter-observer reliability

learned helplessness
observation
sex differences
trait

Rites of Passage

■ Koff, E. (1983). Through the looking glass of menarche: What the adolescent girl sees.
In S. Golub (ed.), *Menarche*, pp. 77–86. Lexington, Mass: D.C. Heath.

Introduction

Growing up is not something that happens smoothly and gradually. There are events and changes that bring about a shift in the way we see the world and the way the world sees us. Half of the population have a clear sign of their growing maturity when they start to menstruate. The physical changes associated with the first menstruation (*menarche*) have been researched and described in some detail, but there have been relatively few studies of the psychological changes that accompany it.

Koff reports that some writers have suggested that menarche brings with it a number of changes in body image and sexual identification. They suggest the pre-menarcheal girl experiences difficulty in organising and communicating her thoughts. The onset of menstruation is associated with a dramatic shift, and the post-menarcheal girl is seen to organise her thoughts and express herself more clearly. Interviews with post-menarcheal girls found that they experienced themselves as more womanly and began to reflect on their future reproductive roles. They also described more acceptance of their bodies as feminine, and a greater awareness of themselves as female.

Menarche usually occurs relatively late in the sequence of physical changes that occur in adolescence. In fact, girls can develop their secondary sexual characteristics and more feminine appearance as much as two years before menarche. Koff suggests, however, that the onset of menarche, which is a sharply defined event, is the key event around which girls make sense of the changes that are happening to them.

This article combines the results from two studies conducted by the author, both of which used *projective techniques* to explore the perceptions and feelings of the girls in the studies.

THE STUDIES

In the first study, girls from the seventh grade of a US school made drawings of male and female figures on two occasions about six months apart. The researchers were able to divide the girls into three groups:

(1)   34 girls were pre-menarcheal on both occasions;
(2)   23 girls were post-menarcheal on both occasions;
(3)   30 girls were pre-menarcheal on the first occasion and post-menarcheal on the second.

This is a *quasi-experimental design* since the groups selected themselves by their menarcheal status.

The researchers collected the pictures and gave them a 'sexual differentiation score' (measuring how much the male and female drawings were distinguishable by their sex) using a previously developed scale. The hypothesis was that the pictures of the post-menarcheal girls would show greater sexual differentiation than the pictures of the pre-menarcheal girls. The researchers also recorded which picture, male or female, the girls drew first.

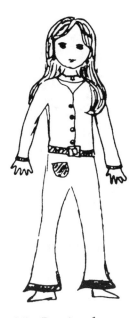

Figure 8.5   *Drawing of a premenarcheal*   **Figure 8.6**   *Drawing of a premenarcheal*
girl, time 1   *girl, time 2*

Source: Figures 8.5–8.10 Koff (1983)

The three groups of girls were distinguishable by the types of drawings they produced. Figures 8.5 and 8.6 show an example of the drawings made by a girl who was pre-menarcheal on both occasions. These show a dramatic contrast with the pictures drawn by post-menarcheal girls, examples of which are shown in Figures 8.7 and 8.8. Perhaps the most interesting pairs of pictures are the ones drawn by girls who changed their menarcheal status between the two drawings, and an example of this is shown in Figures 8.9 and 8.10. The girls in the three groups were approximately the same age, in the same year at school and had experienced the same time gap between the two drawings. The key feature seems to be the menarcheal status of the girls.

Koff reports that, overall, the post-menarcheal girls drew pictures that showed more features of sexual differentiation. Also, among the girls who changed their menarcheal status, there was a significant increase in the sexual features drawn in their second pictures. Another finding was that post-menarcheal girls were more likely to draw their own sex first.

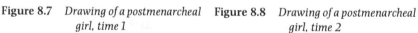

Figure 8.7 *Drawing of a postmenarcheal girl, time 1*   **Figure 8.8** *Drawing of a postmenarcheal girl, time 2*

Figure 8.9   *Drawing of a girl whose menarcheal status changed over course of study – premenarcheal, time 1*

Figure 8.10   *Drawing of a girl whose menarcheal status changed over course of study – postmenarcheal, time 2*

In a second study, Koff and her associates used a sentence-completion task to further investigate the perceptions of the girls. The subjects in this study were 16 pre-menarcheal and 18 post-menarcheal girls. They were given the cue sentence 'Ann just got her period for the first time' and then asked to complete a number of other sentences. Some of the items received similar responses from both groups of girls. For example, when asked to complete the sentence 'When Ann looked at herself in the mirror that night...' the girls gave responses such as 'she felt more grown up', 'she thought she had changed', 'she thought she looked older'.

Some other items, however, did show some differences between the pre-menarcheal and post-menarcheal girls. For example, the sentence 'Ann regarded her body as...' received a number of completions from pre-menarcheal girls about altered body image, such as 'more mature than it was', 'a woman's body', and 'different'. The post-menarcheal girls were less likely to make this sort of response, and some reported no change, for example 'she did before', or 'the same as yesterday'. The authors of this summary are unclear about how this observation fits with the results of the first study (and the original authors argue that it does), which indicated a *changed* perception of the woman's body in post-menarcheal girls.

DISCUSSION

The studies add weight to the suggestion that menarche is an important psychological event for a girl that acts as the turning point in her view of herself and her identity as a woman.

The paper raises a number of other important issues, not least of which is the relative lack of research into the psychology of women. It is quite remarkable that major life events such as menstruation or pregnancy have received so little attention by psychologists.

The study also uses the interesting method of projective techniques. The basic idea of a projective technique is to provide someone with a relatively bland stimulus and let them make of it what they want. Their response is likely to show some characteristics of their thoughts and feelings that they would otherwise find difficult to articulate. The drawings produced by the girls gave a dramatic representation of the effects of menarche, and it is very doubtful whether it would be possible to use interviews or questionnaires to give such a graphic illustration of the psychological changes taking place. Some psychologists might regard this sort of data with suspicion since it does not have numbers attached to it.

The study was carried out on a relatively small sample of US girls, so without further empirical work we cannot generalise the findings to women with a different cultural background. Further studies that explore the experience of menarche in other cultures would give some insight into the processes by which women develop their female identity.

QUESTIONS

1   Why has psychology shown relatively little interest in the behaviour and experience of women?

2   What are projective techniques? What are the advantages and disadvantages of these techniques?

3   Try out the 'draw a female and male' test on your friends and family and look for any systematic difference between the responses.

Suggested Answers start at p. 446

KEY WORDS

adolescence   projective techniques
body image   quasi-experiment
menarche   sexual identity
menstruation   sexual differentiation

9 MEASURING PERSONALITY

We make judgements and statements about people's personality all the time. We use terms that we think other people will understand so that we can share our perceptions of someone's personality. Sometimes these judgements have important consequences, for example in selecting people for jobs or in deciding whether to trust someone with your life savings, or worse, your season ticket or favourite teddy.

Psychologists have tried to produce measuring scales that can provide accurate and reliable information about personality. If this endeavour were to be successful, then it would provide the means for job selection that could remove the bias of selecting people because of their sex or culture or class. However, the task of devising an accurate measurement scale is very difficult, though this difficulty has not inhibited the development of thousands of scales for every personality trait imaginable. The studies in this chapter have been selected to raise some of the issues around the development of personality measurement scales.

The first study by Bem (1974) describes how a scale for measuring masculinity and femininity was developed and tested. The study highlights the complexity of test construction and the importance of relating measurement to theoretical ideas, in this case about gender. The study by Forer (1949) illustrates one of the problems we have to consider with personality tests. We are very *gullible* when faced by expert opinion, and it is not very difficult to impress people with a few simple generalisations about their personality. Forer suggests that we should be very sceptical about the findings from personality tests. Other attempts to measure personal qualities can be found in Part VI on health, where we include a study on coping strategies by Billings and Moos (1981), and a study on the adaptation to stressful life events by Holmes & Rahe (1967).

MEASURING MASCULINITY AND FEMININITY

■ BEM, S.L. (1974).
The measurement of psychological androgyny.
Journal of Consulting and Clinical Psychology, 42, 155–62.

INTRODUCTION

Scales, tests and inventories are part of the psychologist's toolkit, and are of particular interest to psychometricians. The development of such measuring devices is an exacting process, and before they are used to measure anything in the real world their *reliability* and *validity* must be assessed. So it is quite common to see research studies which are devoted to the process of developing a particular scale. Such studies put the scale in question 'on the market' (if the reader is convinced by the processes of assessment which are reported), and allow future users to refer back to see how their measuring device was constructed and what its potential strengths and weaknesses might be.

Bem's famous article is a good example of such a study. It reports the development of a new scale for measuring *psychological androgyny*. The Bem Sex Role Inventory (BSRI) assesses the extent to which masculine and feminine traits co-exist in individuals irrespective of their actual sex. Here we will focus on the process of test development as reported in Bem's paper, but a very brief outline of androgyny is appropriate.

Bem challenges the traditional idea of femininity–masculinity, whereby people are *either* feminine *or* masculine. She also challenges the notion that femininity and masculinity are necessarily to do with being (biologically) female or male. She argues that 'dimensions of masculinity and femininity are empirically as well as logically independent' (p. 155), so that it is possible for someone to be both feminine and masculine ('androgynous') according to 'situational appropriateness' (p. 155). The development of the BSRI, which contains independent feminine and masculine scales, is the first step in the process of exploring these arguments.

THE STUDY

Subjects

Different subjects were used at different stages of the development of the inventory. In the 'item selection' stage, 100 Stanford University under-graduates (50 female, 50 male) acted as the 'judges' (see procedure section below). At the stage of 'psychometric analysis', 723 Stanford under-graduates (279 female, 444 male) and 194 junior college students (77 female, 117 male) were used as subjects. The junior college students were paid. Fifty-six of the Stanford undergraduates (28 female, 28 male) took part in the re-test phase.

Design

This is a paper which documents the development of a psychological measuring scale. The process in this case involved two stages: item selection and psychometric analysis. These stages are described in detail below.

Procedure

Item selection   Initially the author and some student assistants chose 200 words to describe personality characteristics which they judged to be 'both positive in value and either masculine or feminine in tone' (p. 156). One hundred undergraduate 'judges' were asked to rate all of these words on a seven-point Likert scale, according to how desirable each characteristic was in US society for either women, or for men. One set of 50 judges (25 female, 25 male) rated the desirability of each characteristic for women ('In American society, how desirable is it for a woman to be *sincere?*'). The other set of 50 judges (again, half female, half male) rated desirability of each characteristic for men ('In American society, how desirable is it for a man to be *sincere?*'). If a word was rated by men and women in both sets of judges to be significantly more desirable for a woman, then it qualified as a potential 'feminine' item for the inventory. If a word was rated by men and women in both sets of judges to be significantly more desirable for a man, then it qualified as a potential 'masculine' item for the inventory.

Twenty feminine items and 20 masculine items were selected (Bem does not specify how this final selection was made) from those which qualified for the final inventory. The inventory also includes

20 'neutral' items (neither masculine nor feminine) which were incorporated as a measure of social desirability effects in self-rating. The
selection of and rationale for these neutral items is described in detail
by Bem, but is not covered in this summary.

Use of the Inventory   When the inventory is administered, subjects are
instructed to rate themselves on each of the 60 items using a seven-
point Likert scale on which a score of one denotes 'Never or almost
never true' and a score of seven denotes 'Always or almost always true'
(and so forth). A subject's Femininity ('F') score is obtained by adding
up all the ratings for the 20 feminine items, and their Masculinity ('M')
score is obtained by adding up their ratings for the 20 masculine items.
Subjects also receive an Androgyny ('A') score.

The simplest way of calculating 'A' is to subtract the 'M' score from the
'F' score. The closer this number is to zero, the more androgynous the
person. High positive scores on 'A' indicate a feminine sex-typed person,
and high negative scores indicate a masculine sex-typed person. Note
that Bem suggests using a more sophisticated statistical test to calculate
the 'A' score but acknowledges that the simple difference score between
'F' and 'M' can be used instead.

Psychometric Analysis   Once a measuring device has been assembled
it must be tested for its psychometric properties. This is done by administering it to a large sample of the population which it is designed to
measure, and noting various statistical properties of the data which
emerge.

A vital step in this process is the assessment of the reliability of the
measuring device. This involves examining the extent to which it gives
consistent results. Bem did this in two ways. First she looked at the
internal consistency of the scale. If the scale is internally consistent
then a person who scores high on one masculine item will also be likely
to score high on the other masculine items. Her analyses (see the statistical note below if you must) confirmed that the test was internally
consistent.

The second kind of reliability Bem assessed was the *test – retest
reliability* of the inventory. This gives an estimate of the extent to which
the results of the BSRI are consistent over time. Fifty-six of the original
723 Stanford University undergraduate subjects completed the inventory for a second time four weeks after having done their first test.
Their 're-test' scores on each of the 'F', 'M' and 'A' scales were compared

with their original 'test' scores by means of a correlation coefficient (signified by r). The correlations were sufficiently strong to allow Bem to claim a high level of test – retest reliability (for Femininity $r = .90$; for Masculinity $r = .90$; and for Androgyny $r = .93$).

The final statistical property that will be considered in this summary (Bem considers several in the original paper) is the relationship between the 'F' and the 'M' scales. Remember Bem's argument is that femininity and masculinity are 'empirically independent' dimensions. This means that people's scores on the 'F' scale should show no consistent relationship with their scores on the 'M' scale. Calculation of correlation coefficients for the 'F' and 'M' scores for the Stanford undergraduates showed values of nearly zero for r. This supports Bem's assertion of empirical independence for the two dimensions, because the nearer a value of r is to zero (irrespective of whether it is positive or negative), the smaller the relationship between the two variables which have been compared. When a test or scale can be shown to match up to a piece of theory in this way it is said to have a level of *construct validity*.

RESULTS

The most important result of this process of development, aside from the population norms and various statistical properties, is the inventory itself. For copyright reasons we are unable to show the items from the BSRI here. We strongly recommend that you consult Table 1 (p. 156) of the original paper which shows the 60 items organised into three columns of 20; one column for masculine, one for feminine and one for neutral items. The items are mostly single words, although about one-fifth are short phrases. The masculine column contains adjectives such as 'aggressive' and 'self-reliant' (p. 156). The feminine scale lists words such as 'compassionate' and 'understanding' (p. 156). The neutral scale consists of items such as 'friendly' and 'jealous' (p. 156).

DISCUSSION

To say that a measuring device is reliable is to say that it produces *consistent* patterns of results. Assessing the reliability of an inventory like the BSRI is relatively straightforward, since most of the work can be done by means of standard statistical procedures. The evidence that Bem presents suggests that the BSRI does, indeed, give reliable results.

However once reliability has been assessed, the much harder task of considering validity appears. The extent to which a scale is valid is the extent to which it measures what it sets out to measure. For a scale to be valid it must firstly be reliable. But if a scale is reliable this does not in itself mean that it is valid. Imagine a ruler that is wrongly calibrated. It will give perfectly consistent results when used to measure things (it will be perfectly reliable), but the measurements will ·be invalid (and therefore useless). Unfortunately there are no easy statistical means for assessing validity. Sometimes the results of a scale are compared to the results of existing scales which are thought to measure the same thing. This is known as *concurrent validity*. Bem does in fact compare the scores of her subjects on the BSRI with their scores on two other existing masculinity–femininity scales which she administered to them at the same time. The relationship among the various scales was relatively weak, so Bem simply concluded that the scales were measuring different aspects of sex roles. This handy 'get-out clause' always exists in relation to estimates of concurrent validity.

To what extent, then, can the BSRI be said to be valid? That is, to what extent does the Femininity scale really measure femininity? And what about the 'M' and 'A' scales? One way of assessing the validity of the BSRI is to examine the way that the instrument was constructed in the first place. Certainly the care and attention to detail at the stage of item selection is one point in its favour. Bem did not just throw together 40 items that she felt were related to masculinity and femininity. Instead she involved a large number of other people in the selection process (at least 100 others), with the result that the final scales were built on a fair degree of social consensus; consensus that the 20 'F' items really were more 'desirable' characteristics for women than for men in the USA in the 1970s, and likewise for the 20 'M' items.

But even if it was possible to demonstrate that the scales were valid there (in the USA) and then (in the 1970s), this could never ensure that they are valid here (wherever you are reading this) and now. Bem shows great awareness in her article that the BSRI is a culturally specific measuring device, by stressing that the items were assessed for desirability for men and women in the USA. She shows less awareness of the historical specificity of the BSRI, but of course this is something which is always easier to assess in retrospect.

QUESTIONS

1 What are the limitations of using students as the subjects in this study?

2 Bem developed the BSRI in the USA in the 1970s. Why should we be cautious of using this instrument today outside of the USA?

3 What does it mean to say that a test is *reliable*? What does it mean to say that a test is *valid*?

4 What different types of *reliability* do psychologists talk about?

5 What different types of *validity* do psychologists talk about?

Suggested Answers start at p. 446

KEY WORDS

alpha coefficient; Cronbach's alpha (see accompanying statistics note)

androgyny	masculinity
concurrent validity	psychometrics
construct validity	reliability
internal consistency	test – retest reliability
Likert scale	validity

Statistical note

To measure the internal consistency of the scale Bem calculated separate *alpha coefficients* (also known as 'Cronbach's alpha', and signified by α) for the Femininity scale and for the Masculinity scale. Coefficient alpha gives a measure of the internal consistency of the inventory. It works by assessing, statistically, the extent to which responses to the different items on a given scale relate to one another. For example, if the 20 items which make up the masculinity scale really are all measuring a bit of masculinity, then one would expect, on balance, to see a positive correlation among the scores for those items for each subject. In other words, if a given subject rates themselves as '7' on the item 'Acts as a leader', and we assume (as the BSRI does) that 'Acts as a leader' and 'Aggressive' are both measures of 'masculinity', then we would assume that they would be more likely to give themselves a high rating on 'Aggressive' than a person who had rated themselves as '1' on the 'Acts as a leader' item. Coefficient alpha gives a statistical estimate of the extent to which responses to items on a given scale really do relate one to another. Bem cites relatively high alpha values for both the Femininity and the Masculinity scales (α for F =.8; α for M = .86: like a straightforward correlation coefficient the maximum value for α is 1), and so was able to claim that they are reliable in the sense of being internally consistent.

How Gullible Are You?

■ FORER, B.R. (1949). The fallacy of personal validation: A class-room demonstration of gullibility.
Journal of Abnormal and Social Psychology, 44, 118–21.

INTRODUCTION

People appear to have a restless quest for information about themselves. We seek the advice and insight of fortune tellers, friends, counsellors and psychologists. The unfortunate truth is that we tend to neglect our usual critical skills when we deal with the information we receive.

An example of this comes from the work of Furnham & Varian (1988) who looked at how people predict and accept their own scores on psychological tests. In their first experiment, undergraduates tried to predict their own scores and also the scores of a friend on the EPI (the Eysenck Personality Inventory, which claims to measure how extravert and neurotic a person is). They were fairly good at this. Then some other undergraduates were given false feedback (in other words, incorrect results) after completing the EPI. They were more likely to accept positive feedback as accurate than negative feedback, even though it did not have any connection with their actual scores. The results of the first study suggest that we are quite good at predicting the outcomes of personality tests. However, the results of the second study suggest that when the outcomes of the test contradict our predictions, we are inclined to believe the test rather than our own evaluations.

This leads us to a discussion of the *Barnum Effect* (so named after the famous US showman). In brief, the Barnum Effect refers to a powerful tendency to believe information given to us about our personal qualities. This is used to good effect by fortune tellers, astrologers, hand writing experts and various other contemporary shaman. If the 'expert' can say what people are prepared to accept, and can phrase it in such a way that it implies some intimate insight, then there is a good living to be made.

THE STUDY

Forer points out that virtually every psychological trait can be viewed to a greater or lesser extent in everyone. This means that when we read a text book on abnormal psychology we see a connection to our problems and experience; the 'oh, I'm sure I've got that' syndrome. We make this mistake because we lack a reference point for critical comparison, in that we do not know what other people are experiencing. For example, if we read that people with a 'Bashful Syndrome' (made up name) are unsure of themselves in social situations, then we believe it could be us. This is because everyone is sometimes unsure in social situations, but the feeling only becomes noteworthy if you are very unsure of yourself. And you can only make this judgement by comparing yourself to other people and evaluating your unsureness as greater than theirs. This lack of a reference point for comparison makes us vulnerable to statements about ourselves that require a comparison to other people.

Some psychological tests, and psychological therapies, have used *personal validation* to back up the procedure. Personal validation asks the subject or client to say whether he or she agrees with the assessment of the therapist or tester. If they agree, it is seen as evidence for the validity of the test or therapy. However, it seems that people are vulnerable to agreement with certain sorts of comparative statements, so their agreement with the results of the test or therapy is affected by their belief in the test or therapist.

Procedure

Forer tested this observation on his introductory psychology class. During a lecture, he described his Diagnostic Interest Bank (DIB) to his students. In the manner of all the best con tricks, this wetted the appetite of the class and they persuaded Forer to let them take the test (the first rule of a successful con is to appear reluctant!). The class were given the test and told they would receive their personal profiles after the data had been analysed. One week later, each student was given a typed personality sketch with their name on it. The students had requested secrecy and this was encouraged by Forer.

Before the sketches were passed to the students, instructions were given first to read the sketches and then to turn the papers over and complete the following steps:

A. Rate on a scale of 0 (poor) to 5 (perfect) how *effective* the DIB is in revealing personality.

B. Rate on a scale of 0 to 5 the degree to which the personality description reveals *basic characteristics* of your personality.

C. Turn the paper again and check each statement as *true or false* about yourself, or use a question mark if you cannot tell.

When the students looked at their personality sketch they saw 13 statements. If, however, they had looked at the sketch of any of their colleagues they would have seen the same 13 statements. The universal sketch consisted of the following items:

(1) You have a great need for other people to like and admire you.

(2) You have a tendency to be critical of yourself.

(3) You have a great deal of unused capacity which you have not turned to your advantage.

(4) While you have some personality weaknesses, you are generally able to compensate for them.

(5) Your sexual adjustment has presented problems for you.

(6) Disciplined and self-controlled outside, you tend to be worrisome and insecure inside.

(7) At times you have serious doubts as to whether you have made the right decision or done the right thing.

(8) You prefer a certain amount of change and variety and become dissatisfied when hemmed in by restrictions and limitations.

(9) You pride yourself as an independent thinker and do not accept others' statements without satisfactory proof.

(10) You have found it unwise to be too frank in revealing yourself to others.

(11) At times you are extroverted, affable, sociable, while at other times you are introverted, wary, reserved.

(12) Some of your aspirations tend to be pretty unrealistic.

(13) Security is one of your major goals in life.
(p. 119)

After they had completed their assessment of the DIB and the personality sketch, the students were *debriefed* about the study. Forer writes that 'it was pointed out to them that the experiment had been performed as an object lesson to demonstrate the tendency to be overly impressed by vague statements and to endow diagnosticians with an unwarrantedly high degree of insight'. This was Forer's justification for the deception of his subjects.

RESULTS

The results of completing steps A and B are shown in Table 9.1, and graphically in Figure 9.1. The results of completing step C are shown in Table 9.2. The distribution of 'true' responses are shown in Table 9.3, and are graphically represented in Figure 9.2.

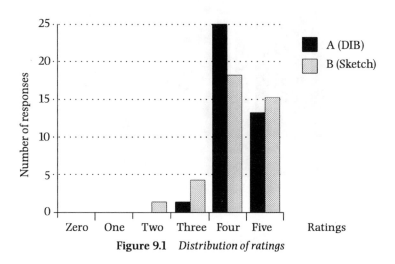

Figure 9.1   *Distribution of ratings*

Table 9.1   Distribution of ratings

Ratings	0	1	2	3	4	5	N
A (DIB)	0	0	0	1	25	13	39
B (Sketch)	0	0	1	4	18	16	39

Source: Forer (1949)

Table 9.2   Distribution of 'true' responses

Number true	5	6	7	8	9	10	11	12	13	N
Frequency	1	0	0	5	5	10	9	7	2	39

Source: Forer (1949)

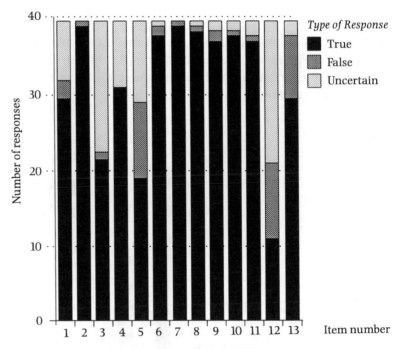

Figure 9.2   *Acceptance of sketch items*

Table 9.3   Group acceptance of sketch items

| | Item number | | | | | | | | | | | | |
Response	1	2	3	4	5	6	7	8	9	10	11	12	13
True	28	38	23	31	18	35	38	37	34	35	34	12	28
False	4	0	1	0	9	3	0	1	3	2	1	9	7
Uncertain	7	1	15	8	12	1	1	1	2	2	4	18	4

Source: Forer (1949)

DISCUSSION

The study suggests that the method of personal validation of therapeutic procedures and personality tests is unsatisfactory. The students in this demonstration found that they were susceptible to messages about themselves from a seemingly credible source.

If we look at a number of personality tests, we can interpret the popularity of these tests as another example of the Barnum Effect. As long as the test provides a plausible, largely positive description that relies on comparisons with the behaviour and experience of other people, then it is likely to be believed.

QUESTIONS

1 Who are the most plausible sources of information about ourselves? In other words what kinds of people do we tend to believe?

2 The subjects in this study were students. How might the results have been different if the study had been carried out on a different subject group?

3 Forer justifies his deception of his students. Do you think this justification is sufficient?

4 Try this demonstration out on someone else, maybe after pretending to read their palm. Do be sure to tell them what it was all about afterwards.

Suggested Answers start at p. 447

KEY WORDS

Barnum Effect   neurotic
debriefing   personal validation
extravert   personality
Eysenck Personality Inventory   trait

10 CULTURAL DIVERSITY

The psychology that you read in most texts is mainly about the experience and behaviour of White people. Psychology courses, conferences and text books do not pay much attention to the diversity of cultures that exist within Western societies and around the world. It is possible to find some reference to cross-cultural studies, but very often the societies under examination are studied by Western psychologists who can only give the perspective of an outsider.

In this collection of studies we have chosen to look at three that say something about the experience of Black people within the Western world. The first is a review by Stephen Jay Gould of the uses of IQ testing. He demonstrates how findings were perverted for political ends, and used in support of racist views of White superiority.

The next two studies look at *identity*. The study by Hraba & Grant (1970) replicates a classic investigation by Clark & Clark (1947), where children were asked to choose between White and Black dolls. Their results suggested a change in the consciousness of Black US children over the intervening 20 years. The paper by Nobles (1976) theorises on Black identity and provides a framework for considering these issues. If you think that Nobles is overstating the case when he refers to scientific racism, then we refer you to an article in *The Psychologist*, the flagship journal of the British Psychological Society. In 1990, it published an overtly *racist* article by Rushton which used nonsensical evidence to mount a case for racial superiority. Scientific racism is sadly still a reality as dominant groups seek to explain their political power through bogus scientific arguments.

MIS-MEASURING INTELLIGENCE

■ GOULD, S. J. (1982). A nation of morons.
New Scientist (6 May 1982), 349–52.

INTRODUCTION

Intelligence is perhaps the most controversial topic in modern psychology. It has created furious debate throughout this century and continues to do so. The issue that creates this controversy concerns whether intelligence is inherited or not. Although this is the way the question is usually framed, the real debate is about whether the differences *between individuals* can be explained by genetic or environmental causes. You might well ask whether this matters at all, but the paper by Gould, which is a short article taken from his book *The Mismeasure of Man*, illustrates how this question can have large social consequences.

If we are going to investigate intelligence, then we need to be able to measure it. The first tests of intelligence were developed in France by Alfred Binet who started his scientific studies by examining the relationship between head size and intelligence. He discovered that there is no relationship between these two factors. He was later commissioned by the minister of public education to develop a technique to identify children in need of special education, and from this the intelligence test was born. The test was used to give an estimate of a child's *mental age* by comparing the child's performance on various tasks with the performance of children of various ages. It was later suggested that the mental age of the child should be divided by the chronological age to give an index of intelligence and so the notion of IQ was developed.

Intelligence Quotient (IQ) = Mental Age/Chronological Age × 100

Subsequently, the calculation of IQ has become more sophisticated. It is now based on *norm referencing*, or in other words it depends on calculating the average performance for your peers then comparing you against the average.

Binet believed that children who were in need of extra help could be identified by these tests, but he vigorously argued against the idea that intelligence is a fixed quantity that cannot be improved by further help.

This approach got sadly lost in the translation of tests into the English language and in their transportation to the USA. In contrast to the approach of Binet, the fiercest supporters of intelligence testing became scientists who believed that individual differences are mainly due to genetic factors, and that a society should scientifically breed a superior group of people (this is referred to as *eugenics*). For example, Lewis Terman who introduced the IQ test to the USA while he was professor of psychology at Stanford University wrote,

> If we would preserve our state for a class of people worthy to possess it, we must prevent, as far as possible, the propagation of mental degenerates.
>
> (Terman, 1921, cited in Kamin, 1977)

This is the basic eugenic argument, that scientists should identify the useless, the stupid and the weak and prevent (or discourage) them from having children. In this way the general population will improve its genetic stock. The crude simplicity of this dogma appeals to some politicians who have used the bogus science to justify oppressive policies.

THE ARTICLE

The article describes one story in the development of intelligence testing. Psychologist Robert Yerkes was concerned to establish psychology as a 'hard' science and thought that mental testing looked a promising route to achieve this. Unfortunately, in 1915, mental testing did not enjoy much credibility, so Yerkes tried to change this.

The outbreak of the Great War (1914–18) in Europe and the subsequent involvement of the United States brought about a massive mobilisation of armies. Yerkes managed to persuade the American military to give mental tests to all army recruits, and as a result he was able to preside over the testing of 1.75 million recruits.

There were three types of test; literate recruits were given a written test called the *Army Alpha*, men who were illiterate or who failed the Alpha were given a pictorial test called the *Army Beta*, and failures on the Beta were to be recalled for an individual *spoken examination*. The Alpha had eight parts made up of the items we recognise today as characteristic of IQ tests, such as analogies, filling in the missing number, and unscrambling a sentence. The Beta test had seven parts including number work and the picture completion task shown in Figure 10.1. Each test took less than an hour and could be administered to large groups.

Yerkes asserted that the tests measured 'native intellectual ability' (cited in Gould, p. 349); in other words intelligence which was unaffected by culture and educational opportunities. But the level of

Figure 10.1 *Part six of examination Beta for testing innate intelligence*
Source: Gould (1981)

cultural and *educational* knowledge required is clearly illustrated in the examples from the tests given below:

Washington is to Adams as first is to.....

Crisco is a: patent medicine, disinfectant, toothpaste, food product.

Christy Mathewson is famous as a: writer, artist, baseball player, comedian.

There were a number of problems in the administration of the tests. In particular, many who were illiterate in English were still allocated to the Alpha test and so scored zero or near to zero. Yerkes had overestimated the level of literacy in the general population and so the queues for the Beta tests became very long leading to the inappropriate re-allocation of men to the Alpha test. Failures on the Alpha test were often not recalled to take the Beta test. This created a systematic bias in the test since recent immigrants who had a poor grasp of English, and Black men who had not been given much, if any, formal education, were unable to score on the Alpha test. Another problem was that even the Beta test required the use of a pencil and the writing of numbers, and many men had never held a pencil in their lives. Gould outlines a number of other problems with the testing procedures which suggest that the data should be looked at with considerable scepticism. However, at the time, the results had a considerable impact, and by the end of the War some of the army camps were using the tests to screen people for officer training.

The tests generated a lot of interest and by 1921, when Yerkes published his findings, he was able to refer to 'the steady stream of requests from commercial concerns, educational institutions and individuals for the use of army methods of psychological examining or for adaptation of such methods to special needs'. Mental testing and psychology had achieved the credibility that Yerkes wanted.

Gould reports that three 'facts' were created from the testing data:

(1) 'The average mental age of White American adults stood just above the edge of moronity at a shocking and meagre 13. Terman had previously set the standard at 16' (p. 351). That is why the title of the article is 'A Nation of Morons', because the *data* showed that the USA was just that.

(2) It was possible to grade European immigrants by their country of origin. According to the test results, the average man of many countries was a moron, with the fair people of Northern and Western

Europe scoring higher than the Slavs of Eastern Europe and the darker people of Southern Europe.
(3) The average score of Black men was 10.4, which was considerably below the White average.

Although the 'finding' that the average American was a moron caused some concern, this was nothing compared to the response to the other two 'facts'. These were used to support the idea of genetic differences between races. Carl Brigham, one of Yerkes' colleagues, argued for a genetic explanation of data and proposed the racial superiority of Nordic people (from Northern Europe). He came up with some remarkable reasoning; for example, his explanation of the low average score of Jewish men despite the very many major accomplishments of Jewish scholars, statesmen and performing artists. Brigham argued that we notice the exceptional performance of some Jews (for example Einstein) because it is unusual against the performance of the average Jew.

This line of argument was threatened by two problems with the data. First, the immigration of different national groups had taken place at different times, and the most recent immigrants, and hence the least familiar with English, were the Slavs and the people from Southern Europe. So if literacy was having an effect on the test scores, then these people would be disadvantaged. Secondly, the data showed that the average score rose with the length of residence in the USA. This is a clear indication that the more experience a person had of the USA the higher their score was on the test, suggesting a cultural bias in the questions. Brigham, however, argued quite bizarrely that this data showed that the early immigrants were the brightest from each national group, and the subsequent immigrants were progressively more stupid.

So, despite the evidence, the eugenic argument took hold and one of the consequences of this was the passing of the Immigration Restriction Act in 1924 by the US Congress. The scientists who supported the eugenics argument lobbied the politicians and, according to Gould, 'won one of the greatest victories of scientific racism in American history' (p. 352). The Act set immigration quotas based on the US population in 1890 (over 30 years prior to the Act). This year was used as the benchmark because immigration from Southern and Eastern Europe had been relatively low before this date.

During the next 20 years, conditions deteriorated dramatically in Europe for Slavs and Jews as the Nazi governments enacted policies of 'racial purity' culminating in genocide. Gould tells how many people tried to flee the political oppression but were denied access to the USA. Estimates suggest that the immigration quotas barred up to *six million* people from southern, central and eastern Europe, a number with some significance in the history of Europe.

DISCUSSION

The article tells one chapter in the giant history of intelligence testing, and in no way attempts to provide a balanced view. It illustrates the human consequences of academic debates, and highlights the need to examine the political context of psychological theory.

One of the striking points to note is that the debate continues, though the evidence has become no more clear. There is no good evidence to support the view that group differences in IQ scores are due to genetic differences. There is also a lack, even today, of a clear operational definition of intelligence, which tends to undermine any line of argument. Likewise the whole idea of 'race' defies definition, with the only sensible conclusion being that race is more a *political* construct rather than a *biological* one.

Finally, how is it that IQ testing has gained such respectability and prominence despite an inability to define the quality it is measuring, and its use in the cause of scientific racism? The best answer must draw on the plausibility of the tests and the excessive respect given to psychologists and their claims (for an example of this, see the study by Forer in the previous chapter).

QUESTIONS

1   Identify the cultural and educational bias in the examples of the Alpha questions contained in the summary, and in the Beta items shown in Figure 10.1.

2   What is scientific racism?

3   What is intelligence? Try and list the skills that you associate with intelligent behaviour.

Suggested Answers start on p. 447

KEY WORDS

chronological age	literacy
cultural bias	mental age
eugenics	norm referencing
genetic	oppression
intelligence	race
IQ – Intelligence Quotient	scientific racism

BLACK DOLLS AND WHITE DOLLS

■ HRABA, J. & GRANT, G. (1970). Black is beautiful:
A re-examination of racial preference and identification.
Journal of Personality and Social Psychology, 16, 398–402.

INTRODUCTION

In 1939, Clark and Clark first reported their work on *racial identification* and preference in Black-American children. They were interested in how racial awareness developed, and devised a novel test using dolls with different skin colour. Clark & Clark (1947) found that Black children preferred White dolls and rejected Black dolls when asked to choose which were nice, which looked bad, which they would like to play with and which were a nice colour. This suggested that Black children had negative attitudes towards themselves and their cultural background.

The studies were replicated a number of times over the next 20 years with similar results. One of the questions that arose from these studies was whether contact with White people in an inter-racial setting, like a nursery, led to greater preference for the White dolls.

The studies have to be seen in an historical context. In the USA during the 1930s many states had policies of *segregation,* and Black people were kept out of White areas and denied access to education, housing, welfare and jobs. The 1960s saw the growth of the *Civil Rights Movement* (most famously, the leadership of Martin Luther King), and the growth of militant Black religious and political organisations and figures (most famously Malcolm X). This led to some improvement in the opportunities for Black people, and a change in their expectations. Since that time, Black people have made advances within US society and occupy an important place in the democratic structure. Despite this, the majority of Black people are still economically disadvantaged and the object of considerable racism.

THE STUDY

Hraba and Grant's study was a replication of Clark & Clark (1947), so they followed the same procedures as far as possible. The children were interviewed individually using a set of four dolls: two Black and two

White, but identical in all other respects. The children were asked the following questions:

(1) Give me the doll that you want to play with.
(2) Give me the doll that is a nice doll.
(3) Give me the doll that looks bad.
(4) Give me the doll that is a nice colour.
(5) Give me the doll that looks like a white child.
(6) Give me the doll that looks like a coloured child.
(7) Give me the doll that looks like a Negro child.
(8) Give me the doll that looks like you.
   (p. 399)

Clark and Clark suggested that items 1–4 measured *racial preference*, items 5–7 measured *awareness or knowledge*, and item 8 measured *racial self-identification*. Hraba and Grant attempted to assess the behavioural consequences of racial preference and identification by asking the children to name the race of their best friends. They also asked the teachers for the same information.

The subjects were 160 children aged between four and eight years who attended primary schools in Lincoln, Nebraska. Eighty-nine of the children were Black (60 per cent of the Black children attending school in Lincoln) and 71 were White. In the town of Lincoln at that time 1.4 per cent of the total population were Black, and in the five schools used in the study the proportions of Black children were 3 per cent, 3 per cent, 3 per cent, 7 per cent and 18 per cent. Also, 70 per cent of the Black children in the study reported they had White friends.

RESULTS

The results provide a comparison of Hraba and Grant's data with that of Clark and Clark, and they also provide a comparison of the responses of Black children and White children.

Table 10.1 shows that, in the Lincoln study, Black and White children preferred the doll of their own 'race'. The White children were significantly more *ethnocentric* on items 1 and 2, there was no difference on item 3 and the Black children were significantly more ethnocentric on item 4. The results are shown graphically in Figure 10.2.

The Clarks had found that Black children preferred White dolls at all ages, though this preference decreased with age. Hraba and Grant found that Black children at all ages preferred a Black doll and this

Table 10.1   Percentage responses to the doll questions

Item	Clark and Clark (1939) Blacks	Lincoln study (1969) Blacks	Lincoln study (1969) Whites
1. 'Play with'			
White doll	67	30	83
Black doll	32	70	16
Don't know/no response			1
2. 'Nice doll'			
White doll	59	46	70
Black doll	38	54	30
3. 'Looks bad'			
White doll	17	61	34
Black doll	59	36	63
Don't know/no response		3	3
4. 'Nice colour'			
White doll	60	31	48
Black doll	38	69	49
Don't know/no response			3

Source: Adapted from Hraba & Grant (1970)

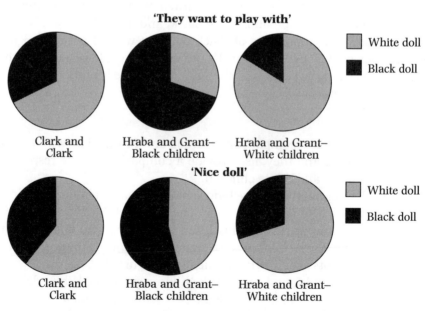

'They want to play with'

White doll
Black doll

Clark and Clark   Hraba and Grant–Black children   Hraba and Grant–White children

'Nice doll'

White doll
Black doll

Clark and Clark   Hraba and Grant–Black children   Hraba and Grant–White children

Figure 10.2   *Choices of doll 'they want to play with' and 'nice doll'*

preference increased with age. The Clarks had classified their subjects by skin colour into three categories: light (practically White), medium (light brown to dark brown), and dark (dark brown to Black). Hraba and Grant used the same criteria. The Clarks found that children of light skin colour showed the greatest preference for the White doll and the dark children the least. Hraba and Grant did not find this trend at all.

For the remaining items on the test (items 5 to 8) Hraba and Grant obtained similar results to Clark and Clark. The children made few errors of racial identification or personal identification. They found that the race of the interviewer had no effect on the choices of either the Black or the White children. Also, there was no apparent connection for both Black and White children between doll preference and the race of friends.

DISCUSSION

The results give a very different picture of doll preference in 1969 to doll preference in 1939. Hraba and Grant suggest a number of explanations for this discrepancy:

(1) Black people were more proud of their race in 1969 than they were in 1939.
(2) Children in Lincoln, unlike those in other cities, might have chosen Black dolls in 1939.
(3) The growth of organisations in the Black community might have enhanced Black pride.
(4) Inter-racial contact might create Black pride.

Whichever interpretation one follows (and after all it is difficult to say what children's preferences for dolls tells us about their self-identity), this replication highlights the fact that social psychological findings are inevitably the product of a particular point in history.

QUESTIONS

1 How did the researchers measure racial identity in this study?

2 How else could you measure racial identity?

3 Why do you think the children in the Clark and Clark study preferred the White dolls?

Suggested Answers start at p. 448

KEY WORDS

civil rights	racial self-identification
ethnocentrism	racism
identity	role model
race	segregation

BLACK IDENTITY

■ NOBLES, W.W. (1976). Extended self: Rethinking the so-called Negro self-concept.
Journal of Black Psychology, 2.
(Also in Jones (1993) *Black Psychology* 3rd ed., pp. 295–305).

INTRODUCTION

The psychology that is presented in mainstream introductory text books is usually described as a psychology of people and behaviour. But what people? And how is that behaviour judged? It is fair to say that most European psychology courses are *Eurocentric*, and tend to describe the world from the viewpoint of White, educated, middle-class people. There are, of course, many other peoples in the world (and many others in Europe), and the way they construct their view of the world and their behaviour has a number of differences from the White Eurocentric account.

One particular group of people who are virtually invisible within mainstream psychology are Black people. The first point we have to consider is whether there is a need for a body of knowledge directed specifically to Black people, that psychology has so far failed to provide. Guthrie (1980) suggests that there *is* such a need and presents the following argument.

One of the major early influences on psychology was Darwinism and the theory of *evolution*. The scientists of the time tended to believe that human differences came from innate causes within people rather than environmental forces in society. The evolutionary approach was twisted to explain the superiority of certain groups in society. Darwin, in dismissing the intellectual abilities of women wrote that the 'less highly evolved female brain... [was]... characteristic of the lower races, and therefore of a past and lower state of civilisation' (in Miles, 1988). A considerable amount of scientific energy went into an attempt to show that some peoples are intellectually and morally superior to others. The 'evidence' produced does not stand up to scrutiny (for further discussion of this point see Gould, 1981). This scientific racism is at the heart of the *eugenics* movement (the attempt to selectively breed a 'superior' group of people) and the early work on individual differences.

Psychology is not politically neutral. It is always influenced by the society and the times it is written in. At its worst, it has been used to provide a scientific justification for oppressive practices. A much quoted example is the diagnosis of the 'mental illness' *drapetomania* in Black American slaves. This condition was characterised by the irresistible urge to run away from the slave plantations. Today, we would not interpret the escape behaviour of slaves as a sign of mental disturbance.

Guthrie suggests that historical factors such as Darwinism and eugenics not only influenced early behavioural scientists, but also have a continuing effect on modern psychology. This effect makes it important to develop a psychology of Black people. One such contribution is the *Afrocentric* approach exemplified by the Nobles paper. The Afrocentric approach aims to dislodge Western civilisation from its self-appointed position as the yardstick by which every other culture is defined, and attempts to put the African factor at the centre of any research on Black people.

THE PAPER

Nobles' account does not present any empirical research, but asks us to re-evaluate the standpoint of contemporary psychology. He suggests that the position of the social scientist is similar to that of the colonial master and his subject people. Table 10.2 shows the comparison between political colonialism and scientific colonialism.

Nobles suggests that the two most important themes in European/American science are:

(a) Survival of the fittest.
(b) Control over nature.

These themes are reflected in the European/American emphasis on 'competition', 'individual rights', 'independence' and separateness. In psychology this leads to an emphasis on *individuality, uniqueness* and *difference*.

By contrast, the themes of the African world view are:

(a) Survival of the people.
(b) Being one with nature.

These themes are reflected in the African values of 'cooperation', 'interdependence' and 'collective responsibility'. The psychological emphasis would then be on *commonality, groupness* and *similarity*.

Table 10.2 Similarities between political and scientific colonialism

Colonialism manifested by	Political colonialism	Scientific colonialism
Removal of wealth	Exportation of raw materials and wealth from colonies for the purpose of 'processing' it into manufactured wealth and/or goods	Exporting raw data from a community for the purpose of 'processing' it into manufactured goods (i.e. books, articles, wealth)
Right of access and claim	Colonial Power believes it has the *right* of access and use for its own benefit anything belonging to the colonised people	Scientist believes she/he has unlimited *right* of access to any data source and any information belonging to the subject population
External Power Base	The centre of power and control over the colonised is located outside the colony itself	The centre of knowledge and information about a people or community located outside of the community or people themselves

Source: Nobles (1976)

These two approaches are summarised in Table 10.3. Nobles argues that the lives of Black people in Europe and America are interpreted within the history and psychological framework of the European world view. To understand the psychology of Black people, he continues, it is necessary to interpret their behaviour and experience within an African perspective.

The tradition of European philosophy connects the notion of self with the experience of independence. The European self is believed to develop by establishing your uniqueness or separateness from other people. Your differentness from other people is used to define your individuality. On the other hand, the African philosophical tradition views the self as being centred on the identity of the people, rather than individual differences. Nobles argues that in understanding the traditional African conception of self we must consider the belief that 'I am because We are, and because We are therefore I am'. A person's self-definition is dependent on the definition of the people.

Table 10.3   Differences between African and European world views

European world view		African world view
Individuality ⟶ Uniqueness ⟶ Differences ⟶	Psychological emphasis	⟵ Groupness ⟵ Sameness ⟵ Commonality

Competition ⟶
Individual rights ⟶
Separateness and
  independence ⟶
	Values and customs	⟵ Co-operation
		⟵ Collective responsibilities
		⟵ Co-operateness and
		  interdependence

Survival of the fittest ⟶ Control over nature ⟶	Ethos	⟵ Survival of the people ⟵ One with the tribe ⟵ Experiental communality

Source: Nobles (1976)

DISCUSSION

The paper by Nobles provides a powerful criticism of the methods and the theories of contemporary Western psychology. It challenges the assumption that psychological theories and concepts can be applied to all people in all situations. The ideas presented in the paper make it essential to see Western psychology as being just one of many possible accounts of human behaviour and experience. Also, it is important to recognise that Western psychology is a product of the various cultural and historical influences that have formed society. In other words, it is not the detached and 'objective' science that it is often assumed to be.

The Afrocentric approach suggests that most of Western psychology should be rejected because it is culturally inappropriate for Black people. According to this view, it is as psychologically constraining and deforming as the shackles that were used to physically enslave Black people.

The Afrocentric approach is one opposing view to mainstream Western psychology. It is not without its critics, however, and perhaps the most controversial feature of the Afrocentric approach is the suggestion that the differences between peoples are biologically based. Nobles & Goddard (1984) write that Black Americans are, 'African in nature and American in nurture' (p. 39).

The criticisms that are made of other attempts in psychology to explain differences between people in terms of genetics can also be used here. For example, it is not clear that we can define a political concept like race in biological terms. Also, the various attempts to disentangle the effects of nature and nurture in psychological qualities have had a remarkably unsuccessful history in psychology. One of the major problems is that the variation between individuals within a group is often so great that it makes the marginal differences between groups quite meaningless.

Another criticism of the approach concerns its attempt to describe the 'true' identity of Black people. This attracts the same criticisms that are made of other personality theories that attempt to fit people within a rigid framework developed by the researcher. An alternative approach is to allow people to describe their own experience within their own framework.

These criticisms challenge whether it is possible to define and measure the Afrocentric personality, but they do not challenge the central force of the argument which requires Western psychologists to re-evaluate their theories and data.

QUESTIONS

1   Think about the other areas of psychology you have studied and suggest which of them have been insensitive to cultural differences.

2   Take another study in psychology and imagine that it had used subject groups of different ethnic background. In what way do you think the results would have been different?

3   In your everyday life, think of examples of behaviour that show co-operation or collective responsibility (African self image). Then think of examples of behaviour that show separateness or competition (Western view of self).

4   A common exercise for exploring self concept is to try and give 20 answers to the question 'Who am I?'. Start each answer with the phrase 'I am ...' How many of your answers refer to features of your personality (for example, generous), how many refer to groups that you belong to, and how many refer to things that you do. Have you described yourself by your differences to other people, or your connection to other people?

Suggested Answers start at p. 448

KEY WORDS

Afrocentric	eugenics
co-operation	Eurocentric
colonialism	evolution
competition	identity
drapetomania	scientific racism

(Acknowledgement: Thanks to Patrick Hylton, Department of Applied Social Studies, The Nottingham Trent University, for help in producing this summary.)

11 ABNORMALITY

When music is discussed, everyone has an opinion. Personally, I like Tamla music. But ask me what I like about it, and I struggle to analyse what I find exceptional in the songs. I can recognise the music, and I know how I feel about it, but I don't know how I recognise it.

People find it easy to make judgements of 'oddness' in other people. 'He's never been quite right, you know', is a familiar judgement from a street-corner conversation. In a similar way to our judgement of music we also find it hard to say what it is that is so odd about the person. And we would find it harder still to classify that oddness.

Psychological diagnosis is an attempt to classify oddness in people. It is a difficult process that is steeped in controversy. Observers often cannot agree on a diagnosis for a patient, and classifying a person can lead to the carers ignoring signs and symptoms that do not fall into the diagnostic pattern. Despite these problems, diagnosis is attempted because it has some benefits, one of which should be effective treatment.

The psychological diagnosis of personality has a long history. The Greeks, for example, recognised such diagnoses as senility, alcoholism, mania, melancholia, and paranoia. The first comprehensive system of psychological disorders was created in 1896 by Emil Kraepelin (see Kraepelin, 1913). He believed that mental disorders have the same basis as physical ones, and that the same diagnostic principles should be applied: that is, the careful observation of symptoms. Other diagnostic systems were suggested by, among others, Eugen Bleuler, Adolf Meyer, and Ernst Kretschmer. Clearly, though, the more systems in operation, the greater the opportunity for confusion. So in 1952 the Diagnostic and Statistical Manual of Mental Disorders (DSM) was developed and approved by the American Psychiatric Association. A revised version, DSM IV, is widely used today. A diagnosis is arrived at using *family resemblances*. If you think of a big family that you know, then you will notice that most of the family members have some similar physical features, yet each member of the family is different from the others. It is a similar recognition process with mental disorders. Each person who has a particular condition has some similar features in their behaviour to other people with the same condition.

This chapter contains four studies that look at the issues around abnormality and its treatment. The study by Rosenhan (1973) challenges the ability of professional workers to identify the sane from the insane. The study by Smith & Glass (1977) attempts to evaluate how effective treatment is for a variety of psychological conditions. The key issue here is how can you measure 'getting better' in a psychological sense? Does it just mean smiling more? The study by Thigpen & Cleckley (1954) describes the famous case of a young woman with a multiple personality. This condition still causes some controversy amongst professional workers though it captured the public imagination through the film 'The Three Faces of Eve'. The last study by Lang & Lazovik (1963) looks at the effectiveness of behaviour therapy in the treatment of a phobia.

You Don't Have to be Mad to Work Here. You Don't Even Have to be Mad to Be In Here...

■ Rosenhan, D.L. (1973). On being sane in insane places. *Science, 179,* 250–58.

Introduction

How do you know when someone is odd? What judgements do you make to assess someone as being not just 'different', but 'abnormal'? We make these judgements in everyday life, and it is necessary in a number of social situations to be able to identify 'abnormal' behaviour and to respond appropriately. Mental health workers have to make judgements about whether someone is psychologically 'abnormal' and needing specialised help. The definition and categorisation of abnormality is both difficult and controversial, and the way we make these definitions varies between societies.

Rosenhan starts his paper with a simple question, 'If sanity and insanity exist, how shall we know them?' (p. 250). His study is designed to look at the categorisation of abnormality and to question whether madness, like beauty, is in the eye of the beholder.

The Study

The research question is: 'do the salient characteristics that lead to diagnoses [of abnormality] reside in the patients themselves or in the environments and contexts in which observers find them?' (p. 250). This was tested in this study with the further question: 'If "normal" people attempt to be admitted to psychiatric hospitals, will they be detected as being sane, and if so, how?'

Eight sane people (a graduate student, three psychologists, a paediatrician, a painter and a 'housewife') attempted to gain admission to 12 different hospitals, in five different states in the USA. They telephoned for an appointment, and arrived at admissions complaining that they had been hearing voices. They said the voice, which was unfamiliar and the same sex as themselves, was often unclear but it said 'empty', 'hollow', 'thud'. These symptoms were chosen because they simulated an *existential crisis* (Who am I? What is it all for?) which could arise from concerns about how meaningless your life is. They were also chosen because there is no mention of existential psychosis in the literature.

The 'pseudopatients' gave a false name and job (to protect their future health and employment records), but all other details they gave were true including general ups and downs of life. After they had been admitted, the pseudopatients stopped simulating *any* symptoms, except possibly nervousness, fear of exposure as a fraud, and their inevitable reaction to the novelty of the situation. They took part in ward activities, and spent time writing notes about ward staff and patients. Each pseudopatient had been told they would have to get out by their own devices by convincing staff they were sane.

RESULTS

All of the pseudopatients disliked the experience and wished to be discharged immediately. Not one of the pseudopatients was detected, and all but one were admitted with a diagnosis of *schizophrenia*. This diagnosis was made without one clear symptom of this disorder. They remained in hospital for 7 to 52 days (average 19 days), and were eventually discharged with a diagnosis of *schizophrenia* 'in remission'. Visitors to the pseudopatients observed 'no serious behavioural consequences'. Although they were not detected by the staff, many of the other patients suspected their sanity (35 out of 118 patients voiced their suspicions).

In a follow-up study, a teaching and research hospital which was aware of the first study was informed that during the next three months one or more pseudopatients would attempt to be admitted into hospital. Each staff member rated on a 10-point scale each new patient

Table 11.1   Judgement of all admission patients as to the likelihood that they are pseudopatients

Number of patients judged	193
Number of patients confidently judged as pseudopatients by at least one staff member	41
Number of patients suspected by one psychiatrist	23
Number of patients suspected by one psychiatrist AND one other staff member	19

Source: Rosenhan (1973)

as to the likelihood of their being a pseudopatient. Table 11.1 shows a record of these ratings. Around *ten per cent* were suspected by one psychiatrist *and* another staff member. However, no pseudopatients attempted to be admitted during the period, so the staff were rating their regular intake.

General observations

While the pseudopatients were in the psychiatric hospitals their normal behaviours were entirely overlooked or misinterpreted. For example, nursing records for three of the pseudopatients showed that the writing was seen as an aspect of their pathological behaviour: 'Patient engages in writing behaviour'. Rosenhan notes that there is an enormous overlap in the behaviours of the sane and insane. We all feel depressed sometimes, have moods, become angry and so forth, but in the context of a psychiatric hospital, these everyday human experiences and behaviours were interpreted as pathological. In another incident a psychiatrist pointed to a group of patients waiting outside the cafeteria half an hour before lunchtime. To a group of registrars (trainee psychiatrists) he suggested that such behaviour was characteristic of an *oral-acquisitive syndrome*. However, a more likely explanation would be that the patients had little to do, and one of the few things to anticipate in a psychiatric hospital is a meal.

The pseudopatients carried out a simple observation of behaviour of staff towards patients that illustrates the experience of being hospitalised on a psychiatric ward. The pseudopatients approached a staff member with a simple polite request, for example 'Pardon me, Mr/Ms/ Dr X, could you tell me when I will be presented at the staff meeting?' Table 11.2 shows how the staff responded to this request. Rosenhan carried out a similar study in a university with students asking university staff a simple question. In the university study, nearly all the requests were acknowledged and responded to. This was not the case in the psychiatric hospital where the pseudopatients were treated as if they were *invisible*.

The overwhelming experience of hospitalisation for the pseudopatients was one of *depersonalisation* and *powerlessness*. The patients were deprived of many human rights such as freedom of movement and privacy. For example, their medical records were open to all staff members, regardless of status or therapeutic relationship with the patient. Personal hygiene was monitored and many of the toilets did not have doors. Some

Table 11.2 Self-initiated contact by pseudopatients with psychiatrists, nurses and attendants

Response	Percentage making contact with patient	
	Psychiatrists	Nurses and attendants
Move on with head averted	71	88
Makes eye contact	23	10
Pauses and chats	2	2
Stops and talks	4	0.5
NUMBER OF RESPONDENTS	13	47
NUMBER OF ATTEMPTS	185	1283

Source: Rosenhan (1973)

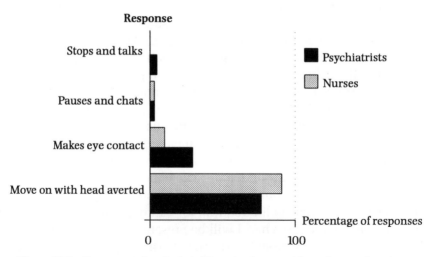

Figure 11.1 *Responses of medical staff to a simple request from the pseudopatients*

of the ward orderlies would be brutal to patients in full view of other patients but would stop as soon as another staff member approached. This indicated that staff were credible witnesses but patients were not.

Strangely, the pseudopatients were given a total of 2100 medication tablets, though only two were swallowed. The rest (2098) were either pocketed or flushed down the toilet. Often, when the pseudopatients visited the toilets to dispose of their tablets they found the medication of other patients which had already been placed there. As long as the patients were co-operative, then their behaviour went unnoticed.

The pseudopatients kept records of the amount of time the nurses stayed in the ward offices (around 90 per cent of the time), the number of times medical staff came onto the ward, and the amount of time spent with patients by the physicians. They noted that the total time a patient spent with psychiatrists, psychologists, registrars and so forth was, on average, under seven minutes per day.

DISCUSSION

Rosenhan claims that 'it is clear we cannot distinguish the sane from the insane in psychiatric hospitals' (p. 257), though many would argue that this conclusion overstates the case. However, his study did illustrate a failure to detect sanity, and, in the follow-up study, a failure to detect insanity. It also illustrated the depersonalisation and powerlessness created by psychiatric hospitals.

Rosenhan points out that behaviour in the institution was systematically reinterpreted according to the *expectations* of the staff. These expectations were created by the labels of sanity and insanity. He suggests that instead of labelling a person as insane, however, it is more useful to discuss behaviours, the stimuli that provoke them and their correlates.

Rosenhan makes an interesting methodological point about the nature of participant observation. He notes that, although he and the other pseudopatients had very negative experiences in the psychiatric hospitals, their accounts do not describe the experience of real patients who did not have the comfort of believing that the diagnosis was false.

QUESTIONS

1 What criteria were used to diagnose the pseudopatients as mentally disturbed?

2 List the similarities and differences between pseudopatients and 'real' patients.

3 List some behaviours that you regard as 'abnormal', and try to say why they are abnormal.

4 What criticisms can you make of the methods used in this study?

Suggested Answers start at p. 449

KEY WORDS

abnormal

depersonalisation

diagnosis

existential

insanity

normal

pathological

powerlessness

pseudopatient

psychosis

schizophrenia

Shrink Wrapped: The Choice of Therapist

■ Smith, M.L. & Glass, G.V. (1977).
Meta-analysis of psychotherapy outcome studies.
American Psychologist, 32, 752–60.

Introduction

Do psychotherapies work? That is, do people with psychological problems get better as a result of receiving therapy? And which types of therapy work best? There are so many varieties, such as behavioural (see Lang & Lazovik, 1963, Chapter 11 of this volume), psychodynamic (see Freud, 1909, Chapter 14 of this volume), humanistic (Rogers, 1951), transactional (Berne, 1968), gestalt (Perls, 1969), and that is only a selection.

Many *evaluation studies* have been carried out which look at the question of the effectiveness of various kinds of therapy. But, as with all areas of the psychological literature, the findings are scattered among hundreds of different volumes of different journals. Smith and Glass' paper is an attempt to draw together the results of these disparate studies. They collated the data from a large number of primary publications (375 studies in all) and attempted to draw general conclusions about psychotherapy from the patterns that were revealed. This investigative strategy is known as *secondary research* or *meta-analysis*.

The Study

Subjects

The subjects in the primary studies were clients of psychotherapists. So in a sense the subjects of this meta-analysis were all the subjects of the 375 original studies, estimated to be some 50 000 in number divided across experimental and control conditions. The average age of clients in the primary studies was 22 years, and they received on average 17 hours of therapy.

Design and procedure

The authors identified 375 studies of the effectiveness of psychotherapy within the psychological literature. All the studies selected had a quasi-experimental design. That is, they were based on comparisons between treated and untreated groups, or between groups receiving different kinds of therapy.

For all the studies at least one 'effect size' was calculated. This was a numeric representation of 'the magnitude of the effect of therapy' (p. 753) as shown by each of the 375 primary studies. For some studies there were several outcome measures, so overall 833 effect sizes were calculated (see the statistical note below).

The effect sizes of each study were then taken as values of the dependent variable (the effectiveness of psychotherapy). These values were then related systematically to a variety of independent variables, the most important of which were level of treatment (the basic treatment versus no treatment comparison), and type of therapy (psychodynamic, Adlerian, eclectic, transactional analysis, rational-emotive, gestalt, client-centred, systematic desensitisation, implosion, behaviour modification). It is these two independent variables which are examined in the results section below.

The details of the various statistical manipulations in this study are pretty impenetrable, so only two basic findings are dealt with. The reason for the complexity of the statistical procedures is the need to cope with data that have been collated from completely different studies with different designs and measurement procedures. Within each primary study important variables such as the experience of the therapist(s), length of therapy, original diagnosis of the clients' problems, and length of time between treatment and evaluation would have been controlled for. You would expect all these variables (and probably many others) to have significant effects on the efficacy of the therapy. But across the different studies no such control exists, so various statistical procedures are used to try and adjust the data to allow for such variables, and to examine how much effect they may have had on the overall findings of the secondary analysis.

RESULTS

The results relating to both independent variables (level of treatment and type of therapy) are reported in terms of comparisons of means and standard deviations of effect sizes.

Level of treatment (treatment versus no treatment)

The mean effect size for the treated group (approximately 25 000 subjects who received some kind of therapy) fell 0.68 of a standard deviation above the mean effect size of the untreated group. This means that the average client in the treated group (the client that experienced the median size of therapeutic effect) was better off than 75 per cent of the untreated control subjects.

Additionally only 99 of the 833 effect sizes (12 per cent) were negative (meaning that in this small number of cases the clients were on average *worse* off than before the therapy).

Type of therapy

By comparing the average effect sizes for subjects who had received different kinds of therapies with the average effect sizes for control subjects, the authors were able to draw up a league table (or rank ordering) of the effectiveness of ten different therapies. This rank ordering is shown in Table 11.3. The higher the value in the right hand column of Table 11.3, the greater the estimated effect of the therapy; the nearer the value in that column gets to 50, the smaller the difference between the treated and untreated groups, hence the smaller the effect of the named therapy.

Discussion

Smith and Glass concluded from their meta-analysis that psychotherapies do work. That is, more people improved in one way or another having been through a course of therapy than would have improved spontaneously with no treatment.

Table 11.3   Rank ordering of ten types of therapy

Type of therapy	Median treated person's percentile status in control group
Systematic desensitisation	82
Rational-emotive	78
Behaviour modification	78
Adlerian	76
Implosion	74
Client-centred	74
Psychodynamic	72
Transactional analysis	72
Eclectic	68
Gestalt (N.B. based on only 8 measures)	60

Source: Adapted from Smith & Glass (1977)

The rank ordering of the different therapies is interesting, but by Smith and Glass' own admission should not be taken too literally, since there was no way of controlling against important confounding variables. For example, systematic desensitisation came out 'top', but this may have been due to the fact that systematic desensitisation deals with more easily 'treatable' problems than, say, gestalt psychotherapy. Smith and Glass' data supports this notion by showing that fear and anxiety reduction is more readily achieved through therapy than is personal change and 'adjustment'; desensitisation deals with the former, gestalt psychotherapy with the latter.

The final comparison that Smith and Glass made was between behavioural therapies (implosion, systematic desensitisation, behaviour modification) and non-behavioural therapies (psychoanalytic, Adlerian, client-centred, rational-emotive, eclectic, transactional analysis). Their conclusion was that there are 'negligible differences in the effects produced by different therapy types' (p. 760).

Statistical note

Smith and Glass calculated the effect size for each study by taking the mean difference between the treated subjects and the control subjects on the outcome measure of the study, and dividing this by the standard deviation of the control group on the outcome measure.

QUESTIONS
1   What particular problems are faced in researching the effectiveness of psychotherapies?
2   Although Smith and Glass' conclusions look very convincing, having been based on a detailed analysis of hundreds of studies with thousands of subjects, what factors might still have biased the overall pattern of findings in favour of the case for psychotherapy?

Suggested Answers start at p. 449

KEY WORDS

behavioural psychotherapy
effect size
evaluation study
humanistic
humanistic psychotherapy
median
psychodynamic

psychodynamic psychotherapy
psychotherapy
quasi-experiments
secondary research (meta-analysis)
spontaneous remission
standard deviation

THE THREE FACES OF EVE

■ THIGPEN, C.H. & CLECKLEY, H. (1954).
A case of multiple personality.
Journal of Abnormal and Social Psychology, 49, 135–51.

INTRODUCTION

Our definition and understanding of 'abnormality' is affected by the culture we live in. Some explanations fit neatly into the general view of life that prevails in a particular culture at a particular time. Some phenomena, on the other hand, challenge our view of life and are regarded with much greater scepticism. The many 'supernatural' experiences that people report are an example of this. Religious visions, and visions of deceased loved ones are commonly reported but do not fit into our current explanations of the world. These experiences, therefore, become marginalised and ignored.

One relatively rare observation of abnormality is the person with multiple personalities. This condition is not to be confused with schizophrenia or other psychotic disorders since the sufferers do not show the disturbances of emotion, perception and reality testing associated with psychosis. The multiple personality challenges our view of people, and receives considerable scepticism as a result. Thigpen and Cleckley recognise this scepticism but suggest that their case study of a unique individual is evidence for the existence of this condition.

THE CASE STUDY

The patient (referred to as Eve White in the study) had been referred for therapy to one of the authors because of 'severe and blinding headaches'. She also complained of 'blackouts' though her family were not aware of anything that would suggest a real loss of consciousness or serious mental confusion. The patient appeared to have a number of complex, but relatively unexceptional marital conflicts and personal frustrations. She showed amnesia for a recent trip, and the therapists used *hypnosis* to restore that memory.

The first sign of anything unusual in the case was when a letter arrived some days after the hypnosis. It was written in a confident hand and concerned her therapy, but at the bottom of the page there was a childish postscript written in a different hand (see Figure 11.2). On her next visit Eve White denied sending the letter though she remembered having begun one which she had not finished. During the interview she became distressed and asked whether hearing an imaginary voice indicated that she was insane. She reported that she had on several occasions briefly heard a voice addressing her. During this conversation Eve White suddenly put both hands to her head as if in pain. After a tense moment of silence her hands dropped, and the therapist observed a 'quick, reckless smile'. In a bright voice she said: 'Hi there, Doc'!

The demure and retiring Eve White had changed into a confident and relaxed person, with a very different physical presence. She crossed her legs and 'the therapist noted from the corner of his awareness something distinctly attractive about them, and also this was the first time he had received such an impression' (p. 137). This new person 'had a childishly daredevil air, an erotically mischievous glance, a face marvellously free from the habitual signs of care, seriousness and underlying distress' (p. 137). The voice and language structure were different, and to the therapist it appeared to be an entirely different woman.

Over the next 14 months, a series of interviews totalling over 100 hours explored the behaviour and experience of Eve White and the other woman, Eve Black. Although Eve Black could sometimes appear unexpectedly, she could only be 'called out' by the therapists when Eve White was under hypnosis. Eve Black had been in existence since early childhood, and when she was 'out' Eve White was not aware of what was happening. In contrast, when Eve Black was not out she was aware of what was happening. This loss of awareness by Eve White, and the coming out of Eve Black to be mischievous, led to a number of incidents in childhood where Eve White was punished for wrong doings she was unaware of. Some of these incidents, revealed during the therapy, were later substantiated in interviews with her parents and her husband.

Eve Black was irresponsible and shallow, looking for pleasure and excitement. She succeeded in concealing her identity from Eve White, and also from her parents and husband. She denied marriage to the man, who she despised, and denied any relationship to Eve White's daughter. Her unpleasant behaviour, harshness and occasional acts of violence observed by the husband and parents were attributed to unaccountable fits of temper in a woman who was habitually gentle and considerate.

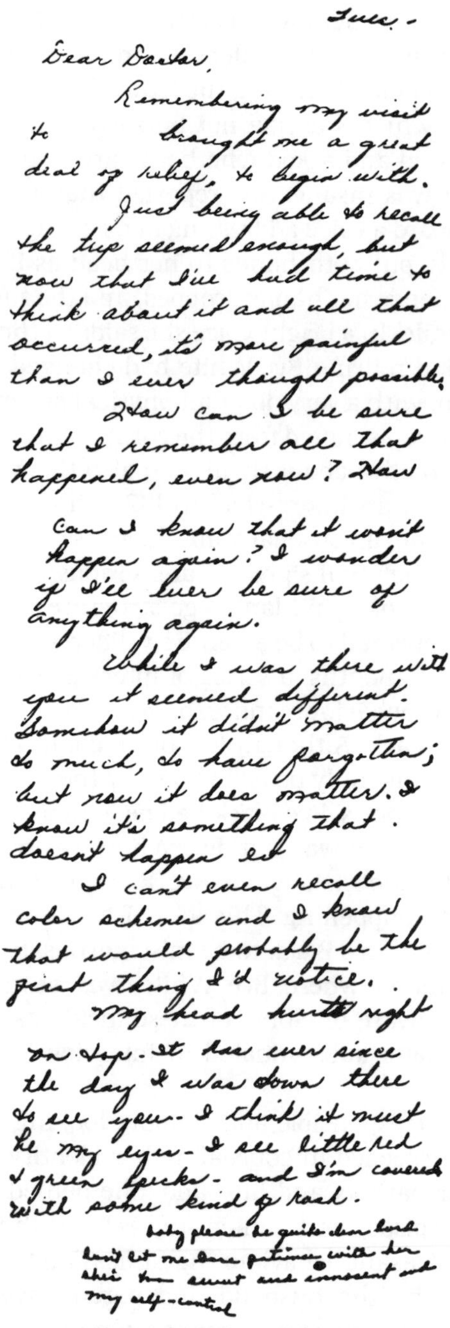

Figure 11.2   *Letter from Eve*
Source: Thigpen & Cleckley (1954)

Both personalities were given a series of psychological tests with the following results:

IQ scores – White 110, Black 104;
Memory function – White was far superior;
Rorschach (ink-blot) – profile of Black far healthier; the personality of White was repressive, and Black was regressive.

During the therapy sessions it became clear that Eve Black had little compassion for Eve White, and could not be persuaded to help with the therapy. However, as Eve White became aware of the other personality she became able to prevent her 'getting out' on occasions, and so negotiation was necessary for Eve Black to get more time 'out'.

As the treatment progressed, Eve White's headaches started to recur and she started to experience more 'blackouts'. Eve Black denied responsibility and said that she also experienced lack of awareness during these blackouts. The general state of mind of Eve White deteriorated and confinement was considered. It became easier for the therapist to call up whichever personality he wanted to examine, and childhood experiences were investigated under hypnosis. During one such episode, Eve White appeared to relax into a sleepy state. After a while her eyes opened and she stared blankly around the room before looking at the therapist and saying: 'Who are you?' It appeared that a third personality had emerged who called herself Jane. This new character had full awareness of the other two, but neither of them could be aware of her.

The three personalities were subjected to *electroencephalogram* studies (EEG; see the study by Dement & Kleitman, 1957, Chapter 6 of this volume), and it was possible to make a clear distinction between the readings of Eve Black and the other two personalities.

The therapy then continued of the three women in the same body. To the therapists, it appeared that Jane was the person most likely to bring a solution to the troubled mind, and that her growing dominance over the other personalities appeared to be an appropriate resolution. However, they point out that 'we have not judged ourselves as wise enough to make active decisions' about how the drama should develop, and they note the moral problems with 'killing' one or more of the personalities.

DISCUSSION

What does this all mean? Could the therapists have been conned by a successful actress? They assert that the performance could not have continued so long and so consistently. Was the woman psychotic? The answer appears to be 'no', since she showed no other symptoms of psychosis. Thigpen and Cleckley ask us to judge whether they became so involved that they lost their sense of judgement and overdramatised the result.

They remained convinced that they had witnessed three personalities within the same body. They noted that this observation created as many problems as it solved, not least of which was the question of what we mean by *personality*. In everyday speech we refer to dramatic changes in personality with phrases like 'he's a new man' or 'she's not herself' or 'he's been re-born.' So, maybe our personalities are not as fixed or stable as we like to believe.

Thigpen and Cleckley finished their account with a plea for psychiatry and psychology to consider a wider range of behavioural and experiential phenomena, even when they do not fit into established theories.

A postscript to this remarkable story came in the revelation in 1975 by Eve that she had experienced many other personalities before the original therapy and after it. She recalled a total of 22 and suggested that the fragmentation of her personality had been to protect herself from things she could not bear.

QUESTIONS

1 What were the main differences between Eve White and Eve Black?

2 What is the difference between multiple personality and schizophrenia?

3 Give some examples of the therapists' involvement with their patient.

4 What problems with the case study method does this study highlight?

Suggested Answers start at p. 450

KEY WORDS

abnormality	multiple personality
case study	psychological tests
electroencephalogram	psychosis
hypnosis	Rorschach ink-blot

FEAR TODAY, GONE TOMORROW

■ LANG, P.J. & LAZOVIK, A.D. (1963).
Experimental desensitisation of a phobia.
Journal of Abnormal and Social Psychology, 66, 519–25.

INTRODUCTION

Many people experience fears that seem to be irrational; for example a fear of spiders or heights (the famous French philosopher Jean Paul Satre had a fear of being chased by a giant lobster). For some people the fear becomes so great that it interferes with their everyday life. These fears are often referred to as phobias and psychologists have tried to explain how they develop and how they can be alleviated. One technique for alleviation is systematic desensitisation which is a *behaviour therapy.* The paper by Lang and Lazovik provides a good illustration of this therapy, and evaluates its effectiveness in treating snake phobias. A contrasting style of treatment (*psychoanalytic psychotherapy*) is illustrated in Chapter 14 of this book which describes one of Freud's famous case studies.

The authors cite Wolpe (1958) as the originator of the therapy, which is usually discussed in connection with the theory of classical conditioning. The idea of systematic desensitisation is that people with phobias are gradually taught to respond to the phobic object (or situation) with muscle relaxation rather than with fear. The procedures are described below, and are based on the notion of *reciprocal inhibition:* that is, the response of relaxation is incompatible with a response of fear (you cannot be both fearful and relaxed at the same time). So the stronger the relaxation response becomes, the more it inhibits the old fear response.

One criticism of behaviour therapies such as systematic desensitisation comes from the psychoanalytic perspective. As Lang and Lazovik point out, behaviour therapists are not usually interested in the original causes of the phobia. They focus on treating and alleviating the behavioural symptoms. Psychoanalysts argue that in treating only the symptoms, behaviour therapies leave the root causes of the problem untouched. So while the behavioural symptoms of, say, the snake phobia might indeed be alleviated, they will ultimately be replaced by another set of symptoms which have the same root cause. This is known as *symptom substitution*. The behaviour therapists counter with the argument that the so-called 'symptoms' *are* the problem, and that alleviating them will not necessarily lead to symptom substitution.

THE STUDY

This study has a simple experimental design in which a number of snake-phobic students were allocated either to one of two treatment conditions, or to one of two control conditions. The experimental subjects received desensitisation therapy; the control subjects did not. A variety of measures were used to assess the effectiveness of the therapy, including a follow-up examination of the subjects' anxiety levels six months after the original investigation, and an assessment of whether any symptom substitution had occurred.

Subjects

Twenty-four snake-phobic students from the USA participated. They were selected on the basis of questionnaires and interviews which explored their susceptibility to the phobia. Only those judged to have a strong phobia (for example, those who reported an unpleasant response to seeing a snake) were included in the study. The assignment of subjects to the four conditions was done 'essentially at random, although an effort was made to balance roughly these groups in terms of intensity of fear and motivation to participate in the experiment' (p. 521). Five therapists were involved in the desensitisation procedures, and each worked with between two and four of the experimental subjects.

Design

A four-condition independent measures (between subjects) design was used, with two experimental conditions and two control conditions. The main independent variable was whether the subjects received a desensitisation programme or not. The dependent variable was measured by making a direct observation of the subjects' behaviour when faced by a real-life snake (the 'Snake Avoidance Test'), and by getting subjects to rate the level of their fear when faced by the live snake.

Procedure

The two experimental groups both received a period of training and a period of desensitisation. During the training phase of five 45 minute sessions, the subjects constructed an *anxiety hierarchy*. This was a list of 20 situations which involved snakes, and which were rank-ordered from 'most feared' to 'least feared'. For example, seeing a picture of a snake might have been an item towards the 'least feared' end of a subject's scale, whilst holding a snake would most likely have been towards the 'most feared' end. Each subject constructed their own personal hierarchy in consultation with their therapist. After the hierarchy had been completed, the subjects were taught deep muscle relaxation (Lang and Lazovik refer to the methods of Jacobson, 1938, in this regard), and then introduced to the process of hypnosis. All training and therapy was done on a one-to-one basis.

The desensitisation phase involved eleven 45 minute sessions. During these the subjects gradually worked through their hierarchy of fears. The process started with hypnosis and deep muscle relaxation. The subjects were then instructed to imagine the least feared item on their list. When they were able to do this without any fear response (when they could relax completely when imagining the situation described in the item) they moved onto the next item on the list. When they could relax whilst imagining this item, they progressed to the next, and so on, until they reached the most feared item. They would only move to the next most feared item on the list if they had successfully learnt to relax in response to the previous one. Of the 13 experimental subjects, seven completed 16 steps or more in their hierarchy, and six completed 14 steps or less.

The strength of each subject's phobia was tested in the following ways. The subject was brought into a room with a snake 15 feet away in a glass cage. An experimenter, who took no part in the other aspects of the study, encouraged the subject to come into the room, to approach the snake, and if possible to touch it or hold it. If the subject actually touched the snake they passed the Snake Avoidance Test. If they refused to touch the snake then they were asked to approach as near as they could, and the distance they ended up from the snake was measured. The score they were assigned on this basis was on a 19-point scale, with 1 indicating 'held snake', 2 indicating 'touched snake', 3 indicating 'approached to within one foot', 4 indicating 'approached to within two feet', and so forth, to 19 which indicated 'refused to enter room'. The

Table 11.4 The snake avoidance test: experimental design

Group	Experimental procedures				
E_1	Test 1	Training	Test 2	Desensitisation	Test 3
E_2		Training	Test 2	Desensitisation	Test 3
C_1	Test 1		Test 2		Test 3
C_2			Test 2		Test 3

Source: Lang & Lazovik (1963)

higher the score, then, the stronger the avoidance of the snake. All subjects were asked at this point to rate the fear they were experiencing on a 10-point 'fear thermometer'. In addition, the subjects completed a Fear Survey Schedule (FSS) at the beginning and end of the experiment, and were interviewed by the experimenters. The FSS listed 50 phobias which were rated by the subjects on a 7-point scale according to their subjectively judged susceptibility to each fear. Snake phobia was included in this list. In Table 11.4 the sequence of events for each group of subjects is detailed. The 'Test' phases involved all the measures described in this paragraph. Note that 20 of the original subjects were re-tested after six months.

RESULTS

For the experimental subjects 'the percentage of increase [in numbers passing the test] from Test 2 to Test 3 yielded a t of 2.30, $p < .05$. A similar test of the control subjects was not significant' (p. 522). The scores for this measure are shown in Table 11.5. The therapeutic gains appear to have been maintained for most experimental subjects over the ensuing six months.

Table 11.5 Number of subjects who held or touched the snake during the avoidance test

Group	N	Test 1	Test 2	Test 3
E_1	8	1	1	5
E_2	5	–	1	2
C_1	5	0	0	0
C_2	6	–	1	2
E_1 and E_2	13	–	2	7
C_1 and C_2	11	–	1	2

Source: Lang & Lazovik (1963)

Table 11.6 Mean snake avoidance scale scores at Tests 2 and 3, mean change scores, and the Mann–Whitney U-test

Group	Test 2	Test 3	Change score	U
Experimental	5.35	4.42	.34	34.5*
Control	6.51	7.73	−.19	

*$p < .05$.
Source: Lang & Lazovik (1963)

The average distance measures on the 19-point Snake Avoidance Test are shown in Table 11.6. Note that the average distance *decreased* between Test 2 and Test 3 for the experimental subjects, whereas the average distance *increased* for the control subjects. The data from Table 11.6 are shown graphically in Figure 11.3. A 'change' score was computed for each subject using a simple formula to calculate how much closer (or further away) the subject had stood on Test 3 than on Test 2. The positive average change score for the experimental groups indicates that they were standing (on average) nearer at Test 3 than at Test 2, whereas the minus score for the control subjects indicates the opposite. A Mann Whitney U test showed statistically significant differences between the individual change scores of all the experimental subjects when compared with all the control subjects ($p < .05$).

The subjects' self ratings on the FSS and on the Fear Thermometer also indicated therapeutic gains for the experimental subjects in

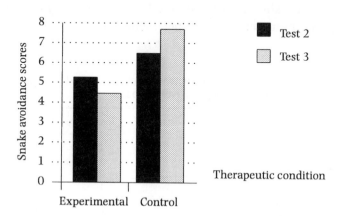

Figure 11.3 *Snake avoidance scores for the experimental and control groups at test 2 and test 3*

comparison with the control subjects, but no statistically significant differences across the groups were found.

Subjects who completed more than 15 items on their hierarchy during desensitisation showed significantly greater therapeutic gains on 'nearly all measures employed in this experiment' (p. 523). These subjects also showed an *overall decrease* in self-reported phobic responses on the FSS. All the subjects who completed all 20 steps of their hierarchy were able to touch or hold the snake during Test 3.

DISCUSSION

The measures used by Lang and Lazovik suggest that desensitisation therapy is effective in reducing the intensity of snake phobias. Perhaps the most convincing data come from the snake avoidance test, which gives a direct behavioural indication of the subjects' levels of fear. Of the 13 experimental subjects, seven were able to touch or hold the snake during Test 3, whereas of 11 control subjects only two were able to touch or hold the snake. Furthermore, all the subjects who completed all 20 steps of their hierarchy were able to touch or hold the snake during Test 3.

The fact that the experimental subjects who completed more than 15 items on their hierarchy showed an overall decrease in self-rated anxiety on a range of phobias (as measured by the FSS) suggests that, in this instance, symptom substitution was not taking place. Indeed this indicates (albeit somewhat weakly) that desensitisation of one phobia *may* lead to a decrease in overall levels of anxiety. The six month follow-up is a strong point of this study. It indicates that the therapeutic gains were not just temporary improvements.

As with all studies, a number of questions spring to mind in relation to the results. One of these has to do with the effects of demand characteristics on the behaviour of the subjects (see Orne, 1962, Chapter 21 of this volume). Presumably the experimental subjects knew they were receiving therapy, and were being compared with a group of control subjects who were not receiving therapy. One wonders whether this might have had some effect on the outcome measures, since all the subjects would have had a pretty clear idea of what was expected of them during each testing phase. And demand characteristics of the initial interviews and questionnaires concerning subjects' levels of snake phobia may also have played a part. If these measures had overestimated the levels of anxiety which each subject experienced in response to snakes, then the therapeutic 'gains' may not have been gains at all.

Nevertheless, one study cannot address all these issues, and the cases for and against the effectiveness of procedures such as systematic desensitisation are ultimately built over a period of time, and over sequences of investigations. This study lends support to the proposition that systematic desensitisation is an effective treatment for phobias.

QUESTIONS

1   Why does this study not necessarily mean that systematic desensitisation, in itself, is an effective treatment of phobias?

2   What was the reason for having two experimental groups, when the only difference between them was that one group was tested prior to initial training, and the other group was not?

Suggested Answers start at p. 451

KEY WORDS

anxiety hierarchy
behaviour therapy
demand characteristics
hypnosis
phobia

psychoanalysis
reciprocal inhibition
symptom substitution
systematic desensitisation

PART IV

DEVELOPMENTAL PSYCHOLOGY

Developmental psychology is sometimes understandably but misleadingly thought of as child psychology: understandably because the major part of the literature in developmental psychology is about children; misleadingly because it gives the impression that psychological development stops as the child enters adulthood. A truly comprehensive developmental psychology should concern itself with the whole *lifespan* of human development. Having said this, the studies summarised in this part reflect the traditional pre-occupation with children. The studies that have been selected for inclusion have been chosen in order to give a fair reflection of the literature as it is, rather than trying to show how it should be.

Attachment is the subject of Chapter 12. Studies of attachment look at the way in which babies and children bond with adult caregivers, and focus on the consequences of problems that can occur during the course of this complex process. Perhaps the most famous name to be associated with attachment is Bowlby, who popularised the controversial notion of *maternal deprivation* (Bowlby, 1951). His work is not represented here, but the summaries of Harlow (1959), Koluchová (1972) and Hodges & Tizard (1989b) provide a good introduction to the area.

The studies that have been included under the heading Moral Development in Chapter 13, address the issue of how children make sense of moral issues, and how this sense-making develops into the moral reasoning of the adult. Kohlberg's (1968) studies, based as they are on the work of Piaget, provide the most usual starting point in this respect. But his stage theory of how children's moral reasoning develops is contested by Gilligan & Attanucci (1988). The investigation by Bandura,

Ross & Ross (1961) is not normally thought of as a study of moral development, but its focus on *behaviour* offers a welcome contrast to studies which look at children's abstract and theoretical moral *judgements*.

Chapter 14, on Classic Approaches, includes work to do with two of the all-time-great figures in developmental psychology: Piaget and Freud. Ironically, neither was a developmental psychologist! Piaget's approach is touched upon in the summary of Samuel & Bryant's (1984) paper, which provides a small methodological critique of one of his research procedures. Freud's case history of Little Hans provides an insight into the influential *psychoanalytic* approach to psychology. And Watson & Rayner's (1920) study of Little Albert, although not a classic in its own right, ensures that the traditions of *behaviourism* do not go unrecognised in this volume.

Finally, Chapter 15 deals with the development of language. The child's eventual mastery of language is perhaps the single most impressive and important achievement of childhood. The first two studies in this chapter show how language development can be traced right back to the moment of birth (and probably before). The final study of the chapter deals with the work of a sociologist, Labov, who looked at the issue of how to assess children's language competence, and made a series of methodological and political points that are relevant to the whole field of developmental psychology.

One final word. The studies that are included in this part are not the only ones in this book that relate to developmental psychology. In a very real sense all of psychology is developmental since it is the study of things (people and processes) which change and develop over the course of time. For too long psychology as a whole has tended to study static snapshots of people, frozen in time and space, and thereby has risked missing some things which lie at the very core of human existence.

12 ATTACHMENT

Attachment refers to a strong emotional tie between two people. In developmental psychology, the term attachment is often taken to mean the emotional tie between the infant and the adult care-giver. It is a popular belief in this culture that the emotional experiences we have in our early years will have an important effect on our adult behaviour and experience. This belief has received considerable support from some psychologists, for example John Bowlby.

In 1951, Bowlby produced a report for the World Health Organisation in which he suggested that 'mother love in infancy and childhood is as important for mental health as are vitamins and proteins for physical health'. (see Bowlby, 1965, p. 240). The clear implication of this is that mothers are a crucial part of a child's development and that many of the problems of later life can be traced back to inadequate mothering. While it is clear that the evidence supports the value of a warm and stable emotional environment for a child, it does not support the notion that this environment must be created by the biological mother. The problem lies in the choice of the term 'mothering' to describe the process of caring for a child. A *mother* is a woman who gives birth to a child, whereas *mothering* is a collection of activities that can be carried out by anyone, though most commonly this person is the mother.

Bowlby presented a considerable amount of evidence that illustrated the negative effects of early experience. It showed that children brought up in institutions who were not given the opportunity to develop stable emotional bonds failed to thrive and develop in the same way as children brought up in family homes. Bowlby concentrated on the emotional bond with the mother, though there are many other features of the institutions that affected the development of the children. The report led to a change in the way that children are cared for in institutions and helped to raise the standards of child care generally.

Bowlby's work stimulated a lot of other research studies which have used a variety of methods in an attempt to broaden our understanding of attachment. Some work has looked at attachment processes in animals, and the first study in this chapter describes the famous (possibly infamous) work of Harlow (1959) with rhesus monkeys. This link between animals and people is very controversial and can only be made if, like Bowlby, you believe that the attachment between mother and child is biologically pre-programmed. Another rich source of information are the various case studies of children brought up in severely deprived circumstances, and the study by Koluchová (1972) is an example of this work. The third example of work in this field is the longitudinal study of Hodges and Tizard (1989b), which looks at the development of a number of children who spent their infancy in institutions before being adopted into families.

There are no simple answers or straightforward theories to describe any type of human relationship, least of all the relationships between children and their parents. Despite this, or maybe because of this, psychologists need to study attachment, because the everyday beliefs that we have about it affect the development of social policies which deal with children.

Can You Hear Me Mother?

■ Harlow, H.F. (1959). Love in infant monkeys.
Scientific American, 200, 68–74.

Introduction

What is love? And how do we develop our bonds of affection? These are
major questions for psychologists though they have turned to some
unlikely sources for the answer. One of these unlikely sources has been
the field of comparative psychology and the work of Harry Harlow and
his associates.

Harlow's work developed from an unfortunate accident that
occurred in the primate colony he was responsible for. Harlow wanted
to reduce infant mortality in the animals and create a sturdy and
disease-free colony for use in various research programmes (Harlow &
Harlow, 1962). He separated the animals from their mothers, and from
all social contact at birth, and put them in a controlled and isolated
environment. The primary objective of a reduced mortality rate was
achieved, but at the cost of their psychological health and social competence. The monkeys sat in their cages and stared fixedly into space,
circled their cages in a repetitive and stereotyped manner, clasped
their head in their hands and rocked, and developed self-injurious com-
pulsive habits. Harlow suggested that it was possible to observe similar
behaviour patterns in disturbed children and adults. When these monkeys were put together, they were unable to develop a characteristic
social structure and, most remarkably, were totally unable to mate.
They could make the right movements, but not in the right order! Any
attempts to encourage mating produced vicious assaults. Some of the
females were eventually impregnated but were unable to nurture their
young and would just brush them off or would abuse them. Harlow
and his team decided to investigate these phenomena, and in a famous
series of experiments looked for the important factors in the development of affectional bonds and 'normal' social behaviour.

The Study

Harlow observed that the isolated monkeys became quite attached to the
gauze nappy pads that were placed on the floor of their cages. They

showed some distress when the pads were removed once a day for cleaning, and the attachment seemed similar to a human baby's attachment to a teddy or a blanket. The researchers used this observation as a starting point for their experiments on the importance of nursing and body contact in the development of attachment.

The researchers made two *surrogate mothers*. One was a bare wire frame with a wooden head and a crude face. The other model had a covering of terry cloth over the frame and a more monkey-like face. They placed eight newborn monkeys in individual cages with equal access to both the cloth and wire 'mothers'. Four of the infants received their milk from one mother and four from the other. The milk was provided via a nursing bottle with a nipple protruding through the frame. The two models (Harlow continually referred to the models as 'mothers', but this is not an acceptable description of them) proved to be *physiologically* equivalent; the monkeys in the two groups drank the same amount of milk and put on the same amount of weight. However, the models were not *psychologically* equivalent; all the monkeys spent more time clinging to the cloth model regardless of whether they were being fed by it or not.

The results showed the importance of bodily contact for young monkeys. Harlow went on to say:

> all our experience indicates, in fact, that our cloth covered mother surrogate is an eminently satisfactory mother. She is available 24 hours a day to satisfy her infant's overwhelming compulsion to seek bodily contact; she possesses infinite patience, never scolding her baby or biting it in anger. In these respects we regard her as superior to a living monkey mother, though monkey fathers would probably not endorse this opinion.
> (p. 70)

This strange mixture of *anthropomorphism* and stereotyped attitudes about the role of mothers and mothering give us more insight into contemporary attitudes than into the development of affectional bonds.

In the next phase of the study, Harlow subjected the monkeys to stressful situations to see how they would respond. In one example they were presented with a mechanical teddy bear (bigger than themselves) which walked towards them playing a drum. The monkeys who had been fed by the cloth model climbed onto this model to reduce their anxiety. The monkeys who had been fed by the wire model also went to the cloth model under this stress.

In another test, the monkeys were taken to a strange situation which was a much larger room than they were used to, and which contained a number of unfamiliar objects. The monkeys would 'hide' in the corner and cover their heads with their arms. However, if the cloth model was put in the room the monkey would rush to it and climb on it. Then it would start to explore the room using the model as a base. It would check out the objects one by one and return to the model continually. Harlow suggested that this response can also be seen in young children.

A final test involved giving the monkeys the opportunity to press a lever that opened a window. Previous research had shown that monkeys will do this just to look out, and will press the lever more often to view some stimuli (another monkey for example) than for others (a bowl of fruit perhaps). The experimental monkeys pressed the lever to look at the cloth model as often as they did to look at another real monkey. In contrast they showed very little interest in the wire model.

Other studies showed that the monkeys had a slight preference for a rocking model over a rigid model, though no preference for a heated model over a non-heated model. Also, if the monkeys were raised with the cloth model for five months, then separated from it for 18 months, they still showed the same level of attachment when they were re-united.

DISCUSSION

Harlow, and a number of other researchers, saw this work as an important contribution to our understanding of human attachment. In particular, the work disputes the importance of feeding in the development of attachment (cupboard love), and at the time of these studies this was an important challenge to Freudian ideas about child development.

The objections to Harlow's conclusions are numerous and come, in part, from his own subsequent work. The monkeys who were 'reared' by the cloth 'mothers' but were otherwise kept isolated, still grew up to be socially inept. The 'mothering' provided by these models was woefully inadequate. However, monkeys that were kept with a cloth model in isolation from other monkeys, but who were allowed to play with three other young monkeys for one hour every day, grew up to be indistinguishable in their social behaviour from monkeys who had been reared by their natural mothers. The crucial ingredient for the healthy psychological development of the animals was by this account shown to be *social contact*, and not contact comfort, or even mothering.

QUESTIONS

1   What are the major findings of the study?

2   What are the problems in making generalisations from this study to the behaviour of children?

3   What behaviours did Harlow notice in the monkeys that were similar to the behaviour of disturbed children?

4   What are the problems with using the terms 'mother' and 'mothering' in the observations of these monkeys?

5   How does Harlow's work make you feel? Was his treatment of monkeys justified?

Suggested Answers start at p. 452

KEY WORDS

affectional bonds	mothers
anthropomorphism	self-injurious behaviour
attachment	social isolation
mothering	surrogate

FAMILY LIFE

■ HODGES, J. & TIZARD, B. (1989b).
Social and family relationships of ex-institutional adolescents.
Journal of Child Psychology and Psychiatry, 30, 77–97.

INTRODUCTION

One of the major questions which developmental psychologists have studied is whether or not there is a *critical period* in the first stages of human development, and, if there is, how long it extends after birth. By 'critical period' we mean a stage during which the child is highly 'malleable', when the occurrence of damaging experiences might have long term (perhaps life-long) consequences.

Koluchová's (1972) work (which is also summarised in this chapter) deals with this issue by means of a longitudinal case study. Hodges and Tizard's investigation which is summarised here is also longitudinal, but with a larger sample of children. Their subjects spent the first two years of their lives in institutional care, before being either adopted or returned to their biological parents. They were followed up and assessed at various stages until the age of eight (see for example Tizard & Hodges, 1978), and were then re-assessed for the purposes of this study at the age of 16. A comparison of this group of children with a matched group who had been with their families throughout their lives provides the basis for a quasi-experimental investigation which could potentially isolate some of the long-term effects of early institutional care, and which would thereby contribute to our understanding of the complex critical period issue.

THE STUDY

Subjects

Thirty-nine children aged 16 were the subjects of this study. They had all been in institutional care until at least two years of age, at which point most of them had either been adopted or restored to biological parents. At the time of the study, 23 of the children were with adopted families (the 'adopted' group), 11 were with their biological parents (the 'restored' group), and five were in institutional care. The paper focuses on 31 of the adopted and restored (that is, 'ex-institutional') children.

All of these children were the subjects of a longitudinal study which had followed their progress until they were eight years old. The original sample had included 65 children at age four, and 51 children at age eight. Relatively high rates of 'subject attrition' are a typical feature of longitudinal research.

Two comparison groups of children were established. One was drawn from the London area, and was made up of 16-year-old children who were matched one for one with the ex-institutional children on the basis of sex, position in the family, whether they were from one- or two-parent families, and the occupation of their family's main bread-winner. The other comparison group comprised a same-sex school friend (of the same age) for each of the ex-institutional children.

Details of the subject sample are included in a companion article (Hodges & Tizard, 1989a) which needs to be read in conjunction with the paper summarised here.

Design

The study reported in this paper was part of a large-scale longitudinal investigation, the data for which were gathered by means of various self-report measures, interviews, and assessment scales. The authors focus on comparisons among the various groups of subject who participated in the study: the adopted group, the restored group, and the comparison groups. They also compare the data from the 16-year-old ex-institutional children with data from the ex-institutional children at age eight.

Procedure

Five principal methods were used to collect data on all the adolescents (including those in the comparison groups):

(1) an interview with the adolescent subject;
(2) an interview with their mother (in some cases with their father present);
(3) a self-report questionnaire concerning 'social difficulties';
(4) a questionnaire completed by the subjects' school teacher about their relationships with their peers and their teachers;
(5) the Rutter 'B' scale. This comprises 26 items and is used for psychiatric screening.

Again, details of the assessment procedures are included in the companion article.

RESULTS

A lengthy results section includes data on the following issues:

- attachment to parents;
- relations with siblings;
- showing affection;
- similarity and assimilation;
- confiding and supporting;
- disagreements over control and discipline;
- involvement in the family;
- peer relationships;
- specific difficulties with peer relations;
- special friends;
- relationships between attachment and peer relationships;
- relationships between current and earlier peer relations;
- overfriendly behaviour;
- relationships to teachers.

In many of these areas differences were apparent among the different groups in the study, but some of them are based on rather too few responses to be meaningful. At the end of the results section the authors summarise the main differences which they observed between the comparison groups and the ex-institutional group as a whole. These were:

(1) The ex-institutional adolescents were more often 'adult-oriented'. For example, teachers rated the ex-institutional adolescents 'as "trying to get a lot of attention from adults" more often than the school comparison group ($p < .05$)' (p. 92). This continued a pattern that had been observed at the age of eight.

Table 12.1   Teachers' assessment of popularity with peers

	Less popular than average	Average	More popular than average	Total
Ex-inst.	12 (39%)	12 (39%)	7 (23%)	31
Matched comparisons	4 (15%)	20 (74%)	3 (11%)	27
School comparisons	6 (21%)	18 (64%)	4 (14%)	28

(Ex-inst. vs matched comparisons $p < .025$.)
Source: Hodges & Tizard (1989)

(2) The ex-institutional adolescents had a greater likelihood of encoun-
tering difficulties in getting on with peers. Table 12.1 shows that the
ex-institutional teenagers were more likely than the matched subjects to be rated 'less popular than average' by their teachers (and
slightly more likely to be rated 'more popular than average').

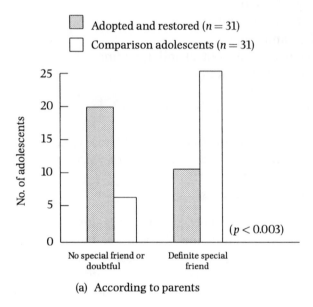

(a) According to parents

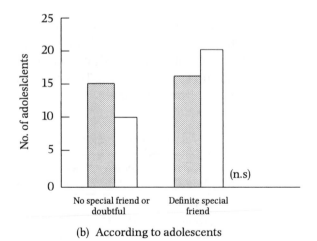

(b) According to adolescents

Figure 12.1   *Number of adolescents with special same-sex friend*
Source: Hodges & Tizard (1989)

(3) The ex-institutional teenagers were 'less likely to have a special friend' (p. 92). There were statistically significant differences in this respect according to the accounts of the mothers ($p < .02$), and the accounts of the adolescents themselves showed the same basic pattern without reaching the level of statistical significance (see Figure 12.1).

(4) The ex-institutional group were 'less likely to turn to peers for emotional support if anxious' (p. 92).

(5) The ex-institutional teenagers were 'less likely to be selective in choosing friends' (p. 92). That is, they were somewhat more likely to be 'friendly with any peer who was friendly towards them, rather than choosing their friends' (p. 91), at least according to the parents' judgements.

Perhaps the most striking differences that the authors report were between the adopted adolescents and the 'restored' adolescents within the ex-institutional group. It appeared that the within-family relationships of the restored group were noticeably different from the within-family relationships of the adopted and comparison groups (indeed the adopted group and the comparison groups showed no major differences in terms of intra-familial relationships). These differences were that the restored adolescents tended to be less attached to their mothers, showed less affection to their parents, identified themselves less with their parents, and had particular difficulties in getting on with their siblings.

Discussion

The study indicates that the adopted children were more able to overcome some of the problems of early institutional upbringing than the restored children, notably the problem of attachment to parents. The authors offer a plausible explanation for this. One of the features of institutional care is the lack of a single, stable caregiver, or pair of caregivers. Children in institutions have to spread their attachments rather thinly over a large number of people: 'By the age of 2, an average of 24 different caregivers had looked after them for at least a week; by 4, the average was 50' (Hodges & Tizard, 1989a, p. 53).

One might expect, then, that forming stable long-term attachments could be a problem for such children. However, Hodges and Tizard noted that the family environments into which the adopted children were subsequently integrated were more suited to counteracting this potential problem than the family environments of the restored children. The financial situation of the adoptive families was often better, they had on average fewer children to provide for, and the adoptive parents were particularly highly motivated to have a child and to develop a relationship with that child. The biological parents in Hodges and Tizard's sample seemed to have been 'more ambivalent about their child living with them' (p. 94).

It seems then, according to Hodges and Tizard's findings, that in terms of stable familial attachments, the negative experiences of early institutional upbringing can be overcome with the right environment and adequate resources. However, the children in this study were still only 16 years old, and it may be that in the longer term they could face problems with the sorts of stable attachments that come in later years outside the family environment. Indeed, the fact that there were differences between the whole ex-institutional group and the comparison groups with regard to relationships beyond the family (friendships and relationships with peers, for example) suggests that the long-term prognosis for them is far from clear.

QUESTIONS

1   How might 'subject attrition' have biased the findings of this study?

2   Can the differences observed between the ex-institutional group and the comparison groups at 16 years of age definitely be put down to the early institutional experiences of the former?

Suggested Answers start at p. 452

KEY WORDS

adolescents	intra-familial relationships
adoption	longitudinal study
adult-oriented behaviour	peer relationships
caregivers	quasi-experiment
critical period	subject attrition

Emotional Deprivation

■ Koluchová J. (1972). Severe deprivation in twins: A case study. *Journal of Child Psychology and Psychiatry, 13,* 107–14.

Introduction

Koluchová's case study describes one of the most severe cases of childhood deprivation on record within the psychological literature. It is a brief, descriptive paper about a pair of Czechoslovakian identical (monozygotic) twin boys who were 'reared from age 18 months to 7 years in social isolation by a psychopathic stepmother and an inadequate father' (p.114). The story is distressing, and shot through with human tragedy despite the author's somewhat bald account. However, Koluchová manages to convey a sense of optimism about the development of the boys' lives subsequent to the period of deprivation. The author was part of a multi-disciplinary team which was involved with the children when they were admitted to hospital.

The boys' mother died after giving birth to them in September 1960, and for the first 11 months of their lives they lived in a children's home. By the age of 18 months they were again living with their father, his new wife and four other children, two of whom were their natural siblings. The authorities only became involved in 1967 after the father had taken the twins to a local paediatrician in order to obtain a certificate granting them exemption from entering primary school. 'Gradually it became clear that this was a case of criminal neglect' (p.108) and a trial ensued. The twins had evidently been brought up in isolation from the rest of the family, unable to go outside or into the main family living room. Their room was unheated and they were periodically locked up in the cellar and beaten. By the time this paper was written the twins had begun to be able to talk about their early experiences, and their accounts matched with the story that had emerged during the court case.

The case of the children, who are referred to as P.M. and J.M., is of interest to psychologists for two reasons. First, psychologists are people, and human dramas such as this must be taken note of by the whole of society. Secondly, psychologists are scientists, engaged in the pursuit of knowledge about the human condition; knowledge which can be turned to good use in improving the quality of human life. Cases such as this, as tragic as they are, provide psychologists with the opportunities to further our understanding of 'normal' childhood development. By examining what appear to be the consequences of the twins' abnormal early experiences we may be able to make advances in our understanding of what constitutes 'normal' development, and further our understanding of what factors contribute to healthy psychological and physical growth. This strategy is a familiar one in abnormal and developmental psychology, and is used to compensate for the fact that formal experimentation cannot be undertaken into these sorts of areas, at least not with people (see Harlow, 1959, earlier in this chapter).

THE STUDY

The effects of the children's five years and six months of social and emotional deprivation were very wide ranging. At seven they could hardly walk, had very poor fine motor skills, and hardly any spontaneous speech. Their play skills were 'primitive', they were 'timid and mistrustful' (p. 109), their ranges of emotional expression were limited, and their I.Q's, had they been measurable, 'would have been within the range of imbecility' (p. 110). They were also unable to understand the meaning of pictures. Koluchová's assessment of their mental age was that they were functioning, on average, at the level of three-year-old children.

After spending some time in a children's home and in a special school for children with learning difficulties, the twins moved into a permanent foster home and into a mainstream school. Their development from age seven to age ten appears to have been relatively rapid, for by that age the Wechsler Intelligence Scale for Children (WISC) showed that they were functioning intellectually at around average levels, with particular gains having been made on verbal components of the tests. It seems that a stable environment had compensated to some extent for the earlier extremes of deprivation, and although the author presents an uncertain prognosis for future development, there is an optimistic feel to the paper. We should note, however, that this account emphasises cognitive and intellectual development. The emotional impact of such experiences will always be much less easy to assess, even though, as Koluchová asserts, 'the most severe deprivation... was probably their poverty of emotional relationships and their social isolation' (p. 113).

During the court case it became essential for the prosecution to demonstrate that the children's disabilities at age seven had been caused by deprivation rather than, as the stepmother had claimed, that they had been 'defective from birth' (p. 110). It is not entirely clear what evidence was used to do this. It may have been some combination of the records of the children's first institutional home which showed no evidence of disability up until 11 months of age, the testimony of neighbours who had noticed unusual things about the family, and the fact that the children's development did seem to speed up substantially after being taken into care. An important upshot of this is that it shows how difficult it is in principle to separate out the influences of nature and nurture, even in detailed investigations of individual cases.

DISCUSSION

Case studies are noted for the richness of data which they produce, and the human dramas that they reveal can be engaging and moving. One of the most notable exponents of this brand of psychology is Oliver Sacks, whose text 'The Man who Mistook his Wife for a Hat' (Sacks, 1986) stands as a classic. But case studies, like all other research methods, have their limitations. The reader of this paper can be left with the feeling that this is *one* person's account of a complex state of affairs in which the author has had considerable license in choosing which aspects of the case to present. Much is made, for example, of the idea that the stepmother was the pivotal character in the story. The father is presented as rather slow and powerless, but less to blame for what happened. Since the reader's access to the case is controlled by Koluchová, one can only surmise about what a different author might have made of this disturbing affair.

A general problem with case studies like this is the balance between scientific interest and the welfare of the child. Getting the balance wrong can be damaging. For example, in a well-reported case from the USA, a girl called Genie had been kept in a back room strapped to a chair until she reached her teens. Sadly, Genie's suffering did not come to an end when she was discovered, but continued at the hands of the scientific community. After her discovery, researchers struggled for access to the disturbed child and some were able to foster her, to help her development and also to facilitate the scientific observation. Distressingly, when the research money ran out, the fostering ended, and Genie then experienced a number of poor foster placements where she was abused and regressed to her non-communicative condition. Later, her mother was able to take more responsibility for her and sued the psychologists for excessive experimentation on the child. For a full account of Genie's story see Rymer (1993).

QUESTIONS

1 What sorts of biases might have entered Koluchová's account?

2 What conclusions can be drawn from this study about 'normal' childhood development?

3 How do psychologists try to establish a healthy balance between scientific interest and the welfare of the child in cases such as these?

Suggested Answers start at p. 453

KEY WORDS

case study
deprivation
I.Q.
monozygotic twin

nature
nurture
Wechsler Intelligence Scale for
    Children (WISC)

13 MORAL DEVELOPMENT

How do we learn right from wrong, good from bad? All societies have rules, some of which are written down and make up 'the law', whereas other rules are less well defined. The questions for psychologists are how do we learn these rules and at what age are we able to make adult moral judgements?

Discussions about the age of moral maturity are very relevant to our everyday judgements of behaviour. In the tragic case where a toddler was taken from a shopping centre in Liverpool, England, and eventually murdered by two ten-year-old boys, we have to ask whether the boys had an adult sense of right and wrong. Events such as this challenge the way we make moral judgements, and in this case the courts found them guilty of murder and the Home Secretary has recommended that they serve no less than 15 years in custody. This judgement suggests that the courts believed the boys to be capable of adult moral judgement. So, at what age would we accept that they were *not* capable of that judgement?

Perhaps the most influential approach to moral development in psychology has been the attempt to describe the development of moral reasoning, first by Piaget (1932) and later by Kohlberg (1968). This approach suggests that the important issue is our ability to think things through, and the more we develop our general cognitive skills, the more developed our moral thinking will be. Interestingly, Piaget suggested that the highest stage of cognitive development (the formal operational stage) does not develop in children until they are about 12 or above. This would place the age of moral maturity some time in the teens and draws into question the decision to treat 10-year-old children as if they are adults. This chapter summarises two papers on this approach. The first is a summary of Kohlberg's (1968) paper, and the second (Gilligan & Attanucci, 1988) is a critical study that highlights some of the limitations of Kohlberg's approach.

The third study in this chapter takes an entirely different approach and looks at moral behaviour rather than moral reasoning. The distinction is an important one because other studies (for example LaPiere, Chapter 2 of this volume) have shown the differences between people's attitudes and behaviour. The moral *judgement* might be sound, but the moral *behaviour* might be duff. Most people believe it is wrong to cheat (in examinations, on your partner, at sports, and so forth) but hands up anyone who has not cheated sometimes. The study by Bandura, Ross & Ross (1961) is one of the most quoted pieces of psychological research and is used in debates on aggression, moral development, socialisation, and the effects of the media.

Both the behavioural and the cognitive approaches highlight the strengths and weaknesses of psychological research. On the one hand they are based on relatively controlled research and provide interesting data for us to interpret. On the other hand, they are carried out in a *social vacuum* since they study how we think and behave when we are alone, whereas in everyday life we obtain instruction on moral issues from family, friends, workmates, and so forth; in other words, from people who we have relationships with. Our moral judgements and behaviour are part of our wider network of relationships and the existing psychological theories do not really account for this.

THE MORAL PRINCIPLE OF JUSTICE

■ KOHLBERG, L. (1968). The child as a moral philosopher.
Psychology Today, 2, 25–30.

INTRODUCTION

How do children understand notions of right and wrong? How do they
reason morally about the world that they find themselves in? Do they
understand the world in the same way as adults (albeit in a less developed way), or are there *qualitative* differences between the thoughts of
children and adults? If there are *real* qualitative differences, what stages
do children go through in their moral thinking as they grow towards
adulthood?

These are all familiar questions in developmental psychology,
inspired to a large extent by Piaget (see the summary of Samuel &
Bryant, 1984, Chapter 14 of this volume). Although Piaget tended to
focus on the logical side of children's thinking, he also studied the development of moral reasoning (Piaget, 1932). Kohlberg drew substantially
upon Piaget's 'pioneering effort' (p. 25) in this respect, and made moral
development the centrepiece of his psychological research.

THE STUDY

'The Child as a Moral Philosopher' summarises the work on moral
reasoning which Kohlberg carried out over a 12-year period in the
late 1950s and 1960s. From his longitudinal and cross-cultural empirical work he developed a stage theory of moral development which is
outlined in the results section below. It is worth noting that the result
of Kohlberg's extensive research is a typology of moral reasoning
based on a 6-stage model of development. In other words, the end
result of this research is a theory which is derived (induced) from the
data. This is a legitimate and recognised approach to research and is
known as an *inductive* strategy. This investigative style can be con-
trasted with the standard experimental approach whereby a theory is
the starting point of the process, and the data are used to test propositions (hypotheses) which have been derived from the theory (a
deductive strategy).

Subjects

Seventy-five boys from the United States formed the cohort of subjects for Kohlberg's work. In addition children from Taiwan, Mexico, Turkey and Yucatan were studied.

Design

The research reported in this paper is both longitudinal and cross-cultural. The 75 boys from the US were studied over a period of 12 years, and compared in terms of moral development with the children from Taiwan, Mexico, Turkey and Yucatan.

Procedure

Kohlberg's research procedures drew heavily on the method developed by Piaget for investigating moral development (see Piaget, 1932). Children were presented with 'hypothetical moral dilemmas' (p. 26), such as 'Should the doctor "mercy kill" a fatally ill woman requesting death because of her pain?', and 'Is it better to save the life of one important person or a lot of unimportant people?' (p. 27). The children were posed the same dilemmas at various points in time over the 12-year period of the study. Their answers were analysed according to the underlying structures of their moral reasoning.

RESULTS

Kohlberg induced a stage theory of moral development from the responses that children gave at different ages to the hypothetical dilemmas. Stage theories hold that there are a set of (invariant) steps which all children go through in the same order without missing any of the steps out, and without returning to earlier steps, though different children will progress at different rates through the sequence. The six stages which Kohlberg identified were subdivided into three 'levels' as follows:

The preconventional level

> *Stage 1* Orientation toward punishment and unquestioning deference to superior power. The physical consequences of action regardless of their human meaning or value determine its goodness or badness (p. 25).

Stage 2   Right action consists of that which instrumentally satisfies one's own needs and occasionally the needs of others . . . Elements of fairness, of reciprocity and equal sharing are present, but they are always interpreted in a physical, pragmatic way . . . (p. 25).

The conventional level

Stage 3   Good-boy – good-girl orientation. Good behavior is that which pleases or helps others and is approved by them. There is much conformity to stereotypical images of what is majority or 'natural' behavior. Behavior is often judged by intention – 'he means well' becomes important for the first time . . . (p. 25).

Stage 4   Orientation toward authority, fixed rules and the maintenance of the social order. Right behavior consists of doing one's duty, showing respect for authority and maintaining the given social order for its own sake (p. 25).

The postconventional level

Stage 5   A social-contract orientation, generally with legalistic and utilitarian overtones. Right action tends to be defined in terms of general rights and in terms of standards which have been critically examined and agreed upon by the whole society . . . The result is an emphasis upon the 'legal point of view' . . . (pp. 25–26).

Stage 6   Orientation toward the decisions of conscience and toward self-chosen *ethical principles* appealing to logical comprehensiveness, universality and consistency. These principles are abstract and ethical . . . they are universal principles of *justice*, of the *reciprocity* and *equality* of human rights, and of respect for the dignity of human beings as *individual persons* (p. 26).

Kohlberg tested the children on 25 'basic moral concepts' (p. 26). Each child's reasoning at any given age was typically at the same stage on about 50 per cent of these concepts. In other words, the structure of each individual child's reasoning tended to be the same even when the content (the basic moral concept in question) changed. Because Kohlberg believed he had tapped into the deep underlying structure of moral reasoning, he believed he should be able to observe the same stages of development in children of other cultures. The content of moral reasoning might vary from culture to culture, but its structure should remain the same. The argument is similar to Chomsky's idea of a 'universal grammar' (see Chomsky, 1957); a deep underlying structure of language which is the same for all languages even though the content (the vocabulary) of those languages is very different.

Kohlberg argues that his empirical data support this position. The children he studied in Taiwan, Mexico, Turkey and Yucatan showed evidence of going through the same stages of moral reasoning as the US children, albeit at a slower rate in Taiwan and Mexico, and at a much slower rate for the children from Turkey and Yucatan who lived in isolated villages. According to Kohlberg's data, the US children made most use of the more advanced stages of moral reasoning.

DISCUSSION

Cross-cultural studies are critically important in psychology, but they must be handled expertly and the results must be interpreted with caution. Kohlberg argued in effect that his research methods were culturally neutral; that is, that they act as an unbiased measure of moral development, irrespective of the background and upbringing of the child that is being measured. If this argument is correct then the US children were more highly developed morally than the children from Taiwan, Mexico, Turkey and Yucatan.

This seems highly improbable for it is not at all clear that morality can be separated from culture in the way that Kohlberg suggests. It is much more likely that the tests he used, having been developed in a given culture, on a sample of children from that same culture, would simply not work very well when transported to other cultures. The net effect of 'not working very well' is to show what *appears* to be poor performance. So, we should be very aware that the differences between ethnic groups is much more likely to be a result of some ethnocentric bias than a reflection of any *real* differences in moral development. This basic line of argument is taken up and developed by Gilligan & Attanucci, in the following study on the issue of gender bias in Kohlberg's work.

QUESTIONS

1   Is it possible to identify an underlying 'structure' of moral thinking and reasoning which is independent of the 'content' of that reasoning?

2   What do you think are some of the strengths and weaknesses of Kohlberg's method of getting children of various ages to respond to these mini moral dilemmas?

Suggested Answers start at p. 453

KEY WORDS

cross-cultural studies
deductive strategies
ethnocentric bias
inductive strategies
longitudinal studies
moral dilemmas
moral reasoning

natural language accounts
post-structuralism
qualitative differences
stage theories
structuralism
universal grammar

THE MORAL PRINCIPLE OF CARE

■ GILLIGAN, C. & ATTANUCCI, J. (1988).
Two moral orientations: Gender differences and similarities.
Merrill–Palmer Quarterly, 34, 223–37.

INTRODUCTION

Before reading this summary you should read the preceding summary of Kohlberg's paper on moral development .

Gilligan & Attanucci challenge Kohlberg's analysis of stages of moral development on two grounds. Firstly, the analysis is argued to be the product of a male perspective on morality; one that over-emphasises the notion of *justice*: 'Psychologists studying moral development have equated morality with justice' (p. 225). Within Kohlberg's system the moral principle of *care* is undervalued and implicitly seen as characteristic of earlier (lower) developmental stages of moral reasoning. Gilligan and Attanucci argue that 'care' is just as important a moral principle as 'justice', and contest the idea that a person who responds to moral dilemmas with a caring perspective is at a lower stage of moral development than a person responding to the dilemma in terms of justice. If, as they suspect, women tend to emphasise the moral principle of care, while men tend to emphasise the moral principle of justice, then according to Kohlberg's stage-theory, women will be consistently found to be behind men in terms of moral development. So Gilligan and Attanucci propose that the principles of care and justice should not be viewed as being characteristic of different *levels* of moral development, rather they should be seen as different, but equally mature, moral orientations (for a more detailed insight into these ideas see Gilligan, 1982). The authors give some illustrative examples of these two orientations at work in their data, and two of these examples are reproduced below.

Excerpt one

I have moral dilemmas all the time, but I have no problem solving them usually. I usually resolve them according to my internal morality... the more important publicly your office is, to me the more

important it is that you *play by the rules* because society hangs together by these rules and in my view, if you cheat on them, even for a laudatory purpose, eventually you break the rules down, because it is impossible to draw any fine lines.
(p. 226, as in original emphasis)

Excerpt two

I have to preside over these decisions and try to make them as non-disastrous as possible for the people who are most vulnerable. The fewer games you play the better, because you are really dealing with issues that are the very basis to people's day-to-day well-being, and it is people's feelings, people's potential for growth, and you should do everything in your power to smooth it.
(p. 226).

The subjects in both these excerpts were lawyers. In the first excerpt a justice orientation is displayed by the person arguing for the necessity to keep within 'the rules', and to defend the legal system which keeps society together. In the second excerpt the arguments are more focused on people's well-being, their needs and their feelings; a care orientation.

Gilligan and Attanucci's second criticism of Kohlberg's work, which is addressed in the design of this study, is that it is grounded in people's answers to hypothetical moral dilemmas. They argue that people's perspectives change when they are confronted by real dilemmas from their own lives, because they then have to consider in their answers what they actually might have to *do*, rather than just responding abstractly according to some high-sounding principle.

THE STUDY

Gilligan and Attanucci's investigation required subjects to generate accounts of moral dilemmas from their own lives, and then to discuss them, all in the context of a detailed interview. The subjects' accounts were analysed and scored according to whether they emphasised one or other of the moral principles of care and justice, or whether they balanced their considerations equally between these two orientations. The authors were also interested in whether there was a relationship between choice of the orientations and gender. Their specific prediction was that female subjects would tend towards the principle of care, and male subjects would focus on the principle of justice.

Subjects

Eighty subjects participated; 34 women and 46 men, all from the USA. The men and women were matched for levels of education and professional occupation. Twenty-one 'minority' students (Black, Hispanic, and Asian Americans) were included in the overall sample.

Design

The study had a quasi-experimental design, in that it capitalised on the pre-existing demographic variable of sex in its 'allocation' of subjects to 'conditions'.

Procedure

Each subject underwent a detailed, one-to-one, tape-recorded interview which lasted two hours. The discussion of moral conflicts took up only part of the interview; the rest of the time was spent discussing related topics, but in relation to a different research study. The questions relevant to this study were:

(1) Have you ever been in a situation of moral conflict where you had to make a decision but weren't sure what was the right thing to do?
(2) Could you describe the situation?
(3) What were the conflicts for you in that situation?
(4) What did you do?
(5) Do you think it was the right thing to do?
(6) How do you know? (p. 229).

The recorded conversations were transcribed and subjected to a content analysis. This involved analysing each interview into 'considerations', 'defined as each idea the participant presents in discussing a moral problem' (p. 230). Each consideration was then assigned either to the category of care or to the category of justice, according to set criteria. The assignment of considerations to the two categories (known as the process of *coding* the data) was undertaken by three independent coders who did not know the sex, age or race of the participants whose material they were analysing. The authors report high levels of *intercoder reliability*, with an overall agreement level of 80 per cent among the coders.

On the basis of this coding process, each subject's dilemma was allocated to one of the following categories. If all the considerations in the dilemma had been coded as 'care' it was labelled 'Care Only'. If all the considerations had been coded as 'justice' it was labelled 'Justice Only'. If at least 75 per cent of the considerations had been coded as care it was labelled 'Care Focus'. If at least 75 per cent of the considerations had been coded as justice it was labelled 'Justice Focus'. Finally, if neither orientation accounted for 75 per cent or more of the considerations, the dilemma was labelled 'Care Justice'.

RESULTS

Most subjects used both moral orientations in their dilemmas (only 31 per cent used *only* care or justice considerations). But most people *favoured* one or other of the orientations, with only one-third of subjects' dilemmas appearing in the combined care/justice category.

A chi-square test on the data presented in Table 13.1 showed that, at the level of $p < .001$, 'Care Focus is much more likely in the moral dilemma of a woman and Justice Focus is much more likely in the dilemma of a man' (p. 231).

Table 13.1   Contingency table showing moral orientation by gender

	Care Focus and Care Only	Justice Focus and Justice Only
Women	12	10
Men	1	30

Source: Adapted from Gilligan & Attanucci (1988)

DISCUSSION

The data support Gilligan and Attanucci's prediction that the moral principle of care is more evident in the accounts of women than in the accounts of men. This finding has implications for work on moral reasoning. The authors point out that if the women's accounts are removed from the data set, the moral orientation of care would be much less easy to see. Since Kohlberg's stage theory of moral development was based on a sample of boys, it is no wonder that his theory seems to have undervalued this orientation. We might also argue that

Kohlberg's work undervalued mature moral orientations of other cultures given that it was developed on a US sample. (See the discussion section of the previous summary of Kohlberg, 1968.)

Among a series of recommendations, Gilligan and Attanucci suggest a close examination of the moral orientation of care, including an analysis of how it develops into a mature moral orientation. The discussion section of the paper provides an interesting analysis of the tension between care and justice perspectives:

> The tension between these perspectives is suggested by the fact that detachment, which is the mark of mature moral judgment in the justice perspective, becomes the moral problem in the care perspective, that is, the failure to attend to need. Conversely, attention to the particular needs and circumstances of individuals, the mark of mature moral judgment in the care perspective, becomes the moral problem in the justice perspective, that is, failure to treat others fairly, as equals.
> (pp. 232–33)

The tension is evident in Gilligan and Attanucci's data to the extent that most people focus on one or other of the orientations in their accounts. This suggests that people find it difficult to juggle with both orientations at once. On the other hand, the fact that most of the subjects at least acknowledged their non-preferred orientation (a minority talked in terms of *only* one of the perspectives) suggests that both orientations are generally known and available as ways of reasoning. Perhaps the mark of truly mature moral reasoning is the ability to synthesise two apparently competing principles within the same line of thinking?

QUESTIONS

1   Why are the authors keen to claim a high level of inter-coder reliability in the process of assigning the 'considerations' to the different
categories?

2   How convincing do you find Gilligan and Attanucci's data? Can you
see any problems with their method of content analysis?

3   Consider the following dilemma (adapted from Kohlberg, 1969):

> A man's wife is dying. There is a drug that might help, but it
> costs £10 000 because it took so many years for a struggling
> pharmaceutical company to develop it. The man cannot afford
> this so he breaks into the drug company's office and steals a
> supply. Was he right or wrong to have done this? Why?

Try considering this moral dilemma from the perspective of a justice orientation and then from the perspective of a care orientation. What sorts of factors do you take into account in judging the
man's actions from each perspective? Do the different orientations
lead to the same conclusions about whether he was right or wrong?

Suggested Answers start at p. 454

Key Words

care orientation
coding
content analysis
detachment
gender
inter-coder reliability

justice orientation
moral development
moral dilemmas
moral reasoning
quasi-experimental design

BASHING BOBO

■ BANDURA, A., ROSS, D. & ROSS, S.A. (1961). Transmission of aggression through imitation of aggressive models. *Journal of Abnormal and Social Psychology*, 63, 575–82.

INTRODUCTION

This study looks at how aggressive behaviour develops in children. It has attracted a lot of attention from a number of academic disciplines and is still quoted in many texts despite its age. There are two social issues that the study addresses. First, is aggression an *innate* feature of our behaviour? And to look at one particular aspect of this issue, can we say that male aggression towards women is a feature of 'natural' male behaviour or is it learnt? These questions have a bearing on how we develop social policies to deal with aggressive behaviour. The second issue, which follows on from the first, is if aggression is *learnt* then *how* is it learnt?

Bandura's approach is an extension of *behaviourism* and basically sees people as being moulded by their life experiences. It looks at how we are affected by the rewards and punishments that we experience every day. Bandura is a leading figure in Social Learning Theory which attempts to extend the concepts used in operant and classical conditioning to explain complex human social behaviour. Key concepts in this approach are *reinforcement* and *imitation*.

THE STUDY

In this study, Bandura set out to demonstrate that if children are passive witnesses to an aggressive display by an adult, they will imitate this aggressive behaviour when given the opportunity. More specifically, the study was guided by the following predictions:

> ... subjects exposed to aggressive models will reproduce aggressive acts resembling those of the models ...

> ... the observation of subdued non-aggressive models will have a generalized inhibiting effect on the subject's subsequent behaviour ...

... subjects will imitate the behaviour of a same-sex model to a greater degree than a model of the opposite sex...

... boys will be more predisposed than girls towards imitating aggression...
(p. 575)

Subjects

Thirty-six boys and 36 girls aged between 37 to 69 months were tested. The mean age was 52 months. They used one male adult and one female adult to act as role models.

Design

The study had three major conditions; a control group, a group exposed to an aggressive model, and a group exposed to a passive model. The children who were exposed to the adult models were further subdivided by their gender, and by the gender of the model they were exposed to. In other words there were three independent variables. A summary of the groups is shown in Table 13.2.

This is quite a complicated design that appears to cover a lot of different possibilities. However, the number of children in each group is quite small, and the results could be distorted if one group contained a few children who are normally quite aggressive. The researchers tried

Table 13.2 Bandura's eight experimental groups

Control group – 24 subjects
Eight experimental groups (each with 6 subjects)
- Aggressive model condition – 24 subjects
- Non-aggressive model condition – 24 subjects

Aggressive model condition

6 boys with same-sex model	6 boys with opposite sex model	6 girls with same-sex model	6 girls with opposite sex model

Non-aggressive model control

6 boys with same-sex model	6 boys with opposite sex model	6 girls with same-sex model	6 girls with opposite sex model

to reduce this problem by pre-testing the children and assessing their aggressiveness. They observed the children in the nursery and judged their aggressive behaviour on four 5-point rating scales. The rating scales were:

(a) physical aggression;
(b) verbal aggression;
(c) aggression towards inanimate objects;
(d) aggressive inhibition.

A composite score for each child was obtained by adding the results of the four ratings. It was then possible to match the children in each group so that they had similar levels of aggression in their everyday behaviour. The observers were the experimenter (female), a nursery school teacher (female), and the model for male aggression. The study reports that the first two observers 'were well acquainted with the children' (p. 576).

A disadvantage of using rating scales in this way is that different observers see different things when they view the same event. This might mean that the ratings will vary from one observer to another. To check the inter-rater reliability of the observations, 51 of the children were rated by two observers working independently and their ratings were compared. The high correlation that was achieved ($r = .89$) showed these observations to be highly reliable, suggesting that the observers were in close agreement about the behaviour of the children.

Procedure

The children were tested individually. In stage one they were taken to the experimental room which was set out for play. One corner was arranged as the child's play area, where there was a table and chair, potato prints and picture stickers, which were all selected as having high interest for these children. The adult model was escorted to the opposite corner where there was a small table, chair, tinker toy, mallet and Bobo (a five-foot inflatable doll). The experimenter then left the room.

In the non-aggressive condition, the model assembled the tinker toys in a quiet, subdued manner, ignoring Bobo. In the aggressive condition the model started to assemble the tinker toys, but after one minute turned to Bobo and was aggressive to the doll in a stylized and distinctive way. The aggression was both physical (for example 'raised the

Bobo doll, picked up the mallet and struck the doll on the head', p. 576), and verbal (for example, 'Pow!', and 'Sock him in the nose', p. 576). After 10 minutes the experimenter returned and took the child to another games room.

In stage two, the child was subjected to 'mild aggression arousal'. The child was taken to a room with attractive toys, but after starting to play with them the child was told that these were the experimenter's very best toys and she had decided to reserve them for the other children.

Then the child was taken to the next room for stage three of the study. The experimenter stayed in the room 'otherwise a number of children would either refuse to remain alone, or would leave before termination of the session'. In this room there was a variety of toys, both non-aggressive (three bears, crayons and so forth) and aggressive toys (for example, a mallet peg board, dart guns, *and* a three-foot Bobo). The child was kept in this room for 20 minutes, and their behaviour was observed by judges through a one-way mirror. Observations were made at five-second intervals giving 240 response units for each child.

The observers recorded three measures of imitation in which they looked for responses from the child that were very similar to the display by the adult model:

(1) imitative for physical aggression;
(2) imitative verbal aggression;
(3) imitative non-aggressive verbal responses.

They also looked at two types of behaviour that were incomplete imitations of the adult model:

(1) mallet aggression;
(2) sits on Bobo.

In addition, they recorded three types of aggressive behaviour that were not imitations of the adult model:

(1) punches Bobo;
(2) non-imitative physical and verbal aggression;
(3) aggressive gun play.

By looking at the results we can consider which children imitated the models, which models they imitated, and whether they showed a general increase in aggressive behaviour rather than a specific imitation of the adult behaviours.

RESULTS

The results are summarised in Table 13.3. They show that:

- the children who saw the aggressive model made more aggressive acts than the children who saw the non-aggressive model;
- boys made more aggressive acts than girls;
- the boys in the aggressive conditions showed more aggression if the model was male than if the model was female;
- the girls in the aggressive conditions also showed more *physical* aggression if the model was male but more *verbal* aggression if the model was female;
- the exception to this general pattern was the observation of how often they punched Bobo, and in this case the effects of gender were reversed.

Table 13.3 Mean aggression scores for experimental and control subjects

| Response category | Experimental groups | | | | Control group |
| | Aggressive | | Non-aggressive | | |
	Female model	Male model	Female model	Male model	
Imitative physical aggression					
Female subjects	5.5	7.2	2.5	0.0	1.2
Male subjects	12.4	25.8	0.2	1.5	2.0
Imitative verbal aggression					
Female subjects	13.7	2.0	0.3	0.0	0.7
Male subjects	4.3	12.7	1.1	0.0	1.7
Mallet aggression					
Female subjects	17.2	18.7	0.5	0.5	13.1
Male subjects	15.5	28.8	18.7	6.7	13.5
Punches Bobo					
Female subjects	6.3	16.5	5.8	4.3	11.7
Male subjects	18.9	11.9	15.6	14.8	15.7
Non-imitative aggression					
Female subjects	21.3	8.4	7.2	1.4	6.1
Male subjects	16.2	36.7	26.1	22.3	24.6
Aggressive gun play					
Female subjects	1.8	4.5	2.6	2.5	3.7
Male subjects	7.3	15.9	8.9	16.7	14.3

Source: Bandura, Ross & Ross (1961)

DISCUSSION

One of the issues commented on by Bandura, Ross and Ross is the affect that the gender of the model had on the children. They noted that the aggression of the female model had a confusing effect on them. For example one of the children said, 'Who is that lady? That's not the way for a lady to behave. Ladies are supposed to act like ladies...' (p. 581), and another child said, 'You should have seen what that girl did in there. She was just acting like a man. I never saw a girl act like that before. She was punching and fighting but no swearing' (p. 581). On the other hand, the aggressive behaviour of the male model fitted more comfortably into a cultural stereotype of appropriate behaviour. For example, one boy said, 'Al's a good socker, he beat up Bobo. I want to sock like Al' (p. 581), and one of the girls said, 'That man is a strong fighter, he punched and punched and he could hit Bobo right down to the floor and if Bobo got up he said, "Punch your nose". He's a good fighter like Daddy' (p. 581).

If we look back at the questions we raised in the background section of this summary, then what can we learn from the study? First, is aggression innate? Like all examples of the nature–nurture debate, it is very hard to get clear evidence one way or the other. This study shows that aggressive behaviour can be learnt, but it does not offer any evidence on the question of whether some features of aggression are also innate. On the issue of male violence, it is worth noting that the children in this study already had an expectation that men will behave more aggressively than women. This was shown by the children's comments.

The second question was how is aggression learnt? Bandura believes that we can learn by being witnesses to the behaviour of others, and his study offers some support for this idea. If this is so, then it would suggest that the regular viewing of violent behaviour on television programmes would encourage the learning of violent behaviour in the viewer. A later variation of the experiment (Bandura, Ross & Ross, 1963) showed the children the violent behaviour on a video rather than in real life, and he found they were still likely to imitate the aggression behaviour towards the Bobo doll.

There are, however, a number of reasons why we should be cautious about making too many connections between this study and the everyday experience of children. For example, we have no evidence about any long-term effects of the study, and also, it is very uncommon for children to be in a situation where they are alone with strangers. Much of their experience will be with people they know who will give their opinions on whatever is going on.

QUESTIONS

1   How is aggression measured in this study?

2   How else could it be measured?

3   What are the three independent variables?

4   What ethical guidelines does Bandura appear to break?

Suggested Answers start at p. 455

KEY WORDS

aggression	model
aggression arousal	nature–nurture debate
behaviourism	observation
Bobo	rating scale
correlation	reinforcement
imitation	reliability
inter-rater reliability	Social Learning Theory
male violence	

14 THE CLASSIC APPROACHES

There are arguably three classic approaches in developmental psychology that represent three very different traditions in psychology. In this chapter we have decided to illustrate each approach with one study, though the influence of all three approaches appears throughout this volume.

One simple classification system of human behaviour and experience is to distinguish between *cognitive, affective* and *behavioural* features. In other words, what we think (cognitive), how we feel (affective) and what we do (behavioural). The most important theorist in the cognitive tradition is Jean Piaget who became interested in how his own children developed their way of interpreting the world. He devised a range of delightful puzzles for children that highlight the unique characteristics of child thought. His approach is not without its critics and the paper we have chosen provides a re-evaluation of some of his tests, and gives a further insight into the way children think and make sense of the world.

The work of Freud gives us some insight into the emotional development of children, and his theories have been very influential on Western culture and social policy during this century. The work of Bowlby (1965) on attachment, for example, is heavily influenced by Freudian theory. In this chapter we have chosen one case study from a number of lengthy studies published by Freud. This illustrates the methods that he used as well as the kind of insights that he offers us.

The third classic approach, covering the behavioural aspects of human development, is provided by Behaviourism. The influence of the behaviourists on psychology as a whole has been far reaching, so it is essential to look at their work. Elsewhere in this book we have summarised studies about the shaping of behaviour (Skinner, 1960, Chapter 5), about behavioural therapists (Lang & Lazovik, 1963, Chapter 11) and about imitative learning from a Social Learning Theory perspective (Bandura, Ross & Ross, 1961, Chapter 13). In this chapter we review a famous study about conditioning a phobia.

I Want a Girl, Just Like the Girl, That Married Dear Old Dad

■ Freud, S. (1909). Analysis of a phobia of a five-year-old boy. In *The Pelican Freud Library* (1977), *Vol 8, Case Histories 1*, pp. 169–306.

Introduction

If you had only heard of one psychologist before you opened this book, it was probably Freud. He has a unique place in the history of psychology and a unique place in the development of ideas in the twentieth century. His work provokes strong opinions both supporting and challenging his theories. In this book it is impossible to do justice to the theories or to represent the arguments for or against them. We will just try to give a flavour of Freud's approach which shows some of the strengths as well as some of the weaknesses.

One of the key themes of Freud's work is the importance of the first few years of life in the subsequent development of personality. He suggested that 'the boy is father to the man', meaning that our experiences in childhood have a crucial effect on our adult personality. He believed that children experience a lot of emotional conflict, and their future adjustment depends on how well these conflicts are resolved. Another theme within Freud's work concerns the *unconscious mind*, which is that part of our mind which we are not aware of. Freud believed that the unconscious contains all manner of unresolved conflicts and has a powerful effect on our behaviour and experience. He argued that many of these conflicts will show up in our fantasies and dreams, but the conflicts are so threatening that they appear in disguised forms, in the shape of symbols.

Freud was a practising therapist who developed his theories from his observations of his patients, and his reflections on his own experience. He wrote the case histories in terms of his recollections and interpretations of the interviews and did not keep complete on-going records.

The study that we have chosen for this book is unusual in two respects. Firstly it is the analysis of a child (Hans), and Freud usually dealt with adults. Secondly, the therapy was carried out by correspondence and interview with the boy's father, rather than with the child himself. The study gives some insight into how Freud viewed child development and how he interpreted the seemingly bizarre imagination of the child.

THE STUDY

The report is written in three parts; (a) the introduction, (b) the case history and analysis, and (c) the conclusions.

(a) Introduction (pp. 169–84)

Freud reports how the analysis was conducted through his conversations and correspondence with Hans' father. He notes that it was the special relationship between father and son that allowed the analysis to progress and for the discussions with the boy to be so detailed and so intimate. The first reports of Hans are when he was 3 years old. At this age he developed a lively interest in his 'widdler' (penis), and also those of other people. On one occasion he asked 'Mummy, have you got a widdler too?'

The parents recorded numerous extracts of conversation with Hans which show his concerns and their attitude towards him. When he was about three years and six months old his mother told him not to touch his widdler or else she would call the doctor to come and cut it off. Around the same time, Hans' mother gave birth to his sister Hanna, and Hans was told that the stork had brought the baby. (It was common at that time – 1906 – to keep children ignorant of information about fertility, and so stories about babies being flown in by giant birds were common lies told to keep children quiet).

Hans expressed jealousy towards his sister though this diminished after a few months. His parents also recorded that Hans had considerable interest in other children, especially girls, and formed emotional attachments with them. Throughout this time, the main theme of his fantasies and dreams was widdlers and widdling.

(b) Case history and analysis (pp. 185–59)

Just before Hans was five, his father wrote to Freud about his son. He described the main problem as follows: 'He is afraid a horse will bite him in the street, and this fear seems somehow connected with his having been frightened by a large penis' (p. 185). From this time on, the father provided Freud with considerable detail of conversations with Hans, and together they tried to make sense of what the boy was experiencing and tried to resolve the fear of the horses. Freud noted that the fear of the horses had developed just after the child had experienced some anxiety dreams about losing his mother, and around the time he had been warned about playing with his widdler. Freud reasoned that the boy, who liked to get into bed with his mother, had a repressed longing for her, and had focused his *libido* (sexual energy) on her.

One month later, the correspondence revealed that the phobia (which Hans refers to as his 'nonsense') was much worse. Hans' father made a connection between the phobia and Hans' interest with his widdler, so he said to him 'If you don't put your hand to your widdler any more, this nonsense of yours'll soon get better' (p. 193).

Hans' anxieties and phobia continued and he was afraid to go out of the house for fear of the horses (note that in the early twentieth century horses were used in many forms of transport including freight carts, buses and cabs). One night, Hans told his father of a dream/ fantasy which his father immediately summarised as follows: 'In the night there was a big giraffe in the room and a crumpled one: and the big one called out because I took the crumpled one away from it. Then it stopped calling out: and I sat down on top of the crumpled one' (p. 199). This dream/fantasy was interpreted by Freud and the father as being a reworking of the morning exchanges in the parental bed. Hans liked to get into his parent's bed in the morning but his father often objected (the big giraffe calling out because he had taken the crumpled giraffe – mother – away). Both Freud and the father wondered about the significance of the giraffe and whether the long neck was a symbol for the large adult penis, but Hans rejected this idea.

Hans was taken to see Freud, who asked him about the horses he was frightened of. Freud was interested by certain aspects of the description, for example the black bits around the mouth. He reasoned that the horse was a symbol for his father, and the black bits were a moustache. After the interview, the father recorded an exchange with Hans where the boy said 'Daddy, don't trot away from me!' (p. 207); bear in mind that we are dealing with an English translation from the original German text which makes some idioms sound rather odd.

Hans' fear of horses developed and he became particularly frightened about them falling over. He described an incident where he witnessed this happening (later verified by his mother). Throughout this analysis the parents continued to record copious examples of dialogue and the father asked many leading questions to help the boy discover the root of his fear. For example:

Father: When the horse fell down did you think of your daddy?
Hans: Perhaps. Yes. It's possible.
(p. 213).

Hans started to develop a particular interest in toilet functions, especially 'lumf' (a German word denoting faeces). Hans had long discussions with his father about lumf, the birth of his sister, the colour of his mother's underwear and his liking for going into the toilet with his mother or the maid. He also describes his imaginary friend called Lodi who he had named after 'saffalodi' a German sausage. Hans' father pointed out to the child that the sausage looked a little like lumf, and Hans agreed.

During this period the fear of the horses declined and two final fantasies marked a change in Hans and an apparent resolution of his conflicts. First, he described a fantasy where he was married to his mother and was playing with his own children. In this fantasy he had promoted his father to the role of grandfather. In the second fantasy, he described how a plumber came and first removed his bottom and widdler and then gave him another one of each, but larger.

(c) Discussion (pp. 260–303)

Freud divided his discussion of the case to offer three points of view:

(i) Support for his Theory of Sexuality   Freud believed that children could provide valuable evidence, writing 'I do not share the view... that assertions made by children are invariably arbitrary and untrustworthy' (p. 261). He saw the conversations with Hans as providing powerful support for his view that children have an interest in sexual matters from a very early age. In particular, the case study provided support for his theory of the *Oedipus complex* in which the young boy wishes his father will go away so that he can have exclusive intimacy with his mother. Freud believed that much of Hans' problem came from the conflict caused by this desire. The final fantasy of being married to his mother supported this idea.

(ii) The Nature of Phobias   Freud noted that 'Little Hans' parents were determined from the very beginning of his illness that he was neither to be laughed at or bullied, but that access must be obtained to his repressed wishes by means of psychoanalysis' (p. 275). This appears to have been a successful strategy, though Freud wrote that therapeutic success was not the primary aim. The main aim of the therapy was to allow Hans to gain conscious control of his unconscious wishes, to undergo a journey of self discovery.

Freud referred to Hans' recollection of seeing a horse fall down and reasoned that this event alone was not enough to explain the development of the phobia, even though it became the focus for his various anxieties. The real causes of phobias lie in the hidden conflicts of the unconscious mind. The implications of this line of thinking are far-reaching, particularly with regard to potential treatment. It would not be enough, in Freud's opinion, to treat the fear of horses directly, for this would only be tinkering with the symptoms of a deeper problem. One may be able to get rid of horse phobia by, say, a behavioural treatment, but *symptom substitution* would most likely occur, and the unconscious conflicts would simply manifest themselves in another form. It is worth contrasting Freud's ideas with the behavioural approach to treating phobias (Lang & Lazovik, 1963, Chapter 11 of this volume).

(iii) Views on Life and Children   Freud starts this last section of the report by contesting the idea, inescapable in the reader, that Hans is in some way a very strange child. He points out that Hans was able to express fears and wishes that many children do not have the opportunity to articulate, and as a result had been able to resolve conflicts that would remain unresolved in other children. Freud notes that there is no sharp distinction between the neurotic and the normal, and that many people constantly pass between normal and neurotic states. He goes on to make some comments about education, suggesting that (in his time) it was largely concerned with controlling people rather than encouraging self-awareness. He suggests that psychoanalysis would be one way of helping someone to become '... a civilised and useful member of society' (p. 303).

Postscript

Thirteen years after the case study was published, 'Little Hans', at 19 years old, appeared at Freud's consulting room. He declared that he was fit and well and had suffered no troubles during adolescence. He had no recollection of the discussions with his father, and described how when he read his case history it 'came to him as something unknown' (p. 304).

EVALUATION

It is difficult not to be intrigued by this case study but it is equally difficult not to be sceptical about some of the reasoning made by Freud and Hans' father. We will leave you to draw your own conclusions, though we do recommend that if you find the study at all interesting then you should read more of the case studies that appear in the collected writings of Freud. *The Pelican Freud Library* is a good place to start.

The case study of little Hans raises a number of issues that still provide some controversy today:

(a) Reliability of Child Evidence   Freud had no trouble in accepting the evidence of a child, and suggested that children are no more likely to tell lies than adults. This idea was not acceptable at the time, and it is only very recently that the evidence of children has been given much weight in situations such as police inquiries and court proceedings.

(b) Disturbed Behaviour should be Treated rather than Controlled   Freud notes in the study that Hans' father asked him to emphasise the severity of Hans' symptoms so that readers of the study would not think that Hans should just have been given a 'sound thrashing' to solve his problem. We still have the debate today about whether children should be punished or helped for bad behaviour. Many people favour the 'help' approach (until *their* car is stolen, of course).

(c) Sexuality of Children   Freud sees Hans' talk about sexual and bodily matters as reflecting his perfectly normal interest and emotional involvement in these things. This was not a commonly held view at the time, though it is something that we are more likely to accept today.

When you read the report it is hard not to smile at some of the comments made by Hans, and the way they were dealt with by his father. For example, Hans had played happily for many months with his 'imaginary friend' Lodi, but his father discovered the source of the name (sausage, see above) and suggested that this sausage looked like lumf. His father was telling Hans that his imaginary friend was really a turd!

QUESTIONS

1   How do you think people show their unconscious wishes in their behaviour?

2   What criticisms can you make of Freud's method of collecting data?

3   What differences are there between the attitudes of Hans' parents and the attitudes of parents today?

4   Freud comments that education was largely concerned with controlling people rather than encouraging self-awareness. How has education changed from Freud's time compared to today?

Suggested Answers start at p. 455

KEY WORDS

case history
dreams
libido
lumf
Oedipus complex
personality
phobia

psychoanalysis
repression
self discovery
sexuality
symbols
therapist
unconscious mind

Piaget's Cognitive Approach

■ Samuel, J. & Bryant, P. (1984). Asking only one question in the conservation experiment. *Journal of Child Psychology and Psychiatry, 25,* 315–18.

Introduction

How do children think? Are their thought processes just a scaled down version of adult thought processes, or are they altogether different? Swiss psychologist Jean Piaget (that's Jean as in French for 'John') carried out some remarkable studies on children that had a powerful influence on our theories of child thought (see for example, Piaget, 1952). He argued that children's thinking is qualitatively different from the thinking of adults. For readable and interesting introductions to Piaget's work we suggest you try Donaldson (1978) and Boden (1979).

Piaget's theory of cognitive development suggests that children develop their ability to think through a series of *maturational* stages. In brief the child progresses through the:

(a) *Sensory Motor Stage* (birth to around 18 months), during which the child is learning to match their senses (what they see and hear, and so forth) to what they can do.
(b) *Pre-operational Stage* (18 months to about 7 years), during which the child is learning to use symbolism (and language in particular), and is developing some general rules about mental operations.
(c) *Concrete Operational Stage* (7 to around 12 years), during which the child is able to use some sophisticated mental operations but is still limited in a number of ways; for example, the concrete operational child tends to think about the world in terms of how it is, and finds it hard to speculate on how it might be.
(d) *Formal Operational Stage* (12 years and above), which is the most sophisticated stage of thinking and is mainly governed by formal logic.

Piaget said that the different quality of thought in these stages can be seen in the errors which children make with certain problems. He devised a number of ingenious tests of child thought to illustrate this different style of thinking. The most famous of these tests concern the pre-operational stage. In this stage Piaget said that children's thought has the following features:

(i)   they are unable to *conserve*. For example, they do not appreciate that if you change the shape of an object it keeps the same mass;

(ii) they are unable to *reverse* mental operations. If they have seen some action take place they can not mentally 'rewind the tape';

(iii) they rely on their *intuitions* about what they can see rather than what they can reason;

(iv) they are perceptually *egocentric*, finding it difficult to imagine a view from any other viewpoint than their own.

An example of one of Piaget's tests is carried out with some Plasticine or child's modelling clay. The child is shown two lumps of Plasticine the same shape and size. The adult asks, 'Which one is bigger?' and the child replies 'They're both the same'. Then, in full view of the child, the adult rolls out one of the lumps of plasticine into a sausage shape. The adult now asks the same question and many pre-operational children answer, 'The sausage is bigger'. Piaget believes that the child does not realise that the mass of the object stays constant (conserved) even though its shape has changed. If children at this developmental stage were able to 'rewind the tape' of the adult rolling out the clay, if they were able to reverse the adult's actions in their minds, they would realise that the Plasticine was still the same size. Because they cannot conserve and cannot mentally reverse the process, the children use their intuition to answer the question. One of the pieces of Plasticine *looks* bigger than the other, so they answer that it *is* bigger than the other.

The Plasticine example is a test of conservation of mass. Piaget used other tasks to explore number and volume conservation. Number conservation tasks involve lining up two rows of buttons. The rows have the same number of buttons each, and are of equal length, so that each button in one row is directly opposite and level with a button in the other row. The child is asked whether there are more buttons in one row or the other. The experimenter then bunches up one of the rows without removing any buttons. The child is asked again whether there are more buttons in one row than in the other. The child who cannot conserve number answers that the longer row now has more buttons.

Volume conservation tasks are done with two identical beakers each with exactly the same amount of fluid in them. The child is asked if one beaker has more fluid in than the other, or if they contain the same amount. The fluid from one beaker is then poured into a taller, thinner beaker (or into a shorter, fatter beaker), again without removing any of the liquid. The child is asked the conservation question again, and the non-conserving child answers that there is now more (or less) fluid in the different shaped beaker.

The work of Piaget captured the imagination of developmental psychology and many students mounted expeditions to primary schools armed with Plasticine, counters and beakers to try out Piaget's tests. In the 1960s and the 1970s, these tests were thought to give real insight into the qualities and limitations of child thought. However, from the late 1970s onwards, there has been a growing body of evidence that suggests that Piaget's methods led to underestimation of the cognitive abilities of children.

THE STUDY

Samuel and Bryant devised their study to see whether children could really conserve after all, and whether the results that people usually obtain when they carry out one of Piaget's tests are due to the structure of the test rather than the limitation of child thought. They were particularly concerned with the way in which the traditional conservation task involved asking the child the same question twice. The traditional Piagetian procedure would start with a question like 'is there more Plasticine in this lump or in this lump or are they the same size?' to which the child would answer 'they're the same size'. The experimenter would then deliberately alter the experimental materials in full view of the child (perhaps rolling one of the lumps into a sausage), and then repeat the first question. Now there are all sorts of reasons for suspecting that some children might interpret this whole procedure as meaning that the experimenter wants them to give a different answer to the question when it is asked for the second time. One such reason (you might think of others) has to do with the fact that children are only usually asked the same question twice when they have got the answer wrong the first time. So repeating the question might be leading the child to believe that 'they're the same size' was the wrong answer. In short, Samuel and Bryant were concerned that the failure of some children on the conservation task might be more to do with the *demand characteristics* of the research procedure (see Orne, 1962, Chapter 21 of this volume) than failure to reason logically.

For this reason, they designed a study in which half of their sample of children were only asked the conservation question once, after the materials had been altered by the experimenter. The other half of the sample were asked the conservation question twice, as in the standard Piagetian procedure. If, as they hypothesised, the 'one question' group of children tended to give more correct responses on the task than the 'two question' children, this would suggest that their concerns about demand characteristics were warranted.

Subjects

The subjects were 252 children from Devon, England, between the ages of five years and 8 years, 6 months (8; 6). The sample was divided into four age groups of 63 children each. The mean ages of the four groups were (i) 5;3 (ii) 6;3 (iii) 7;3 and (iv) 8;3.

Design

The main independent variable of interest was manipulated across three conditions:

(1) *Standard.* They carried out the conservation task in the way that Piaget described, asking the children about the size of the objects before and after the shape was changed.
(2) *One judgement.* In this condition they only asked the children about the size (or number, or volume) of the objects after the transformation.
(3) *Fixed-array control.* In this condition the children just saw the objects after they had been changed, and not before.

Children from each age group were allocated to one of the three conditions, giving an independent measures design (each child only performed in one of the conditions), with equal average ages across the three conditions.

The researchers carried out mass, number, and volume conservation tasks with each child. Each child was given four trials with each type of task, and the order of the tasks was systematically varied between the children.

RESULTS

The researchers recorded whether the children made an error in judgement on any of the tasks. An error was recorded when they said that one lump was bigger than the other, or one row had more counters than the other, or one glass had more liquid than the other. The results are summarised in Table 14.1 and Table 14.2. The data of Table 14.1 are shown graphically in Figure 14.1.

The researchers carried out a number of sophisticated statistical tests and drew the following conclusions:

(a) *Age*: there was a significant difference between every age group. Each group of children made fewer errors than all the groups that were younger than them.

(b) *Conditions*: the children made significantly fewer errors on the one judgement task than on the other two tasks. The children also made significantly fewer errors on the standard task than the fixed-array task.

(c) *Materials*: the children made fewer errors on the number task than on the other two tasks.

Table 14.1 Mean errors of judgement for all the tests
(maximum possible error = 12, minimum possible error = 0)

	Experimental condition		
Age	Standard	One judgement	Fixed array
5 years	8.5	7.3	8.6
6 years	5.7	4.3	6.4
7 years	3.2	2.6	4.9
8 years	1.7	1.3	3.3

Source: Samuel & Bryant (1984)

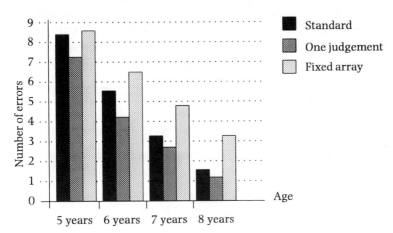

Figure 14.1 *Average number of errors made by the children (maximum possible error = 12, minimum possible error = 0)*

Table 14.2   Mean errors of judgement for all ages
(maximum possible error = 4, minimum possible error = 0)

Test	Experimental condition		
	Standard	One judgement	Fixed array
Mass	1.5	1.2	1.7
Number	1.5	1.0	1.5
Volume	1.8	1.6	2.5

Source: Samuel & Bryant (1984)

DISCUSSION

The study confirms Piaget's observation that children will make errors in the conservation tasks he devised. However, the study also shows that children will make fewer errors in these tasks if the procedure is changed slightly. This shows that the reason for at least some of the errors is to do with the task itself rather than the way children think. Samuel and Bryant conclude that the important question is not whether children possess an intellectual skill, but how and when they decide to apply that skill.

The studies by Samuel and Bryant and other researchers that challenge the original theories of Piaget are sometimes described as having refuted Piaget's ideas. This is very far from the case, for basic insights from Piaget still hold good. Children have different thought processes to adults and these can be seen in the errors they make in cognitive tasks. In the above study, the children made conservation errors in all the conditions, and the frequency of these errors reduced with age. But one message that Samuel and Bryant's work leaves us with is the importance of paying close attention to the details of research procedures, for even minor alterations can have an effect on the results.

QUESTIONS

1   What do developmental psychologists mean by conservation?

2   Why do adults have problems carrying out studies on child thought?

3   Piaget believes that adult thought is very logical. Give some examples of adult thought that are not logical.

Suggested Answers start at p. 456

KEY WORDS

concrete operational stage
conservation
demand characteristics
egocentrism
formal operational stage

intuitive thought
maturation
pre-operational stage
reversibility
sensory-motor stage

THE TALE OF LITTLE ALBERT

■ WATSON, J.B. & RAYNER, R. (1920). Conditioned emotional reactions.
Journal of Experimental Psychology, 3, 1–14.

INTRODUCTION

Can fear be taught? This was the main question behind this study by Watson and Rayner. They wanted to demonstrate that behaviourist theory could be applied to humans. The study is usually described by referring to the concept of classical conditioning developed by the Russian physiologist, Ivan Pavlov. Pavlov studied the salivation response in dogs and noticed that food in the mouth will stimulate salivation. This natural link between *stimulus* and *response* is called a reflex. Pavlov presented his dogs with a neutral stimulus (such as a bell) before putting the food in their mouths. After this had been repeated a few times the dogs began to associate the bell with the arrival of the food and would salivate to the sound of the bell: they had learnt a new *stimulus–response (s–r) relationship* (see Figure 14.2). Pavlov and Watson believed that a lot of human learning could be explained in terms of learnt s–r relationships, and the study described below is often cited as an illustration of this.

Watson and Rayner were specifically interested in whether our emotional responses can be conditioned using the principles outlined above. The idea is that by the time we are adults we have a very complex repertoire of emotional responses which can be elicited by all sorts of stimuli. Watson and Rayner believed that these complex s–r relationships are built upon a few basic unconditioned ones, through the processes of classical conditioning . Their study, which is one of the most famous (or perhaps infamous) in the history of psychology, involved conditioning an infant to respond with fear to the sight of a rat. In this case, they used the unconditioned response of fear to a loud noise.

THE STUDY

Subjects

The subject of this investigation was an infant named Albert B. Little Albert (as he is now popularly known) was the son of a wet nurse in a

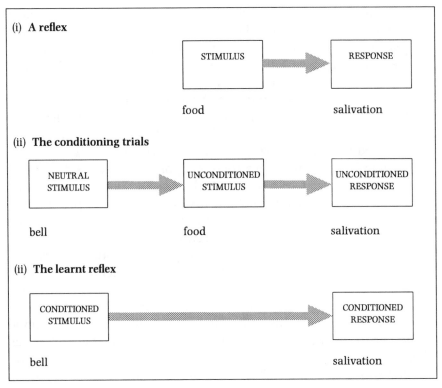

Figure 14.2 *Classical conditioning*

children's home, and was nine months old at the beginning of the study. 'He was on the whole stolid and unemotional. His stability was one of the principle reasons for using him as a subject in this test' (p. 1).

Design

This was a single-case laboratory experiment which took place over approximately four months. Baseline behavioural observations were made in the first phase of the study. A 'treatment' phase followed, and subsequent behavioural observations were made to assess the effects of the treatment.

Procedure

At nine months of age, Albert was tested with various stimuli to examine whether or not he exhibited a fear in response to them. Some of the neutral stimuli that were used at this stage were a white rat, a rabbit, a dog, a monkey, masks with and without hair, cotton wool and burning newspapers. They were demonstrably 'neutral' stimuli since none of them elicited anything like a fear response from the child. In fact, Albert's most common response was to play with the objects.

The unconditioned stimulus which Watson and Rayner used in the baseline phase of the study was the sound made by striking a four-foot steel bar with a hammer, just behind the child. Naturally this sudden noise caused the child to cry, presumably through fear. At the age of eleven months and three days the conditioning process started. The white rat was presented to Albert. As he reached out to touch it 'the bar was struck immediately behind his head' (p. 4). The process was repeated once on the first day, and a further five times one week later. The conditioning was 'topped-up' with two more pairings 17 days later.

Twelve days after the first treatment a variety of stimuli were presented to Albert in order to examine the effects of generalisation. These included his toy blocks, a rabbit, a dog, a fur coat and cotton wool. These were presented to Albert periodically during the next few sessions. The white rat was also presented periodically without the sound of the bar to test the extent and duration of the initial conditioning. Observations of the child's behaviour were made in the form of laboratory notes for each session. The results of the study are presented in the form of excerpts from these notes.

RESULTS

The following are excerpts from the laboratory notes cited in the paper.

First treatment session

White rat suddenly taken from the basket and presented to Albert. He began to reach for rat with left hand. Just as his hand touched the animal the bar was struck immediately behind his head. The infant jumped violently and fell forward, burying his face in the mattress. He did not cry, however.
(p. 4)

Just as the right hand touched the rat the bar was again struck. Again the infant jumped violently, fell forward and began to whimper.
(p. 4)

Second treatment session (7 days after first)

> When the rat nosed the infant's left hand, the hand was suddenly withdrawn...It is thus seen that the two joint stimulations given the previous week were not without effect.
> (p. 4)

> Joint stimulation with rat and sound. Started, then fell over immediately to right side. No crying.
> (p. 4)

> Rat suddenly presented alone. Puckered face, whimpered and withdrew body sharply to the left.
> (p. 5)

Third treatment session (12 days after first)

> Blocks... offered. Played readily with them, smiling and gurgling.
> (p. 5)

> Rat alone. Leaned over to left side as far away as possible, then fell over....
> (p. 6)

> Rabbit alone. The rabbit was suddenly placed on the mattress in front of him. The reaction was pronounced. Negative responses began at once. He leaned as far away from the animal as possible, whimpered, then burst into tears.
> (p. 6)

> Dog alone. The dog did not produce as violent a reaction as the rabbit. The moment fixation occurred the child shrank back...(p.6).

> [The cotton wool] was placed on his feet. He kicked it away but did not touch it with his hands.
> (p. 7)

Fourth treatment session (17 days after first)

> Rat alone...The response was much less marked than on the first presentation the previous week. It was thought best to freshen up the reaction by another joint stimulation...Just as the rat was placed on his hand the rod was struck. Reaction violent.
> (p. 7)

Rabbit alone. Leaned over to left side as far as possible. Did not fall over. Began to whimper but reaction not as violent as on former occasions. (p. 7)

On this same day... Albert was taken into a large well-lighted lecture room belonging to the laboratory... The situation was thus very different from that which obtained in the small dark room. (pp. 8–9)

Rat alone. No sudden fear reaction appeared at first. The hands, however, were held up and away from the animal. (p. 9)

Follow up session (1 month and 18 days after first treatment)

Santa Claus mask. Withdrawal, gurgling, then slapped at it without touching. When his hand was forced to touch it, he whimpered and cried. (p. 10)

Fur coat. Wrinkled his nose and withdrew both hands, drew back his whole body and began to whimper as the coat was put nearer. (p. 11)

Blocks. He began to play with them as usual. (p. 11)

The rat... touched his hand. Albert withdrew immediately, then leaned back as far as possible but did not cry. (p. 11)

DISCUSSION

Albert's behaviour as recorded by Watson and Rayner does suggest that emotional responses to stimuli can be learnt. Before conditioning, Albert was not afraid of the white rat; after conditioning (comprising seven pairings of noise and rat) he did appear to be afraid of it. The learnt emotional response generalised to stimuli which had a similar appearance to the white rat, such as cotton wool, a rabbit, and a Santa Claus mask. The conditioned emotional responses were maintained for over one month.

The study is cited very widely in psychological literature despite it being based on the evidence from one case. Interestingly, it is often incorrectly reported in many text books with some adding a happy ending by suggesting that Albert's fear was deconditioned by Watson and Rayner. Harris (1979) reviewed the various descriptions of this study that appear in the psychological literature and suggested that the story of Little Albert has developed like a myth with each generation of psychologists retelling the story to illustrate their own position.

Needless to say, the work carried out by Watson and Rayner would be quite unacceptable today. They intentionally caused their subject, a very young infant at that, to become distressed. The matter of fact recording of observations like Albert jumping violently and burying his face in the mattress show a curious detachment from what was clearly an upsetting experience for the child, and from what should have been an upsetting experience for the researchers. Their argument that Albert was sufficiently stable emotionally to withstand the procedures with no lasting effect is not convincing, especially in the light of their argument in another part of the paper that '[conditioned emotional responses] persist and modify personality throughout life' (p. 12). Furthermore, Albert left the hospital before any therapeutic strategies could be used to remove the conditioned emotional response.

A sensible evaluation of the study must take into account its historical and cultural context. We must bear in mind that at the beginning of the 20th century there may have been a much greater faith than exists today in the capacity of science to provide answers to societies' problems. Maybe Watson and Rayner believed that a greater good would come out of this child's distress, in terms of improved insights into the important issue of human learning, and in terms of developing treatments for people who show extreme and irrational emotional behaviour.

QUESTIONS

1   Why did the experimenters move Albert to a different room in the fourth session?

2   What behavioural strategy might the authors have used to reverse the conditioning which had occurred?

3   Watson and Raynor's methods were unacceptable by today's standards. What methods could we use instead to study things such as phobias?

Suggested Answers start at p. 456

KEY WORDS

baseline measures	reflex
behaviourism	single-case experiment
classical conditioning	stimulus–response (s–r) relationships
generalisation	treatment phase
learning	unconditioned stimulus
neutral stimulus	

15 COMMUNICATION

Communication is a basic feature of all living things. Human beings love to communicate and devise all manner of ways to get messages from one person to another. We also communicate in a lot of unconscious ways, and pass messages about our *intentions*, our *attitudes*, and our *emotions*. We even invent communications with things that can't respond, like trees or our cars. The basic ingredients of communication are a sender, a message and a receiver, though it is worth noting that the message which the sender sends is often not the same as the message the receiver receives.

Human beings are arguably unique in possessing the ability to communicate with language (though see the article by Gardner and Gardner, Chapter 5 of this volume, on language development in chimpanzees). This language is able to produce an infinite number of messages, convey abstract ideas and refer to events that took place years ago and in other parts of the world. These features distinguish *language* from *communication* which usually has a simple message that is located in this place and at this time. Imagine a type of non-verbal communication that says 'I loved you last Thursday fortnight but I feel a bit iffy about you today'. Your non-verbal communication cannot convey messages with this degree of precision, but your language can.

So, a major question that has occupied developmental psychologists concerns how children learn the quite remarkable skill of language. As with most other areas of psychology, the nature–nurture debate has been played out in relation to language acquisition. Skinner and Chomsky represent the two opposing standpoints, with Skinner asserting that language is *learnt* (the 'nurture' position) and Chomsky arguing for an *innate* linguistic capacity. The first two studies reported in this chapter reinforce the common-sense notion that right from birth (and probably from before birth), the human skill of language emerges out of a potent *mixture* of biological potential (nature) and social context (nurture). The studies look at how language is mixed in with other communication skills such as movement and rhythm, and how we are able to adjust our language when we are talking to infants.

One political battleground in this field has been the area of educational performance and language style. An argument developed during the 1960s about the quality of language spoken in different social classes, with the basic proposition being that the standard English of the upper and middle classes is a superior form of language and conveys messages of greater sophistication than working-class talk. In order to highlight this important issue we have described one piece of the influential work of the sociolinguist Labov, who refutes these notions of linguistic superiority.

The Dance of the Neonates

■ Condon, W.S. & Sander, L.W. (1974). Neonate movement is synchronized with adult speech: Interactional participation and language acquisition.
Science, 183, 99–101.

Introduction

In the 1960s and 1970s, W.S. Condon and Adam Kendon started to publish work on non-verbal behaviour and 'interactional synchrony' (see for example, Condon & Ogston, 1966, and Kendon, 1970). Their intriguing empirical work was suggesting that the body movements of interacting people are synchronised in an extraordinarily complex way. Furthermore, they claimed that these body movements are coordinated with the rhythms of speech. The notion of interactional synchrony became a controversial issue in the literature of developmental psychology when Condon and Sander published the paper that is summarised here, claiming that the same sorts of synchronies between speech and non-verbal behaviour could be detected even in new-born babies.

The Study

The study is based on a microanalysis of sound films of new-born babies ('neonates') who were either being spoken to directly, or who were being played tape-recordings of adult human speech and other kinds of sounds. The authors were interested in whether the movements of new-born babies are synchronised with speech sounds in the same way that adults' movements seem to be. They cite evidence from Condon & Ogston (1966) that adult speakers coordinate their movements with their own speech (so called 'self-synchrony'), and that listeners coordinate their movements with the speech of speakers ('interactional synchrony'). Furthermore, they cite evidence from Condon & Brosin (see Condon & Brosin, 1969) that people with disorders such as aphasia, autism and schizophrenia display 'marked self-asynchronies' (in other words a *lack* of coordination between their own speech and movement).

Condon and Sander's claim is that the coordination of speech and movement is so *fine-grained* that it happens at a level well beyond our normal conscious awareness. This is why the frame-by-frame analysis (a systematic microanalysis) of a permanent audio-visual record is necessary. The sound-film that the authors used yields 30 frames of film *per second*, and the detailed examination of these frames, going backwards and forwards again and again over the same short sequences, allows for the identification of complex features of behaviour and speech which we simply cannot perceive in real time.

The paper actually presents the findings of six studies, but for the purposes of this summary they will be treated as one.

Subjects

Sixteen neonates were studied. Fourteen of these babies were between 12 to 48 hours old, and two were 14 days old.

Design

This study is an example of a systematic and highly structured observation. The authors characterise their method as a 'frame-by-frame microanalysis of sound films' (p. 99), whereby very brief sequences of audio-visual records are inspected in great detail. Since the film record provides 30 frames per second, the observational analysis can be fine-grained. The study was designed in order to examine the relationships between human speech sounds and babies' movements.

Procedure

A total of approximately five hours of sound film was collected from the 16 participating babies, of which approximately one hour was suitable for analysis given that each baby spent large periods of time asleep! Fourteen of the neonates were filmed whilst laying in their crib, and two were held. The infants were filmed in a variety of contexts, including:

(1) being spoken to directly by an adult male speaking US English;
(2) being played an audio tape of an adult male speaking US English;
(3) being played an audio tape of disconnected vowel sounds;
(4) being played an audio tape of tapping sounds;
(5) being played an audio tape of an adult speaking Chinese.

Short sequences of the sound-film of each infant were inspected frame-by-frame, again and again. Changes in the direction and speed of movements of all the infant's moving body parts were recorded. Particularly crucial to the reported analysis was the identification of the frame numbers which marked changes in direction or speed of any of the moving body parts. The audio record was also 'segmented' in this fashion and frame numbers which marked speech boundaries between phonemes (the component sounds of speech), syllables and words were identified. The extent to which changes of direction and speed in the movement of body parts coincided with speech boundaries was recorded and is summarised in the results section below.

RESULTS

Table 15.1 shows the way in which 93 per cent of the changes in speed and direction of movement of baby E's body parts corresponded with the boundaries of speech segments within a 30 second period (892 frames of film). The much lower level of agreement between the movements of baby C and the sound track of the adult talking to baby E are shown in the row labelled 'study 3' (the authors confusingly refer to their different analyses as different 'studies'). This suggests that this correspondence of movement and speech segments for baby E was not just happening by chance.

Table 15.2 shows how 87 per cent of changes in speed and direction of baby A's movements coincided with the boundaries of speech

Table 15.1 Correspondence of infant movements with live speech

Study	Total frames	Total discrepancies	Agreement (%)	Estimated range of agreement*
1	892	65	93	91.3–94.5
2	336	21	94	90.7–96.4
3	336	119	65	59.0–70.0

Baby E's motion segmentation was compared with the speech segmentation of the adult for the total sequence (study 1) and for the first 336 frames only (study 2). In study 3, baby C's motion segmentation during 336 frames of silence was compared to the first 336 frames of speech segmentation on the sound track of baby E
* This column gives, for $p = .025$, the maximum risks of overestiming the lower limit and of underestimating the upper limit for random samples having the percentage of misses in studies 1 to 3.
Source: Condon & Sander (1974)

Table 15.2   Correspondence of infant movements with recorded speech and non-speech sounds

Study	Sound	Baby	Total occurrences	Total discrepancies	Agreement (%)
4	Speech (word boundaries)	A	146	19	87
5	Disconnected vowels	E	167	97	42
		C	124	51	59
6	Tapping sounds	E	27	15	44
		C	34	16	53

Source: Condon & Sander (1974)

segments from the tape recorded adult speaker. Note the much lower levels of synchronisation between the movements of babies C and E, and disconnected vowel and tapping sounds.

Condon and Sander's original illustration of synchronised speech and movement is reproduced in Figure 15.1. The figure should be read from left to right and downwards rather like a musical stave. The speech is transcribed above each section of the figure ('come over an' see who's over here'), and is split into speech segments along the row headed 'phonetics'. Each line in the figure represents one body part moving, and the arrows denote when there is any change in speed or direction of movement in that body part. Note that the arrows occur at the boundaries of the speech segments (which are marked on the first 'stave' by vertical lines).

DISCUSSION

The results show that the movement of the new-born babies was synchronised with adult speech sounds. That is, changes in direction and speed of moving body parts occurred precisely in coordination with the speech segments that the researchers had identified. The synchronisation appeared to be just as strong when an unfamiliar language was played. Much lower levels of synchronisation of movement were observed with ordinary rhythmic tapping sounds and with disjointed spoken vowel sounds. This seems to suggest that babies, at birth, are somehow tuned into the sounds and structure of normal adult speech. Perhaps we are born *prepared* in this way for the learning of *any* language.

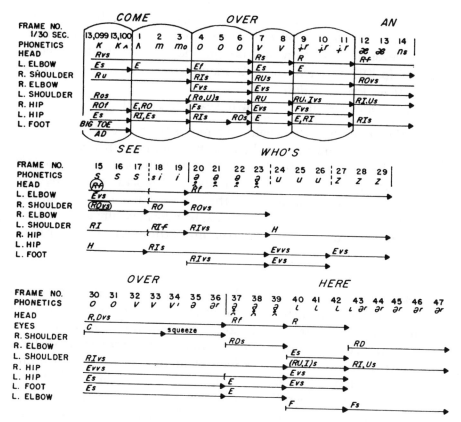

Figure 15.1 *Frame by frame microanalysis of sound and movement*
Two-day-old neonate moving synchronously with adult speaking, 'Come over an see who's over here.' The transcription read vertically shows that the infant's configurations of movement coincide with the articulatory segments of the adult's speech. Definition of descriptive notation: *F*, forward or flex (depending on body part); *H*, hold; *D*, down; *E*, extend; *C*, close; *RI*, rotate inward; *RO*, rotate outward; *AD*, adduct; and *U*, up. Lower case letters refer to speed: *s*, slight; *f*, fast; and *vs*, very slight.
Source: Condon & Sander (1974)

The authors are very clear that they have not simply observed 'responses' on the part of the infants to the 'stimulus' of adult speech. They argue for a much more sophisticated understanding of communication which focuses on the enmeshment of interactions between babies and adults; a kind of interactional ballet. For example, they observed that the synchronies appear between speech and movement *when the baby is already moving*. This suggests that the speech sounds are not 'causing' the baby to move, and that the interactions that they have studied must themselves be understood as part of a 'more macroscopic level of regulation and organization of the infant–caretaker system' (p. 101). As such, the authors are clearly operating within an *interactional level of analysis*.

They conclude with the following exciting speculation:

> If the infant, from the beginning, moves in precise, shared rhythm with the organization of the speech structure of his [sic] culture, then he participates developmentally through complex, sociobiological entrainment processes in millions of repetitions of linguistic forms long before he later uses them in speaking and communicating. By the time he learns to speak, he may have already laid down within himself the form and structure of the language system of his culture.
>
> (p. 101)

But before we get too carried away with the seductive qualities of this research it is important to bear in mind that Condon and Sander's findings remain controversial. Work on interactional synchrony has been criticised on a number of grounds (see Rosenfeld, 1981, for a useful critique of the literature). Some claim that the methods of frame-by-frame microanalysis are not sufficiently reliable (it is difficult for observers to agree when the changes in speed and direction of movement in a body part actually occur; McDowall, 1978a), and that the levels of synchrony reported by Condon and Sander occur so infrequently that they can be attributed to chance factors (if enough body parts are moving for enough of the time that someone is speaking, then some of them will inevitably fall at the boundaries of speech segments; see McDowall, 1978b).

It is certainly the case that Condon and Sander did not provide an exhaustive account of their methods in this article. For example, it is evident that they were highly selective in choosing which sequences of analysed film they reported. But their methods and ideas have received support from a number of quarters (see for example, Austin & Peery, 1983, and Gatewood & Rosenwein, 1981) and the work remains intriguing and highly suggestive.

QUESTIONS

1   Why are the authors especially interested in the finding that there is 'a synchronisation of infant movement organization with the articulatory segments of adult speech *as early as the first day of life*'? (p. 99; emphasis added).

2   Why is it so essential in this study to have a film record of the infants' movements?

3   What is the significance of the comparisons they made between US English speech sounds, Chinese speech sounds, disconnected vowel sounds and tapping sounds?

4   Why did they use taped speech sounds some of the time?

5   Two of the infants were held in one of the studies that the authors report: what problems might this cause in terms of interpreting results obtained from these two children?

Suggested Answers start at p. 457

KEY WORDS

aphasia
asynchrony
autism
interactional level of analysis
interactional synchrony

language
microanalysis
neonate
schizophrenia

LISTEN WITH MOTHER

■ FERNALD, A. (1985). Four-month-old infants prefer to
listen to motherese.
Infant Behavior and Development, 8, 181–95.

INTRODUCTION

When adults talk to babies, they talk in a different way from how they
talk to adults. They tend to adopt a tone of voice and style of expression
which has been somewhat misleadingly labelled 'motherese'. The label
is misleading since all adults seem to talk in this way to babies, not just
their mothers. Motherese is characterised by relatively high pitched
speech, and varied and exaggerated intonation; adult-to-adult speech
tends to be lower in pitch, and more monotonous. It has been suggested
that motherese actually plays an important role in the infant's development of language (Snow, 1979). Among other things, it is more interesting to the baby than adult-to-adult (or 'adult-directed') speech, and so
engages their attention for longer. Presumably, the more a baby focuses
on language, the more opportunity there is for learning. Fernald's study
set out to discover whether babies prefer listening to motherese than to
normal adult talk. If they do, this would give some support to the suggestion that motherese enhances the interactions between adults and
infants.

It is not easy to find out what a baby likes listening to, because it is
very difficult to tell exactly what a baby *is* listening to at any given
moment in time. Babies do not have to move their heads in the direction
of a sound in order to attend to it. One way of tackling this problem is
to use *operant techniques* (for a description of these techniques see the
study by Skinner, Chapter 5 of this volume). With operant techniques
the baby has to do something to make a particular sound occur. Fernald cites Glenn & Cunningham's (1983) work in which babies had to
learn to operate a switch which allowed them to listen to either one of
two possible sounds. Once they had learnt the basic skill, a measure of
preference could be obtained by observing how long they spent listening to each sound.

The Study

Fernald used a variation on this operant theme. She placed the infants in a room with one loudspeaker on each of the side walls. Out of one speaker could be played 8-second bursts of a woman talking to her own infant. Out of the other speaker could be played 8-second bursts of the same woman talking to another adult. In other words, motherese was played from one speaker, and adult-to-adult speech came from the other. The babies could cause an 8-second burst of speaking to come from one or other speaker by turning towards it. So if infants turned towards the motherese speaker, they would hear motherese. If they turned towards the adult-to-adult speaker they would hear adult-to-adult talk. Exactly how this worked is described in the procedure section, below.

Before the experimental trials, each infant was given four training trials. This was to show them that one type of speech sound was to come from one side of the room and another type of speech sound was to come from the other. The first training trial consisted of the speaker on one side of the room playing one 8-second burst of either motherese or adult-directed speech. The infant's gaze would tend to be attracted by this sound, causing them to turn in the direction of the sound. If they did not turn, then the mother, whose lap the infant was sitting on, was instructed to swivel her chair to the side from which the sound came. The next training trial consisted of an 8-second burst of the other kind of speech (depending on what kind of speech had been played in the first training trial) from the other speaker. Again the infant would tend to turn in the direction of the sound. This whole process was repeated for the third and fourth training trials.

The difference between the training trials and the experimental trials was that in the experimental trials the infant had to turn in the direction of one of the speakers in order to cause speech sounds to be played from it, rather than just responding to the sounds as they had done in the training trials. Fernald's hypothesis was that the infants would turn more often in the direction which caused motherese to be played, than in the direction that caused adult-directed speech to be played.

Subjects

The data come from tests on 48 four-month-old infants, 21 of whom were female, 27 of whom were male.

Design

This experiment was based on operant techniques. It uses a kind of repeated measures design in which the dependent variable was measured by counting the number of times out of 15 trials that the infant turned in the direction which caused a burst of motherese to be played.

Two important and potentially confounding factors were controlled against. These were:

1. Side of presentation of motherese (left or right).
2. The order of presentation of motherese and ordinary adult speech in the training stage (motherese first or last).

From the 48 infants, 12 heard motherese on the left, and heard motherese first in the training trials; 12 heard motherese from the right, and first in the training trials; 12 heard motherese from the left, and second in the training trials; 12 heard motherese from the right, and second in the training trials. So *all* possible combinations of left/right and first/second are accounted for in this *factorial* design. This ensures that if a tendency to turn in the direction of motherese is found, a sceptic cannot argue that this was only because motherese was always heard, say, on the left-hand side (and perhaps babies tend to prefer *any* sounds which are played on their left-hand side).

Procedure

The laboratory was divided into two rooms. In the main room sat the mother with the infant subject on her lap. The mother wore headphones and listened to music throughout the experiment. In the adjoining room sat a judge and the experimenter. A one-way mirror separated the rooms, and a camera in the main room could be monitored by the judge in the adjoining room. The judge and the experimenter actually performed different tasks, but in the interests of a straightforward summary we will refer to them as the 'experimenters'.

On the wall directly in front of the child was a video camera, and just above this was a green light. Each trial began with the green light going on to attract the child's attention to the mid-line of the room. When the experimenters were satisfied that the child was looking at the green light (they could observe this by monitoring the picture from the video camera) the light was switched off. Nothing then happened until the child turned their head at least 30 degrees in one direction or the other. As soon as they did turn their head 30 degrees an 8-second burst of speech came from the speaker on the side of the room which they had turned towards. After the 8-second burst the sound would stop and the green light would then go on once again to attract the child's attention back to the mid-line of the room. The next trial was begun once the experimenters were satisfied that the infant was looking at the green light once more.

There are a number of important things to note about the procedure. First, for each trial no sound was heard from either side of the room until a 'criterion head-turn' of 30 degrees had spontaneously been made by the infant. The experimenters judged when this had occurred by monitoring the child's movements through the video camera, a task that they practised before the experiment began. Secondly, half the infants heard motherese from the right speaker and adult-to-adult speech from the left speaker, whilst half heard motherese from the left speaker and adult-to-adult speech from the right speaker. Thirdly, the voice that the child heard was not their own mother's.

RESULTS

Thirty-three out of 48 of the infants turned more often in the direction that caused motherese to be played than in the direction that caused adult-directed speech to be played. A binomial test on the relative proportion of infants who turned most often in the direction of motherese compared with the proportion that turned most often in the direction of adult-directed speech showed the differences in these proportions to be statistically significant at the level of $p < .01$. The mean number of head-turns in the direction of motherese (8.73) was shown to be significantly greater than the mean that would have been expected by chance (7.5) by a t-test which compared the means ($p < .05$).

DISCUSSION

The data support Fernald's experimental hypothesis. Overall, the babies made more head-turns in the direction of motherese than in the direction of adult-directed speech. This suggests that, on average, the babies preferred to listen to the motherese speech sounds, and in turn this preference suggests that motherese does play a useful role in infant language development.

The evidence from this one study is, of course, not compelling. Just because infants appear to prefer to listen to this kind of speech does not necessarily mean that it actually helps their language development. Babies prefer to eat very sugary and salty foods, but this does not mean that these foods help their physical development. By four months of age, perhaps they are just more used to hearing motherese. Furthermore, some infants actually seemed to prefer adult-directed speech; two babies turned every time in the direction which caused adult-to-adult speech sounds to be played. However, the results of one research study should never be interpreted in isolation from the body of literature out of which it has emerged. Fernald's data should be considered within the context of other work which shows how particular features of motherese are well suited to the needs of the infant (see for example Snow, 1979). This bigger picture suggests that adults talk to babies in a way that facilitates their language development.

QUESTIONS

1 Why did the speech sounds on both sides of the room, whether adult-directed or motherese, come from the same woman speaker?

2 Why were the speech sounds not recorded from the infants' own mothers?

3 Why did half the babies hear motherese from the left, and half hear it from the right?

Suggested Answers start at p. 458

KEY WORDS

confounding variables
factorial design
language
language development

motherese
operant techniques
t-test
training trials

TALKING PROPER

■ LABOV, W. (1969). The logic of nonstandard English.
In P.P. Giglioli (ed.) *Language and Social Context*, pp. 179–215.
Harmondsworth, England: Penguin. Originally in *Georgetown Monographs on Language and Linguistics*, 2, 1–31.

INTRODUCTION

In this important paper Labov, a sociolinguist, set out to challenge the basic principles of language deprivation theory. Deprivation theory (or deficit theory) had been used to explain the consistent trend of underachievement in schools among ethnic minority groups and working-class children, both in the United Kingdom and in the United States. The idea was that children from these backgrounds lacked some of the key language skills that enabled non-minority and middle-class children to succeed in schools. The empirical basis of the theory was the poor performance of these children (relative to their White and middle-class counterparts) on language assessments carried out by school teachers and researchers.

It is important to note from the outset that the relatively poor performance of these groups of children in their schoolwork and on language assessments is not in dispute (see for example Scarr, 1981). Indeed, Labov reports data from a 1968 study which shows that the Black New York City children that he and his colleagues were working with lagged more than two years behind the national norm on reading tests. What is at stake in this article is what this all means. To deprivation theorists the apparent deficit in language skills shown by Black and working-class children pointed to, and was caused by, a form of 'cultural deprivation' (Labov cites Deutsch *et al.*, 1967, as leading proponents of this perspective). The homes of these children were supposed to have an impoverished *linguistic* environment which prevented them from developing the full range of verbal skills which enabled White middle-class children to succeed in school.

The work of the British educationalist Basil Bernstein (1959, 1960) was influential in this respect. Although it is unclear whether Bernstein really was a 'deficit' theorist (Edwards, 1979), his work is strongly associated with this line of thinking. It was Bernstein who had framed the notion of *restricted* and *elaborated* linguistic 'codes' (originally 'public' and 'formal' codes, respectively); the former being a rather concrete and limited form of language which was characteristic of working-class speakers; the latter a more symbolic and flexible way of speaking which was available to middle-class speakers. The restricted code was seen as being less useful, less powerful, less adaptive than the elaborated code, and was thought to be the result of the relationships and linguistic environment within the working-class household. Translated into the terms of deprivation theory, these ideas resulted in extreme assertions such as:

> the language of culturally deprived children... is not merely an underdeveloped version of standard English, but is a basically non-logical mode of expressive behavior.
> (pp. 183–84, cited by Labov from the work of Bereiter *et al.*, 1966)

The language of Black US inner-city children in particular was seen from this perspective as deficient in verbal skills and limited in its grammar. Labov's article is specifically based on research with Black New York City children, but class issues are never far from the surface since they were 'children from urban ghetto areas' (p. 182). He contests vigorously and empirically two key related features of the language deprivation tradition. Firstly he argues that these children are not deficient verbally. True, they perform poorly on tests of verbal skills, but there are, he asserts, important non-linguistic reasons for this. Secondly, he argues that the language of the Black New York City child is not inferior to the dominant English dialect of the United States; it is simply different (although this argument is not dealt with here). An important part of Labov's reasoning has to do with the shortcomings of the methods of investigation and assessment which have traditionally been used in this field. In this respect his arguments are relevant to the whole enterprise of social science.

METHODOLOGICAL CONSIDERATIONS

Labov's methods could be described as *qualitative*. He avoided testing the children, preferring instead to involve them in informal discussions. He and his colleagues had learnt from experience that:

> ... the social situation is the most powerful determinant of verbal behavior and... an adult must enter into the right social relation with a child if he wants to find out what a child can do.
> (p. 191)

The relatively poor verbal performance of Black New York City children in previous studies had not been due to any spoken language deficit. Instead, it had been caused artificially by the inhibiting and intimidating social context of the traditional research procedures that had been used. These would often involve a White middle-class adult, who knew little of the children or of their worlds, asking unusual and (to the child) irrelevant questions.

The empirical work which lay behind this paper was carried out by an experienced Black interviewer who knew the children's neighbourhood well, and had insights into their interests and aspirations. The work with one particular eight-year-old child (Leon) is documented. To allow Leon to demonstrate his true verbal competence, the interviewer paid particular attention to the conditions under which the discussions took place. Four key strategies are specifically noted: having a supply of potato chips available; bringing along Leon's best friend; sitting on the floor (to reduce the height imbalance between adult and child and the implications of power that this can hold); using taboo words and discussing taboo topics. The aim was to make the research situation one in which Leon felt able to talk.

The data which emerge from such a research strategy are transcripts of discussions which allow the children's spoken language to be examined in some detail. Labov used the data to illustrate his argument that previous assessments of Black New York City children's language had seriously underestimated their verbal skills. He also used the data to show the structure and sophistication of the children's language, which is different from, but not inferior to, standard US spoken English. However, this latter argument is not covered in this summary.

RESULTS AND DISCUSSION

The following is an extract of a conversation between Leon and the interviewer (CR) before the strategies mentioned in the method section (above) were implemented:

CR: Well – uh – did you ever get into a fight with a guy?
Leon: Nope.
CR: That was bigger than you?
Leon: Nope.
CR: You never been in a fight?
Leon: Nope.

CR: Nobody ever pick on you?
Leon: Nope.
CR: Nobody ever hit you?
Leon: Nope.

It is not difficult to see how Leon's monosyllabic performance in this situation could lead an interviewer to believe that his verbal skills were under-developed. But Labov argues, and goes on to demonstrate, that Leon's verbal performance in this situation is not a good measure of his verbal competence. Take, for example, the following exchange from the second session with Leon when the strategies mentioned above had been implemented:

CR: ... but I wanted you to tell me about the fight that you had.
Leon: I ain't had no fight.
{ Greg: Yes you did!   He said Barry,
{ CR: You said you had one! You had a fight with Butchie,
{ Greg: An' he said Garland ... an' Michael.
{ CR: an' Barry...
{ Leon: I di'n'; you said that Gregory!
{ Greg: You did.
Leon: You know you said that!

Leon is still defensively trying to deny that he had been fighting, but the stilted monosyllabic talk has been replaced with an active and competitive verbal performance. In Labov's view, the reason for Leon's poor performance in the first meeting was nothing to do with Leon himself, but was instead to do with the social situation of that interview. Labov's more general point is that this type of social situation tends to be created whenever children are tested or assessed in some way at school. As a result, children like Leon were being systematically disadvantaged by having their true abilities underestimated. There are all sorts of ways in which underestimations of this type can be damaging. The *belief* that a child has poor verbal and intellectual skills may in the long run *cause* that child to have poor verbal and intellectual skills (see Rosenthal & Jacobson, 1966, on the self-fulfilling prophecy; summarised in Chapter 21 of this volume).

Overall, Labov's article provides a convincing and dense refutation of the suggestion that cultural deprivation and verbal deficits lie behind Black (and working-class) children's problems in schools. The children that Labov studied were not deficient in verbal skills, and neither were they 'culturally deprived' in the way that some psychologists had claimed. Indeed the idea that the causes of their problems should be looked for within the children, or within their home environment, or within their relationships with their parents, is typical of an ethnocentric and reductionist perspective; a perspective which is unfortunately taken too frequently by psychologists. For this reason it is important that the work of social scientists from disciplines other than psychology is familiar to psychologists. It is the sociologist who is more likely to point out that the problems faced by Black children in New York City schools arise from the experience of being Black and interacting with the institutions of a White society, and not from inadequate parenting or deficient intellect.

QUESTIONS

1   Labov's data is qualitative and taken from a limited sample of interviews with children. What objections could you raise with this approach?

2   How would Labov defend his research strategy against these objections?

Suggested Answers start at p. 458

KEY WORDS

class	linguistic environment
cultural deprivation	qualitative data
deficit theory	restricted codes
elaborated codes	self-fulfilling prophecy
ethnocentric	social situation
language	sociolinguist
linguistic competence	

PART V

COGNITIVE PSYCHOLOGY

Cognitive psychology is about mental processes such as remembering, perceiving, understanding and producing language, solving problems, thinking and reasoning. It is an area of psychology which deals with abstract, invisible things which are not easy to pin down and define. Try asking yourself the question 'what is thought?'. Then when you have answered that go onto the next question, which is 'where is thought?'. The slipperiness of the notions that cognitive psychology deals with make it a particularly difficult area to study!

One of the central concerns of cognitive psychology is with the question of how information gets processed by the brain. It is not difficult to see why this is such an important question. The ability to act in ways which are recognisably human depends upon the ability to make sense of the world in which we live. Our contact with that world is via our senses; sight, hearing, smell, touch and taste. But the data that are picked up by our senses are raw, and most require processing and interpretation if they are to be useful to us. Our actions are at least partly based upon the processing and interpretation that goes on, so understanding these cognitive processes can help us understand what we do. The quantity and variety of work that explores these issues is huge and, like all sciences, this work ranges from the highly theoretical (see for example the following summaries of the papers by Craik & Lockhart, 1972, and Searle, 1980) to the directly applicable (see the summaries of Loftus & Palmer, 1974, and Baron-Cohen, Leslie & Frith, 1985).

Within cognitive psychology can be found all the standard dialogues and debates which are encountered in psychology as a whole. For example, should we study human cognition in highly controlled laboratory conditions (like Ebbinghaus, 1913) or would it be better to aim for a higher level of ecological validity at the expense of precision and replicability, as in Bartlett's work? The summary of Bartlett (1932) provides descriptions of these competing approaches. Should we always try and study cognitive phenomena by making direct observations of people's performance on tasks, or is it acceptable to rely on self-reports of cognition? Young, Hay & Ellis (1985) took this latter, slightly unusual approach in their study of face recognition. And what about the nature–nurture controversy? How many of our cognitive skills do we learn through experience, and how many just unfold through maturation on the basis of inheritance? Gibson & Walk (1960) addressed this issue in the famous 'visual cliff' study. Finally, how much influence does culture have on our cognitive processes? Do all humans think and perceive in the same way, or are there differences across cultural divides? Deregowski's (1972) paper on picture perception tackles this important issue.

In this part, we have included some studies that look at the issues of perception, memory and mind. There are also a number of studies in other parts of this book that can be included under the broad heading of cognitive psychology. For example, the papers on social cognition in Chapter 2, and the papers on communication in Chapter 15. The cognitive approach is currently the most influential area of psychology, and though it starts from the core topics contained in this chapter it has far reaching theoretical and practical implications.

16 MEMORY

We take our memory for granted until it fails us. Then we experience all kinds of irritating phenomena, such as the feeling that the thing we want to recall is on the tip of our tongue but we can't quite remember it. On other occasions our memory will surprise us and we will recall unusual pieces of information or personal events for no obvious reason. Sometimes our memory plays tricks on us and we remember things that never happened. For example, do you have any memories of events where you can see yourself doing something? If, like many other people, you have 'memories' like this then it is obvious that they cannot be an accurate record of what you perceived at the time, because you could not have seen yourself. Your memory has made the event into a mental home movie and then sold it to you as a record of the event.

The study of memory is as old as the discipline of psychology, dating at least as far back as the work of Ebbinghaus in the 1880s (see Ebbinghaus, 1913). Indeed Ebbinghaus' investigations of his own memory are the starting point for our summary of one of Bartlett's influential studies (Bartlett, 1932). Bartlett is notable for trying to study the characteristics of everyday remembering, rather than the abstract properties of experimentally induced memories.

Loftus & Palmer's (1974) analysis of the accuracy of eyewitness testimony illustrates how cognitive psychology can be put to work in addressing important, real-life questions. People put a lot of faith in evidence supplied by eyewitnesses, both in the context of the courtroom and in the context of everyday conversations about events. The faulty memories of some of Loftus and Palmer's subjects suggests that the testimony of eyewitnesses should perhaps be regarded more sceptically.

Craik & Lockhart's (1972) exposition of their levels of processing framework for memory research is an example of a paper which addresses a theoretical problem, and which is principally of interest to cognitive psychologists engaged in the study of memory. Their emphasis on the process of 'remembering', rather than on the structure of 'memory', resonates with Bartlett's earlier analyses.

REMEMBERING PICTURES

■ BARTLETT, F.C. (1932). *Remembering: A Study in Experimental and Social Psychology*, pp. 177–85. Cambridge: Cambridge University Press.

INTRODUCTION

The earliest systematic work on the psychology of memory was carried out at the end of the nineteenth century by Ebbinghaus (see Ebbinghaus, 1913). He undertook a range of highly controlled experiments to discover the characteristics of human memory. To control for past knowledge he studied how well meaningless material could be remembered and re-learnt. The studies were methodical, and provided a wide range of findings which had a major influence on the way memory research was conducted, and the type of theories that were developed.

Bartlett criticised Ebbinghaus' work on the grounds that, in attempting to avoid the difficult problem of past knowledge by using nonsense material, it confined itself to a very artificial situation, and therefore lacked *ecological validity*. He also suggested that Ebbinghaus concentrated too closely on the material that was being remembered, and ignored other important features like the attitudes of the subject and their prior experience. In contrast, Bartlett's book describes a series of studies into the memory of meaningful material like stories (most famously 'The War of the Ghosts') and pictures.

Bartlett used two main methods in his studies. In one (the method of *repeated reproduction*), a single person is asked to keep remembering the same material over a period of time. The changes in the remembering are analysed to discover any systematic distortions. In the second method (the method of *serial reproduction*), the material is reproduced by the first subject. This reproduction is seen by the second subject who then makes their own reproduction. This new reproduction is seen by the next subject and so on, resulting in a 'chain' of remembering. When we pass on material in a spoken form in this way it is sometimes referred to as a Chinese whisper (after a children's game), and you will know from experience how distorted a message can become as it passes from one person to another.

THE STUDY

In his studies on serial reproduction, Bartlett used three types of material; (1) folk stories (2) descriptive passages of prose, and (3) pictures. The folk stories were used because of the range of social information they carry and the unusual quality of many of them. The prose passages were used as a contrast to the stories. In this summary we will look at the picture material.

The pictures were shown to subjects who were then given something to do for around 15 to 30 minutes before being asked to reproduce the drawing. Simple, but ambiguous, pictures were used and as many as 20 reproductions were collected for one chain.

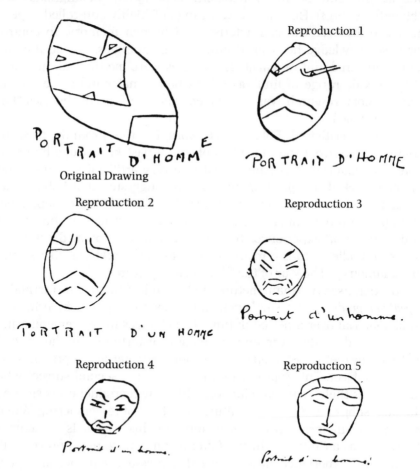

Original Drawing

Reproduction 1

Reproduction 2

Reproduction 3

Reproduction 4

Reproduction 5

Figure 16.1 *Example of successive reproductions*

RESULTS

(i) Transformation to conventional representations

Whenever the material was meant to represent a common object but contained some unfamiliar features, then these features were transformed during the course of the serial reproduction. In the drawings shown in Figure 16.1, all the characteristics of the original drawing which have any peculiarity are lost. The face is tilted upwards immediately, becomes oval and then round, acquires eyes, a nose and a mouth, and becomes a conventional representation of a face. The face continues to have some elaborate features up until the title change on reproduction 7, when the elaboration declines and disappears.

(ii) Elaboration

There were two frequent types of elaboration. In the first type, as the whole figure was gradually being transformed, certain relatively

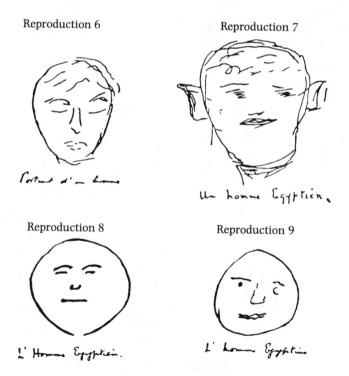

Reproduction 6

Reproduction 7

Reproduction 8

Reproduction 9

Figure 16.1 *Continued*

disconnected material was elaborated into some characteristic that naturally belonged to the new setting. In the second type, some details were simply enhanced.

Figure 16.2 is an example of the first type of elaboration. The drawing is a representation of the Egyptian 'mulak', a conventionalised reproduction of an owl, which may have been used as the model for our letter 'M'. The elaboration of certain features, for example the tail of the cat, can be seen to develop from the original sweep of the lines in the owl. However, by the 10th reproduction, the tail is actually sweeping in the other direction to the original drawing, and the cat has also acquired whiskers and a bow!

Figure 16.2   *Example of successive reproductions*
Source: Bartlett (1932)

(iii) Simplification

Whenever there was a design which was not easily categorised (because it was odd or unfamiliar), there was a strong tendency to elaborate this into a recognisable form. Once in this form, the feature would then be simplified into a conventional example of this feature or form. If the chain continued, then elaboration developed from the new simplified drawing until it once again became ambiguous and started to simplify and change form again.

(iv) Naming

The verbal labels affected the reproductions of the drawings. One subject described their memorisation of the mulak as follows:

> I visualised throughout and gave names to the parts. I said to myself: 'a heart at the top, then a curve and a straight post down to a little foot at the bottom. Between these two a letter W, and half a heart half-way up on the left hand side'.
> (p. 183)

This subject produced a drawing that followed this description but showed massive changes from the original picture.

(v) Preservation of detached detail

When there was some detail that was detached from the main image and in a form that was representative (like decoration), then it tended to remain unchanged.

DISCUSSION

Bartlett suggested that we base any learning on our existing *schemas* (which are ways of categorising information in the world based on our past experience). When these conflict with what is being remembered, then distortions occur to make the material more in keeping with our world view; to make it fit into our existing schemas. Bartlett's argument is that learning and memory are active processes involving *effort after meaning*. The process of recall involves a constructive component, in that we use what we have retained, along with our existing schemas to re-create the original. The distortions, elaborations and simplifications that he observed in the serial reproduction of pictures support this perspective.

Bartlett's work was criticised as being too vague, and his predictions as being relatively untestable. The following 40 years saw memory researchers concentrating on controlled laboratory studies using material of limited meaning. However, over the last two decades there has been a growing emphasis on meaningful material and how it is recalled in real-life situations.

The studies on remembering, by Bartlett, make continued reference to the cultural context of material, and show an awareness that people with different experiences will interpret, memorise and recall the same material in very different ways. This was another feature that was ignored by psychologists for a number of years, and highlights the value of Bartlett's original studies.

QUESTIONS

1 Identify some advantages of controlled laboratory studies of memory.

2 Identify some disadvantages of controlled laboratory studies of memory.

3 What are the main causes of distortion in memory according to Bartlett?

4 Try the method of repeated reproduction on yourself – find a picture in a book, and draw it from memory every day for two weeks. Only look at the previous day's drawings when doing each new one

---

Suggested Answers start at p. 459

KEY WORDS

cultural context	re-learning
ecological validity	repeated reproduction
effort after meaning	schema
memory	serial reproduction

Eyewitness Testimony

■ Loftus, E.F. & Palmer, J.C. (1974). Reconstruction of
auto-mobile destruction; An example of the
interaction between languagae and memory.
Journal of Verbal Learning and Verbal Behavior, 13, 585–89.

Introduction

'I saw it with my own eyes, I can tell you exactly what happened.' This
statement carries a lot of weight when we are trying to find out about
an event. The evidence of eyewitnesses is a very important part of criminal trials, but is our memory as trustworthy as we believe it to be? The
work of Bartlett (1932; see the previous summary in this text) tells us
that remembering is an inaccurate process that is distorted by expectations, values and cultural norms. So, can we really believe the evidence
of our own eyes?

When we are describing an event, one of the possible causes of distortion might be the suggestions given to us by other people. In particular, they might suggest how we should remember the event through
leading questions. A leading question is simply one that, either in its
content or the way it is phrased, suggests to witnesses what answer is
desired, or leads them to the desired answer. An example of a leading
question in everyday conversation might be 'Do you like my new
outfit?'. This is not a request for serious evaluation of the cut, colour
and style of the clothes, but a request for reassurance that we do not
look stupid.

The First Study

The 45 student subjects were shown seven film-clips of traffic accidents.
The clips were short excerpts from safety films made for driver education. Following each clip, the students were asked to write an account
of the accident they had just seen. They were also asked to answer
some specific questions, the critical one of which involved the speed of
the vehicles involved in the collision. There were five conditions in the
study (each with nine subjects) and the independent variable was
manipulated by means of the wording of the questions. The basic

Table 16.1   Speed estimates for the
verbs used in the estimation of
speed question

Verb	Mean estimate of speed (mph)
Smashed	40.8
Collided	39.3
Bumped	38.1
Hit	34.0
Contacted	31.8

Source: Loftus & Palmer (1974)

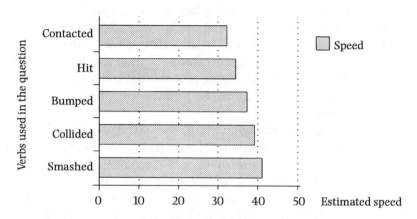

Figure 16.3   *Speed estimates for the different verbs used in the witness question*

question was 'About how fast were the cars going when they ***** each other?'. In each condition, a different word or phrase was used to fill in the blank. These words were; *smashed, collided, bumped, hit, contacted.* The results are shown in Table 16.1 and graphically in Figure 16.3.

The results show that the phrasing of the question brought about a change in speed estimate.

THE SECOND STUDY

A similar procedure was used. The 150 student subjects saw a short (one minute) film which contained a 4-second scene of a multiple car accident, and were then questioned about it. Fifty of the subjects were asked 'How fast were the cars going when they *hit* each other?; 50 of the subjects were asked 'How fast were the cars going when they *smashed into* each other?'; and 50 of the subjects were not interrogated about the speed of the vehicles.

One week later, the subjects returned and, without viewing the film again, they answered a series of questions about the accident. The critical question was 'Did you see any broken glass?', which was part of a longer series of questions and was placed in a random position on each subject's question paper. There was, in fact, no broken glass in the film. Table 16.2 shows the responses of the students to this question, with the data shown graphically in Figure 16.4.

These results show a significant effect of the verb in the question on the mis-perception of glass in the film.

Table 16.2   Response to the question 'Did you see any broken glass?'

| | Verb condition | | |
Response	Smashed	Hit	Control
Yes	16	7	6
No	34	43	44

Source: Loftus & Palmer (1974)

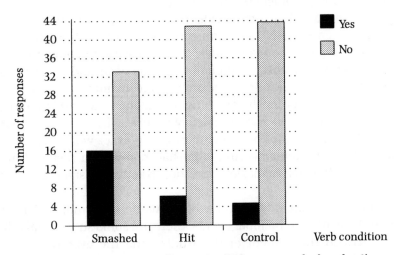

Figure 16.4   *Response to the question, 'Did you see any broken glass?'*

DISCUSSION

There are two possible interpretations of the findings from study one. First, they could be due to a distortion in the memory of the subject created by the verbal label which had been used to characterise the intensity of the crash. Secondly, they could be due to response-bias factors, in which case the subject is not sure of the exact speed and adjusts his or her estimate to fit in with the expectations of the questioner (see Orne, 1962 on demand characteristics; Chapter 21 of this volume).

In trying to account for the findings of the second study, Loftus and Palmer suggest that two kinds of information go into a person's memory of a complex event. The first is the information obtained from perceiving the event, and the second is the other information supplied to us after the event. In this case the 'other' information came from the speed question which had been posed to 100 of the subjects.

One of the difficulties with the finding that our memories are so susceptible to influence, is that it contradicts our feeling that we are capable of recalling exact details of events. Neisser (1981) reported the case of John Dean, who gave eyewitness testimony at the Watergate hearings in the USA which eventually resulted in the impeachment of President Nixon. Dean was reported to have an extremely accurate memory. He recounted conversations in very precise details, and testified on oath that these were exactly what he had heard. There was no doubt that he, and others who worked with him, were convinced that he had an eidetic (photographic) memory for detail.

Some time after Dean gave evidence, it was discovered that The President had been secretly taping all conversations in the White House. When these tapes were made public it was possible to compare Dean's testimony with an accurate record of what had been said. Interestingly, Dean's memory was found to be inaccurate in almost every detail, although his memory for the meaning of what had occurred in the conversation (the gist of it) was completely accurate. He had remembered what had been said, not by remembering the exact words which had been used, but by remembering what had really been meant. But he had no idea that his memories were not exactly the same as a tape-recording.

Although the laboratory studies on eyewitness testimony offer some clues to the way we remember events, there are some substantial differences between the content of the studies and the everyday activity of remembering. For example, when the subjects were giving their estimates of speed, they did not have any personal involvement in the judgement and had not taken any part in the event. When we are telling a story about an event we have witnessed in everyday life, we often have some involvement in the people or the action, and we are often explaining our own behaviour as part of the action.

QUESTIONS

1   What controls were used in this study?

2   What are the differences between laboratory studies of eyewitness testimony and the behaviour of eyewitnesses in everyday life?

3   List as many factors as you can that might influence your memory of an event?

4   What are the problems with using students in this study? Do you think there would have been different results with a different subject group?

Suggested Answers start on p. 459

KEY WORDS

demand characteristics
eidetic memory
expectations
eyewitness

leading question
memory
response-bias

MODELS OF MEMORY

■ CRAIK, F.I.M. & LOCKHART, R.S. (1972). Levels of processing: A framework for memory research. *Journal of Verbal Learning and Verbal Behavior, 11*, 671–84.

INTRODUCTION

Craik and Lockhart's theoretical paper set out to challenge the widely accepted 'multi-store' model of memory (see Atkinson & Shiffrin, 1968), and to replace it with a new framework for memory research centred on the concept of *levels of processing*. This summary of their paper gives a brief description of the multi-store model, reviews Craik and Lockhart's objections to it, and then examines their arguments in favour of the levels of processing approach which they advocate.

THE MULTI-STORE MODEL

According to the multi-store model of memory, the three 'stores' which make up memory (the *sensory register, short-term memory*, and *long-term memory*) are differentiated one from another in terms of how much information they can store, how long they can store it for, what format ('modality') they store it in, if and how forgetting occurs, and also by their place in the sequence of information processing that goes to make up 'memory'.

The first store in the sequence is known as the sensory register. Incoming information can enter this store without being attended to, and can be held (in the case of visual information at least) for up to one second (Sperling, 1960) before it decays spontaneously. The information is probably stored in the same modality as the input (Atkinson & Shiffrin, 1968); in other words visual information is stored visually, auditory information is stored acoustically and so forth. This means that the information is relatively uninterpreted and is for a brief moment a 'literal copy of [the] input' (Craik & Lockhart, p. 672). The storage capacity of the sensory register is large, since a lot of information can be taken in without ever being attended to.

The tiny fraction of the information in the sensory register which is attended to then passes into the next store, known as short-term memory (STM). Craik & Lockhart cite Peterson & Johnson (1971) who showed that information in STM is stored in an *acoustic* format. STM traces have a duration of several seconds: Peterson & Peterson (1959), for example, estimated the duration to be from 6–12 seconds, after which the memory trace decays. But the most striking characteristic of STM is its limited capacity and the consequent ease with which information held within it can be disrupted or displaced. Miller (1956) estimated the total capacity of STM to be approximately seven *chunks* of information, with a chunk being a unit of whatever material is being presented (letters, words, numbers, dates, phrases and so forth).

From STM the information passes into long-term memory (LTM), providing it has not been forgotten by decay or displacement. Long-term memory may have a limitless capacity (can you imagine your long-term memory being full?), and memory traces can last a lifetime. It is uncertain how forgetting from LTM occurs, if indeed it does occur. There is general agreement that the information in LTM tends to be coded *semantically*. That is we store information in our LTM according to its *meaning*. Figure 16.5 shows the structure of the three-stage (multi-store) model.

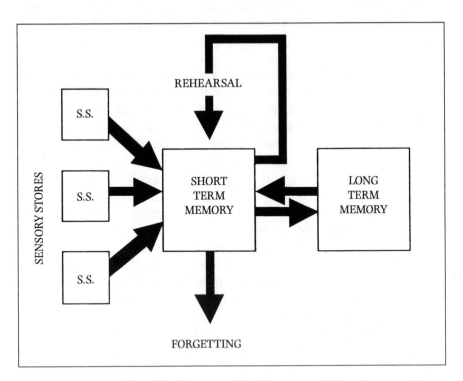

Figure 16.5 *Traditional multi-store model of short-term and long-term memory*

THE PROBLEMS WITH MULTI-STORE MODELS

The core of Craik and Lockhart's objection to the multi-store model is that the characteristics which distinguish the stores from each other are poorly specified and appear to be too dependent on the research paradigms that have been used to investigate them. For example, the fragility of STM memories has been put down to limitations of capacity. But it is unclear whether this means *storage* capacity or *processing* capacity. That is, do we lose things from STM because bits of information get displaced by new bits of information, or is it because STM can only actively handle (process) small quantities of material at the same time? The psychologists who support the multi-store model have tended to favour the former (storage) interpretation, and dealt in 'numbers of chunks' that can be recalled from experimental tasks. Craik and Lockhart clearly favour the latter interpretation, as the phrase 'depth of processing' might indicate. They are also unhappy with the notion of a 'chunk' of information, for if STM really can deal with data at any level of abstraction (one moment dealing with seven physical features, the next moment coping with seven phrases), then it must be very flexible with regard to the format of data it can accept as input.

This latest point leads into another related objection, though before seeing what that objection is we need to take a step back temporarily. The whole rationale of the multi-store model rests on the stores being identifiably different in a number of respects. Of course all information has to be processed, and some stages of processing will come before other stages. So as Craik and Lockhart point out, you can always put boxes round different stages in the sequence and call this stage 'the sensory register', this next stage STM, and this other stage LTM. But unless the different stages really *are* distinguishable one from another, above and beyond the simple observation that 'one comes before another', what is the point of having the boxes at all?

Now the objection that stems from this point is that gradually, through empirical work, the distinguishing features of the stages have been broken down. One example of this relates to how information is coded in each of the stores. Craik and Lockhart argue that originally the basis for discriminating between STM and LTM was established by Conrad (1964) and Baddeley (1966), who showed that coding in STM was primarily acoustic, and that coding in LTM was primarily semantic. However, STM has been shown to be able to accept other formats for information, including visual formats (the authors cite the work of Kroll *et al.*, 1970), and even semantic formats (they cite Shulman, 1970 and 1972 in support of this assertion). Indeed, if STM can work with chunks of information such as meaningful phrases, then one would suspect that some semantic representation was being used. It is widely agreed that LTM works with semantically encoded information. So perhaps STM and LTM are not so different in this respect after all, in which case one major reason for naming them as separate stages is gone. On the basis of this, and other arguments, the authors propose that the multi-store model is not a useful model of memory.

THE LEVELS OF PROCESSING FRAMEWORK

The levels of processing approach does away with the idea that memory is made up of a series of stores, and that information has to pass through each of these stores in turn (sequentially). According to the levels of processing framework, the initial analysis of incoming information is carried out in *primary memory* by a *limited-capacity central processor*. This processor can handle information very flexibly. The modality in which the information is handled is determined partly by the nature of the information itself, and partly by the purpose of remembering. In other words, if we are trying to remember the six figures in a telephone number for a few seconds while we dial, primary memory will handle the material in an acoustic or articulatory format (we will repeat the numbers to ourselves over and over again until we dial). If, on the other hand, we are listening to someone talk and trying to understand what they are saying, then the incoming data will surely be dealt with semantically. In fact primary memory, according to this theory, is virtually an attentional system. Craik and Lockhart's suggestion that some of the characteristics of memories are related to the *function* of those memories is a welcome one. The multi-store tradition dealt comparatively little with this issue, but one would surely expect that the nature of a memory will relate to the reason for attending to the to-be-remembered information in the first place.

The result of processing in primary memory is the *memory trace*. The key feature of the levels of processing approach is that the durability of the memory trace is affected by the *depth* at which the incoming information has been processed. Depth, in this context, has to do with the *meaningfulness* of the processing; the 'greater [the] degree of semantic or cognitive processing' (p. 675), the greater the depth. So if incoming information is processed semantically, it will tend to be remembered better (the resulting memory trace will be more persistent) than material that has just been processed according to, say, its physical features. A simple example might illustrate this point. If you listen to someone saying a sentence in your own language, you will be able to remember and repeat back what was said with relative ease, because you have been attending to the meaning of the words (deep processing). If on the other hand someone says the same sentence, but in a foreign language, you will have great difficulty in repeating what was said, because you will only have been able to attend to the sounds of the words (shallow processing of physical sound features). Notice that in this approach the capacity of primary memory is limited not in terms of storage (as in the multi-store model) but in terms of *processing* capacity. Information that is understandable and meaningful can be handled very efficiently by primary memory. But the same quantity of meaningless information, which can only be analysed in terms of its physical features, will be beyond its capabilities.

In support of their framework, Craik and Lockhart present a re-evaluation of existing data from empirical studies on incidental learning, selective attention, sensory storage, the serial position curve, repetition and rehearsal effects, and the distinction between STM and LTM. They show how the findings of these studies are compatible with their depth of processing approach. For example, in studies on incidental learning, subjects are asked to perform certain tasks on a set of experimental stimulus materials (a word list, for example). Tasks that have been used include crossing out all the vowels, copying down the words, rating words for pleasantness, finding rhymes for each word, estimating the frequency of the occurrence of the words in the English language. These are known as *orienting tasks* because they determine the way in which the subjects look at the material; in short they determine the way the material is processed. Once they have performed the required task, subjects are asked unexpectedly to recall the words they have been oriented towards. Subjects that performed a task which forced them to process the words semantically (estimating the pleasantness of the words, for example) are able to recall more words on average than subjects who performed tasks which forced them to process the words non-semantically (crossing out all the vowels, copying down the words, and so forth). In other words, the deeper the processing, the more durable the memory.

CONCLUSION

Craik and Lockhart summarise their basic position as follows:

> Specifically, we suggest that trace persistence is a function of depth of analysis, with deeper levels of analysis associated with more elaborate, longer lasting, and stronger traces.
> (p. 675)

In doing away with the various traditional memory stores they are not arguing anything particularly new or revolutionary. They rightly resist calling their approach a 'theory'. Instead they claim simply to have described 'a conceptual framework...within which memory research might proceed' (p. 681). In this respect they have been successful, for their depth of processing framework has underpinned a large amount of research into memory processes. The quantity of work that an approach inspires is one indicator of its usefulness.

QUESTIONS
1   What are the three stores that make up memory within the multistore model?
2   What are the most important ways in which the three stores are differentiated from each other?
3   What might be a suitable alternative word for 'depth' (as in 'depth of processing')?
4   In an experiment with the following conditions, which condition would you expect to produce the best remembering for items on a word list? Rank order the conditions according to your expectations of subjects' performance on a recall task: condition (a)   repeating the words over and over again; condition (b)   thinking of bizarre visual images to go with each word; condition (c)   putting the words into a sentence; condition (d)   thinking of a rhyme for each word.

Suggested Answers start at p. 460

KEY WORDS

chunking	multi-store model
depth of processing	orienting task
forgetting	processing capacity
incidental learning	semantic coding
information procesing	sensory register
long-term memory (LTM)	serial position curve
memory	short-term memory (STM)
memory trace	storage capacity

17 PERCEPTION

Perception has to do with the taking in and making sense of the vast array of sensory information that we experience. Perception should not be confused with sensation. *Sensation* refers to the raw physical data which impinge upon our senses. *Perception* refers to the processes that occur in the mind which convert these sensations into a representation of the world that we can make sense of. This is an important issue to bear in mind because perceptions are not, and should not be thought of as, direct internal copies of the outside world. Any given perception is, in fact, a miraculous feat of cognition, but one that happens so invisibly to us that we do not appreciate how much cognitive effort, how much internal work and processing is really involved. For example, consider Deregowski's (1972) work on the three-dimensional perception of pictures, summarised in this chapter. In Western cultures we tend to see pictures in three-dimensions. But of course pictures are really two-dimensional representations of three-dimensional scenes and objects. We reconstruct the extra dimension by means of internal cognitive processes.

One of the debates in the study of perception is over the importance of 'top-down' or 'bottom-up' explanations. A *bottom-up* explanation is one that looks at the sensations we obtain from the environment and examines how we use these to create our perceptions. *Top-down* explanations look at the various higher mental processes that affect the way we perceive things. For example, our *expectations* have an affect on what we perceive, as shown in the simple drawing below (Figure 17.1). If the drawing is read from side to side then the middle item appears to be the letter 'B', but if it is read from top to bottom it appears to be the number '13'. So, which is it? It is neither and it is both, and the interpretation depends on the expectations we have of the figure as well as its simple shape.

One of the phenomena of perception is our ability to recognise people. Sometimes we are able to pick people out in a crowd, and those

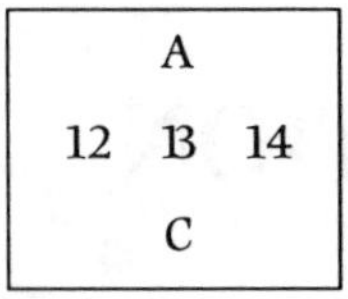

```
        A
  12   B   14
        C
```

Figure 17.1   *The effect of context on the perception of a simple shape*

of you who have done 'Where's Wally' puzzles (go on, you can admit it) will be able to recognise the skills involved in this. Sometimes our normally expert performance breaks down and we make mistakes in attempting to recognise faces and people. Such breakdowns give us fleeting glimpses of the processes that occur when everything is working normally. The summary of Young, Hay & Ellis' (1985) study of errors in face recognition is provided as an example of this strategy (see also Sperry, 1968, on hemispheric disconnection; Chapter 6 of this volume).

The chapter starts with a summary of Gibson & Walk (1960). This is a classic study of cognitive development, in which the researchers investigated babies' abilities to read the depth cues which allow us to perceive distance in three-dimensional visual arrays.

Walking Off a Cliff

■ Gibson, E.J. & Walk, R.D. (1960). The 'visual cliff'.
Scientific American, 202, 64–71.

Introduction

What does a newborn baby see when it first opens its eyes? This is a question which has puzzled philosophers and psychologists for many years, though unfortunately it is impossible to provide a full answer. The question is significant because it bears on the important nature–nurture debate within the field of visual perception. Finding an answer might allow us to understand which of our perceptual abilities are inborn, and which abilities we have to learn.

There are a number of ways of investigating the nature–nurture question, though all of the methods produce evidence that is open to more than one interpretation. One of the methods is to investigate *neonates* (new-born animals or babies) and try to assess their abilities. Since neonates have had little opportunity for learning, it is reasonable to suggest that any abilities they have are inborn (see Condon & Sander, 1974, Chapter 15 of this volume). However, this method presents a few problems since neonates, and especially human babies, cannot do a lot. Also, just because a baby does not respond to certain visual stimuli does not mean that it does not see them or understand them. It might mean that it is unable to respond.

One solution to this problem is to work with older babies who are better able to respond. This is the solution that Gibson and Walk chose in studying a sample of babies who could already crawl. The down side of this strategy is that the older the babies get, the more opportunity they will have had to learn any skills and abilities that they demonstrate. To compensate for this, they also studied a variety of animal neonates which were only 24 hours old.

The investigation of the abilities of human babies and animal neonates has progressed with the development of ingenious pieces of apparatus that can explore specific responses. An example of this is the 'visual cliff' which Gibson and Walk invented to examine whether young babies and animal neonates are able to perceive depth. The visual cliff is made up of a thick piece of glass placed over a wooden box. Under the glass is a

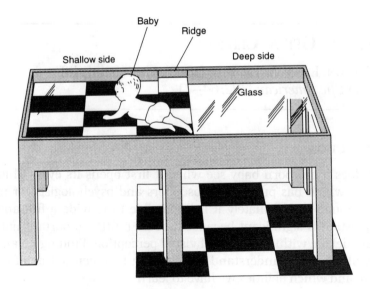

Figure 17.2 *The visual cliff*

change of levels, as shown in Figure 17.2. The baby is placed in the middle of the glass, and its mother tries to get it to crawl either over the shallow end of the apparatus or over the deep end of the apparatus. If babies crawl over the shallow end but refuse to crawl over the deep end it suggests that they are able to perceive depth.

THE STUDY

Subjects

Gibson and Walk tested 36 infants ranging in age from 6 months to 14 months. They also tested a variety of animal neonates including lambs, chicks, rats, kittens and turtles.

Results

(i) Children   Of the 36 children, nine stayed where they were and did not crawl in either direction. All of the 27 crawlers moved onto the shallow side at least once, and only three crawled over the deep side. Many of the infants crawled away from mother when she tried to encourage them to crawl over the deep side, and others stayed in the middle and cried. Some of the children peered through the glass and then backed away. Others

patted the glass yet despite this tactile reassurance still did not cross the 'cliff'. This suggests that babies that can crawl can also perceive depth.

(ii) Animals   Chicks tested at 24 hours after birth never made a mistake and always hopped onto the shallow side. Lambs and kids tested at 24 hours after birth always chose to go onto the shallow side. Rats went over the deep side as often as the shallow side. However, rats tend to use tactile cues when moving around (a common feature of nocturnal animals), and if the glass was lowered so that it was further away than the length of the rats' whiskers, then the rats used their visual sense and chose the shallow side 95 per cent of the time. Turtles chose the shallow side only 76 per cent of the time and chose the deep side on 24 per cent of the time. These creatures, however, are aquatic and so have much less reason to fear depth. These results suggest that animals are able to discriminate depth as soon as they are able to move around, and this has obvious survival value.

Perception of depth is aided by a number of different 'depth cues' (pieces of information in the two-dimensional image that suggest depth). Gibson and Walk continued their studies to look at two of these depth cues; pattern density and motion parallax.

(1) Pattern Density   If you move away from a pattern such as a check, then the elements of the pattern get smaller as you move away and the pattern appears to get more dense. Gibson and Walk put two different patterns either side of the middle section of the apparatus but at the same depth. The only difference was the type of pattern. One pattern was a small check and the other pattern was a large check. If pattern density is an important cue then the animals will choose the large check side because the narrow check suggests depth. They found that rats chose the large check, but one-day-old chicks showed no preference. This suggests that, for some animals at least, this cue requires some learning.

(2) Motion Parallax   As the observer moves, nearer objects appear to move faster. A good example of this is the view from a moving train where telegraph poles at the side of the train track appear to move much faster than the trees in the distance. The relative speed of the objects gives us a clue to how far away they are. Gibson and Walk investigated this cue by changing the pattern on the deep side so that it would produce the same image as the pattern on the shallow side. They did this by making the check bigger and more spaced out. Rats and chicks both continued to avoid the deep side which suggests that they used the cue of motion parallax from a very early age.

DISCUSSION

At first glance, the study suggests that some animals are born with the ability to perceive depth. However, the apparatus only allows the subjects to be tested after they start to move, and they might have already had some experiences that encouraged the learning of this skill. The most we can say about humans from this study is that babies as young as six months can perceive depth. In the end, then, this study leaves the question of whether this ability is inborn or learnt unanswered.

Nevertheless, the visual cliff has provided interesting insights into factors which affect depth perception. Later work showed another important ingredient in the way children make sense of their perceptual world. Sorce *et al.* (1985) put one-year-old infants on a visual cliff and got their mothers to wait at the other side. The mother was asked either to keep an expression of fear on her face, or to keep a happy and interested expression. The infants who saw the fearful face did not crawl across, but the infants who saw the happy face, looked down to check the cliff again and then crawled over. If, however, the babies were put on a flat plane with no visual cliff, they crawled over without checking with mother. In this study, then, the babies used social information to back up their perception of the environment.

It is worth noting the practical and ethical problems with the study. In particular the failure of 25 per cent of the babies to respond at all, and the number of babies who appeared to become very distressed at the sight of their mother enticing them over a cliff.

QUESTIONS

1 What are depth cues? And how many can you identify?

2 Give *one* piece of evidence from the study that suggests that some aspects of depth perception are innate.

3 Which pieces of evidence from the study suggest that some aspects of depth perception are learnt?

4 What is the nature–nurture debate?

5 Why do psychologists explore the nature–nurture debate?

Suggested Answers start at p. 460

KEY WORDS

depth cues	neonates
innate	pattern density
motion parallax	perception
nature–nurture debate	visual cliff

WHY DID THE ANTELOPE CROSS THE ROAD?

■ DEREGOWSKI, J.B. (1972). Pictorial perception and culture. *Scientific American, 227,* 82–88.

INTRODUCTION

This is a review article which tries to answer the question 'do pictures offer us a lingua franca for inter-cultural communication?' (p. 82). In other words, are pictures seen and understood in the same way in different cultures? Are pictures a universal means of communication which transcend culture and language? The answer provided by Deregowski is 'no!', and is based on empirical work which dates back to the studies of Hudson (1960).

Hudson (1960) had noted difficulties among South African Bantu workers in interpreting depth cues in pictures. Such cues are important features of two-dimensional representations (pictures) of a three-dimensional world, for they convey information about the spatial relationships among the objects in the picture. A person using depth cues will extract a completely different meaning from a picture than will a person who is not using such cues.

On the basis of his observations, Hudson constructed a test of three-dimensional picture perception which was used in many parts of Africa with subjects from different tribal and linguistic groups. The test comprised several pictures which contained within them various combinations of three depth cues: familiar size, overlap, and perspective. *Familiar size* refers to the cue whereby objects which are further away in the picture are drawn smaller than objects of the same size which are closer. The *overlap* cue is simply the effect of a nearer object obscuring parts of a more distant object. *Perspective* is given by the convergence of lines depicting edges which are parallel in the real world, but which appear to come together as they move into the distance. The classic example of this is the way that we draw a road or a railway line as it disappears into the distance.

The pictures were drawings of various combinations of the following elements: an antelope, an elephant, a person, a tree, a road, some hills and a flying bird. An example is given in Figure 17.3. The test involved showing the pictures to subjects and asking questions such as

Figure 17.3   *Pictorial depth perception*
Pictorial depth perception is tested by showing subjects a picture such as the above illustration. A correct interpretation is that the hunter is trying to spear the antelope, which is nearer to him than the elephant. An incorrect interpretation is that the elephant is nearer and is about to be speared. The picture contains two depth cues: overlapping objects and known size of objects. The bottom illustration depicts the man, elephant and antelope in true size ratios when all are the same distance from the observer.
Source: Deregowski (1972)

'what do you see?', 'what is the man doing?', and 'which is nearer, the antelope or the elephant?'. The questions were asked in the subject's native language. Correct responses to the questions indicated that the person was interpreting the depth cues as intended, and resulted in them being classified as a three-dimensional perceiver. Incorrect responses were taken to indicate that the subject was seeing the picture in two dimensions.

Deregowski summarises Hudson's findings as follows:

> The results from African tribal subjects were unequivocal: both children and adults found it difficult to perceive depth in the pictorial material. The difficulty varied in extent but appeared to persist through most educational and social levels.
> (pp. 84–85)

This summary is slightly at odds with Hudson's original data which show that the samples of school children that were tested showed much higher rates of three-dimensional perception than the adult samples. Some samples of adult subjects (57 illiterate Black mine labourers, for example) contained no three-dimensional perceivers (Hudson, 1960).

Further evidence that some subjects really were perceiving the picture in two dimensions was provided by a number of follow-up studies. One of these involved Zambian schoolchildren who had previously been labelled by Hudson's test as either two- or three-dimensional perceivers. Their task was to copy two figures. One of the figures was a straightforward trident shape. The other was the familiar trident illusion figure, in which the three prongs seem to merge into only two prongs at the handle (see Figure 17.4). Efforts to see this figure as a three-dimensional object cause perceptual confusion. The subjects had to lift a flap to see each figure, and could only draw when the flap was

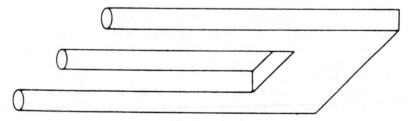

Figure 17.4   *Ambiguous trident is confusing to observers who attempt to see it as a three-dimensional object. Two-dimensional perceivers see the pattern as being flat and are not confused*
Source: Deregowski (1972)

put down again and the figure was obscured from view. Those children who had been labelled as three-dimensional perceivers found the trident illusion figure harder to replicate and spent more time looking at it than they did at the ordinary trident. Two-dimensional perceivers spent the same amount of time looking at each of the figures.

Deregowski discusses other cross-cultural differences in picture perception. He notes, for example, the fairly consistent preference among African children and adults for split-type drawings over perspective-type drawings. Split-type drawings (see Figure 17.5) show all the important features of an object which could not normally be seen all at once from the same perspective. Perspective drawings give just one view of an object, with features that cannot be seen from that perspective not represented in the picture. He notes that in some cultures split

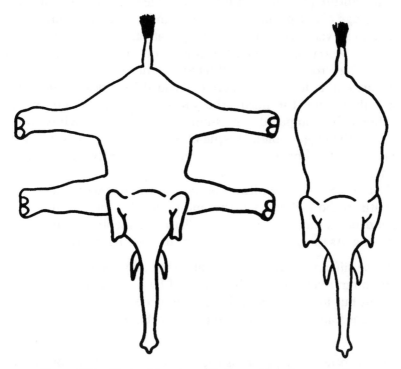

Figure 17.5 *Elephant drawing split-view and top-view perspective*
The split-elephant drawing (*left*) was generally preferred by African children and adults to the top-view perspective drawing (*right*). One person, however, did not like the split drawing because he thought the elephant was jumping around in a dangerous manner.

Source: Deregowski (1972)

drawing has been developed 'to a high artistic level' (p. 88), whereas in other cultures the perspective style is more common. The evidence that he draws on from art historians, anthropologists, and from the empirical work leads him to the conclusion that pictures are not a universal medium of communication, since they are perceived and produced in different ways by people of different cultures.

DISCUSSION AND EVALUATION

There is not enough cross-cultural work in psychology. For too long European and US researchers have conducted most of their empirical work in Europe and the USA, assuming that general principles of human behaviour and experience can be derived from such work. History and culture play such an important role in who and what we are, that findings about people at one time and in one place are unlikely to generalise very well to other people at other times and in other places. The worrying side effect of this is that the longer the literature of psychology remains so dominated by the perspectives of such a small range of cultures, the more embedded becomes the notion that these cultures are the norm, the yardstick against whom everyone else should be compared. Cross-cultural psychology, whilst not the answer to the bigger political issue of 'who's psychology is it anyway?', at least keeps the important issue of cultural diversity on the academic agenda.

As a piece of cross-cultural psychology, Deregowski's paper leaves one with mixed feelings. On the one hand, the effort to address the question of cultural differences in picture perception is worthy and interesting. As the author points out in his opening paragraph:

> These differences merit investigation not only because improvement in communication may be achieved by a fuller understanding of them but also because they may provide us with better insights into the nature of human perceptual mechanisms.
> (p. 82)

On the other hand, there is the nagging feeling that somehow the 'Western' interpretation and perceptual handling of pictures is implicitly privileged by the author. He does acknowledge the 'high artistic level' of split-style drawings, for example, but also suggests that children of *all* cultures produce this style of drawing at a certain stage of development. Is there an implication here that split-style drawing may represent a developmental stage of a *culture*, and that for the purposes of greater efficiency Western cultures have grown out of this stage, and into the more 'mature' perspective-style stage? Are we to infer that three-dimensional perception of drawings is more advanced than two-dimensional perception, rather than simply being a different interpretation of abstract symbols and conventional depth cues? This feeling of discomfort with the article is reinforced right from the start with some quotations from missionaries working in Africa at the turn of the twentieth century. For example:

> When all the people were quickly seated, the first picture flashed on the sheet was that of an elephant. The wildest excitement immediately prevailed, many of the people jumping up and shouting, fearing the beast must be alive, while those nearest to the sheet sprang up and fled. The chief himself crept stealthily forward and peeped behind the sheet to see if the animal had a body, and when he discovered that the animal's body was only the thickness of the sheet, a great roar broke the stillness of the night.
> (attributed to Mrs Donald Fraser, and cited by Deregowski, p. 82)

Whether this anecdote constitutes qualitative anthropological data, or whether it should be regarded as straight out of the dominant discourse of British colonialism is perhaps a matter for debate.

QUESTIONS

1   In the trident test, children who had been labelled as three-dimensional perceivers found the trident illusion figure harder to replicate and spent more time looking at it than they did at the ordinary trident. Why does this suggest that they were, indeed, perceiving the figure in three-dimensions? Equally, children labelled as two-dimensional perceivers spent an equal amount of time looking at the two figures and did not find one figure harder to replicate than the other. Why does this indicate that these children were, in fact, perceiving in two-dimensions?

2   What does ethnocentrism mean?

3   Why should we regard ethnocentrism as a problem in psychology?

Suggested Answers start at p. 461

KEY WORDS

cross-cultural studies
depth cues
ethnocentrism
illusions

perception
perspective
representations

Will the Real Ralph Richardson Please Stand Up

■ Young, A.W., Hay, D.C. & Ellis, A.W. (1985). The faces that launched a thousand slips: Everyday difficulties and errors in recognizing people.
British Journal of Psychology, 76, 495–523.

Introduction

Recognising other people is something we do so skilfully and effort-lessly that we are not even aware of doing it; not, at least, until we experience difficulties or make errors in the process. Such difficulties and errors are of interest to psychologists because they may give clues about how we recognise people, and about the underlying processes of 'person perception'. One way of trying to understand more about an everyday psychological process is systematically to examine instances when people's normally faultless performance breaks down. Gregory's work with visual illusions, for example, is based on the approach of forcing errors in perceptual processes (see Gregory, 1973). Errors like these can bring to light the features of a process which we are otherwise completely unaware of, both as people and as psychologists.

The article which is summarised here set out to investigate the everyday errors which people make when trying to recognise someone; errors such as forgetting a name, mistaking a face, not recognising someone we know. The authors' method is relatively naturalistic, since the data they collect come from subjects' own diary records of these phenomena, rather than from controlled laboratory studies. On the basis of their data, the authors speculate about the cognitive processes which underlie person recognition.

The Study

Subjects

Twenty-two people (11 female, 11 male) between the ages of 20 and 40, who were mainly students at Lancaster University in the UK, volunteered to take part in this study in return for a fee payable at the end of its eight-week duration. The subjects are referred to by the authors as 'diarists'.

Design

This was a diary study. Diary studies involve subjects keeping records (usually daily) about some feature of their everyday experience, so they qualify as a self-report method. The records in this case were a mixture of checklists, rating scales, and free-form description.

Procedure

Subjects kept records of incidents in which they had experienced difficulties or made errors in the process of recognising someone. A record for each incident was to be completed as soon as possible after it had occurred. The individual record sheets required that certain types of information regarding the incident were noted. Among other things, subjects were asked to:

- describe the incident briefly;
- identify the sources of information, such as facial features, voice and so forth, that had been available to them in the (mis)recognition process;
- estimate how well they knew the person (on a scale of one to five);
- judge (again on a Likert scale) how certain they had been that they had identified the person correctly;
- say whether there were any adverse conditions for recognition, such as obscured vision, stress, intoxication;
- describe briefly how the incident ended (how did they end up recognising the person correctly, if at all?);
- record if they were unable to recall certain details about the person, such as their occupation, their appearance, the sound of their voice, their name, and where they were usually seen;
- estimate how long the incident lasted.

The diaries lasted for eight weeks, the first of which was regarded as a training week. The results are based on the data collected from the final seven weeks of records. In addition to the data collected from the main record sheets, subjects were also asked to record information about instances of seeing people who resembled other people, even

Figure 17.6 *Some faces in a crowd often look a bit familiar even when they are not*
Source: Jill Furmanovsky/Camera Press London

though the resemblance did not cause any error in recognition. The 'resemblance' part of the study is not considered in this summary.

RESULTS

From the 922 completed records, the authors constructed a classification system based on seven types (and associated subtypes) of error or difficulty in person recognition. These types of error were derived from an analysis of the brief initial descriptions. The other data on each record were then used to highlight general characteristics of each type of error. Below are the four most common types of errors and difficulties, with one example description supplied for each subtype, and a brief indication of some of their key characteristics as summarised by the authors.

Person unrecognised

I knew that Raquel Welch was in the film, but I didn't recognise her when she came on.
(p. 500)

These are the most general errors considered in the data. A surprisingly large proportion of the temporarily unrecognised people were 'highly familiar' (42 per cent), and more than one quarter were people who the subjects would have expected to encounter at the time and place of the recorded incident.

Person misidentified

First Subtype: Unfamiliar Person Misidentified as Familiar Person

> I was waiting for the phone. A lot of people were walking past. I thought one of them was my boyfriend.
> (p. 505)

These misidentifications tended to be momentary, and to occur when viewing conditions were poor. They tended to end when the subject was able to see the person properly.

Second Subtype: One Familiar Person Misidentified as Another

> I was watching television. I knew that both Ralph Richardson and John Gielgud were present at the function being shown; but I mistook John Gielgud for Ralph Richardson. I realized my mistake when the real Ralph Richardson stood up.
> (p. 505)

These mistakes tended to happen most frequently for public figures known through the mass media. The person who the subject (wrongly) thought it was, tended to be more familiar to the subject than the person it really was.

Person seemed familiar only

First Subtype: Familiar Person Successfully Identified

> I was at the theatre when I saw someone in the audience I thought I knew. I didn't know who she was till I saw her with her sister and parents, who I know better.
> (p. 507)

The difficulties in recognition in these cases were generally when the person was not well known to the subject, and was seen in an unfamiliar context. The mental searching used to resolve the uncertainty could take some time.

Second Subtype: Incident Not Ended When Record Made

> I went to a meeting at the Trades Hall. I don't usually go there. I was sure I knew someone who was there, but after two hours I still can't think why or from where.
> (p. 507)

Third Subtype: Person Found to be Unfamiliar

> I just thought the person looked familiar, as she waved, and I thought it was at me. I waved back, then realised I didn't know her. She was waving at someone else.
> (p. 508)

Generally the duration of these incidents was short, and the difficulty was associated with adverse viewing conditions. Most of the incidents were resolved either when the subject got a better view, or when they spontaneously realised their mistake.

Difficulty of retrieving full details of person

First Subtype: Difficulty Successfully Resolved

> I saw another student walking past, but I couldn't remember his name, even though I'd been talking about him only a few days ago. Someone had to tell me it.
> (p. 508)

The most common failing in these cases, was retrieval of the person's name. The subjects tended to be very certain that they had recognised the person correctly, and could retrieve other bits of information about them: nearly all could recall the person's occupation; most were able to recall the person's voice (if it had not been heard); but less than half were able to recall the person's appearance if the person had not been seen. Bits of the name were sometimes available, in terms of first letters, or 'sounds like...', or even first names. Subjects reported using recall strategies such as going through the alphabet, focusing on the person's appearance, or just waiting for the name to come.

Second Subtype: Incident Not Ended When Record Made

> I met another student I knew from the reading party in Alexandra Square. I couldn't remember her name. I think there is a 'J' in it. It might be Jackie or Julie, but I don't know.
> (p. 509)

These incidents were similar to those in the first sub-type, particularly with respect to the likelihood of different bits of information being lost. Occupation was most often remembered, followed by where the person was normally seen, followed by the sound of their voice, then their appearance, and, most difficult of all, their name.

DISCUSSION

The model of person recognition which this data set is used to support is based on the notion of 'recognition units' and 'person identity nodes'. The idea is that recognition units are activated by different sources of information (facial features, voice and so forth). These units in turn activate the 'person identity node' of the resembled person (each person that we know is represented by an individual node), which in turn makes available other information about the resembled person. Usually this additional information confirms the resemblance and the person is recognised. On occasions, the person identity node wrongly confirms the resemblance and the person is misidentified. Sometimes insufficient recognition units are activated, and no identity node cannot be accessed. This would equate to the feeling that someone is familiar, without being able to recall who they are. Such a feeling is more common when we are dealing with unfamiliar people because, so the theory goes, the person identity nodes of unfamiliar people require much more information in order for them to be activated than do the nodes which represent familiar people.

Young *et al.*'s study is included in this collection principally because it is a good example of an infrequently used method of data collection; the diary method. Diary methods offer the possibility of looking at areas of people's lives which normally remain inaccessible to the research psychologist. A researcher cannot, for example, follow someone around for seven weeks observing slips of action; not, at least, without having a substantial effect on the behaviour of the person they are observing. Questions one and two, below, ask about the relative merits and drawbacks of diary methods.

QUESTIONS

1   What are some of the strengths of diary methods?

2   Identify some of the weaknesses of diary methods.

3   Try and record any face recognition errors that you catch yourself making. Compare your recognition errors with the ones described by Young, Hay and Ellis.

Suggested Answers start at p. 461

KEY WORDS

diary method   person perception
face recognition   qualitative data
Likert scale   recognition units
naturalistic methods   self-report methods
person identity nodes

18 MIND

In this chapter, the final two studies of part V address important philosophical issues to do with the nature of the mind. The remarkable thing about human beings is that we are able to reflect on our own experience and describe this experience to each other. One of the puzzles that emerges is that even when we know about how the brain works and we can describe our cognitive processes, we still cannot account for our unique personal experience of the world. We are all aware that we have a *mind*, but what is it and how does it work? The first study in this chapter (Baron-Cohen, Leslie & Frith, 1985) is about autistic children and tests the hypothesis that the central deficit of autism is a failure to develop a 'theory of mind'. In other words, the claim is that autistic children and adults are not very good at understanding what is going on in someone else's mind. The authors were able to show that autistic children tended to fail on a task which 'normal' children are consistently able to achieve by about the age of four. An adequately developed theory of mind (something that we take so much for granted that we are not even aware of having one) may be an essential prerequisite for effective interaction and communication among people.

In a completely different vein, and a more theoretical one at that, Searle (1980) took issue with certain ideas that have emerged from the field of artificial intelligence about the nature of the mind. The key question here is whether computers can think and whether they can be like people. This is a common theme in science fiction which blurs the distinction between people and machines. The classic silent film *Metropolis* explores this idea and suggests that technology will one day make us unable to tell the difference between a human being and a mechanical copy. Some psychologists suggest that it is possible for machines to mimic human thought, and computer programmes have been developed which at first glance show some of the signs of thought. Searle, however, challenges this view and argues that compu- ters can be a good tool for studying thinking, but cannot in themselves actually think. This remains an important argument because of the growing influence of computers in cognitive science, and their impact on how we think about the mind.

AUTISM AND THEORIES OF MIND

■ BARON-COHEN, S., LESLIE, A.M. & FRITH, U. (1985). Does the autistic child have a 'theory of mind'?
Cognition, 21, 37–46.

INTRODUCTION

Autistic children and adults have difficulties interacting with others, they also have difficulties communicating with others, and they tend to engage obsessively in a restricted range of activities. Various attempts have been made to discover the origins of autism and to identify a core deficit which can account for the typical range of behavioural symptoms of the syndrome. Bettelheim's (1967) psychoanalytic approach focused (unhelpfully) on poor parenting; Tinbergen & Tinbergen's (1983) ethological work directed attention towards interactions within families; and Lovaas (1979) took the typical behaviourist line and suggested that we should concentrate on the symptoms of autism rather than look for any underlying cause. In contrast to all these, the study summarised below emerged from a *social-cognitive* approach to understanding autism.

According to Baron-Cohen, Leslie & Frith (1985), the core feature of autism has to do with the autistic person's characteristic way of understanding other people (hence the label social-cognitive). They argue, specifically, that most autistic people do not develop a 'theory of mind' (Premack & Woodruff, 1978). That is, most autistic people do not seem to understand the notion that people, including themselves, have thoughts and beliefs about the world. Because this is such a taken-for-granted kind of understanding in everyday social life, the full implications of not having an adequately developed theory of mind are not immediately obvious. But the more you think about it the more you realise that social relationships and social interactions are based upon people's beliefs about other people's beliefs. For one thing, this ability to mind read allows us to anticipate what other people are likely to do. For example, an everyday comment such as 'I don't think so-and-so will like that' is based on the assumptions we have about what goes on in that person's mind. In fact if we could not conceive of other people's thoughts and beliefs, social interactions would become literally meaningless (see the example given in Question 1, below).

The Study

How can we investigate a person's theory of mind? How can we find out whether or not someone is able to understand the notion that other people have beliefs? One answer is to set up a task for subjects on which they can succeed only if they are able to attribute a belief state to another person. This is the strategy used by the authors of this study. The task that was set for the subjects in this study is known as the 'Sally-Anne' test (see Wimmer & Perner, 1983), which is a test of *false belief*. It is one that children who are developing 'normally' can usually succeed at by the age of four or five.

Subjects

Three groups of children were selected: 20 autistic children with a mean chronological age (CA) of 11;11 (11 years, 11 months) and a mean verbal mental age (vMA) of 5;5; 14 Down's syndrome children with a mean CA of 10;11 and a mean vMA of 2;11; and 27 'normal' children with a CA of 4;5 (who were assumed to have vMA's equivalent to their CA). Note that the estimated mental ages of the autistic children were higher than the estimated mental ages of the other groups of children.

Design

This was a straightforward quasi-experiment whereby the three experimental conditions were defined by the three groups of children who participated. The dependent measure was success or failure on the Sally-Anne test which is described below.

Procedure

The children were tested one at a time. They were seated behind a desk opposite the experimenter. On the desk were two dolls, Sally and Anne. Sally had a basket in front of her, Anne had a box. After introducing the dolls, the child's ability to name them was tested (the 'Naming Question'). The test unfolded as follows. Sally takes a marble and hides it in her basket. She then 'goes for a walk' and leaves the room. Whilst she is away, and therefore unknown to her, Anne takes the marble out of Sally's basket and puts it in her own box. Sally returns and the child is asked the key question 'Where will Sally look for her marble?' (the 'Belief

Figure 18.1 *Experimental scenario*
Source: Baron-Cohen, Leslie & Frith (1985)

Question'). The correct response is to point to or name Sally's basket; that is, to indicate that the child knows that Sally believes the marble to be somewhere where it is not. The incorrect response is to point to Anne's box. Two control questions are also asked: 'Where is the marble really?' ('Reality Question'), and 'Where was the marble in the beginning?' ('Memory Question'). Each child had two goes at this test. The second time round, a new location for the marble was introduced: the experimenter's pocket. The basic procedure is illustrated in Figure 18.1.

The only way for children to succeed in this task (other than by luck) is to attribute a belief to Sally. They have to be able to appreciate that Sally has beliefs about the world which can differ from their own beliefs, and which happen in this case not to be true.

RESULTS

The difference in performance on the belief question between the autistic children and the other children (as shown in Table 18.1) is reported by the authors as being statistically significant at the level of $p < .001$.

Table 18.1   The percentage of correct responses to each of the four
'Sally-Anne' questions

	Autistic children	Down's syndrome children	'Normal' children
Naming question	100	100	100
Reality question	100	100	100
Memory question	100	100	100
Belief question	20	86	85

DISCUSSION

All the children answered all the 'naming', 'reality' and 'memory' questions correctly. However, the belief question created more problems for the autistic children. Whereas at least 85 per cent of the 'normal' and Down's syndrome children gave the correct response to the belief question, only 20 per cent (4 from 20) of the autistic children were able to do so.

The 16 autistic children who gave the wrong response on both trials pointed to where the marble really was rather than to where Sally must believe it to be. Apparently, most of the autistic children were unable to appreciate that another person has their own beliefs which may not match up with how things really are. The results of the study lend support to the notion that autistic children may have underdeveloped 'theories of mind'.

Of course one study can never cover all the angles of such a complex topic. One question that immediately springs to mind in relation to this study has to do with its ecological validity. Specifically a sceptic might argue 'So, autistic children do not attribute beliefs to dolls. Might this not indicate that they have a more developed theory of mind than the experimenter who seems to think that a lump of plastic can think in the same way as a person?' The objection has been addressed by Leslie & Frith (1988) who were able to replicate the pattern of results in a study which used the same procedures, with the exception that Sally and Anne were replaced with real people.

The theory of mind hypothesis has been receiving support from a number of different sources, and certainly stands as a plausible core deficit of autism. It sits comfortably with the growing consensus among experts that the causes of autism are organic (that is, that autism is caused by some sort of physical damage to the brain).

Furthermore, it suggests that 'theory of mind' is an innate human capability which, in the absence of damage to the brain, unfolds as the child matures. Readers who are interested in the topics of autism and theory of mind are referred to the excellent books by Frith (1989) and Happé (1994).

QUESTIONS

1   How important do you think a theory of mind is for everyday social interaction?

2   Why does the experiment rely on *false* belief?

3   Why was the memory question asked?

Suggested Answers start at p. 462

KEY WORDS

autism   organic causes
chronological age   quasi-experiment
Down's syndrome   Sally-Anne test
ecological validity   social-cognitive
false belief tests   theory of mind

I'm Sorry Dave, I Can't Do That

■ Searle, J.R. (1980). Minds, brains and programs.
The Behavioral and Brain Sciences, 3, 417–57.

Introduction

The aim of those who work in the field of Artificial Intelligence (A.I.) is to build and programme computers to behave 'intelligently'. One area of A.I. has focused on programming computers to 'understand' natural language inputs. Natural language, in this context, means the sort of language that people use in their everyday lives, as opposed to the highly structured and inflexible language of computer programming. Some workers in the field wish to achieve artificial natural language understanding for the sake of it, simply because it would be useful if we could converse with computers without having to learn the obscure commands that are currently required. Others wish to find out more about how humans understand language by building computer models which allow them to test key aspects of their own theories.

Boden (1977) gives a detailed description and analysis of key natural language understanding programmes, including Weizenbaum's ELIZA, Winograd's SHRDLU and Schank's SAM. All of these programmes are able to handle various kinds of natural language inputs. ELIZA was able to respond to a user's input as if it were a non-directive psychotherapist. SHRDLU could converse about a virtual toy-blocks world. SAM was able to answer questions about, and provide synopses of, short stories that it had been told. But the question which springs to mind in relation to all of these programmes is, 'do they really understand the language?' It is the issue of *understanding* that Searle tackles in this famous article.

Searle begins by distinguishing between two positions within the field of artificial intelligence: strong A.I. and weak (cautious) A.I. The weak A.I. position holds that the computer is a very useful and powerful tool for studying cognition. Computer programmes can be written which put into practice theoretical models of cognitive processes. The performance of these models can be studied and compared with human performance. The models themselves are susceptible to detailed critical analysis because the discipline of writing a working computer programme requires the model builder to be precise and explicit about every detail of their theory. Searle has no argument with the weak A.I. position.

The strong A.I. position, on the other hand, holds that 'the appropriately programmed computer really *is* a mind, in the sense that computers given the right programs can be literally said to *understand* and have other cognitive states' (p. 417; emphasis as in original). Whereas weak A.I. operates on the assumption that computer models are only *simulating* cognition and understanding, strong A.I. assumes that the models are *duplicating* cognition and understanding. The Chinese Room Gedankenexperiment (thought experiment), which Searle describes in this paper, challenges the claims of strong A.I.

PROCEDURE

Thought experiments are a non-empirical form of investigation widely used in philosophy. The idea is that a mental scenario is constructed, and then the full implications of every element of that scenario are thoroughly thought out, taking each line of reasoning to a logical extreme. The Chinese Room is one such thought experiment, and a simplified version of it is described below.

The best way of thinking about the Chinese Room scenario is to imagine yourself as the central character. You are locked in a room on your own and given (perhaps through a letter box in the door) a card with a Chinese character on it (see Figure 18.2). You understand no Chinese, so the character just looks like a complex squiggle. In the room you have a pile of other cards which have Chinese characters on them. You also have a set of instructions, written in English (which you do understand), and these tell you how to match up the symbol that has just been posted through the door with one of the symbols in your own pile. The matching that you do is based on the distinctive patterns and shapes of the symbols which are described in the English instructions. You then post the correct symbol from your pile back out of the letter box in the door. This sequence of events is repeated again and again, and gradually you are able to perform the whole process pretty quickly.

Now, in artificial intelligence terms the person outside the room who is posting in the Chinese symbols is the computer user, you are the computer's central processor, the Chinese symbols which come in to the room are questions, the symbols which you post out of the room are answers, and the English instructions are the computer programme. To the user,

Figure 18.2   *Examples of Chinese characters*

who is a native Chinese speaker, it appears that you are able to under-stand Chinese, since the answers you give to the questions happen to be sensible and appropriate. In fact the answers you give are indistinguish-able from the answers that a native Chinese speaker might give. How-ever, if you have imagined yourself into this scenario it should be clear to you that you do not understand Chinese. All you have done is fol-lowed some rules which tell you how to manipulate certain symbols on the basis of a rather straightforward pattern matching exercise.

DISCUSSION

One of the targets of Searle's thought experiment was the *Turing test* (Turing, 1950), which was proposed as a hallmark test of whether a computer could think and understand. In the Turing test a subject communicates via a computer keyboard with two 'people' who are hid-den from view; one of these people is a real person, and the other is a computer programme. If the subject cannot reliably identify which is the computer and which is the person, then the computer programme has passed the test and can be said to be able to think and understand.

The Chinese Room scenario suggests that the ability to make responses in a language which are indistinguishable from those of a native speaker is not, in itself, sufficient to demonstrate *understanding*. Under certain circumstances ELIZA can pass the Turing test. But when it is revealed how the programme works it becomes clear that its use of rather unintelligent pattern-matching strategies (rather like the ones you use in the Chinese Room) in no sense amounts to understanding. Searle argues that the Turing test, which is 'unashamedly behavioristic and operationalistic' (p. 423), does not provide a measure of understanding.

Searle's original article is complex, dealing as it does with difficult philosophical issues such as intentionality and the causal powers of the brain. It is rounded off by a number of invited peer commentaries which challenge and develop his ideas. Searle is allowed the last word with a lengthy rejoinder to his critics. His conclusion:

> I conclude that the Chinese room has survived the assaults of its critics. The remaining puzzle to me is this: why do so many workers in AI want to adhere to strong AI? Surely weak AI is challenging, interesting, and difficult enough.
> (p. 456)

QUESTIONS

1   One of the most entertaining thought experiments was dreamt up by Dennett (Hofstadter & Dennett, 1981). Imagine having your brain removed by key-hole surgery, placing it in a life-sustaining solution in a glass container (like one sees in science-fiction films), and replacing all the severed nerve connections by means of mini radio transmitters (this takes a bit of imagination!). Your body then moves to the other side of the room and looks at your brain (you can still see because your eyes have been reconnected via the radio transmitters). Now ask yourself the question 'where am I?' Are you over there, or over here, and who, in any case, is doing the asking?. If your body commits a murder which bit of you should be locked up? (Safety note: don't try this at home kids.)

2   What does Searle mean when he asserts that the Turing test is 'behavioristic'?

3   What famous film is our title for this summary taken from?

Suggested Answers start at p. 463

KEY WORDS

artificial intelligence (A.I.)
Chinese room
Gedankenexperiment –
   thought experiment
natural language

strong artificial intelligence
Turing test
understanding
weak artificial intelligence

PART VI

HEALTH PSYCHOLOGY

Health psychology is relatively new and it is quite different from the traditional areas of psychology. For the best part of this century the different sub-disciplines of psychology, which are represented in the other parts of this book, have become more and more specialised, and more and more separate from each other. Some of the early psychologists like John Watson (see Chapter 14) carried out a range of research on such topics as the habits of the sooty tern, the behaviour of children in nursery classes, and the effect of health education films on a person's attitudes. Today, it is uncommon for psychologists to work outside their narrow specialism.

The study of health has reversed the trend towards specialisation because it looks at the wide range of factors that affect out health and our health behaviour. Our health is clearly affected by a whole variety of *biological events* including diseases and changes in body chemicals. However, our health is also affected by our *personal behaviour* including our choice of certain actions that are risky (for example, eating a meat pie from a street trader), and also our response to various bodily conditions. Furthermore, our behaviour is affected by the *social world* we live in with its expectations of how we should behave, and its explanations of various health conditions. So, psychology needs to integrate all the specialised areas of the subject in order to deal with specific health problems.

The major concerns of Health Psychology are outlined by Taylor (1990) as follows:

(a) *Health Promotion*   Over the past century there has been a decline in the incidence of acute infectious disorders such as tuberculosis,

351

measles and polio. At the same time there has been an increase in 'preventable' disorders such as lung cancer, cardio-vascular disorders, substance abuse and vehicle accidents. They are preventable because we develop the disorder mainly because of something we do; for example, lung cancer is relatively rare among non-smokers. Psychologists are interested in devising effective ways to encourage healthy behaviour.

(b) *Do Psychological States Cause Illness?* Or to put it another way, is there a disease-prone personality type? A major research area has been around Friedman & Rosenman's (1959) description of the Type A behaviour syndrome which is characterised by competitive drive, impatience, hostility, and rapid speech and motor movements. We have summarised an article on this topic in this part of the book.

(c) *Cognitive Factors in Health and Illness* Cognitive factors include our attitudes and our attributions, and the way we explain our experiences. In this collection we include a study on the concept of locus of control.

(d) *Stress and Coping* Stress is a topic that generates a lot of concern and a lot of research. The first three papers in this selection look at different issues around stress.

(e) *Lifestyle and Health* There are numerous factors in the way we live that contribute to ill health, and many of them are difficult to investigate because of the complex way we conduct our everyday lives. Some of the issues examined under this heading include, substance use, nutrition, exercise, and accidents.

(f) *Using the Health Services* Psychologists are interested in how patients interact with health professionals, how they experience hospitals, and why patients do not comply with instructions from doctors.

(g) *Pain* This is one of the puzzles of modern science, and we include a paper on the phenomenon of phantom limb pain.

(h) *Issues Associated with Chronic Diseases* A considerable amount of research has looked at the psychological variables associated with a range of specific disorders. The following list gives some indication of the breadth of the research areas; cardiac disorders, diabetes, disability, geriatric medicine, gynaecology, renal care, terminal care, cancer in children, AIDS. In this collection we include a description of one paper on the topic of AIDS.

19 STRESS AND COPING

Stress. We all have it, we all talk about it, we all blame it for all manner of things, but do we know what it is? Stress is part of our way of explaining ourselves and our behaviour. It is thought to cause a range of emotional, physical and social problems, but we do not seem to be able to remove it or identify its causes. Perhaps it is a good idea to start with one or two definitions.

We can think of the stress experience as being made up of two major components: stressors and the stress response. *Stressors* represent stimulus events that require some form of adaptation or adjustment, for example looking at your bank statement, or developing an illness. Stressors usually stimulate a relatively stereotyped set of responses; the stress response. This *stress response* is a complex pattern of reactions that has physiological, cognitive, emotional and behavioural components.

The issues for psychologists include how to measure stress and how to identify stressful behaviour patterns. One of the ways of measuring stress is to identify all the stressful events that have happened to you over a given time period. The early work by Holmes & Rahe (1967) has been very influential in this area and we include a summary of their original work.

When something happens to us, we might experience it as stressful, or we might experience it as challenging or exciting. One of the factors that will affect this interpretation is how much we feel able to cope with the event. So, when we are looking at stress it is also important to look at the issue of coping. Coping can be defined as the process of managing external or internal demands that are perceived as taxing or exceeding a person's resources. Our ability to cope will affect our experience of stress, and so our resources for coping and our ways of coping are important issues for psychologists to study. The paper by Billings & Moos (1981) looks at their attempt to classify the ways that people cope with everyday events.

The final paper in this collection on stress looks at the particular stresses of having AIDS. This paper takes a relatively unusual, but very fruitful, approach to the research and records some extensive interviews with people with AIDS, giving some general insights into stressors, and the ways that people cope with AIDS. It also describes some of the psychological effects of chronic disease.

LIFE IS STRESS

■ HOLMES, T.H. & RAHE, R.H. (1967). The social re-adjustment rating scale.
Journal of Psychosomatic Research, 11, 213–18.

INTRODUCTION

What are the events and experiences that affect our level of stress, and how can we measure the stress level on an individual? This is the question that Holmes and Rahe tried to address with their Social Re-adjustment Rating Scale. The scale looks at the stresses caused by major life events (the sort of events that we experience as difficult to deal with) and is based on previous research which had found that some social events that required a change in life style were associated with the onset of illness.

The paper describes the development of the Social Re-adjustment Rating Scale. This involved the collection of data which aimed to quantify the stress created by different events.

THE STUDY

An opportunity sample of 394 people (details are shown in Table 19.1) completed a pencil and paper test. The test consisted of 43 life events

Table 19.1   Characteristics of the sample

Group	Number in group
Male	179
Female	215
Age <30	206
Age 30–60	137
Age >60	51
Single	171
Married	223
Lower class	71
Middle class	323
White	363
Black	19
Oriental	12
Protestant	241

'empirically derived from clinical experience'. The subjects were given the following written instructions (instructions (b) and (c) are paraphrased):

(a) Social re-adjustment includes the amount and duration of change in one's accustomed pattern of life resulting from various life events. As defined, social re-adjustment measures the intensity and length of time necessary to accommodate to a life event, *regardless of the desirability of this event.*
(p. 213)
(b) Rate the events according to the amount of adjustment you think they require. Give your opinion of the average degree of re-adjustment necessary rather than the extreme.
(c) The first event on the list, 'marriage', is given an arbitrary value of 500. Look at each of the other events and consider whether it requires more or less re-adjustment than marriage, and whether it will take more time or less time to re-adjust. Give a number to each of the other events based on the 500 for marriage.

RESULTS

The Social Re-adjustment Rating Scale is shown in Table 19.2. The values were calculated from the average score given to each event, divided by 10. So the value for marriage, which was given to the subjects as 500, therefore became 50.

The researchers compared the responses of the different groups of people in their sample and found a startling degree of agreement. They calculated 16 correlations to compare the different groups and all but one showed an agreement of $r > .9$. The exception was the comparison of White subjects with Black subjects where the correlation was $r = .82$. Overall, then, it appears that the evaluation of stress is fairly constant across many groups of US society tested by Holmes and Rahe.

DISCUSSION

To measure your personal stress score, tick off the events that have occurred to you in a given time, usually 12 months or 24 months, and add up the re-adjustment values. A number of studies, by Holmes and Rahe in particular, have shown a connection between high ratings and subsequent illness and accident, though according to Sarafino (1994)

Table 19.2   Social re-adjustment rating scale

Rank	Life event	Mean value
1	Death of spouse	100
2	Divorce	73
3	Marital separation	65
4	Jail term	63
5	Death of close family member	63
6	Personal injury or illness	53
7	Marriage	50
8	Fired at work	47
9	Marital reconciliation	45
10	Retirement	45
11	Change in health of family member	44
12	Pregnancy	40
13	Sex difficulties	39
14	Gain of new family member	39
15	Business re-adjustment	39
16	Change in financial state	38
17	Death of a close friend	37
18	Change to different line of work	36
19	Change in number of arguments with spouse	35
20	Mortgage over $10 000	31
21	Foreclosure of mortgage or loan	30
22	Change in reponsibilities at work	29
23	Son or daughter leaving home	29
24	Trouble with in-laws	29
25	Outstanding personal achievement	28
26	Wife begin or stop work	26
27	Begin or end school	26
28	Change in living conditions	25
29	Revision of personal habits	24
30	Trouble with boss	23
31	Change in work hours or conditions	20
32	Change in residence	20
33	Change in schools	20
34	Change in recreation	19
35	Change in church activities	19
36	Change in social activities	18
37	Mortgage or loan less than $10 000	17
38	Change in sleeping habits	16
39	Change in number of family get-togethers	15
40	Change in eating habits	15
41	Vacation	13
42	Christmas	12
43	Minor violations of the law	11

Source: Holmes & Rahe (1967)

the correlation between rating and illness is only about $r = .3$ which is not a very strong relationship.

There are a number of problems with this method of measuring stress. For example, how commonly do the life events in the scale actually occur? A study of nearly 2800 adults by Goldberg & Comstock (1980) used a modified version of the scale and found that 15 per cent of the subjects experienced none of the events in the prior year (this seems hard to believe since one of the events is 'Christmas'), and 18 per cent reported five or more events. The number of events increased with the number of years of schooling, and, for adults, decreased with age from early adulthood to old age. It is debatable whether the scale can pick up these population differences and measure stress effectively for all people.

Other criticisms concern the items in the scale which are vague or ambiguous. Also, some of them will have greater value for some groups in society rather than others. There is also the issue of individual differences in our ability to cope with stressful events. It is worth noting, however, that the measurement of psychological phenomena is a singularly difficult enterprise, and it is usually easier to come up with criticisms of existing attempts than to devise better ways of doing things.

The stressful life-event approach to stress and illness generated a considerable amount of research, not least because the Social Re-adjustment Rating Scale developed by Holmes and Rahe provides a relatively straightforward way of measuring stress. It also conforms to everyday notions of the effect of dramatic events in our lives. In accounts of personal experience recorded in news reports it is not unknown for people to say how a particular event, such as unexpected bereavement, or desertion by a loved one has 'shattered my life'. But Kanner et al. (1981) argued that the minor stressors and pleasures of everyday life might have a more significant effect on health than the big, traumatic events assessed by the Holmes and Rahe scale, particularly in view of the cumulative nature of stress.

Kanner et al. (1981) developed a scale to explore these small events, which they called the Hassles and Uplifts Scale. They administered the checklist to a 100 middle-aged adults once a month for 10 months. The Hassles scale was found to be a better predictor of psychological problems than life-event scores, both at the time and later. Scores on the Uplift scale, however, only seemed to relate to symptoms in women. The men in the study seemed relatively unaffected by uplifts.

QUESTIONS

1 Identify three items in the scale that are likely to have different values for men and women, and say why.

2 Identify three items in the scale that are likely to have different values for people of different ages, and say why.

3 The scale was devised in the USA in 1967. What differences would you expect if you made up a similar scale today?

4 What other causes of stress, other than major life events, can you think of?

Suggested Answers start at p. 464

KEY WORDS

coping	Social Re-adjustment Rating Scale
correlation	stress
hassles	stressors
life events	uplifts

STRESS? I CAN HANDLE IT!

■ BILLINGS, A.G. & MOOS, R.H. (1981). The role of coping responses and social resources in attenuating the stress of life events.
Journal of Behavioral Medicine, 4, 139–57.

INTRODUCTION

How are you coping? This is a common enough question, though the answers we give are usually in terms of *how well* we are coping, rather than *what means* we are using to cope. But, what do we mean by coping? Coping has been defined by Lazarus & Folkman (1984) as the process of managing external or internal demands that are perceived as taxing or exceeding a person's resources. The development of health psychology has brought about a framework for investigating coping, which has tended to focus on three different aspects: the mechanisms involved in coping, the experience of coping, and different strategies for going about coping. The model of coping put forward by Lazarus and Folkman suggested that the stress experience is moderated by two basic *appraisals*; the first of these is an appraisal of the level of threat, and the second is an appraisal of the person's own resources for dealing with it (see Figure 19.1).

One of the important problems for psychologists is to find some way of measuring coping so we can find out exactly how people cope, which methods of coping are most effective for which situations, and how we can improve the coping strategies of people who are struggling.

The previous paper, by Holmes and Rahe, looked at stressful life-events, how to classify them, and how to estimate their effect on the individual. Some psychologists have suggested, however, that the way that people handle stressful events may be one important set of influences on the long-term effects of the stress. The paper by Billings and Moos attempts to *operationalise* and classify the coping responses used by a non-clinical, adult community sample.

THE STUDY

Billings and Moos begin by reviewing the various approaches to coping. One approach sees coping as a set of psychological processes (such as

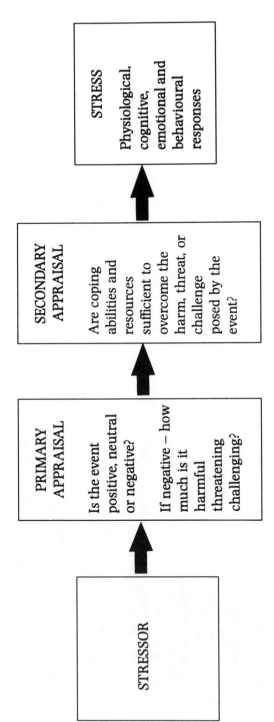

Figure 19.1 *The experience of stress*

Table 19.3   Composition of method and focus of coping measures

Coping items	Method of coping			Focus of coping	
	Active cognitive	Active behavioural	Avoidance	Problem focused	Emotion focused
Tried to see positive side	X				X
Tried to step back from situation and be more objective	X				X
Prayed for guidance and strength	X				X
Took things one step at a time	X			X	
Considered several alternatives for handling the problem	X			X	
Drew on my past experiences: I was in a similar situation before	X			X	
Tried to find out more about the situation		X		X	
Talked with a professional person (e.g. doctor, clergy, etc.)		X		X	
Took some positive action		X		X	
Talked with spouse or another relative about the problem		X		X	
Talked with a friend about the situation		X		X	
Exercised more		X			
Prepared for the worst			X		X
Sometimes took it out on other people when I felt angry or depresssed			X		X
Tried to reduce the tension by eating more			X		X
Tried to reduce tension by smoking more			X		X
Kept my feelings to myself			X		X
Got busy with the other things in order to keep my mind off the problem					X
Didn't worry about it; figured everything would probably work out					X

Source: Billings & Moos (1981)

denial) which protect the individual from external and psychological threats. The most well-known example of this approach is the idea of *ego-defence mechanisms*. This approach limits itself to looking at how we maintain a psychological and emotional balance, and does not include the cognitive and behavioural responses directed at changing the stressor or avoiding it. Another approach has looked at the *methods of coping*, and attempted to classify the responses into cognitive and behavioural strategies. Alternatively, a further approach has looked at the *focus of coping* and categorised the strategies into problem-focused strategies and emotion-focused strategies. Billings and Moos attempted to combine the methods of coping and the focus of coping approaches in their analysis.

Subjects

The researchers contacted a random selection of families in the San Fransisco Bay area. A further sample of matched families were selected from a population of families with an alcoholic member. A questionnaire was mailed to 360 families, and 294 replied (an 82 per cent response rate). Twenty-seven were single-parent families, and 267 were families with two parents present. The ethnic distribution was 82 per cent White, five per cent Mexican-American, four per cent Asian, three per cent Black and six per cent other background. This distribution was quite close to the proportions of different peoples in the general population, and the average income of the sample families also matched the average for the area.

The survey

The researchers collected data on four types of measures:

(1) *Negative life change events*, using a modified version of the Social Re-adjustment Rating Scale (see the study by Holmes and Rahe);
(2) *Coping responses*: respondents were asked to indicate a recent personal crisis or stressful event and then answer 19 yes/no items which looked at how they dealt with the event. The items were selected from previous inventories and a review of the research (see Table 19.3);
(3) *Social resources*, measured by two indices: a quantitative measure of the number of relationships and amount of activity with family, friends, relatives, friends and co-workers, membership of clubs and

organisations etc. Also a qualitative measure that looked at cohesion, expressiveness and conflict within the family;

(4) *Three mood and symptom dimensions*: depression, anxiety, and stress-related physical symptoms.

RESULTS

The results showed some small gender differences with women reporting more emotion focused strategies, and more avoidance and active behavioural strategies than men. Billings and Moos also looked at the coping strategies for different events and these results are shown in Table 19.4. Although there are some notable differences, the major observation is of the relative consistency of response to a variety of events.

The indices of coping and social resources appeared to have an effect on the relationship between the stressful event and the person's ability to deal with it, and also provided some information about how stressful the events were. The relationship between social resources and coping is seemingly very complex and contradictory. For example, the death of a loved friend or partner causes stress and reduces the available support, but the remaining social relationships may be used and even strengthened when dealing with the loss.

Table 19.4 Mean percentage of coping responses for each type of stressfull event

Coping measures	Type of event					
	Illness	Death	Economic	Children	Other inter-personal	Other non-inter-personal
Method of coping						
Active cognitive (% yes of 6)	62	58	67	66	67	55
Active behavioural (% yes of 6)	70	56	56	60	67	57
Avoidance (% yes of 5)	24	23	21	26	29	19
Focus of coping						
Problem focused (% yes of 6)	54	40	53	49	54	51
Emotion focused (% yes of 11))	39	35	37	41	41	55

Source: Billings & Moos (1981)

Overall, Billings and Moos suggested that it may not be possible to identify 'positive' or 'negative' types of coping because of this complex relationship between coping, social support and the event to be dealt with. However, they noted that more reliance on active attempts to deal with the event and fewer attempts to avoid dealing with it were associated with less stress.

DISCUSSION

One of the strong features of the study is its attempt to deal with an everyday aspect of human experience and to consider it in the widest possible social context. This is also, of course, the weakness of it as well, because the data that come out of it are not clear cut, and the measures they use can only make crude estimates of the variables they are examining.

The research generally suggests that dealing with a stressful situation is better than avoiding it. However, some studies find the reverse. For example, Cairns & Wilson (1984) found that people who lived in areas of Northern Ireland which had a high degree of sectarian violence tended to have a higher level of psychological disorder than people who lived in more peaceful areas, particularly if they had a realistic appraisal of the amount of violence that was going on. But those who adopted a coping mechanism which the researchers termed denial, in which they inaccurately perceived there to be relatively little violence, seemed to have lower levels of disturbance. The suggestion being that if you are in a situation where reality really *is* threatening, then being unrealistic about how dangerous it is may help you to cope!

QUESTIONS

1   What variables did the researchers measure?

2   How did they measure them?

3   Suggest one other way that you could measure coping?

4   What factors affect your ability to cope with an unpleasant experience?

Suggested Answers start p. 464

KEY WORDS

appraisal
coping
ego-defence mechanisms
emotion-focused coping
denial
life events

problem-focused coping
qualitative measures
quantitative measures
social resources
social support
stress

AIDS AND UNCERTAINTY

■ WEITZ, R. (1989). Uncertainty and the lives of persons with AIDS.
Journal of Health and Social Behavior, 30, 270–81.

INTRODUCTION

AIDS (see Table 19.5) was always going to be different to other diseases. It made us discuss taboo topics like sex and drugs, it made us watch embarrassing television demonstrations of how to put a condom on a carrot, and it made us accept that the only protection from it is to change our behaviour. Doctors have got no cures to offer, but psychologists have studied behaviour for over a century so surely they can tell us something. The health threat posed by AIDS presented psychology with a very real challenge and provoked a large body of research.

The research into AIDS has raised a whole range of issues including how much we know about what people actually do, and how we can research issues of personal behaviour. In this particular study, Weitz was interested in how people who had developed AIDS managed to deal with the disorder and how they made sense of their lives. She decided to use extensive interviews with a relatively small number of people and from her data she derived some themes that tell us something about the experience of having AIDS, and also give some general insights into how people deal with chronic disease.

Table 19.5   AIDS

AIDS stands for Acquired Immune Deficiency Syndrome

HIV stands for Human Immunodeficiency Virus

It is generally believed that AIDS is caused by HIV. It attacks one type of white blood cells – the T helper lymphocytes – reduces the competence of immune system, and makes body vulnerable to attacks by malignancies and infections

If someone is infected with HIV they can continue without any symptoms for several years. Alternatively, they might develop a number of symptoms including swollen glands, weight loss, diarrhoea, fever and fatigue. This collection of symptoms are referred to as AIDS RELATED COMPLEX (ARC)

The diagnosis of AIDS also requires identification of malignancy or infection not associated with a healthy immune system

THE STUDY

This study concentrates on the issue of uncertainty which has been recognised as crucial for chronically and terminally ill people, and a major source of stress in their lives. The feeling of uncertainty occurs when someone lacks a cognitive framework to understand their condition or situation, and when they cannot predict outcomes of their behaviour or condition. Few people tolerate uncertainty well, and they deal with it in a variety of ways. Two basic coping strategies have been identified:

(a) *Vigilance* – where people try and research possible diagnoses and so predict how their condition will develop, and
(b) *Avoidance* – where people try and protect themselves against unpleasant knowledge by attributing symptoms to less harmful conditions, and not seeking medical advice.

These strategies create frameworks that allow the people to explain their situation to themselves and increase their sense of personal control.

Method and sample

Between July 1986 and March 1987, Weitz interviewed 25 residents of Arizona (USA) who had AIDS or AIDS-related complex (ARC). Four to six months after the initial interview 13 were re-interviewed (two declined to participate further, two had moved without leaving a forwarding address and eight had died or suffered brain damage in the interim). The interviewees were mainly men who described themselves as homosexual or bisexual, plus two heterosexual women who were intravenous drug users.

Respondents all referred themselves to the study from support projects or from the gay community. The sample was compared against populations of people with AIDS, and it was found that on issues of religion, geographical location and mode of transmission, the sample was representative of the population. However, the sample underrepresented people with Kaposi's sarcoma (a skin cancer), people of colour, and older people.

Each interview lasted from two to five hours at the respondent's or the interviewer's home. From the vast amount of material gathered from these interviews, Weitz was able to identify seven themes in the respondents' descriptions of their situations.

RESULTS

The findings are summarised under seven questions which are each the source of some uncertainty.

(1) *Will I Get AIDS?* Fear of contracting AIDS is a big issue for gay and bisexual men. Among the respondents some assumed they had the infection long before diagnosis, whereas others developed theories that reduced their personal risk. Obtaining a test for the presence of HIV ought to reduce some uncertainty, but all except two of the respondents had initially declined to take a test. They reasoned that if they tested positive then it would increase their uncertainty and increase their sense of stigma. A positive test would not tell them if or when they would develop AIDS so they would, in fact, be worse off than not knowing. They avoided the test until it was quite clear that they had developed AIDS.

(2) *What Do My Symptoms Mean?* The symptoms of AIDS build up gradually, and it is possible to blame the symptoms on a variety of causes. For example, several men blamed their night sweats and exhaustion on the Arizona heat, and others confused their AIDS symptoms with the side effects of drug use. When the symptoms continued, the respondents found themselves in a position experienced by many people who develop chronic illnesses such as multiple sclerosis. They were anxious about their symptoms, but did not have the social support for adopting a sick-role because they had not received a diagnosis.

(3) *Why Have I Become Ill?* The respondents had all tried to come up with a reason for their illness, and although some had integrated it into religious experience (for example, believing that AIDS was a test from God), most of them had underlying attributions of personal guilt. On the whole, they blamed their promiscuity, homosexuality, lack of forethought, or drug use, but they were still left with the question 'Why me?'.

(4) *Will I Be Able to Function Tomorrow?* In common with many other chronic disorders, AIDS causes unpredictable flare-ups and remissions. This made it very difficult to plan anything, even as simple as going shopping with someone the following Tuesday, because they did not know how they would feel on that day. As a consequence they tended to avoid plans, both long and short term, to avoid disappointment.

(5) *Will I Be Able to Live With Dignity?* Fear of death is minimal compared to the fear of what life may become. In particular, the respondents feared neurological impairment (which is common in people

with AIDS), and disfigurement by Kaposi's sarcoma (which occurs in ten per cent of people with AIDS). They especially feared the unusual illnesses whose effects they could not predict. One respondent said:

> I'm not [as] afraid of getting infections from people as I am from inanimate objects like fruits and moldy tile ... I know what a cold is like ... [It's] something I have experienced. I've never experienced a mold infection.
> (p. 277)

(6) *Will I Be Able to 'Beat' AIDS?* Can we beat death and live forever? The simple answer is 'no', but it did not stop the respondents from wondering whether God or medicine would be able to cure them. They reported various behaviours that they hoped would preserve or improve their health. These included prayer, a change of diet, exercise, and attempts to enhance the will to live. Some had also managed to illicitly obtain experimental drugs that were being used in trials that were attempting to find a cure for AIDS.

(7) *Will I Be Able to Die With Dignity?* The uncertainty about how prolonged their final days would be led some of the people with AIDS to sign living wills to prevent physicians keeping them alive by extraordinary means, and some had made plans to commit suicide.

Weitz acknowledges that uncertainty is a central problem for people with many disorders, but she believes that it will have a particularly large impact on people with AIDS. This is because:

(a) They are more likely to know before diagnosis that they are at risk.
(b) They are likely to feel guilt over behaviours that led to the illness such as drug use or sexual choices.
(c) They have difficulties in obtaining accurate diagnosis.
(d) They have difficulty in predicting the effects, since AIDS causes more extensive and less predictable physical and mental damage than other illnesses.
(e) Since it is a new disease, people with AIDS are more likely to lack answers to questions about treatment and prognosis.

Weitz goes on to draw some policy implications including the suggestion that care workers should consider using the technique of *stress inoculation*. Janis (1983) suggests that people handle stress most effectively if they feel they are in control of their lives. To this end stress inoculation involves:

(1) giving people information about what to expect, which is realistic but which still allows them to maintain optimism,
(2) encouraging people to identify possible actions that can help them to survive and to find internal and external resources that allow them to take those actions,
(3) helping people to develop their own plan for responding to the situation.

DISCUSSION

The study uses a very small sample of people but produces findings that appear to have some general relevance to health psychology as a whole. An important methodological comparison to make is between these relatively unstructured interviews and the tightly controlled questionnaires that are used for investigating Type A behaviours (see the following study by Friedman & Rosenman) or for examining locus of control (see Langer & Rodin 1976, also in the following chapter). The comparison is between *quantitative data* (the scores from the questionnaires), and *qualitative* data (from Weitz's interviews). The qualitative data are clearly more difficult to obtain and also more difficult to interpret, but give an opportunity for the researchers to explore the complex experiences of the people they are studying.

QUESTIONS

1 Why were people with the disfiguring Kaposi's sarcoma and people of colour missing from the sample?

2 What are the problems with this type of qualitative research?

3 Look at question three under the heading 'Results' (above). What other disorders might involve a sense of guilt in the people who develop them?

Suggested Answers start at p. 465

KEY WORDS

AIDS	people of colour
attributions	qualitative data
avoidance strategies	quantitative data
chronic disease	stigma
coping strategies	stress inoculation
Kaposi's sarcoma	uncertainty
living wills	

20 HEALTH BEHAVIOUR

All of us engage in behaviours that have some health risk. It might be an excess of alcohol, or it might be our eating habits, a lack of exercise, risky sexual behaviour or dangerous sports. The problem for psychologists is to find out which behaviours are associated with illness, and to find out how we make our decisions to behave in the way we do.

An obvious starting point would be to look at our attitudes and beliefs. If we believe something is unhealthy then, surely, we won't do it. Unfortunately, it is not as simple as that, and the study by LaPiere (see Chapter 2) illustrates how our behaviour often does not connect with our attitudes. One of the attempts to describe how we take decisions is the Health Belief Model of Becker & Rosenstock (1984). According to this model, the likelihood that someone will take preventive action depends directly on two assessments that they make; (a) evaluating the threat, and (b) a cost–benefit analysis.

The factors that influence a person's *perceived threat* of illness include the perceived seriousness of the health threat, how susceptible the person believes themselves to be, and what social cues there are to encourage them to do something about it. The *cost–benefit* assessment, on the other hand, looks at whether the perceived benefits exceed the perceived costs. The costs might be financial, situational (difficult to get to a health clinic), or social (don't want to acknowledge getting old). The benefits might be improved health, relief from anxiety, and reduced health risks.

The model has attracted a large amount of research and much of it is supportive of the basic theory. However, there is no standard way of measuring the variables in the model such as perceived susceptibility. Also, there are a number of health behaviours that do not fit the model, such as habits (for example teeth brushing), and delay in reporting heart attacks.

In this chapter, we have chosen to look at one attempt to match up a pattern of behaviour to a number of health problems, and also to look

374 INTRODUCING PSYCHOLOGICAL RESEARCH

Table 20.1 Type A and Type B behaviour pattern

Classifying behaviour into Type A or Type B is usually done by interview or by questionnaire. Examples of questions are:

1. 'Has your partner or friend ever told you that you eat too fast?'
   Type A's are likely to say, 'Yes, often'
   Type B's are likely to say, 'Yes, once or twice' or 'No'

2. 'How would your partner, or best friend, rate your general level of activity?'
   Type A's are likely to say, 'Too active, need to slow down'
   Type B's are likely to say, 'Too slow, need to be more active'

3. 'Do you ever set deadlines or quotas for yourself at work or at home?'
   Type A's are likely to say, 'Yes, once a week or more often'
   Type B's are likely to say, 'Only occasionally'

4. 'When you are in the middle of a job and someone (not your boss) interrupts you, how do you feel inside?'
   Type A's are likely to say, 'I feel irritated because most interruptions are unnecessary'
   Type B's are likely to say, 'I feel O.K. because I work better after an occasional break'

at an attempt to manipulate a cognitive variable to improve someone's health. The pattern of behaviour is the *Type A* syndrome where research has suggested a connection between an aggressive and hostile lifestyle and heart disease. This research was started by Friedman & Rosenman (1959), and the method of classifying people is usually by questions such as the ones in Table 20.1. A similar method is used to investigate how people experience their level of control over their lives. The work on *locus of control* was started by Rotter (1966) who suggested that people can either see themselves in control of their own lives or they see themselves as being controlled by events. The article by Langer & Rodin (1976) which we summarise, looks at how people were encouraged to take more control of their lives and so improve their health. The final article in this chapter, on phantom limb pain (Melzack, 1992), gives a flavour of the complexities of the relationship between psychology and health, and illustrates the connection between biological and psychological variables.

Type A or Not Type A

■ Friedman, M. & Rosenman, R.H. (1959).
Association of specific overt behaviour pattern with
blood cardiovascular findings.
Journal of American Medical Association, 169, 1286–96.

Introduction

Do some lifestyles make people more vulnerable to disease? 'You'll make yourself ill with worry' mutters the helpful voice in our ear, but is there any evidence for this? Are we justified in associating high-stress behaviour with certain health problems such as heart disease? Friedman and Rosenman investigated this and created a description of behaviour patterns that has generated a large amount of research and also become part of the discussions on health in popular magazines.

Text books and articles often describe their work as referring to the Type A Personality, though, at least in the original paper, the authors describe a *behaviour pattern* rather than a personality type. The difference between these two things is that a personality type is what you *are*, whereas a behaviour pattern is what you *do*. The importance of this distinction comes in our analysis of why we behave in a particular way ('I was made this way', or 'I learnt to be this way'), and what can be done about it. It may be easier to change a person's pattern of learnt behaviour than it is to change their nature.

The Study

On the basis of previous research and their own clinical experience with patients, Friedman and Rosenman devised a description of Pattern A behaviour that they expected to be associated with high levels of blood cholesterol and hence coronary heart disease.

Pattern A Behaviour:

(1) An intense, sustained drive to achieve your personal (and often poorly defined) goals.
(2) A profound tendency and eagerness to compete in all situations.
(3) A persistent desire for recognition and advancement.

(4) Continuous involvement in several activities at the same time that are constantly subject to deadlines.
(5) Habitual tendency to rush to finish activities.
(6) Extraordinary mental and physical alertness.

Pattern B behaviour, on the other hand, is the opposite of Pattern A, characterised by the relative absence of drive, ambition, urgency, desire to compete, or involvement in deadlines.

The authors also described a third behaviour pattern (Pattern C), which was similar to Pattern B but also included a chronic state of anxiety and insecurity. This third pattern was investigated by examining the health of 46 blind men, some of whom were institutionalised and many of whom were unemployed. The differences in this group from the other people in the study, and the differences in the way the data were collected, make comparisons difficult, so for the rest of this summary we will concentrate on Pattern A and Pattern B.

Subjects

The researchers asked business people to put forward the names of people in their organisation who predominantly showed the Pattern A behaviour. Over 96 per cent of the selected subjects agreed to take part in the study. They came from a range of businesses and held both executive and non-executive positions. All were men. In total, 83 men were studied in Group A with around half being between 40 and 50 years old. Group B were selected to match the subjects in Group A in terms of their physical appearance, and differing only in terms of their behaviour pattern. Group B was predominantly made up of union officials and accountants.

Procedure

Each subject was given a personal interview about their family history of heart disease, past and present illnesses, hours of work and sleep, smoking habits, activity and dietary habits. Then the interviewers investigated whether the pattern of behaviour was fully developed. This judgement was based on the body movements, tone of voice, gesturing, air of impatience of the subject, and also their self report of their own level of drive, competitiveness and sense of urgency. Of the 83 men in

Group A, 69 were judged to have a fully developed behaviour Pattern A, and in Group B, 59 of the men were judged to have a fully developed behaviour Pattern B.

All the men were asked to keep a full diary of their food and alcohol intake for seven days. The subjects were given code numbers to protect their anonymity and encourage accurate reporting. The data were then analysed by dieticians who were not aware of the identity of the subjects.

A number of physiological measures were taken including:

(a) serum cholesterol level;
(b) blood coagulation (clotting) time;
(c) electrocardiograph readings;
(d) test for arcus senilis (inspecting the eyes to look for an opaque ring around the cornea which is caused by the breakdown of fatty deposits in the bloodstream).

RESULTS

A summary of the key features of the data is shown in Tables 20.2 and 20.3. Group A subjects had been selected for their Pattern A behaviour, and also differed from Group B in that they worked longer, exercised more, smoked more, drank more alcohol but ate fewer fats.

In the physiological measures, there was relatively little difference in the blood clotting time of the two groups (though if the data were analysed for only the fully developed behaviour pattern subjects, then the

Table 20.2 A comparison of the subjects who displayed Pattern A and Pattern B behaviours

	Number of subjects	Weight (lbs)	Hours work/week	Hours exercise/ week	Number of smokers
Group A	83	176	51	10	67
Group B	83	172	45	7	56

	Cigarettes/ day	Alcohol calories/day	Total calories	Fat calories
Group A	23	194	2049	944
Group B	15	149	2134	978

Source: Adapted from Friedman & Rosenman (1959)

Table 20.3   A comparison of blood and illness for Group A and Group B

	Average clotting time (minutes)	Average serum cholestrol (mg/100 ml)	% of subjects with arcus senilis	% of subjects with signs of coronary heart disease
Group A	6.9	253	38	28
Group B	7.0	215	11	4

Source: Adapted from Friedman & Rosenman (1959)

blood of Group B was found to clot significantly slower, which is a healthy response). Group A subjects showed considerably higher (and therefore worse) cholesterol levels, and a higher incidence of arcus senilis. The most striking difference, however, was the incidence of coronary heart disease, where over a quarter of the men in Group A showed signs of the disorder.

DISCUSSION

The first question to consider is how we can explain the difference in health of the two groups of subjects. It is unlikely to be diet since the two groups appeared to have similar food intakes and, in fact, the Group A subjects ate less fat than Group B. Exercise is unlikely to be the answer either since Group A carried out more exercise then Group B. Friedman and Rosenman concentrated their explanations on the behaviour patterns shown by the two groups of men. Could it be that the competitive style of life leads to coronary heart disease? It is an appealing conclusion, but there are at least two other possible sources of the health problems. Table 20.2 shows that Group A contained more smokers and their average consumption of cigarettes was far higher than Group B. Since this study was carried out, there has been a growing acknowledgement of the serious health risks of smoking which include a high incidence of coronary heart disease in heavy smokers. The other factor is the alcohol intake which was 30 per cent higher in Group A.

The idea that people can be categorised into simple types has an appeal to a range of practitioners because of the implications for predictions of future health, and predictions of job performance. The relationship between personality type and ill health is far from straightforward however, as Ragland & Brand (1988) discovered in their follow-up of a study started in 1960. Their original study used measures of the Type A behaviour pattern to identify 257 men who subsequently had coronary heart disease in 1969, and they found that, in the first eight years of the investigation, the measure of Type A behaviour was successful in predicting the development of coronary heart disease. However, in the follow-up conducted some 22 years later, the initial behaviour pattern of the men was compared with their subsequent mortality rates. Ragland and Brand found that among the 231 men who survived the first coronary event for 24 hours or more, those who had initially displayed a Type A behaviour pattern died at a rate much lower than the men who displayed a Type B behaviour pattern (19.1 versus 31.7 per 1000 person-years). This subsequent finding was rather unexpected. It may indicate that people who display the Type A behaviour pattern respond differently to a coronary event than do people who display the Type B behaviour pattern. Alternatively, Type A behaviour patterns may cease to be a risk factor after such an event. People may take warning and change their lifestyle.

The lasting appeal of the Type A behaviour pattern is its simplicity and plausibility. Unfortunately, health is rarely that simple and the interaction of stress with physiological, psychological, social and cultural factors cannot be reduced to two simple behaviour patterns. However, the work has focused attention on the role of lifestyle in health, and provided a stimulus for a range of research projects and therapeutic interventions with coronary-prone patients.

QUESTIONS

1   The study was conducted exclusively on men. Do you think they would have obtained different results for women?

2   What criticisms can you make of their selection of subjects?

3   What other factors in lifestyle might affect our health?

Suggested Answers start at p. 465

KEY WORDS

anonymity	lifestyle
cholesterol	personality type
coronary heart disease	self report
diet	smoking
habits	stress
health risks	Type A behaviour pattern

In Control

■ LANGER, E.J. & RODIN, J. (1976). The effects of choice and enhanced personal responsibility for the aged: A field experiment in an institutional setting.
Journal of Personality and Social Psychology, 34, 191–98.

INTRODUCTION

How in control do you feel? Psychologists in the field of health have investigated how much the experience of being in control will affect the long-term health of patients. This work stems from the ideas of Rotter (1966) who suggested that people differ in the way that they experience their *locus of control*; in other words, where they feel the control over events in their life comes from. Some people perceive themselves as having an *external* locus of control, which means they do not feel that they can personally control events. They see their lives as being controlled by outside forces. On the other hand, some people perceive themselves as having an *internal* locus of control, which means they experience themselves as exerting personal control over events in their lives. For people with an external locus of control it seems as though things happen to them. Those with an internal locus of control feel that they themselves make things happen.

Rotter suggested that locus of control is a significant factor in psychological well-being. Feeling unable to control events, feeling yourself to be a 'victim of circumstance', is inherently stressful for the human being. Moreover, because such people experience a higher level of stress, an external locus of control can lead to ill-health and psychological problems. Rotter developed a questionnaire to classify people as either 'external' or 'internal', and some sample items are shown in Table 20.4 (from Rotter, 1966, pp. 13–14).

The process of ageing involves changes in behaviour and choices that can create a lessened sense of control. Declining physical powers can create a lowered self-esteem, and this can combine with a lowered sense of usefulness to create a feeling of declining mastery of your fate. The generally negative attitudes towards elderly people in this society further enhances their dependency, and they may adopt passive and incompetent roles. Langer and Rodin cite a study by Ferrare (1962)

Table 20.4   Locus of control

The I–E scale asks you to choose one of two alternatives from items such as:

1.   (a) In the case of the well-prepared student there is rarely, if ever, such a thing as an unfair test.
(b) Examination questions are often so unrelated to course work that studying is really useless.

2.   (a) The average citizen can have an influence on government decisions.
(b) This world is run by the few people in power, and there is not much the little guy can do about it.

3.   (a) Most people do not realise the extent to which their lives are controlled by accidental happenings.
(b) There is no such thing as 'luck'.

4.   (a) What happens to me is my own doing.
(b) Sometimes I feel that I do not have enough control over the direction my life is taking.

People with an internal locus of control tend to choose 1a, 2a, 3b, 4a; and people with an external locus of control tend to choose the alternatives.

---

concerning the effects on geriatric patients of the ability to control their place of residence. Of the subjects who said that they did not have any other alternative than moving to a specific old peoples' home, eight died in the first four weeks of residence and a further 16 died within 10 weeks of residence. By comparison, of the people who felt they did have a choice, only one died during the same period. All of the deaths were classified as unexpected because there had not been any 'warning of the impending disaster' (p. 193).

THE STUDY

Langer and Rodin attempted to assess the effects of enhanced personal responsibility and choice in a group of nursing-home patients. In particular, they wanted to find out whether the ability to make specific choices would have a general effect on their experience of their own level of control and competence. The study was based in a nursing home rated by the local authorities (State of Connecticut, USA) to be offering quality medical, recreational and residential facilities. They describe the home as large, modern, clean and efficient, and it appeared to be cheerful and friendly. They selected to study two out of the four floors in the home because the patients on these floors had similar health and socio-economic status.

The aim of the study was to encourage a sense of responsibility and control in the residents on one floor, and compare their long-term progress and general level of health with the control residents on the other floor. This study is an example of a field experiment. The experimental floor had eight males and 39 females who took part in the study, plus 11 other residents who were too uncommunicative or bedridden to take part. The control floor had eight males and 35 females, plus nine people unable to take part. The average age of the residents and their average length of stay in the home was similar for both groups.

The nursing home administrator gave a talk to both groups which he introduced as some information about the home. The main points of the talk to the experimental group were:

(a) you have the responsibility of caring for yourselves;
(b) you can decide how you want your rooms arranged;
(c) you can decide how you want to spend your time;
(d) it's your life;
(e) it's your responsibility to make complaints known.

They were also offered a plant as a present, told that there was a movie showing in the home on Thursday and Friday, and asked which night, if any, they would like to go.

The control group were given a similar talk with the change that their personal responsibility and control was not emphasised. So, for example, they were given the present of a plant rather than offered it, and told that they would be scheduled to see the movie one night or the other, and told how the staff tried to make their rooms nice.

Three days later, the administrator visited all their residents individually and repeated the previous message. To the experimental group he said:

Remember what I said last Thursday. We want you to be happy. Treat this like your own home and make all the decisions you used to make. How's your plant coming along?
(p. 194)

He said the same to the residents on the control floor, but left out the bit about decision making.

Measurements

The researchers measured the sense of responsibility in the residents using two types of questionnaire which were given one week before the communication and three weeks after:

(a) A research assistant who was not aware of the hypothesis or manipulation, interviewed the residents about their sense of control, happiness and level of activity. The research assistant also made a judgement about how alert the resident was (on an 8-point scale).
(b) The nurses who staffed the two floors, and who were also unaware of the experiment, completed nine 10-point scales on the mood and activity of the patients, together with questions about their other activities like reading, visiting, talking and so forth.

A summary of some of the results is shown in Table 20.5, and these data are represented graphically in Figure 20.1. These indicate some substantial differences between the two groups after three weeks. The effect was noticeable in the self reports, the interviewer ratings and the nurse ratings. When the scores for the individual residents were examined it showed that 93 per cent of the experimental group, but only 21 per cent of the control group were judged to have improved. Sadly the researchers did not measure the plants to see how they were doing.

Table 20.5   Average scores for self-report, interviewer ratings and nurse ratings for the experimental and control groups

	Experimental group Change score	Control group Change score
Self report		
Happy	0.28	−0.12
Active	0.2	−1.28
Perceived control		
Have	0.16	0.41
Want	−0.05	0.17
Interviewer rating		
Alertness	0.29	−0.37
Nurse ratings		
General improvement	3.97	−2.37
Change in time spent:		
visiting patients	6.78	−3.29
visiting others	2.25	−4.17
talking to staff	8.22	1.6
watching staff	−2.14	4.64

The data are presented as *change scores* which are calculated by subtracting the second assessments from the first assessments
Source: Langer & Rodin (1976)

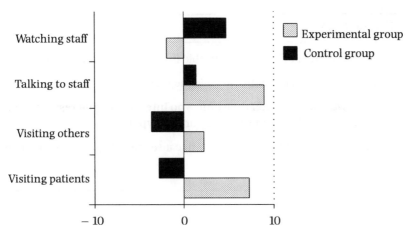

Figure 20.1 *Change in self-reports of the residents*

DISCUSSION

The researchers went back to the home after 18 months (Rodin & Langer, 1977) and found that the experimental group were still improved in comparison to the control group. They were in better health and fewer had died. Overall, the authors' work suggests that a minor intervention had achieved a substantial effect on the health and well being of the residents in the old people's home.

One of the important problems with studies like this was pointed out by Langer and Rodin. The welfare of the residents must be carefully considered, and it could be very damaging to create a sense of enhanced control only for that control to be taken away after the study is completed. The effects of being in an institution are described elsewhere in this book (see the studies by Haney, Banks & Zimbardo, 1973, and by Rosenhan, 1973, in Chapters 3 and 11 respectively), and there is a pressure to reduce the power of residents. The study raises some harsh questions about the treatment of people in residential establishments and the effects of that treatment on their quality of life and their general health.

The concept of locus of control has been applied in a number of health settings other than institutions. It has been found to be useful in a range of disorders such as diabetes and kidney disease which require long-term treatments and strict adherence to diet. The sense of control that the patient feels over their disorder has an effect on their general health (see Lau, 1982).

QUESTIONS

1 How was the independent variable in this study manipulated?

2 How was the dependent variable measured?

3 Why was the research assistant who interviewed the residents not aware of the design of the study or the hypothesis?

4 Make a list of features that enhance a sense of loss of control in an old people's home.

Suggested Answers start at p. 465

KEY WORDS

ageing	internal locus
external locus	interview
field experiment	locus of control
institution	questionnaire

WHERE DOES IT HURT?

■ MELZACK, R. (1992). Phantom limbs.
Scientific American, April, 90–96.

[This summary contains a number of technical terms, particularly labels for parts of the brain. It is not essential to know the structure of the brain to understand the general points of the study so try not to be put off by the terms like 'thalamus' or 'cortex'.]

INTRODUCTION

Why do we feel pain? The answer to this question is nowhere near as straightforward as it might appear. The most obvious suggestion is that injury to the body causes tissue damage, which in turn causes the sensation of pain. However, there are a number of phenomena that challenge this simple notion. First, some people are born without the ability to feel pain, but this is very rare and also it is a health threatening condition. More commonly, people report *episodic analgesia* for events when they are injured but do not feel the pain until some minutes or hours after the injury: the injuries range from minor abrasions to broken bones or even limb loss. Melzack *et al.* (1982) described how 37 per cent of people reporting to an emergency clinic with a variety of injuries reported no pain until some minutes or hours after the injury. He observed six characteristics of episodic analgesia:

(1) the condition has no relation to the severity or the location of the injury;
(2) there is no simple relationship to circumstances – some of the injuries occurred during military combat, whereas others occurred in more mundane settings such as work;
(3) the victim can be fully aware of the nature of the injury but feel no pain;
(4) the analgesia is instantaneous;
(5) the analgesia lasts for a limited time;
(6) the analgesia is localised to the injury – the patient might experience no pain at the severed limb but complain about the needle prick for an injection.

A further challenge to the pain–tissue damage connection comes from the observations that we can have pain without injury. Many headaches have no known damage or explanation of cause. And some pain, for example that caused by small kidney stones, is out of all proportion to the injury. But the most dramatically puzzling thing of all is the experience of pain after healing, and, in particular, *phantom limb* pain. This occurs in people who have lost a limb, often in an accident, who still experience the presence of that limb (a phantom) and sometimes experience pain in it as well.

THE STUDY

The phenomenon of phantom limbs (see Figure 20.2) has been recorded for over a century, and their 'existence' raises a number of questions about how our senses work, and how we interpret sensory

Figure 20.2   *Shaded areas represent the most common examples of phantom limbs*

information. This paper provides a review of the evidence on phantom limbs and proposes a way of understanding this phenomenon.

Phantom limbs have the following remarkable features:

(a) A vivid sensory quality and precise location in space – at first people might try to walk on a phantom leg because it feels so real.

(b) In most cases a phantom arm will hang down at the side when the person sits or stands, but moves in co-ordination with other limbs when the person is walking.

(c) Sometimes it gets stuck in an unusual position – for example, one person had a phantom arm bent behind them, and could not sleep on their back because the limb got in the way.

(d) Wearing an artificial arm or leg enhances the phantom, and it often fills the extension like a hand fits a glove.

(e) Phantoms have a wide range of sensations including pressure, warmth, cold, dampness, itchiness and different kinds of pain (around 70 per cent of amputees suffer pain in the phantom).

(f) Patients perceive phantoms as an integral part of the body – even when a phantom foot is felt to be dangling in the air several inches below the stump and unconnected to the leg, it is still experienced as part of the body and moves appropriately.

(g) Phantoms are also experienced by some people with spinal injury, and some paraplegics complain that their legs make continuous cycling movements producing painful fatigue, even though their actual legs are lying immobilised on the bed.

Explanations of phantom limbs

An early explanation was that the cut nerve ends, which grow into nodules called *neuromas*, continue to produce nerve impulses which the brain interprets as coming from the lost limb. Working on this hypothesis, various cuts have been made in the nerve pathways from the neuromas to the brain in an attempt to remove pain. These cuts sometimes bring about short-term relief, but the pain usually returns after a few weeks, and the cuts do not remove the phantom.

A further theory suggested that the source of phantom limbs was in the excessive spontaneous firing of nerve cells in the spinal cord that had lost their normal sensory input from the body. However, evidence from spinal injury patients shows that people with complete breaks in the spinal cord can still feel pain in the lower body. Therefore, the spinal cord cannot be the source of these sensations and phantoms.

A more recent approach has been to look for a cause in the brain, and in particular the sensory cortex and the thalamus. Although there is some evidence to support the role of these brain structures, Melzack concludes that this explanation cannot account for all the phenomena of phantoms, and that the simple 'electrical wiring diagram' approach to the brain will not provide the answers to this puzzle.

Melzack's model

Melzack suggests that the brain contains a *neuromatrix* – or network of neurons. This neuromatrix responds to information from the senses and also generates a characteristic pattern of impulses that indicate the body is whole and is also your own. He calls this pattern the *neurosignature*. It may be helpful to think of it as a mental hologram that builds up a picture of your body in the mind. If a limb is removed, the sensations cease from that region but the hologram is still created in the neuromatrix (sounds more like Dr Who every minute!).

The matrix has at least three major nerve circuits:

(a) Sensory pathways passing through the thalamus and sensory cortex.

(b) Emotional and motivational pathways passing through the limbic system.

(c) Pathways associated with the recognition of self, which is commonly thought to involve the parietal lobe of the cortex. Studies of people with damage to the parietal lobe have shown problems with their sense of self, for example some patients have been known to push one of their own legs out of bed because they were convinced that it belonged to a stranger.

Melzack offers the image of a musical piece. He suggests that the neurosignature is like the basic theme of the orchestral piece. The collective sound changes as the instruments play their parts (the sensory input), but the product is continually shaped by the underlying theme (the neurosignature) which provides continuity for the work even as the details of its rendition change.

Melzack suggests that the matrix is largely pre-wired (or innate), and offers the evidence that very young children can experience phantoms after amputation, and people born with limbs missing can experience vivid phantoms. The matrix also responds to experience, as shown by the gradual disappearance of some phantoms, though it is interesting to note that they can sometimes re-appear years later.

DISCUSSION

The phenomenon of phantom limbs creates a number of medical problems; for example, how to reduce the pain in parts of the body that do not exist. It also raises doubts about some major assumptions in psychology. One of these assumptions is that sensations are produced by stimuli affecting the senses, and that perceptions that occur without these stimuli are abnormal – or hallucinations. However, phantom limbs tell us that the brain does more than just detect and analyse sensory inputs. It also generates perceptual experience even when there are no sensory inputs. We do not need a body to feel a body.

This view has implications for how pain can be treated. Many people suffer long-term, debilitating pain, and the traditional approaches of surgery or large doses of medication have only produced limited relief. Modern approaches are making more use of cognitive and motivational approaches to pain relief with considerable success.

The phenomenon of phantom limbs highlights the problems with simple reductionist explanations of behaviour and experience (the attempt to explain all our complex feelings and behaviour in terms of simple biological responses). Maps of the brain that describe it like a car engine saying which bits are responsible for which functions are clearly too simplistic. The experience of pain appears to involve a complex interaction of sensory information, emotional feelings and cognitive evaluations. It will take a very sophisticated model to fully describe all this. If you are at all interested in the complex issue of pain after reading this summary, then you might consider consulting Melzack & Wall (1985).

QUESTIONS

1   What is the evidence that shows pain is not a direct result of tissue damage?

2   How can pain be measured?

3   Why is the inability to feel pain a health threatening condition?

4   Remember a physically painful experience that you have had – what made the pain worse and what made the pain better? Categorise the things you identify into cognitive, physiological and emotional factors.

Suggested Answers start at p. 466

KEY WORDS

analgesia	pain
cognitive	phantom limb
cortex	reductionism
neuroma	spinal cord
neuromatrix	thalamus

Part VII

METHODOLOGY

One of the themes of this book is methodology, and in the studies described in previous chapters we have attempted to highlight how each study was carried out. The importance of this is that if you do not know how the evidence was gathered, then it is difficult to evaluate its worth. Any choice of method is limiting in some way on the final outcome of the study. If the researchers chose an experimental design, then it was likely to be very tightly controlled and only allow a limited range of responses from the subjects. On the other hand, if they chose a case study approach, then there is a limitation on the generalisations that can be made. So, the choice of method for a study affects the outcome of that study.

In this part we include some studies that raise some general points about the conduct of psychological research. For bluffing students who want to gain the maximum effect in their essays from the minimum of research, these studies are for you. These are pieces of work that have a bearing on a large proportion of psychological evidence, and so can be referred to in most essays. The studies by Orne (1962), Rosenthal & Fode (1963), Rosenthal & Jacobson (1966), and Sears (1986) come into this category.

Psychology uses the methods of the natural sciences (biology, chemistry and physics) but there are some big differences between the subject matter of physics and the subject matter of psychology. For example, if you are carrying out a physics experiment on the momentum of toy cars running down an inclined plane, it is very unlikely that one of the cars will suddenly stop rolling down the plane and say, 'Stuff this for a lark, I'm going out for a pint.' However, in a psychology experiment, this is a very real possibility. In other words, the subject matter of psychology (yes, it's usually about people) make choices about their behaviour, and they may choose to co-operate or not. So, in the natural sciences, it is possible to experiment *on* things, in psychology it is only possible (and desirable) to experiment *with* people.

The study by Orne looks at the influence of the social situation of the experiment on the behaviour of the subjects. The studies by Rosenthal and his colleagues look at the effect of the research expectations on the outcome of studies. The study by Sears looks at the choice of subjects for psychological investigation and speculates on how this has affected our view of people. All of these studies raise big question marks about the conclusions we can draw from psychological research.

The final two studies are included here partly because they did not seem to fit anywhere else, and partly because they provide examples of less familiar research methods. The study by Potter & Edwards (1990) illustrates the relatively recent development of discourse analysis as a method of investigating meanings in the social world. In particular, it makes a number of criticisms about the way that social psychological research has traditionally been undertaken. The final study looks at another method used to investigate people's beliefs and perceptions of their world. In this case the method comes from George Kelly's Personal Construct Theory, and looks at the belief systems of managers.

21 FRAMEWORKS AND APPROACHES

DEMAND CHARACTERISTICS

■ ORNE, M.T. (1962). On the social psychology of the psychological experiment: With particular reference to demand characteristics and their implications. *American Psychologist, 17*, 776–83.

INTRODUCTION

One problem with studying people is that their behaviour and experience change as a result of being studied. This means that we can never be certain in psychological research that we are finding out about how people really are. This holds true for all research methods, to a greater or lesser extent, but it is particularly true of experimental methods. Orne's paper looks at why this might be the case. His review article begins with a brief discussion of some of the social psychological characteristics of the psychology experiment. It moves on to a discussion of *demand characteristics*, examining what they are, how they might affect research findings, and what can be done about them. The paper includes a number of references to both informal and formal psychology experiments conducted by Orne and his colleagues.

THE PSYCHOLOGICAL EXPERIMENT AS A SOCIAL SITUATION

The experimental situation is one which takes place within the context of an explicit agreement of the subject to participate in a special form of social interaction known as 'taking part in an experiment'.
(p. 777)

Orne's first point is that the psychological experiment, involving as it does an interaction between experimenter(s) and subject(s), should be regarded as a social situation. In other words a psychology experiment always takes place in a particular social context. In everyday life we expect people's behaviour to be affected by the social contexts in which they find themselves. For example, imagine being in a pub, a church, a football ground, and a shopping centre. If someone bumps into you in the shopping centre, you are likely to say 'Well really!', but at a football ground you wouldn't even notice it. In a church if someone put a plate in front of you then you might put money in it, but if the plate appeared in a pub you might flick your ash in it. Orne argues that the psychology experiment is not exempt from this principle: the behaviour of subjects in an experiment will be affected by the social context created by that experiment.

One feature of any social context which can be expected to have an affect on behaviour is the relationship between the people involved. In an experiment, the proceedings are dominated by the experimenter–subject role relationship. There are characteristics of this relationship which make the psychological experiment a particularly potent and rather unusual social situation.

For example, within this role relationship experimenters find themselves with an unusual degree of power over their subjects. This is partly because in agreeing to take part in an experiment in the first place the subject:

> implicitly agrees to perform a very wide range of actions on request without inquiring as to their purpose, and frequently without inquiring as to their duration.
> (p. 777)

Orne gives the following examples of subjects' 'remarkable compliance' (p. 778) to the demands of an experimenter. They are taken from informal pilot experiments which he and his colleagues carried out. The first involved a psychologist asking a few acquaintances for a favour. When they agreed they were asked to do five press-ups. Their reaction tended to be to ask 'why?', with a degree of puzzlement. Another group of acquaintances were asked if they would take part in an experiment. When they agreed they were asked to do five press-ups. Their reaction tended to be to ask 'where?'. This suggests that people are prepared to do things as subjects that they would not normally be prepared to do in other social contexts.

The second example of compliance is startling. Subjects were set a task which involved them making 224 additions of random digits on each of 2000 sheets of paper. Their watches were taken away and the experimenter told them to continue working until they were told to stop. 'Five and one-half hours later, the *experimenter* gave up!' (p. 777), amazed at the unquestioning diligence of the subjects. In a variation on this task, subjects were instructed to do the calculations on each sheet, then to tear up their answer sheet into at least 32 pieces before continuing with the next one, which was also to be torn up (and so forth). Again subjects tended to continue for several hours at this completely senseless task, simply because they were 'doing an experiment'.

Orne argues that one reason for people's willingness to do things in an experiment that they would not normally do otherwise, is their desire to be 'good' subjects. Generally speaking, subjects want to help the experimenter do a good experiment; we all like to be involved in things which are successful. In addition, since a large proportion of psychological studies are carried out on students, the subject population may also tend to share the goals and values of experimenters in terms of the quest to further human knowledge and thereby to make a positive contribution to society.

What are demand characteristics?

> The totality of cues which convey an experimental hypothesis to the subject become significant determinants of subjects' behaviour. We have labelled the sum total of such cues as the *demand characteristics of the experimental situation*.
> (p. 779)

The insight that the psychology experiment is a kind of social situation is an important one, since it reminds us that the subjects of psychological research are usually people. People do not just passively respond to things that happen to them. They actively try and make sense of what is happening, and act in accordance with their sense-making. There is no reason to assume that people in experiments are any different in this respect to people in any other kind of situation. This implies that subjects will tend to try and understand what is going on in the experiment that they are in, and their behaviour will be affected by whatever understanding they come to.

The most important thing that subjects will try to understand in an experiment is 'what is this person (the experimenter) trying to find out from me?' In other words, 'what is the experimental hypothesis?' Orne argues that subjects will automatically use whatever cues are available in the experimental situation in order to try and work out the experimental hypothesis. The cues can come from a variety of sources, such as the wording of instructions, the manner of the experimenter, the experimenter's known area of research (remember that many psychology experiments are done with students on the experimenter's course!), and so forth. The procedure is another source of information for the subject:

> ... if a test is given twice with some intervening treatment, even the dullest college student is aware that some change is expected, particularly if the test is in some obvious way related to the treatment.
> (p. 779)

We all want to know what is expected of us in social situations, and we tend to act in accordance with our understandings of those expectations. The experimental hypothesis is literally an expectation of how subjects will act in the experimental situation. If subjects come to know the hypothesis, then their behaviour will tend to support it.

The point that Orne is trying to make is that the behaviour of subjects in experiments is a function of two different kinds of variables:

(a) those which are traditionally defined as experimental variables and
(b) the perceived demand characteristics of the experimental situation.
(p. 779)

If experimenters are not careful they may interpret their findings as being a consequence of their manipulation of the independent variable(s), when in fact the data have been artificially produced by the demand characteristics of the situation. Mix the power of the experimenter with a large helping of subject compliance; add some desire to be a good subject; season with some active sense-making, and you have a recipe for a self-fulfilling prophecy (see Rosenthal & Jacobson, 1968, later in this chapter).

Orne gives examples of demand characteristics in operation in the findings of psychological research from his own fields of interest; sensory deprivation research and research into hypnosis. He cites one of his own studies (later published by Orne & Scheibe, 1964) which shows some of the dangers. One group of subjects were told they were in a sensory deprivation study. They undertook a series of tasks, signed release forms and were left on their own in a room which had some visible trappings of sensory deprivation (including a red 'panic' button) for four hours. However, the experimenters had not created any sensory deprivation at all. Another group of subjects were told they were *control* subjects in a sensory deprivation study. They did the same series of tasks and sat in the same room for four hours (only with the panic button removed). Both sets of subjects then repeated the original tasks. The performance of the subjects who thought they had undergone sensory deprivation had deteriorated significantly on a number of the measures in comparison with the control group.

The subjects in the sensory deprivation condition appeared to have a very good idea, at least subconsciously, of the way they were expected to behave. Their behaviour promptly confirmed these expectations. Orne argues that many of the results of sensory deprivation (and hypnosis) studies could have been produced not by sensory deprivation (or hypnosis) but by demand characteristics; that is by people behaving in the way that they believe they are expected to.

What can be done about demand characteristics?

> It is futile to imagine an experiment that could be created without demand characteristics. One of the basic characteristics of the human being is that he will ascribe purpose and meaning even in the absence of purpose and meaning. In an experiment where he knows some purpose exists, it is inconceivable for him not to form some hypothesis as to the purpose, based on some cues, no matter how meagre....
>
> (p. 780)

When experimenting on people demand characteristics are unavoidable, because people will always try to make sense of things. The most popular way of counteracting any systematic influence of such factors in an experiment is by means of deception. Experimenters put a lot of effort into concealing the true purpose of their experiment from their subjects by trying to convince them that they are really studying something completely different. Milgram's work (in Chapter 1 of this volume) is one notable example of this strategy. But deception has its own drawbacks. There are ethical problems with misleading people and besides, many people (especially psychology students) know that experimenters will try to deceive them, and will inevitably try and work out the true purpose of the investigation.

Orne's preferred method of dealing with demand characteristics is to encourage experimenters to be aware of their potential impact on research studies, and to suggest some strategies for assessing what this impact might be. If we can come to understand which aspects of subjects' behaviour are affected by demand characteristics, then we should be able to assess more accurately which aspects are affected by the bona fide experimental variables.

One strategy that Orne recommends is a kind of simulation exercise based on a combination of pre- and post-experimental inquiry. A group of subjects (drawn from the same population as the subjects in the experimental and control conditions) are told about the experimental procedures and asked to guess the hypothesis. They are then asked to behave in a way that they believe subjects would behave after having been given the experimental treatment, only without actually receiving the treatment. If the behaviour of these subjects correlates with the behaviour of subjects who had received the real experimental treatment, then there is a possibility that that behaviour has been produced by the demand characteristics of the situation.

Orne's basic message is that when the subjects of our research are people, we should be aware that they are active sense-makers rather than passive responders. This awareness should affect the way that research is designed and the way in which findings are interpreted.

QUESTIONS

1 Demand characteristics are regarded as a source of 'artefact' in behavioural research. What does the word artefact mean in this context?

2 How can the behaviour of people in demonstrations of stage hypnosis be explained by demand characteristics?

3 Look at some of the other studies in this volume and try to identify any demand characteristics. Can the results be explained by these demand characteristics? Look especially at the quotation from page 779 of Orne's paper about giving a test twice 'with some intervening treatment'. How does this relate to Samuel & Bryant's (1984) investigation of conservation in children (see Chapter 14 of this book).

Suggested Answers start at p. 467

KEY WORDS

artefact	hypnosis
compliance	power
deception	role
demand characteristics	self-fulfilling prophecy
expectations	sensory deprivation
experiment	social situation

DULL RATS AND BRIGHT RATS

■ ROSENTHAL, R. & FODE, K.L. (1963). The effect of experimenter bias on the performance of the albino rat.
Behavioral Science, 8, 183–89.

INTRODUCTION

One of the most important effects to control against in psychological experimentation is the effect of experimenter bias. Experimenters can all too easily find what they are looking for (support for their own hypotheses) by inadvertently influencing the way in which their subjects behave. Quite how such bias happens is unclear, since the most troublesome forms of it happen outside of our awareness. But the chances are it is something to do with the experimenter's *expectations* of how the subjects in the different conditions will behave; people have a tendency to live up to (or down to) the standards that are expected of them (see Rosenthal & Jacobson, 1966, in the following study). Experimenter effects (another term for experimenter bias) are a source of *artefact* in behavioural research, meaning they can be the cause of artificial, non-valid findings (see also the previous summary of Orne's paper on demand characteristics).

THE STUDY

The authors of this study set out to examine whether or not experimenter effects can occur in studies of animal behaviour. They led their student subjects to believe that they were acting as experimenters and gave each one of them five rats which were to be trained over a period of days on a T-maze task (see Figure 21.1). In one condition, a group of students were led to believe that their rats had been specially bred to be 'maze-bright'; in the other condition the students were informed that their rats were 'maze-dull'. In fact, there was no difference between the groups of rats which had all been randomly selected from the same stock. The only differences were in the minds of the student 'experimenters'. If any consistent differences in performance in the rats could be detected across the two conditions, those differences must have been caused by the expectations that the students had of their rats.

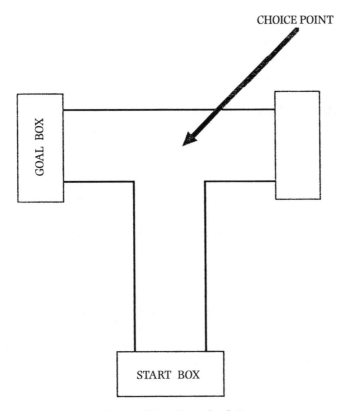

Figure 21.1   *Example of a T-maze*

Subjects

Twelve students taking a course in experimental psychology in a US University acted as subjects in this experiment as part of their course requirements. None of them had any experience in working with animal subjects. In addition, 60 rats, aged between 64 and 105 days old and which had no experience of a T-maze, were used. Throughout the paper the authors refer to the human subjects as 'experimenters' (because that is what the subjects thought they were) and to the rats as 'subjects'. We, on the other hand, will refer to the students as the subjects.

The rats were divided into 12 groups such that every group had a similar mean age. There were two males and three females in each group. 'Several days before the beginning of the experiment [the rats were] placed on a 23-hour food deprivation' (p. 184).

Design

The study used a basic two-condition independent measures experimental design, with subjects' beliefs about the relative ability of their group of rats as the independent variable. Subjects were sorted into pairs according to their estimates of how much they expected to like working with the rats, and then each pair of subjects was split at random across the two conditions. Subjects in one condition believed they were working with maze-bright rats; in the other condition subjects believed they were working with maze-dull rats.

The dependent variable was the mean number of correct responses per rat per day over a five-day period. Other data were also collected, including mean response times for correct responses, and some self-assessment scores from questionnaires that the subjects completed.

Procedure

Subjects were told that the groups of rats with which they would be working had been bred over a series of generations to be either maze-bright or maze-dull. Maze-bright rats would show 'learning during the first day of running. Thereafter performance should rapidly increase' (p. 184). Maze-dull rats should show 'very little evidence of learning' (p. 184). They were led to believe that the aim of the exercise was to give them experience in handling rats, and to give them experience in 'duplicating experimental findings' (p. 184).

Each subject was given a group of five rats labelled either maze-bright or maze-dull according to which condition the subject had been assigned. Needless to say, the rats had actually been divided into maze-bright and maze-dull groups at random.

Subjects were instructed to run their rats ten times for each of five days on a T-maze. The rats had to learn to discriminate between one arm of the maze which was painted white, and the other which was painted dark grey. Running to the darker arm was always reinforced; whilst running to the white arm was never reinforced. The arms were interchangeable, and swapped round at random, so that the rats could not just learn to run in a given direction. The subjects (believing they were experimenters!) recorded success rates per rat per day, time taken for every correct response, and also some post-experimental data on their feelings about their rats and how they had interacted with them.

RESULTS

The data show that the rats which were believed to be maze-bright made, on average, more correct responses each day than the rats which were believed to be maze-dull (Table 21.1 and Figure 21.2). The correct responses of the maze-bright rats were on average quicker than the maze-dull rats on each of the five days (Table 21.2). Furthermore, the rats in the maze-bright condition showed a consistent trend of improvement in terms of number of, and speed of, correct responses over the five-day period. The performance of the maze-dull rats did not improve every day in this way.

In the post-experimental questionnaire subjects in the maze-bright condition reported higher levels of cleanliness, tameness, brightness and more pleasantness in their rats than did subjects in the maze-dull condition. The former also made higher estimates of how often they handled their rats, and how gentle they had been with them.

Table 21.1   Number of correct responses per rat per day

Day	Maze-bright	Maze-dull	t	p (one-tailed)
1	1.33	0.73	2.54	.03
2	1.60	1.10	1.02	ns
3	2.60	2.23	0.29	ns
4	2.83	1.83	2.28	.05
5	3.26	1.83	2.37	.03
Mean	2.32	1.54	4.01	.01

ns = not significant
Source: Rosenthal & Fode (1963)

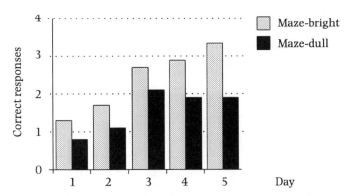

Figure 21.2   *Average number of correct responses per rat per day*

Table 21.2   Mean time in minutes required to make correct response

Day	Maze-bright	Maze-dull	t	p (one-tailed)
1	3.13	3.99		ns
2	2.75	4.76		ns
3	2.05	3.20		ns
4	2.09	2.18		ns
5	1.75	3.20		ns
Mean	2.35	3.47	3.50	.02

ns = not significant
Source: Rosenthal & Fode (1963)

DISCUSSION

The results certainly seem to indicate that the experimenter effect is alive and kicking in studies of animal behaviour. And if rats can be affected by human expectations, how much more powerful are experimenter effects likely to be in studies of human behaviour?

Experimenter bias can have some very serious consequences in scientific tests such as drug trials. If the person administering the drug has an expectation of how it will work, the patient might well behave accordingly. One way of dealing with this is the double-blind design which conceals the experimental hypothesis from the person actually carrying out the experiment as well as from the subject. Alternatively, the person conducting the experiment is not permitted to know which conditions subjects have been allocated to. In this way the experimenter cannot have relevant and biasing expectations. This technique is commonly seen when a new drug is being tested against a placebo. None of the people who administer the drugs or who assess the health of the people taking the drugs know at any stage who is receiving the real thing and who is receiving the placebo.

QUESTIONS

1 How do you think the experimenter effect worked in this case? If the experimenters' expectations really did lie behind the differences in performance in the two groups how might these expectations have been communicated to the rats?

2 Why were the subjects led to believe that the point of the whole exercise was to give them practice in handling rats and in duplicating experimental findings?

3 What are your feelings about animal research? For example, how did you respond to reading about the '23-hour food deprivation'?

Suggested Answers at p. 467

KEY WORDS

artefact
double-blind design
expectations
experimenter effects/bias

placebo
reinforced
single-blind design
T-maze

TEACHERS' BLOOMERS

■ ROSENTHAL, R. & JACOBSON, L. (1966). Teachers' expectancies: Determinants of pupils' I.Q. gains.
Psychological Reports, 19, 115–18.

INTRODUCTION

In 1963, Rosenthal and Fode demonstrated that the behaviour of experimental subjects can be influenced inadvertently, yet powerfully, by the expectations of the experimenter (see the previous study). Experimenters who had certain *expectations* of their subjects actually seemed to *cause* their subjects to behave in accordance with those expectations.

This effect is known as 'experimenter bias', and as such it may only be of interest to social scientific researchers. However, Rosenthal argues that experimenter bias is only one example of a broader psychological phenomenon known as the *self-fulfilling prophecy* or the *expectancy effect*. This is where a person lives up to, or down to, the expectations that significant others have of them in their everyday lives.

THE STUDY

In the study summarised here, Rosenthal and Jacobson set out to discover whether pupils' performance over the course of a school year could be affected simply by the expectations that their class teachers have of them. A proportion of children in an elementary school in the US were labelled as 'bloomers'. That is, they were identified to their class teachers as children who, on the basis of a psychological assessment, were expected to develop particularly rapidly in terms of intellect over the course of the next year. Unknown to the teachers the bloomers had been chosen at random from each of the classes in the school. There was actually no difference at the outset of the study between them and their classmates. If at the end of the year they *had* actually developed more rapidly than their classmates, then this could be put down to their teachers' expectations. And if it can be shown that children perform better because of *high* expectations, then we might be able to make the worrying inference that *low* expectations will cause *poorer* performance.

Subjects

The subjects of this field experiment were the children of a US elementary school. All 18 classes of children were used, which were made up of three streams of children (above average, average, and below average) from each of the six grades (known more commonly as 'years' in the UK system).

Design

The study employed an experimental design, in which subjects were randomly allocated either to the experimental (treatment) condition, or to the control (no treatment) condition. The experimental treatment which was received by 20 per cent of the children was an artificial enhancement of their teachers' expectations of their likely intellectual performance over the course of a school year. No such enhancement of expectations was made for the remaining 80 per cent of control subjects.

Procedure

Flanagan's 'Tests of General Ability' (TOGA; Flanagan, 1960), a nonverbal intelligence test, was administered to all the children of the school. The teachers were deceived into thinking that it was a test designed to spot the onset of 'blooming', or marked intellectual growth during the coming school year. Twenty per cent of the children in each test were identified to their respective teachers as bloomers, apparently on the basis of the TOGA results. In reality, these pupils had been selected at random by the experimenters.

After eight months, the teachers re-administered the TOGA to all children in the school. A change score for each child was computed by comparing their IQ level from this repeat test with their baseline IQ level from the test carried out eight months previously. The IQ gains of the experimental group could then be compared with the IQ gains of the children in the control group, the only difference between the two groups of children having been the teachers' expectations of their likely intellectual growth.

Some of the children were tested for a third time by an independent researcher who did not know which children had been nominated as bloomers. This was to check whether there had been any bias in the teachers' administration of the second test. No such bias was found.

RESULTS

The authors report that for the school as a whole IQ growth was significantly greater for the experimental group than for the control group ($p = .02$, one-tailed). The most marked gains were among the experimental children in grades one and two. Table 21.3 shows the percentages of experimental and control children in the two lowest grades who gained at least ten IQ points over the eight months.

Table 21.3   Percentages of experimental and control Ss gaining 10, 20 or 30 IQ points (first and second grade children)

I.Q. Gain	Control Ss*	Experimental Ss**	χ^2	p†
10 points	49	79	4.75	.02
20 points	19	47	5.59	.01
30 points	5	21	3.47	.04

* Total number of children = 95
** Total number of children = 19
† p one-tailed
Source: Rosenthal & Jacobson (1966)

DISCUSSION

This is clearly a very important topic. If labelling someone actually causes them to behave and develop in accordance with their label, then we need as a society to be very careful about the labels that are given to people.

The results appear to support Rosenthal and Jacobson's hypothesis. However, there have been numerous criticisms of the study (see Snow, 1969, and Thorndike, 1968). For example, the IQ test they employed was not standardised for the age-range of children on which it was used. This means that the results may be meaningless, particularly for the younger children where the biggest effects were observed. There is also some doubt about how much notice some of the teachers took of the lists of bloomers, and about whether expectations really had been created in their minds.

Replication studies have found mixed results, and the effect described by Rosenthal and Jacobson appears not to be as robust as they thought. However, there has been some empirical support for the idea of the self-fulfilling prophecy in schools and a good example of this is the natural (or quasi-) experiment carried out by Seaver (1973).

Seaver's experiment capitalised on the common belief in sibling similarity. Many children are compared to their brothers and sisters when they are at school. Comments such as, 'you'll have to work harder if you want to do as well as your brother' are part and parcel of the social environment of the school. In general there is an expectation that brothers and sisters will be like each other in a number of ways because of their shared environment and their genetic relationship. Seaver assumed that teachers would hold this implicit belief in sibling similarity.

His investigation looked at pairs of siblings, no more than three years apart in age, some of whom were taught by the same teacher in the first year of school and some of whom were taught by different teachers. He hypothesised that a teacher who had taught an older sibling of a pupil would have expectations of that pupil which (if the expectancy effect is to be believed) would lead the child to perform to a similar level of attainment as the older sibling: if the older sibling had been a high performer, the teacher would probably expect the younger one to be a high performer too. Following this line of reasoning, if an expectancy effect is operating there should be a greater level of similarity in attainment between siblings who were taught by the same teacher in the first year than between siblings who were taught by different teachers. This is indeed what Seaver's results showed.

One reason for describing Seaver's work, apart from the fact that it lends some support to the self-fulfilling prophecy effect, is to bring out some contrasts between this quasi-experimental study and the experiment proper of Rosenthal and Jacobson. Rosenthal and Jacobson actually intervened in the lives of their subjects in order directly to manipulate the independent variable of 'expectation'. Seaver's investigation required no such intervention. He capitalised on a set of existing circumstances which naturally created the 'conditions' in his design (unlike Rosenthal and Jacobson he did not *assign* subjects to conditions; he selected subjects who *fitted the requirements* of the conditions). In addition, all his measures came from existing records and independent assessments which did not involve his subjects doing anything. There are a number of drawbacks with this approach, but a very strong advantage is that it did not cause the same ethical problems that Rosenthal and Jacobson's work did.

QUESTIONS

1   Why did Rosenthal and Jacobson not identify a group of 'wilters' (a group of children whose performance was going to fall behind in the coming year)?

2   Are there any ethical problems with identifying a group of children as 'bloomers'?

3   What expectations do other people have of you? Are you affected by these expectations? If so, in what way?

Suggested Answers start at p. 468

KEY WORDS

expectancy effect
experimenter effect
IQ test
labelling

natural (quasi-) experiment
self-fulfilling prophecy
standardisation
treatment

WHO ARE PSYCHOLOGY'S SUBJECTS?

■ SEARS, D.O. (1986). College sophomores in the laboratory: Influences of a narrow data base on psychology's view of human nature.
Journal of Personality and Social Psychology, 51, 513–30.

INTRODUCTION

Psychology is regarded as the scientific study of human behaviour and experience. It attempts to make generalisations about how people behave, what influences that behaviour, and how people make sense of their experience. However, in their studies, who do psychologists use to test their theories? There is considerable diversity in human behaviour and experience, so is this diversity taken into account when studies are designed and conducted?

When a study is designed, it is important to state the target population of people under investigation which, for example, might be 'residents of Nottingham', or 'young people between the ages of 16 and 19'. Once we have stated the target population, we can set about selecting a sample by whatever, usually haphazard, means we choose. A consideration of our choice of sample will tell us how confident we can be about generalising our results from the sample back to the population. The study by Sears looks at the samples that are used in social psychology studies, and assesses how much we can generalise about people on the basis of these studies.

THE STUDY

Sears reports that immediately after the Second World War (1939–45), social psychology used a wide range of subjects in its studies and a variety of locations. The prevailing feeling was that it was important to conduct studies both in the field and the laboratory. However, from the 1960s onwards, a trend developed for laboratory experiments which used the most available subjects – college students. Sears looked at the major journals in social psychology for the years 1980 and 1985 to discover what were the chosen samples and chosen locations of the published research. The results are shown in Table 21.4 and Figure 21.3.

Table 21.4   Subject populations and research sites in social
psychology articles in 1980 and 1985 (data shown
in percentages)

	1980	1985
Subject population		
American undergraduates	75	74
Psychology classes	54	51
Other classes	21	23
Other students	7	8
Adults	18	17
Research site		
Laboratory	71	78
Natural habitat	29	22
Combined		
Undergraduate/lab	64	67
Adult/natural habitat	15	13
Number of articles		
Total	333	187
Empirical and codeable	301	178

Source: Adapted from Sears (1986)

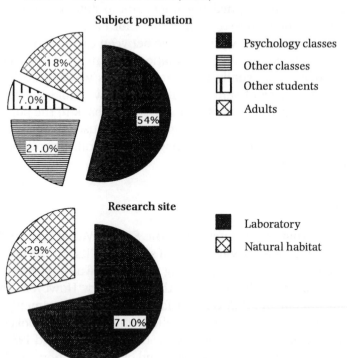

Subject population

- ■ Psychology classes
- ☰ Other classes
- ◫ Other students
- ⊠ Adults

Research site

- ■ Laboratory
- ⊠ Natural habitat

Figure 21.3   *Subject populations and research sites in social psychology articles in 1980*

The table shows that the bulk of psychological research has been carried out on a very narrow subject base of students, and, in particular, psychology students. One explanation for this might be that the prestigious journals that Sears studied have a particular policy towards publications that encourages authors to send in laboratory based studies. To test for this, Sears looked at other publications by the same authors in different journals. The 1980 Psychological Abstracts provided 237 entries by the same authors from a wide variety of journals. The analysis of these articles showed very few differences from the original analysis, and suggested that the results were not peculiar to the mainstream journals.

Another feature to consider might be whether these types of studies are very important in psychology. It might be that the work that has the greatest impact is not presented in these journals. However, Sears describes a study by Findley & Cooper (1981) who coded the articles cited in the most commonly used textbooks in social psychology. They found that the overall proportion of studies that used students as subjects was 73 per cent which was very similar to the publication bias (see Table 21.4). So the curriculum of psychology courses contains the same subject bias as the literature as a whole. Sears goes on to look at other data which suggest that up to 1960, psychologists used adults who were not students in about half of their studies, but since then there has been a consistent dependence on data from students.

Sears considers whether this subject bias presents any problems for social psychology. He notes that one of the potential hazards is the need to test concepts that have been developed in the laboratory in a real life setting to see if they apply. An example of this is provided by the study of Piliavin *et al.*, (1969, described in Chapter 1), who found that the laboratory-developed concept of *diffusion of responsibility* did not apply to their studies of bystander intervention on a New York commuter train.

College students are not very representative of the general population. They come from a narrow age range and are predominantly at the upper levels of educational background and family income. The 17 to 19-year-old young people who make up the majority of subjects in psychology studies have been shown to have a number of unique characteristics which Sears summarises as follows:

(a) their self-concept is unlikely to be fully formed;
(b) social and political attitudes are less crystallised than in later life;

(c) they are more egocentric than older adults;

(d) they have a stronger need for peer approval;

(e) they have unstable peer relationships.

Also, college students differ systematically from other people of the same age:

(f) they are pre-selected for competence at cognitive skills;

(g) they are selected for compliance to authority;

(h) their social and geographical mobility leads to enhanced instability in peer relationships.

It is difficult to disentangle the effects of the choice of subjects from the choice of location. Laboratory studies seem likely to have further effects including:

(i) creating a cognitive 'set' in the subjects, since they are often conducted as part of the student course;

(j) creating a 'set' to comply with the authority;

(k) most studies remove the student from the support of his or her peers to minimise 'contamination' of the individual's responses.

Sears provides an extensive review of modern psychology and shows how its concerns and findings have largely been led by the peculiar features of the US undergraduate. (He comments on several of the studies included in this text, including Schachter & Singer, 1962; Bem, 1974; Nisbett *et al.*, 1973; Asch, 1955; and Milgram, 1963.) He suggests there are four main consequences for psychology:

(1) Psychology tends to view people as having a weak sense of their own preferences, emotions and abilities; they are compliant, their self-esteem is easily damaged, their attitudes are easily changed, and they are relatively unreflective.

(2) Material self-interest, group norms, social support and reference group identification play little role in current research in the USA (though some European psychology is addressing these issues).

(3) Psychology views people as dominated by cognitive processes rather than emotional ones.

(4) Psychological theories treat people as highly egocentric.

He writes:

To caricature the point, contemporary social psychology, on the basis of young students pre-selected for cognitive skills and tested in isolation in an academic setting on academic tasks, present the human race as composed of lone, bland, compliant wimps who specialise in pencil and paper tests. The human being of strong and irrational passions, of intractable prejudices, who is solidly embedded in tightly knit family and ethnic groups, who develops and matures with age, is not that of contemporary psychology; it does not provide much room for such as Palestinian guerillas, southern Italian peasants, Winston Churchill, Idi Amin, Florence Nightingale, Archie Bunker, Ma Joad, Clarence Darrow, or Martin Luther King.

(p. 528)

DISCUSSION

The study produced a damaging criticism of modern psychology. Not surprisingly, it does not get a citation in many introductory psychology texts. The question it leaves us with is, 'What value are the data and theories of modern psychology?' A cynic might be inclined to dismiss much of psychology after reading this paper, but, on the other hand, you might be motivated to try and evaluate the biases in the studies and mentally adjust for them. It might also be worth speculating on the effects of changing the location or the subjects for a number of important studies.

QUESTIONS

1   Why do psychologists use student subjects in their studies?

2   Why do psychologists use laboratories in preference to conducting field studies?

3   Take one of the other studies in this text and speculate on the effects of carrying out the same procedure on a different subject group, for example, factory workers, or time-share salespeople.

Suggested Answers start at p. 468

KEY WORDS

bias	population
cognitive skills	sample
egocentric	self-concept
generalisation	set
haphazard sampling	subject bias
money	students

DISCOURSE ANALYSIS

■ POTTER, J. & EDWARDS, D. (1990). Nigel Lawson's tent: Discourse analysis, attribution theory and the social psychology of fact.
European Journal of Social Psychology, 20, 405–24.

INTRODUCTION

Potter and Edwards write in the area of discourse analysis, an approach to social psychology which takes a critical view of traditional social psychology and which emphasises the role of language (discourse) in everyday life. The term discourse analysis (d.a.) is used in a variety of ways to describe a variety of things; here it refers to the kind of psychology advocated by Potter & Wetherell (1987).

Discourse analysts challenge the common-sense view that language is a purely descriptive medium used to convey information about the real world. They argue that language actually shapes (constructs) the real world, and our views of it. Their ideas may have far-reaching implications for how social psychology should be done. One of the most influential traditions in social psychology, attribution theory, has come in for especially heavy fire from discourse analysis. In this summary we will deal with just one of d.a.'s criticisms of attribution theory; a criticism concerning method, which leads into a more general theoretical argument. The empirical work reported by Potter and Edwards focuses on this particular issue.

Attribution theory (see for example Jones *et al.*, 1972; also Nisbett *et al.*, 1973, in Chapter 2 of this volume) is concerned with discovering the way that we come to conclusions about the causes of our own and other people's behaviour. The usual research procedure of attribution theory involves the presentation of 'vignettes' to research subjects. The vignettes (mini stories) give brief descriptions of pieces of social behaviour. Typically, certain features of the description are systematically manipulated across conditions to create an experimental design. Subjects are asked to judge what caused the behaviour in each vignette, and the effects of the manipulations of the descriptions on the resulting causal judgements are observed.

It is not necessary to understand any more about attribution theory to follow the following critique (though more knowledge would, of course, help!). The vignettes supposedly supply the subjects with certain 'facts' about the situation in question. From these facts, the subjects make inferences about the causes of whatever was done by the characters in the story. The attribution researcher is interested in the inferences that the subjects make. Because the vignettes are descriptive and 'factual' they are thought to 'stand for' the situations they describe. In other words, subjects' interpretations of the vignettes are equivalent to what their interpretations would have been had they *actually* witnessed the events described.

The problem with this, according to discourse analysis, is that the 'facts' of the story are treated by the researcher as a problem-free bit of the whole exercise. They are treated as 'given', as though the person who wrote the vignette had no control over them. They are just gathered together in a neutral description of 'what really happened', and are of no particular interest in themselves. What is of interest to the attribution-theory researcher is how the subjects then go on to interpret the causes of 'what really happened'.

Discourse analysis points out that this whole process is based on a fundamental misapprehension of the relationship between words and reality. For a start, social behaviour is a very complex thing, so any short description of a piece of it must, in principle, rely on a *selection* of facts. This means that the writer of the vignette has already decided for the reader (in this case, for the research subject) what is and what is not relevant. And decisions about the relative relevance of different things are subjective and value-laden. The writer has also, for that matter, decided what constitutes a 'fact' in the first place. As the empirical work of Potter and Edwards in this paper shows, what does and does not constitute a fact is in itself open to argument and interpretation; 'what really happened' in any given slice of social behaviour is itself a matter of opinion.

So, discourse analysis argues that the vignettes that are used in attribution-theory research are not just neutral descriptions of some piece of social behaviour. They are already loaded with meanings and implications by the selection of facts that the writer has chosen for inclusion, and by the things that the writer has chosen to present as facts. For these reasons they cannot just stand for reality, as they are but one version of events. The judgements that the subjects make about the causes of the behaviour described in the vignettes cannot be seen as equivalent to the judgements they would have made if they had directly witnessed the events in question, for those judgements have already been constrained by the version of events that has been imposed upon them.

The argument takes on a greater significance when we realise that the principles that Potter and Edwards are talking about apply just as much to real-life descriptions of events. Every day we encounter other people's versions of events, in the press, on the television, when we are gossiping and so forth. On the basis of these versions, we form our own points of view about the events that have been described. What discourse analysis is arguing is that in forming our own points of view we should be aware that the descriptions we are receiving are never just neutral, factual descriptions of how things really happened. They are always someone's version of what happened. Furthermore, it is generally the case that people want their version of events to be believed, especially when the events in question are important and controversial. The upshot of this is that people will frame their version of events in the most believable and convincing way that they can. And one of the most effective ways of doing this is to make it sound as though they are just giving us a neutral unbiased account of the 'facts'! The empirical work presented by Potter and Edwards in this paper is a study of how people organise and structure their versions of events to try and make them appear factual and credible. They call this the study of *factual discourse*.

THE STUDY

The methods of discourse analysis involve the interpretation of texts. The texts that are typically used are detailed transcripts of naturally occurring talk, although any kind of text can be subjected to a discourse analysis. The materials that Potter and Edwards used in this study were newspaper articles and Hansard (a written record of the talking done within the British House of Commons). The analysis concerned a dispute which took place in Britain in the 1980s between a senior government minister and a group of journalists. The dispute arose from a briefing session in which Nigel Lawson (then Chancellor of the Exchequer; see Figure 21.4) reportedly briefed 10 journalists on an idea to apply means-testing to benefits for old-age pensioners. When the idea was reported in the press, the Chancellor denied having floated it, accused the journalists of having produced 'a farrago of invention'

Figure 21.4   *Nigel Lawson looking for a conspiracy*
Source: Popperfoto

(Hansard, 2 November 1988, cited in Potter & Edwards, p. 411), and argued that their accounts of the meeting were factually incorrect. So the core of the dispute was about what really happened at the briefing meeting, about what really were the facts of the matter. Potter and Edwards' study examines the way in which each side in the argument framed their version of events to make it appear as the more believable. Note that the data that they use are textual, and that the texts are real ones, as opposed to ones that have been created in the laboratory.

The focus of Potter and Edwards' analysis is on the notion of 'consensus' and on how this notion is used *rhetorically* (that is, how it is used in people's arguments) to make a version of events credible. The journalists' side of the story is grounded on the question 'how could 10 journalists all have simultaneously misunderstood what Nigel Lawson was saying?'. As the Guardian put it:

> [In Nigel Lawson's view] the reporters, it seemed, had unanimously got it wrong. Could so many messengers really be so much in error? It seems doubtful.
> (cited in Potter & Edwards, p. 412)

The way in which the journalists and the papers for whom they worked were trying to convince the public that their account of events was truthful was to claim that 10 independent witnesses all agreed on what the Chancellor had said. People tend to find this kind of argument convincing. Potter and Edwards highlight how the point is strengthened in the style of writing in the extract from the Guardian above. The use of the term 'so many' functions to make the consensus appear very big (and all the more convincing for that). They also suggest that the term 'unanimous' is used to emphasise the strength of consensus, which again has the function of making the journalists' account sound convincing and factual.

Nigel Lawson, however, continued to deny this apparently convincing consensus account given by the journalists. In his arguments, he redefined the 'consensus' among the journalists as 'collusion'; the fact that the journalists all agreed on what was said at the meeting did not mean that their account was correct. On the contrary, it meant that they must have got together after the meeting and colluded to create the story:

> Mr. Lawson: ... they went behind afterwards and they thought there was not a good enough story and so they produced that ....
> (Hansard, 7 November 1988, cited in Potter & Edwards, p. 416)

In a sense, the fact that so many agreed unanimously and to such a great extent was being used by Nigel Lawson to strengthen *his* case that there was collusion against him. The unspoken implication might be 'how often do 10 *genuinely* independent journalists agree this much on anything (without having cooked it up among themselves)?'. The title of the paper comes from Susan Crossland's commentary in the Sunday Times (13 November 1988):

> Nobody can say the Chancellor of the Exchequer is not a bold man. Who else would invite 10 senior journalists to his home for a briefing and then state that when his guests departed they went into a tent to concoct a 'farrago of invention?'
> (cited in Potter & Edwards, p. 106)

Discussion

The facts of the matter are clearly at the core of this dispute in this political incident. So any written or verbal account of the incident can only be a version, which would in the normal course of events be subject to refutations by other competing versions. This is in contrast to the attribution theory experiments where the version of events given to subjects is not open to refutation; it is taken as factual and given. Yet, surely the inferences that a subject makes would depend entirely upon which version they happened to be presented.

The facts of the matter about any given event do not speak for themselves. Facts can be presented in many different ways to support many different lines of argument. In this instance the fact that there were 10 journalists present at the briefing is used by both sides to support their own case; the one argument based on consensus, the other on collusion and conspiracy. Discourse analysts argue that we have repertoires of argumentative techniques (*rhetorical strategies*) which we use, often very subtly and skilfully, to convince others that our version of an event is the one they should believe. One of these techniques is to argue that you are presenting a purely factual account.

Politicians' talk generally provides good examples of factual discourse which is used in an attempt to convince others of the truth of their version of events. However, it is not just politicians that do this sort of thing. Discourse analysis argues that this is something that you and I also engage in all the time in our everyday lives. The analysis points to the importance of language in everyday social life, and suggests that we take a more sophisticated view of the relationship between events (on the one hand) and people's accounts of events (on the other).

The authors' analysis of the different sides of the argument, and the rhetorical strategies that both sides used to support their own case is more extensive than indicated above. The function of this summary has been to give a working introduction to discourse analysis, and its challenging perspective on social psychological research.

QUESTIONS

1   Discourse analysts typically work in great depth with data that have been collected from a relatively small number of sources. What might some of the strengths and weaknesses of their approach be?

2   What is the central concern of attribution theory?

3   The text makes the claim that everyone engages in 'factual discourse which is used in an attempt to convince others of the truth of their version of events'. Try and recall a recent situation in which you gave a 'version of events' to someone else. How did you present the 'facts' in order to persuade the other person that you were telling the truth?

Suggested Answers start at p. 468

KEY WORDS

attribution theory
discourse analysis
factual discourse
inference

rhetorical strategies
versions
vignettes

A Repertory Grid Study of Managers

■ Brown, C.A. & Detoy, C.J. (1988).
A comparison of the personal constructs of management in new and experienced managers.
In F. Fransella & L. Thomas (eds), *Experimenting with Personal Construct Psychology*. London: Routledge and Kegan Paul.

Introduction

In 1955, George Kelly published his two volume account of *personal construct theory* (PCT). Kelly's writing was humorous, engaging, and highly critical of mainstream approaches to psychology. In the best traditions of humanistic psychology he offered up an account of people which emphasised their active, sense-making, autonomous nature. Like Freud, his ideas grew out of direct clinical experience (he was a counsellor) and added up to a grand theory of what it is to be a human being.

Kelly's ideas have implications for how research should be done. He argues that what people do is guided by their beliefs about the world. If we want to understand people we have to understand their beliefs. Furthermore, beliefs are best studied from 'within'; only *you* can give me a satisfactory account of *your* particular view of the world. This means that psychological research should start from the perspective of the research participants (subjects), rather than imposing a perspective upon them. Research participants should be fully involved in the research process, and their accounts of their own beliefs and actions should be respected as insightful. Note that researchers who work within a PCT framework often avoid the traditional label of 'subject', preferring more democratic terms such as 'participant' or 'co-experimenter'.

There is one particularly well-known research method associated with personal construct theory; that is the 'role construct repertory test' (see Kelly, 1955, pp. 267–72), otherwise known as the *repertory grid* (or 'rep. grid'). The idea of the repertory grid, as set out by Kelly, is to provide a format through which individuals can express their own view of one part of their world. One way of completing a grid is given in the procedure section below (grids come in all shapes and sizes, with all sorts of procedures attached to them). Very briefly, a grid consists of a cross-tabulation of 'elements' against 'constructs'. The elements determine what the grid is about; they define which particular bit of a person's world is being examined. Elements can be anything, from political systems to works of art, from motor cars to holidays, from insects to buildings; it all depends on what the research is about. Usually the elements in repertory grids are people that the participant knows well. Figure 21.5 shows a typical grid structure before completion.

The constructs are the ideas which the participant uses to organise their understanding of the elements in the grid. Constructs are bipolar dimensions which are defined by the research participant themselves in terms of the labels of the two opposing poles (see 'generating the constructs', below). Kelly believed that our entire belief systems are based on complex collections of bipolar personal constructs which enable us to perceive similarities among, and differences between things.

Label for Construct pole	Elements/Resources									Label for Construct pole
	×	×	×							
		×		×		×				
				×		×		×		
						×	×	×		
	×			×				×		
			×			×	×			
		×			×		×			
			×		×	×				

Figure 21.5 *The structure of a repertory grid*

Note how in each row three cells are marked. These show which elements the subject should think about in order to elicit their construct. There is no significance to the pattern of cells marked; it is up to the researcher (and maybe to the subject) to work out which will be the most productive triads for comparison. Note also that the two poles of each construct are usually written in separate columns on either side of the grid, as shown here.

THE STUDY

Brown and Detoy's study is an investigation of the personal construct systems of managers in a large US business. They were interested for professional reasons in the managers' understandings of managing. The company in question had just begun to develop a new model of management, and they wanted to know in what areas this model differed from the implicit models (personal constructions) of management, which guided the everyday work of the managers themselves.

They set about the study using repertory grid techniques. The elements of the grids which the managers completed were ten people they knew well, five of whom (including themselves) were managers. The grids were designed in this way in order to elicit from the subjects their understandings of management. Using grid techniques means that subjects are not asked to talk about the abstract notion of management, but are encouraged to think about their perceptions of actual managers. This makes the task concrete. It helps to keep research participants' feet on the ground, discouraging them from going off into abstract theoretical notions which may have nothing to do with how they actually see things in their everyday lives.

The authors' expectations, which were grounded in their own professional experience, were that new managers would place more emphasis than experienced managers on social relationships in the work place. Experienced managers on the other hand would be more task oriented (see Bales, 1955, this volume, Chapter 3) and place greater emphasis on productivity. This led to the hypotheses that there would be a higher percentage of 'social interaction' constructs in the grids of the new managers than in the grids of the experienced managers, and that conversely there would be a higher percentage of 'forcefulness' constructs in the grids of the experienced managers than in the grids of the new managers. Judgment of whether constructs were to do with social interaction or to do with forcefulness were made in accordance with Landfield's (1971) content analysis scheme for personal constructs (see below).

Research participants

Forty-one new managers and 33 experienced managers employed by a large US company participated in the course of a management training programme. New managers were defined as those who had been in post less than six months, experienced managers were those who had been in post for over six months.

Design

This study had a quasi-experimental design, and used repertory grid techniques for data collection. Content analysis was used to deal with the resulting data.

Procedure

All subjects completed repertory grids during a management training session. The procedure for completing the grids (which were administered by an independent psychologist) was as follows.

Generating the Elements   The research participants were given a list of 10 role titles. These were:

- the best manager you know;
- the next best manager you know;
- the worst manager you know;
- a manager you would rate as average;
- yourself;
- your father;
- your mother;
- your best friend;
- a favourite teacher;
- a person at work with whom you usually feel comfortable.
  (p. 428)

Each role title was represented by a column in the repertory grid. Participants were instructed to write the name of a specific person who fitted each role title above the appropriate columns, using 10 different people in all. These were the elements in the grid. Note that although the role titles were the same for each participant, the actual people selected to fill each role would have differed from grid to grid.

Generating the Constructs   The participant's attention was then drawn to the first row of the grid. Three of the cells in this row were marked. They were instructed to think of the three people whose names were in the columns denoted by the marked cells, and to ask themselves the following question: 'are two of them alike in some important way that is different from the third person?' (p. 429). The participant's task was to find descriptive labels for the way in which the two were similar, and the way in which the third person was different. These labels represented the participant's first bipolar personal construct, since they would be of the form

'(These two are) Male – (This other one is) Female', or '(These two are) Assertive – (This other one is) Passive', or '(These two are) Good with People – (This other one is) Awkward socially', and so forth.

After creating their first personal construct the participant was instructed to focus on row two of the grid matrix, in which three different cells were marked. Again, they were required to think of the three people who were indicated by the marked cell, and ask themselves the similarity–difference question cited above. This led to the creation of their second bipolar personal construct. This process of 'triadic elicitation of personal constructs' was repeated, using different triadic combinations of the people in the grid until no new constructs were forthcoming. On average, each subject generated between eight and nine constructs. The group as a whole generated 637 constructs. Because half of the elements in each person's grid were managers, the constructs that were produced provide insights into the way subjects 'construe' the role of manager and the task of managing.

Content Analysis

The 1274 construct labels (637 bipolar constructs, incorporating two labels each) were categorised according to a modified form of Landfield's (1971) coding scheme. Six categories in all were used:

- Social Interaction.
- Forcefulness.
- Organisation.

Table 21.5 Examples of the construct labels from new and experienced managers assigned to the 'social interaction' and 'forcefulness' categories

Social interaction		Forcefulness	
Experienced managers	New managers	Experienced managers	New managers
friendly	tactful	effective	authoritative
patient	diplomatic	a doer	demanding
outgoing	sensitive	assertive	money motivated
good listener	friendly	high energy	corporate
empathy/kind	outgoing	dynamic	dominating
supportive	social	decisive	aggressive
understanding	understanding	motivated	
thoughtful	good with people	dedicated	
considerate	receptive		

Source: Adapted from Brown & Detoy (1988)

- Intellective.
- Morality.
- Personality Attributes.

The details of Landfield's content analysis are not relevant here. The two most important categories were 'social interaction' and 'forcefulness'. Examples of the construct labels assigned to each of these are provided in Table 21.5.

The categorisations were made by 'an outside judge, who was given the descriptions of the categories but was unaware of the hypotheses under examination' (p. 430).

RESULTS

As predicted, there was a higher proportion of constructs relating to social interaction in the grids of new managers than in those of experienced managers: 32 per cent of all the new managers' constructs were classified as 'social interaction', whereas only 13 per cent of all the experienced managers' constructs were put in that category. In contrast, experienced managers' grids included a higher proportion of constructs related to forcefulness (24 per cent) than did the grids of new managers (16 per cent). No assessments of statistical significance were made in relation to any of the data in this study.

DISCUSSION

The raw data of the study appear to support the authors' hypotheses, although without tests for statistical significance it is unclear what status should be given to the differences reported above. However, to focus on this issue would be to miss the whole point of the exercise. The data from the research were fed back to the participants as part of their training course and were the springboard for discussion about the nature of management and about the role of managers in the organisation. This is a crucial point and relates back to the assertion (made in the introduction to this summary) that in personal construct theory research participants (subjects) should be fully involved in the research process. In other words, the raw data from this study were for them as well as for the investigators. So the results of this kind of study are much more than just the numbers reported in the results section. As a piece of *action research* the results are more to do with the managers' professional development and personal insights which the piece of research helped to bring about. The grids, and the analysis of the grids, were in a sense the starting point for this particular research process, rather than the end of it.

QUESTIONS

1   Why was the categorisation done by an 'outside judge'?

2   How do we know that the categorisation was done sensibly? What could have been done to convince us that it had been?

3   Why are the results reported in terms of 'proportions' of construct types in the grids of the new and experienced managers?

Suggested Answers start at p. 469

KEY WORDS

action research
autonomy
bipolar
content analysis
constructs
elements
inter-coder reliability

personal constructs
personal construct theory
repertory grid
research participants
social interaction
task orientation
triadic elicitation

Suggested Answers

Part I   Social Psychology

Chapter 1   Social Pressure

Eight Out of Ten Owners Said Their Cats Preferred It

1   The features that enhanced conformity include the use of strangers rather than friends, the choice of students as research participants, and the meaningless nature of the task.

2   I conform to a range of social norms. For example, behaving politely with people even when I don't like them, trying to appear reasonably presentable in public, eating with a knife and fork, and so forth.

3   Positive aspects of conformity include the reduction in social conflict, and the greater predictability of people and situations. Negative aspects include not thinking for yourself and a loss of individuality.

4   The central criticism is that the study is not true to life (not *ecologically valid*). In particular the subjects had no emotional involvement in the task and the study was carried out in an unusual social context.

Helping Behaviour

1   The major problems are to do with control, ethics and authenticity.

2   The advantages are that you can observe people engaging in natural behaviour rather than responding to experimental requests

in a restricted environment, and as a result the outcome is much less predictable and also more relevant to general discussions about human behaviour and experience.

3 We are not told the answer to this so we can only speculate. A reasonable speculation is that the researchers were too embarrassed, scared or ashamed to conduct this themselves. The students wanted to earn some money and maybe had fewer social inhibitions.

4 The major problems come from the possible distress caused to the travellers, the deception of the travellers, and the possibility that the incident could have precipitated a nasty confrontation.

5 Just think of what people do in cities and how they live, and that should provide a whole range of questions that psychologists might be interested in. For example, one of the major leisure pastimes at the moment is shopping, and people spend hours looking at products that they might never buy.

Be a Good Boy and Do As You Are Told

1 There are numerous possible explanations including the location of the study, the demand characteristics of the study, the social obligations put on the subjects, the unusual nature of the task they were performing, and the tendency for people to accept the commands of people in authority.

2 Advantages for the individual include less aggravation and more acceptance. Advantages for society include greater social order.

3 Disadvantages for the individual include less control of your own behaviour, and doing things you don't want to do. Disadvantages for society include a lack of dissent and therefore no pressure for social change.

4 You name them. The major ones include the deception about the true purpose of the study and the distress caused to the subjects. Also it was not made clear to the subjects that they could withdraw at any time, and they were offered financial incentives to behave in ways they might not approve of.

5 Milgram did not intend to cause distress and was surprised about the results. Also, the authors of this text believe that the Milgram study has made an important contribution to our understanding of human behaviour.

CHAPTER 2 SOCIAL COGNITION

Is She Really Going Out With Him?

1   In this study the task of the coder was to decide whether each reason given was 'situational' or 'dispositional'. Coding is a somewhat subjective process, and consequently can be unreliable. An independent coder allows the investigator to assess the level of 'inter-rater' (or 'inter-coder' or 'inter-observer') reliability in their coding scheme. The greater the agreement between the different coders, the higher the inter-rater reliability of the coding scheme. The independent coder was not allowed to know the experimental hypothesis so that there could be no systematic biasing of their coding in favour of the experimental hypothesis. This is to guard against the self-fulfilling prophecy of 'experimenter effects' (see Rosenthal & Fode, 1963, Chapter 21 of this volume).

2   Nisbett *et al.*, would predict that most of your explanations should be situational. Try and think of dispositional alternatives for each situational explanation that you have written.

I'm Not Prejudiced, But...

1   For example, I have an attitude that we should protect the environment but I never manage to take my newspapers or bottles to the recycling centres. Also I have an attitude that exercise is a good thing but I rarely exercise.

2   There are numerous possible reasons including the opportunity to act on your attitude, habit, the behaviour might be too sensible or boring, it might take too much effort, or some of your attitudes might conflict with each other.

3   The methodological problems include the Chinese people not knowing about the study, their American accents, the general lack of controls and the 50 per cent return rate on the questionnaires (though in truth this is quite a good return for postal questionnaires).

Changing Our Minds

1   The answer to question two has, on the face of it, nothing to do with the cognitive dissonance hypothesis. If, nevertheless, the same pattern of differences across the conditions was observed in the

responses to this question it would indicate that there was something else going on in the experiment instead of (or as well as) the expected cognitive dissonance effects. It would indicate that there was some more general difference across the conditions than the one intended by the experimenters.

2   This is so that the research can be replicated (exactly) to check the reliability of the reported results. The more unusual the research methods, the more detailed the account needs to be, because the reader is likely to be unfamiliar with the procedures that were used.

CHAPTER 3   SOCIAL ROLES

The Prison Simulation

1   The prisoners became immersed in their roles so that the prison became very real to them, they became passive and dependent and they behaved in degrading ways towards each other.

2   One argument says that the study was ethically sound because it went through various ethics committees. But the luxury of hindsight suggests that there were a number of ethical violations including the deception about the arrest, the distress to the prisoners, and their failure to realise that they could leave the study whenever they wanted.

3   Your choice, but we would suggest the 'Milgram Defense', which is that the results illuminate our understanding of human behaviour and the distress caused in the study is justified by this outcome.

4   Students were chosen because of their availability and their willingness to carry out something like this for a relatively small amount of money. However, as the study by Sears (see Chapter 21 of this volume) suggests, students may behave in very different ways to other adults.

Behaviour in Groups

1   The *sequence* of acts can be examined. One important criticism of social psychology has been that it tends to present a rather static view of human interaction, when in fact one of the key features of human interaction is the way that it unfolds over the course of time. Obtaining data on the sequence of events in his studies

allowed Bales to examine the typical stages of decision-making within groups. The methods he used in this respect are known as 'sequential analysis' (see Bakeman & Gottman, 1986).

2   Firstly there is the complexity of the thing which is being observed. There may be too much going on within the group to be recorded by one observer, though it should be noted that a skilled observer will be able to 'see' and record a lot more than a novice. The second reason might be that any kind of research in psychology requires the researcher to address the issue of reliability. In this context, one thing Bales would need to establish is the level of 'inter-observer' (or 'inter-rater') reliability that was achieved. In order to make this estimate he must have at least two observers, working independently, doing exactly the same observational task. The records of these two independent observers can then be compared. The more similar their records are, the higher the level of inter-observer reliability in the study. If necessary, the comparison can be made 'statistically' by means of a correlation coefficient. If there is not sufficient agreement across the two observers the observation schedule may need altering, or the observers may need more training.

3   The behaviour of the group members might have been altered by their awareness of being observed. It is important that we as readers of the study know this so that we can properly evaluate the study. There are no easy ways around this problem of *reactivity* in psychological research; often the only thing we can do is be honest and open about our research procedures, and allow for these inevitable difficulties in our interpretations of our findings.

Chapter 4   Prejudice

The Robber's Cave

1   *Competition* leads to *conflict* which leads to *ethnocentrism*.

2   (a) Observations of behaviour, (b) friendship choices, (c) the target practice judgements.

3   The distress to the children, the lack of informed consent, the inability to leave the study, etc.

4   Competing groups include sports teams, sports supporters, work groups, gangs, political parties, and so forth.

5 The advantages include the spontaneous behaviour of the children, and the ability to generalise the results to other social situations involving children.

The Jigsaw Technique

1 So that claims could be made about the effectiveness of the jigsaw group technique itself. If the control groups were not receiving some sort of special input, then any change in the jigsaw children could be put down simply to extra attention or extra tuition; factors that we already know will have beneficial outcomes. Having said this, the matching of programmes for equivalence is fraught with difficulties and can be the basic cause of any controversy that arises concerning the interpretation of the data in evaluation research. Anyone who does not believe the findings can usually claim that the programmes under comparison were not equivalent in some important and confounding respect.

2 Read our account of Sherif (1956) which is also summarised in this chapter.

The Minimal Group Studies

1 It is worth noting that teenage boys are perhaps the most competitive groups of people in our society. It is an age when people take part in more games, and are part of a competitive education system. The choice of subjects clearly enhanced the results, and it would be interesting see what results would be found in a study on people, say, in a retirement home.

2 A harder question than it appears. You would probably say that you are a member of your family group, friendship group, your class or work group, but it is difficult to go much beyond that. However, it is very easy to know who is on your side, rather than not on your side, even though it is not always easy to identify the group to which you both belong.

PART II   COMPARATIVE AND PHYSIOLOGICAL PSYCHOLOGY

CHAPTER 5   LEARNING

The Flight of the Killer Pigeons

1   By means of shaping using positive reinforcement.

2   Pigeons have better visual acuity, better vigilance skills, and less fatigue at the task. They are smaller, cheaper to use and have no emotional involvement with the task.

3   You're on your own here, but if you believe that a war can be justified, and if you believed that the use of animals might prevent further loss of life, then you could argue for using animals in this way. However, this argument depends on the importance you put on human life over animal life.

4   Coastguard spotters looking for life rafts in a vast expanse of ocean, or maybe as quality control inspectors looking for the dodgy potato on a conveyor belt.

5   There are no straightforward answers to this question, but it is worth considering very carefully. For example, can the apparently complex things that people do always be broken down into simpler units? If they can, then studying the learning of simpler animals like pigeons may offer insights into human learning.

Learning to be Helpless

1   Because the dogs in the yoked control condition had to receive, on average, the same overall duration of electric shocks in phase one as those in the escape condition. If they had not, then any differences across the two groups in phase two could have been attributed to the different amounts of electric shock administered in phase one. The dogs in the escape condition could terminate the shocks, so their performance had to be measured first in order to know

how long each shock should last on each trial for the dogs in the yoked control condition.

2   When considering a question like this try not to think in 'slogans'. Questions relating to the ethics and morality of psychological research are never quite as straightforward as they are sometimes made to appear.

3   A good example might be unemployment. The unemployed often experience multiple rejections in their search for work, and they can come to believe that the problem is something to do with them rather than their situation. In this circumstance they may well learn to be helpless and believe there is nothing they can do to get work.

Talking to the Animals

1   For example, a dog bark is an immediate response to something happening now. Dogs cannot bark to tell a story about something that happened last Tuesday. Another example is bird song which can convey such things as threat, or the position of the bird or the mating ambitions of the bird, but it is very stereotyped and limited in the range of things it can communicate.

2   People can communicate, for example, by touch, by tone of voice, by the way they walk, and by a whole range of non-verbal communication techniques.

3   The strengths are the level of detail and the depth of understanding they achieve with Washoe. The disadvantages include their tendency to overgeneralise from their one animal case study, and from their emotional involvement with Washoe which maybe clouds their judgement about the chimp's true abilities.

4   The difficulties include the speed of movement of the chimp's hands, the tendency of chimps to move around their environment at high speed, and the difficulty in recognising when a sign has been made.

5   There may be all sorts of linguistic and non-linguistic cues which signal when someone is about to hand over the conversation to their communication partner. Obvious ones are to do with intonation and gaze.

CHAPTER 6 BIO-PSYCHOLOGY

A Brain of Two Halves

1 The short presentation of the stimulus ensures that there is no time for automatic eye movements which would 'spread' the information across both sides of the visual field and therefore across both sides of the brain.

2 Because any visual information will be transmitted to both sides of the brain, unless it can be restricted to one side of the field of vision (which can only be achieved when very brief visual displays are used: see answer one above).

3 Examining the behavioural consequences of certain kinds of brain damage may help researchers to make inferences about the normal functions of the damaged areas of the brain, by documenting what things the brain damaged subject is unable to do. Since researchers cannot deliberately cause brain damage in people, in order to perform proper experiments they must rely on the opportunistic study of people who have experienced damage 'naturally'. Note that researchers have felt able to cause intentional brain damage in animals in order to carry out such experiments.

How do you Feel?

1 Independent measures experiment. The independent variables are the information about the adrenaline injection given to the subjects, and the situation they are put in (euphoria situation or anger situation).

2 Observation of behaviour, and self report by questionnaire with a single value of emotion arrived at by taking the anger rating from the happiness rating.

3 For example, a checklist of bodily experiences such as knee tremble, clammy skin, etc., or by using other self-report scales about experiences such as warmth, or anxiety or excitement, etc.

4 The major violation of ethical standards is the deception of the subjects.

5 It is likely the results would be very different. See the study by Sears in Part VII for some suggestions of what these differences might have been.

To Sleep, Perchance to Dream

1 The results tell us something about the relationship of REM with the experience of dreaming, but there are big variations between individuals.

2 The sample is restricted and so generalisation is suspect. The sample is all adult, mainly male, rather small, and culture specific. On the last point it might be interesting to look at the relationship between REM and dreaming in a culture where dreams are talked about more openly.

3 The controls include the location, using the usual sleeping time of the subjects and asking them to avoid stimulants and depressants.

4 The interesting point here is the tension between the need for control and the need to create a situation as near to everyday life as possible. Rather than suggesting further controls it might be useful to look at how to create a more ecologically valid design.

5 Consider factors such as familiarity, privacy, and a change in night-time habits.

CHAPTER 7   ETHOLOGY

The Colony of Monkeys

1 Advantages include the richness of the data, and the opportunity to see development over time. The disadvantages include the time taken to collect data and the difficulty in collecting it. An ambitious longitudinal study is not always a good career move for an academic because of the potentially long gap between beginning the work and publishing it!

2 For example, which matriline it belonged to, who it groomed and who groomed it.

3 Inbreeding (mating with family members) tends to bring out any genetic weaknesses that exist within a family. The survival and the development of a species depends on matings between unrelated individuals so that the genetic weakness is thinned out and genetic variations develop. In the case of these monkeys, the males only mate outside the troop they were born in.

4 The differences include the closeness to water, the relative lack of trees in the early days of the colony, the protection from predators and the provision of food.

5   Your answers here are speculative and therefore no better than ours, but we suspect that the presence of predators would change the structure of the troops and make them more cohesive and less competitive.

A Fishy Tale

1   Ethological observation, and experiment.

2. The sign stimuli include colour of the fish, shape of the fish, orientation of the fish and movement.

3   For example, the sight of blood creates a sense of shock, a smile creates a feeling of warmth, and a baby's cry produces a feeling of concern.

4   The major difference is that *all* sticklebacks behave like this and *all* male sticklebacks will make these nests in the breeding season. It is not possible for a group of sticklebacks to get together one year and say 'I'm fed up of this territorial nonsense, let's form an anarcho-syndicalist collective for this mating season.'

5   For example, going out for a walk when you are angry so that you avoid an argument.

Rat City: The Behavioural Sink

1   The controls include the type of animal, the structure of the environment, the steady supply of food and water and the removal of the young after the population's size reached 80 animals.

2   The main problems are the artificial environment and the artificial species (laboratory rats are specially bred and would be unlikely to survive in a natural environment).

3   The rats were hypersexual, and part of their activity was homosexual, but the description of them as homosexual suggested that they exclusively chose to mate with other males. The choice of the term probably tells us more about Calhoun's attitudes than it does about the rats.

4   The study could be used to illustrate the human problems associated with the inner city such as increased levels of child abuse and child neglect, the high incidence of personal crime such as assault, the

concentration of mental ill health and social pathology, also the high incidence of male aggression, and the general breakdown of social order. But bear in mind that connections between the rats and city life are very slight, if they exist at all.

5   For example, 'harem', 'homosexual', and 'somnambulist'.

PART III   HUMAN DIVERSITY

CHAPTER 8   GENDER

Girls Just Want to Have Fun

1   If reference 'A', for example, had always referred to the candidate as a woman, and the candidate described by that reference had been picked most often for the high-status job, a sceptic could have argued that the description of the candidate in reference 'A' was simply better than in the other references, and that the choice actually had nothing to do with the terms 'woman' and 'girl'. Although all four references were very carefully matched (so that the description in one should not be better than any of the others), the technique of changing which references used the term 'girl' and which used the term 'woman' for each subject gives an extra level of experimental control.

2   Some examples: man, mankind, chairman.

3   One familiar male justification for using 'pet' names and labels to address and refer to women (such as 'love', 'dear', 'the girls' and so forth) is that they are endearing, friendly positive terms. This may be the case (it certainly is not always the case). But Kitto's work suggests that even if the terms are meant well, they still may be contributing to sexual inequality.

Learning to Fail

1   The observers recorded teachers' feedback to the children and noted whether it was positive or negative, conduct or work-related, intellectual or non-intellectual. They also noted the type of attributions the teacher gave for the children's successes and failures.

2   They might also have looked at the response of the children to the feedback.

3   Any situation which you feel unable to have much effect on can cause helplessness. The concept has been applied to noisy environments, unemployment, homelessness and domestic violence.

4   One difference might be the copious praise given to the children to cheer them up.

Rites of Passage

1   The most obvious reasons are that the subject of psychology, and the general scientific community are male dominated. Also, it is difficult to carry out empirical studies on experience, hence the use of projective tests in this study.

2   The aim of a projective technique is to provide someone with a relatively bland stimulus and let them make of it what they want. The theory is that a person's response is likely to show some characteristics of their thoughts and feelings that they would otherwise find difficult to articulate. The major advantage is the information that can be obtained about thoughts and feelings, and the high level of personal disclosure that can occur. The main problem is getting people to agree on what this information means.

CHAPTER 9   MEASURING PERSONALITY

Measuring Masculinity and Femininity

1   Remember that the 'subjects' in this study were actually used in the development of the BSRI. Tests and scales (and inventories) can only legitimately be used on members of populations from which they have been developed. This may mean that the BSRI is only able to tell us about gender identity in students, unless it can be shown that students are representative of some wider population(s).

2   Because notions of femininity and masculinity differ from culture to culture, and change over the course of time. This means that even if Bem had developed a valid measure of these constructs there is no guarantee that it will generalise across time and place. You should have noticed that questions 1 and 2 touch upon very similar themes.

3   A reliable test is one that gives stable and consistent scores. A valid test is one that measures what it purports to measure. Make sure that you understand this distinction and that you can use these important terms appropriately.

4   Test–retest reliability; internal consistency; inter-observer reliability; split-half reliability; parallel forms reliability. Try and find out what these different labels mean.

5 Face validity; concurrent validity; construct validity; criterion (or predictive) validity. Consult a good textbook to find out what these different labels mean.

How Gullible Are You?

1 The sorts of people we believe when they tell us something about ourselves are doctors, scientists, experts, teachers, psychologists, and so forth.

2 Older people might be less gullible (see the study by Sears in Part VII); they also might be more defensive about personality tests, and less trusting of psychologists.

3 Up to you to decide. I suspect his students learnt a valuable lesson about the value of psychometric tests even though they were deceived along the way.

CHAPTER 10   CULTURAL DIVERSITY

Mis-measuring Intelligence

1 The first question refers to US Presidents. Washington was the first and Adams was one of the others, and his place in the order of Presidents is the answer to this question. So if you do not know your US history you cannot score on this question. Crisco is a consumer product and if you are very poor then you might not have come across it. Christy Mathewson was a baseball player and you have to know about sports to get this. In the Beta test picture 15, for example, refers to 10-pin bowling, and picture 18 is a gramaphone.

2 Scientific racism refers to the attempt to justify the political power of some groups (usually nation states) by seeking to show the superiority of this group over others. Science was also used to justify male power over women and early studies produced 'evidence' about the smaller size of female brains and hence their diminished intellectual power.

3 Tricky question, but you might think that some of the following are examples of intelligent behaviour – scoring high on a maths test, solving a crossword puzzle, playing a defence splitting pass in football, being able to empathise with someone. On the other hand you

might regard the following as examples of unintelligent behaviour – burning the toast again, forgetting to take your wallet when you go out, buying a timeshare apartment after receiving a 'hard sell'. The general point to be drawn from this exercise is that the notion of intelligence is applied to such a wide range of behaviours that it is very hard to believe that it is just one quality.

Black Dolls and White Dolls

1   By examining the answers that were given to their question no. 8.

2   A difficult question, though Patrick Hylton, one of our colleagues at The Nottingham Trent University, is working on this at the moment to produce accounts of Black identity in 1990s Britain using interviews and Q sorts.

3   One possible answer could be the lack of appropriate Black role models at that time. If you look at any old films made between 1930 and 1945 then you will see very few Black actors, and when they do appear then they are usually playing the parts of villains or servants. Although there are now many more models for Black children, it is remarkable how blinkered our everyday culture can be. For example, on a day to day level, it is still very difficult in this country to buy Black dolls, or birthday cards with Black children featured in the pictures. It could be argued, additionally, that the scarcity of Black dolls in the 1930s would have made the dolls that Clark and Clark used appear 'unusual' and hence less appealing to all the children.

Black Identity

1   The answer depends on your knowledge of psychology, but the obvious areas to consider are any dealing with social relationships, such as attachment, or attraction, or conformity, or nonverbal communication, or aggression or emotional expression. One of the classic areas is moral development (see Chapter 13), where Kohlberg interpreted the results of his studies as showing that White Americans were more morally developed than any other culture in the world.

2   This is actually a very difficult exercise unless you have some firsthand experience of a non-European culture. We suggest asking someone with that experience to consider this question with you.

3 Examples of co-operation can be found in family life (sometimes, though not at washing-up time), also in team games or any activity that requires a group of people. The most obvious examples of individual competition come from education, where we are always being compared against our peers and there is little or no incentive for co-operation.

CHAPTER 11 ABNORMALITY

You Don't Have to be Mad to Work Here. You Don't Even Have to be Mad to Be In Here...

1 Just the self report of hearing a voice say 'empty' or 'thud'.

2 The similarities include that they have reported feeling unwell, and they have been hospitalised. The differences include the knowledge of the pseudopatients that they are really faking it, and that some people on the outside know this.

3 For example, you might think that being too unhappy to go to work is an abnormal behaviour, or always wearing a bow tie even when you are spending the day at home is unusual. If you make a list of behaviours such as these that you regard as unusual or abnormal, then you could look for some common properties in your list so that you can define what it is that you think abnormal behaviour is made up of.

4 One major criticism is the deception of the hospital staff. Another major criticism asks us to imagine what would happen if we went to a casualty department and complained of stomach ache. How would we be treated? Perhaps Rosenhan was being particularly hard on psychiatric hospitals, especially when it is important for them to play safe in their diagnosis of abnormality because there is always an outcry when a patient is let out of psychiatric care and gets into trouble.

Shrink Wrapped: The Choice of Therapist

1 How do you measure outcomes? That is, how do you measure how much 'better' someone has got after therapy? If people do seem to get better how can you be sure that this improvement is due to the therapy and not due to 'spontaneous remission' (in other words,

how can you be sure that they would not have got better anyway)? These are not insurmountable problems, so think how they can be addressed in the design of studies.

2   You would suspect that most published studies would show a positive effect in favour of psychotherapy. There may be two major reasons for this. Firstly, the people who are most interested in the effectiveness of psychotherapy would be practitioners who have a stake in showing its effectiveness. Secondly, publication of evaluation studies is biased in favour of studies which show statistically significant differences between treated and untreated groups. That is, studies which show no significant differences will tend not to get published as readily as those that do show such differences. Furthermore, it is unlikely that many studies would ever show statistically significant negative effects of therapy (Smith and Glass stated that 12 per cent of their 'effect sizes' were negative). These observations do not invalidate Smith and Glass' conclusions, and are probably in themselves contestable. But it is always important to think critically about what you are being told when you read psychological studies.

The Three Faces of Eve

1   Eve White was withdrawn and inhibited, whereas Eve Black was confident, relaxed, erotic and mischievous.

2   Schizophrenia is a psychotic condition in which people have disturbances of emotion, perception and reality testing. Although schizophrenia is commonly thought to involve a split personality, this is not the case at all. The most striking signs of schizophrenia are the hallucinations (often auditory) that people experience, and the failure to distinguish perceptions that originate in the environment (stimulation from outside the person), from perceptions that start inside the person.

3   The moment that Eve Black appears can be seen in a different way to that described by the therapist. He describes how he noticed Eve's legs for the first time, and notices that she appears erotic to him. He describes this as a change in her personality, but it also signals a change in his perception of her.

4   We have to ask whether this study is unique to the relationship between Eve and her therapists or whether we can generalise it to other cases.

Fear Today, Gone Tomorrow

1   Because although the treatment groups were compared with non-treatment groups, in an effort to rule out the influence of spontaneous remission, the fact that the control groups received no treatment at all, means that the 'desensitisation – no desensitisation' variable was not the only variable that differed across the experimental and control conditions. The most notable confounding variable in this respect was the fact that the experimental groups received a therapy and the control groups received *no* therapy. So the results may only indicate that therapy (in general) is effective against snake phobia; perhaps any old therapy would have had the same effects as systematic desensitisation. It may, for example, just have been the time and interest of another person (which is necessarily given in the course of desensitisation) that helped the experimental subjects to overcome their fear, not the desensitisation process *per se*.

2   This allowed the authors to examine (a) the effects of the pre-therapy training itself, and (b) the effects of repeated exposure to the feared object:

(a) If the subjects in experimental group one ('E_1' in Tables 11.4 and 11.5) had made all their improvement between Tests 1 and 2, rather than between Tests 2 and 3, then this would have indicated that the pre-therapy training was having the therapeutic effect, rather than the desensitisation itself. Note that this did not happen. No more subjects in E_1 passed Test 2 than passed Test 1.

(b) If the subjects in E_1 had improved significantly more than the subjects in experimental group two (E_2) by the time they undertook Test 3, then the desensitisation process itself might not have been responsible for the change. It may have been the fact that subjects in E_1 had been forced to see a live snake twice already (they had had 'repeated exposure' to the snake during Tests 1 and 2), whereas the subjects in E_2 had only received one such exposure (during Test 2). This interpretation would have been further supported had subjects in control group one improved more than subjects in control group two. Check that you understand why.

PART IV   DEVELOPMENTAL PSYCHOLOGY

CHAPTER 12   ATTACHMENT

Can You Hear Me Mother?

1   In monkeys, social isolation from birth will create severe psychological and social disturbance.

2   First, the isolation experienced by the monkeys does not happen to children, even in extreme cases (see the summary of Koluchová in this chapter). Secondly, patterns of human social behaviour are very different from those of the monkey.

3   Harlow observed that the monkeys sat in their cages and stared fixedly into space, engaged in repetitive and stereotyped movements, and developed self-injurious behaviour. All of these sorts of behaviours and habits can be observed in some disturbed children and adults.

4   Neither term is effectively defined by Harlow. The models were not 'mothers' and they provided very little 'mothering', and so the use of these terms confuses what is happening to the monkeys, and encourages us to make connections to human behaviour that may not exist.

Family Life

1   We can never know this, but it may be that the families who refused access to their children at age 16 (this was one of the causes of the subjects dropping out of the study) were more likely to be having child-rearing problems than those that agreed to take part once again. This would have the effect of making the findings rosier than they might otherwise have been.

2   No. One plausible competing explanation (and there are many more) is that the families which took in an extra child (whether by adoption or by having a child restored) at a relatively late stage in that child's development, might have been affected in some unusual way by that event, and that whatever this effect was it may have somehow fed back into the child's subsequent upbringing. In other

words there may have been things going on in these families *after* the child had been (re-) placed which could equally well have accounted for the authors' observations, and which had nothing to do with the child's early institutional experience. Plausible competing explanations for findings are a characteristic of quasi-experiments.

Emotional Deprivation

1   One obvious one may relate to the optimism of the paper. We all need others to think we are doing a good job, and there is no reason to suspect that Koluchová is exempt from this very human need. Is it not possible, then, that some aspects of this case might have been presented in a way that shows the author in a good light? Or maybe this particular case was selected for presentation to a wider audience because things seemed to work out comparatively well (whereas other less successful interventions have gone unreported)? No offence is intended to the author in this respect. We simply want you to think critically about all aspects of psychological research.

2   The first part of your answer to this question should be a statement that only very tentative conclusions can be drawn from one case study! The paper does suggest that it may be possible to compensate quite effectively in later life for early developmental problems. By the age of seven the twins had spent over five years in highly deprived conditions, yet by the age of 11 they were operating at a mental age roughly equal to their chronological age (intellectually, at least). In a small way this challenges the notion that there is a 'critical period' in early childhood during which time our abilities and personality are 'fixed'.

3   By adhering to established ethical guidelines which emphasise the rights of people who participate in psychological research.

CHAPTER 13   MORAL DEVELOPMENT

The Moral Principle of Justice

1   This is a very significant question, the answer to which has far-reaching implications for many key areas in the philosophy and method of psychology. 'Structuralists' would answer 'yes'. 'Post-structuralists' would answer 'no'. We will not take this issue any

further here. We simply want you to know that it is an important question which may crop up again as you study psychology in more depth.

2   Kohlberg's methods allow children to give responses in their own words. This means that the data which are gathered consist of rich, natural language accounts which can be inspected in great detail for evidence of different types of moral reasoning. Furthermore, the method of data collection is relatively simple and portable.

But there are question marks about the ecological validity of Kohlberg's hypothetical dilemmas. For a start, real life dilemmas might be more complex than the ones he used. Furthermore, the judgements that a child makes about the rightness and wrongness of *real* actions may have *real* consequences for that child, whereas decisions about hypothetical situations have no real consequences for anyone. In other words there are many aspects of real life dilemmas that cannot easily be mimicked by hypothetical ones. This may mean that moral judgements made about hypothetical situations are not the same kind of thing as moral judgements made about real life situations. Gilligan & Attanucci (1988) take up this issue in the study which is summarised next.

The Moral Principle of Care

1   The more agreement in processes such as these that can be achieved between independent coders, or observers, the more we can be convinced that the data are not just the product of one person's hair-brained scheme. Inter-coder reliability shows that the data are being handled sensibly, and that a level of consensus has been achieved about their structure and meaning.

2   One problem is that simply counting the number of times a perspective is represented in a piece of talking does not necessarily give a direct indication of the importance of that perspective in the reasoning of the speaker. Imagine the following (hypothetical) account:

> The one overriding consideration is that justice should prevail. That is of paramount importance. I suppose once this principle has been satisfied, then there are issues of need to take account of. We should look at the well-being of the people involved. We

should also take account of their relationships. Maybe we ought to consider their feelings as well.

The 'score' for this unlikely piece of reasoning might (for the sake of argument) be 3 to 1 in favour of the care orientation, and would then be allocated to 'care focus' in the above scheme. Yet the first statement suggests the overarching focus is on justice. So one potential problem with *counting* as a guide to importance is that it takes no account of the *force* of each 'unit' that is counted. For this to be taken into account one might need some kind of *weighting* of units, so that some units count for more than others. The down side of this is that the method then becomes progressively more expensive and clumsy, with probably lower levels of inter-coder reliability in the assignment of weightings.

Bashing Bobo

1   In the pre-test of the children, aggression was measured using four 5-point rating scales: (a) physical aggression, (b) verbal aggression, (c) aggression towards inanimate objects, and (d) aggressive inhibition. During the experiment, a checklist was used with eight categories (see procedure section) making 240 observations at five-second intervals over a period of 20 minutes.

2   There are a number of methods of measuring aggression including physiological measures of arousal, and self-report measures.

3   Aggressiveness/non-aggressiveness of the model; sex of the child; sex of the model.

4   There is no mention of informed consent from parents, and given the high level of distress in the infants it is unlikely that it was obtained. Also the children were not able to leave when they liked, and were coerced into continuing with the study even when they wanted to leave.

CHAPTER 14   THE CLASSIC APPROACHES

I Want A Girl, Just Like the Girl, That Married Dear Old Dad

1   This is an important theme in Freud's work. He believed that we have unconscious wishes and fears which we repress, but which still affect our thoughts, feelings and behaviour. One outlet for

these wishes is through dreams, another is through slips of the tongue (Freudian slips – when we say what we really mean but did not intend to say).

2   What data, you might ask? There are no *quantitative* data, only his reflections and interpretations of the interviews, so we have no way of checking his analyses. Having said this, there is a growing acceptance of *qualitative* data, like Freud's, in psychology today.

3   Difficult to say because of the great variation in parental attitudes within any society. However, Hans' father feels the need to explain why he didn't give Hans a 'good thrashing', and within today's attitudes that seems a little strange. Also, Hans' father seems to be concerned that Hans shouldn't play with his widdler. We can but hope that this particular parental hang-up is dying out.

4   Not a jot.

Piaget's Cognitive Approach

1   The ability to appreciate that changing the *appearance* of something does not affect its *critical attributes* (such as mass, volume or number).

2   The basic problem is to do with communication: do the children understand the question or the task they are given in the way that the adult intends? Can they communicate their thoughts effectively? Also, does their limited attention span affect their performance on the task?

3   For example: (a) buying a ticket on the National Lottery *and* expecting to win; (b) having an extra drink on a Friday night and thinking that you won't regret in the morning.

The Tale of Little Albert

1   To examine whether the fear response generalised to other situations. That is, was Albert afraid of the rat itself, or was he afraid of the rat-in-that-particular-room? The reported response in the new room did appear to be less pronounced than previous responses, leading to the experimenters 'refreshing' the conditioning once again. This indicates to the reader that perhaps there was an element of situational specificity in the original conditioning, although the authors do not comment on this.

2   Systematic desensitisation. See Lang & Lazovik (1963, Chapter 11 of this volume).

3   Perhaps the single most important method for studying this kind of phenomenon is the clinical case study. Case studies can provide detailed analyses of conditions which have occurred 'naturally' (in other words conditions that have not been created by experimental interventions). The case study is a stock method of abnormal psychology, and usually has the key advantage of being part of a therapeutic intervention. In other words, the point of the case study is not only to find out about the condition in question, but also to provide a sound basis for treatment. A number of case studies have been summarised in this book (for example, Freud, 1909; Koluchová, 1972; Thigpen & Cleckley, 1954).

Chapter 15   Communication

The Dance of the Neonates

1   It suggests that what we are dealing with here is an in-born ability.

2   There are a number of reasons for this. One is that the phenomenon that Condon and Sander were studying (if indeed it exists) is so complex and dynamic that to detect it at full speed as it happens is impossible. Only laborious work checking each individual frame of a film record allows us to see *precisely* how movements are coordinated with one another, and how these movements might be coordinated with speech.

3   The fact that the babies synchronised their movements with a spoken language (Chinese) which they could not possibly have heard before (even in the womb) suggests that there may be certain features of speech sounds which are common to more than one (maybe to all?) language(s). The fact that the babies did not synchronise with just any rhythmic sounds suggests that there is something special about the rhythms of *speech* which babies are able to attend to. Since learning language is one of the most important things any baby must do, there would be clear advantages to being able to 'tune into' speech.

4   One reason is to exclude the possibility that the speakers were inadvertently coordinating their speech with the babies' movements.

5   The adults who were holding the children will have been moving with the rhythms of the speech, and the babies in turn may have been coordinating their movements with the adults' movements.

Listen with Mother

1   If the speech sounds on each side of the room had come from different speakers, and the infant had shown a preference for one or other side, then this might have been attributable to a preference for a particular speaker, rather than for a particular style of speaking.

2   The research was trying to establish whether there is something inherently appealing about motherese, irrespective of who is speaking.

3   So that any preference that was shown across the sample of babies as a whole could not be attributable to a general right/left bias in an infant population.

Talking Proper

1   We could ask how typical Leon is of other Black children in New York. Do the data from one 'case' really permit the far-reaching sociological arguments presented by Labov?

     And how selective has Labov been in the excerpts of data which he presents in his paper (he presents a little, but not much more, than is cited in this summary)? The short sequences of talk between CR and Leon do seem to fit well with Labov's ideas; but do they fit a little *too* well? How are we to know as readers whether the reported bits of data are really representative of all the *unreported* bits of data?

2   In response, Labov might argue that his ideas have emerged out of extensive research experience, only a small bit of which can be documented in any one article. The data that he reports in this paper are used to illustrate his ideas, and the 'case study' of Leon helps to bring the whole subject to life in an engaging and concrete way.

Part V   Cognitive Psychology

Chapter 16   Memory

Remembering Pictures

1   The main advantages are the ability to make causal inferences, the clear and unambiguous responses of the subjects and the opportunity for replication.

2   The main disadvantages are that laboratory tasks rarely correspond to the everyday use of memory, and they commonly use meaningless material which the subject has no emotional involvement with.

3   In these studies on pictures, Bartlett found that people made the following systematic errors: (a) Transformation to conventional representations (b) Elaboration (c) Simplification (d) Naming and (e) Preservation of detached detail. These errors may result from the structure of our pre-existing scheme. In his other studies, Bartlett found that attitudes and cultural expectations could also have a substantial effect on our memory.

Eyewitness Testimony

1   The controls include the age of the subjects, the use of video and the location of the experiment. All subjects were asked the same questions (apart from changes in the critical words), and the position of the key question in the second study was randomised.

2   In laboratory studies people get ready to remember something. In real life we often realise we have witnessed 'an event' only after it is all over. Another difference is that in laboratory studies we have no incentive to either remember or forget what we saw. On the other hand, real-life events bring their own incentives. Famous in British gangland history is the event where Ron Kray went into the Blind Beggar public house in South London and shot a member of the rival Richardson gang. Witnesses to the event had very hazy memories about what happened.

3 For example, food, alcohol, emotions, environment, who you were with, what the event meant to you, and so forth.

4 Students are used to remembering useless information, and are unusually good at memory tasks compared with other people (see the study by Sears in Part VII for more information).

Models of Memory

1 The sensory register, short-term memory and long-term memory.

2 The three stores differ in terms of: how much information they can store, how long they can store information for, what modality they store information in, and how (indeed *if*) forgetting occurs.

3 'Meaningfulness' is perhaps the best alternative (if a little clumsy). It reminds us that the more we work with meanings when we are attending to something, the deeper the processing; the less we work with meanings, the shallower the processing.

4 The most likely rank ordering is probably (b)(c)(d)(a), with subjects in condition (b) performing best, and subjects in condition (a) performing worst. (c)(b)(d)(a) would also be a plausible rank ordering. Remember that this question is best answered empirically. Why not conduct a study yourself to find out the answer!

CHAPTER 17 PERCEPTION

Walking Off a Cliff

1 Depth cues are visual information that help us build up a three-dimensional picture in the mind. Examples are the relative size of objects, height in the visual plane, superimposition of objects, pattern density, perspective lines and motion parallax.

2 There are a number to choose from including the choice by the neonate chicks of the shallow side of the visual cliff rather than the deep side.

3 Three babies crawled over the deep side of the cliff. It also appears that the cue of pattern density has little effect on neonates.

4 The nature–nurture debate explores how much of our behaviour and experience is pre-programmed (innate) and how much of it is acquired through experience.

5   The reason why psychologists explore the nature–nurture debate is because it might give us some clues to the *big question* in psychology which is – 'What is a person?' Are individuals and their societies made by their biological make-up, or are they moulded by their environment? There is, of course, a third approach which is to suggest that although we are influenced by biology and the environment, we, in fact, invent ourselves.

Why Did the Antelope Cross the Road?

1   The trident illusion only occurs if the viewer is trying to interpret the figure as three dimensional. If the viewer is not trying to interpret it as a three-dimensional figure, then it should be no harder to copy than the ordinary trident, for under these circumstances both figures are just 'lines on a page'. If, on the other hand, viewers *are* trying to see the figures in three dimensions, then they will be confused by the illusory figure, but not by the ordinary figure. The confusion would cause copying the illusory trident to be harder, and also mean that they would need to look at the illusory figure more in order to copy it accurately.

2   Ethnocentrism refers to the notion of regarding one's own culture as the norm against which other cultures should be compared. It means in effect being unable to see things from the perspective of other people's cultures. It is related to the notion of egocentrism, which refers to one person's inability to see things from another person's perspective.

3   We hope that you can answer this important question for yourself.

Will the Real Ralph Richardson Please Stand Up

1   (a) They can be used to study actions and events which are difficult to arrange to order. In the case of face recognition, it is difficult to imagine how you could reliably cause subjects to *misrecognise* faces in order to conduct a laboratory study. The diary method allows data to be collected about events which happen spontaneously in everyday life.
    (b) Because the data that emerge come from real-life settings, rather than from the laboratory, it can be argued that they have a high level of ecological validity.

(c) Diaries are relatively non-intrusive. The act of keeping a diary record may not effect the behaviour of research subjects as much as, say, the knowledge that they are being observed or the knowledge that they are in an experiment.

(d) Diary records allow subjects to expand upon issues in their own words. They can be rich sources of qualitative data.

2 (a) Diary methods have all the standard problems (and advantages) associated with self-report methods. Are the subjects telling the truth in what they write? Are the data being influenced by factors to do with 'self-presentation'? And so forth.

(b) It is difficult to tell if subjects are keeping accurate and reliable records. Even conscientious subjects are likely to be subject to biases in terms of the selection of events they record. For example, in this study some types of recognition errors might be more noticeable to the subjects than others, or subjects may feel that some types of errors are more interesting to the researcher than others.

(c) Perhaps the hardest problem to cope with when working with diary methods is a practical one: ensuring that subjects actually do keep up with their diaries. Subjects can find the process time-consuming.

CHAPTER 18 MIND

Autism and Theories of Mind

1 Think about the following event which one of the authors witnessed when writing this summary: Two people were standing in a bus queue next to me. Person A asked person B 'when's it due?' Person B answered 'five to', to which person A replied (in a worried voice) 'you're joking'. Understanding this exchange is apparently straight-forward. But one of the preconditions for our understanding is an ability to appreciate that before asking person B about the next bus, person A *probably believed* that there was one coming some time before 'five to'. In making sense of the brief interaction we are already using our own 'theory of mind'. Imagine trying to make sense of this if you were unable to infer what was going on in someone else's mind.

Furthermore, B would only be able to make sense of A's question by assuming that A was waiting for, and talking about, a bus. Again this may appear obvious, but notice that this very assumption is another act of everyday mind-reading. Incidentally, we could have illustrated this point with virtually any piece of conversation or social interaction.

2   Because if you were testing person A's understanding of person B's *correct* belief about a situation (for example), it would be impossible to decide whether person A was really responding in accordance with their belief about B's belief, or whether (on the other hand) they were simply responding in accordance with their own (correct) belief about the same situation. The false belief task ensures that the response is based on what person A believes person B believes.

3   To make sure that any failures on the belief question could not be interpreted as a simple failure to remember where the marble was.

I'm Sorry Dave, I Can't Do That

1   Dennett used this thought experiment as a spring-board for discussing the relationship between mind and body. I'm afraid we cannot provide a one paragraph answer to these sorts of questions!

2   He is making the point that simply focusing on the observable behaviour of a computer (the Turing test focuses on the observable output of the computer) cannot tell us anything very important about how a computer works. Behaviourists were criticised on the same grounds; you cannot tell very much about how a person 'works' from simply studying their behaviour.

3   Stanley Kubrick's science-fiction masterpiece *2001: A Space Odyssey* – The 'speaker' is HAL the spaceship's computer, which conducts natural language conversations with the crew. The sophistication of HAL in this respect is one of the most fictional aspects of the film (see Boden, 1977).

PART VI   HEALTH PSYCHOLOGY

CHAPTER 19   STRESS AND COPING

Life is Stress

1   Item 12: Pregnancy, Item 23: Son or daughter leaving home, and Item 26: Wife begins or stops work, will all be different experiences for men and women for relatively obvious reasons.

2   Item 7: Marriage, and Item 10: Retirement, are clearly age related. Marriage at 70 and retirement at 30 will be very different experiences from marriage at 30 and retirement at 70.

3   The scale is centred on family life, and one of the major changes over the last 30 years has been the growth in the number of people not living in small family units.

4   There are numerous events that can create stress, for example your football team being relegated (or selling their top player to Manchester United), getting a bad mark at college, falling out with your best friend, loosing your favourite teddy bear, etc.

Stress? I Can Handle It!

1   They measured: (a) negative life change events, (b) coping responses, (c) social resources, and (d) three mood and symptom dimensions.

2   All the variables were measured using self report.

3   Another way to measure coping would be to observe people in a variety of stressful situations to see what behavioural strategies they use.

4   There are numerous possible factors including your mood, your confidence, your sense of self-efficacy (belief in your own competence), your sense of helplessness (see the studies by Seligman 1975, and by Dweck & Bush 1976), and your locus of control (see the study by Rodin & Langer, 1977).

Aids and Uncertainty

1   It is likely that people with a disfigurement will be more shy of any social company, and will therefore become more invisible to the outside world. The term 'people of colour' is used by US writers to refer to people who are not White English-speaking Americans, so it includes Black people, and Hispanics and people from Asia. One reason for their absence from the study might be due to a different level of social support within their own communities.

2   One of the problems is that the study cannot readily be replicated because it is so detailed and so personal. Other problems are to do with the time it takes to collect the information, and to do with the reliability of participants' accounts.

3   Many health problems have some guilt attached to them, especially those that are perceived, rightly or wrongly, as the person's own fault. But when it comes down to it, we have probably all experienced guilt at having to take time off work, or having to cancel an arrangement because of illness, even when we really are unwell. Guilt is often not a *rational* response.

Chapter 20   Health Behaviour

Type A or Not Type A

1   The simple answer is 'yes'. The description of the Type A behaviour pattern seems to be very male, and it is unclear how many women would conform to this pattern.

2   The main criticism, other than the lack of women, is that they did not control for smoking or alcohol consumption.

3   Too many to mention, but some examples are your relaxation habits, your exercise habits, your religious beliefs, your family responsibilities, your weekend bungee jumping, etc.

In Control

1   By means of the different information given to the two groups of residents by the administrator.

2   By means of the self reports of the residents, the ratings by the nursing staff, and some assessments of general health.

3   To control against the effects of experimenter bias (see Rosenthal & Fode, 1963, in Chapter 21 of this volume).

3   Examples might be the fixed furniture, no choice over decorations in the living areas, no choice over the menu or meal times, etc.

Where Does It Hurt?

1   (a) Pain without injury, (b) injury without pain, (c) pain out of proportion to injury, and (d) the phenomenon of phantom limb pain.

2   Measurement of pain usually involves self-report methods. For example, the McGill Pain Questionnaire (see Melzack & Wall, 1985), which has items on the location, strength and type of pain experienced by the respondent.

3   Pain is *usually* an adaptive response. In other words it is useful to us to know when our body is being damaged so that we can take steps to allow healing, or to prevent further damage. If you could not feel pain you would not know to drop the plate which is burning hot and which would, as a result, seriously damage your hand. Athletes who use pain-killers to perform whilst they are injured risk making things much worse because they are overriding their body's natural defence mechanisms.

Part VII   Methodology

Chapter 21   Frameworks and Approaches

Demand Characteristics

1   Some kinds of behavioural outcomes of experiments can be artificially produced by the research procedures that have been employed, rather than by the manipulation of the independent variables. Artefact in this context denotes false, artificial, misleading findings about human behaviour, which tell us a bit about how people behave in experiments, but not much about how they behave in more normal situations. In such cases the ecological validity of the research is said to be low. Experimenter bias is another source of artefact which is dealt with in this book (see the study by Rosenthal and Fode which follows).

2   It can be argued that people have an idea about how they should behave under hypnosis. Most people have seen others who have apparently been hypnotised, and know the kinds of things that are expected of a hypnotised person. The behaviour of people in hypnosis stage-shows may be attributable to them acting out these expectations (responding to the demand characteristics of the situation), rather than to any real effects of hypnosis. Orne has conducted much research into hypnosis and demand characteristics (see Orne, 1966).

Dull Rats and Bright Rats

1   Possibly through the gentleness and frequency of handling. Rosenthal and Fode suggest that animal handlers perhaps give 'an extra pat or two for good performance, a none-too-gentle toss into the home cage for poor performance' (p. 188). Perhaps the mood of the experimenter is transmitted through the medium of skin temperature, or muscle tension.

2   This is an illustration of the so-called 'single-blind' design. Subjects are not permitted to know the true purpose of the experiment, or the experimental hypothesis in case they themselves inadvertently (or deliberately) bias the results.

Teachers' Bloomers

1 If their ideas are correct, then inducing low expectations of children would cause those children to perform less well. This would directly disadvantage those children and therefore be morally indefensible.

2 The result of setting up heightened expectations of a group of children will probably be to benefit those children. There can be nothing wrong with that in principle. However, in practice heightened expectations of one group are probably offset in some way by lessened expectations of another group. If, for example, heightened expectations are associated with a little bit more time and attention, then this extra time and attention must come from somewhere, and maybe it is at someone else's expense.

Who Are Psychology's Subjects?

1 Basically, because they are there! Students are readily available to researchers (who often lecture in higher education establishments). Because of the power dynamics within the lecturer–student relationship, students are very likely to 'volunteer' their help. Indeed, in many contexts it is a course requirement that students act as research subjects.

2 Again, the obvious answers are to do with ease and speed. There is considerable pressure in universities to produce publications. Research grants are allocated on the basis of the amount of published material produced by researchers. Therefore it is financially advantageous to publish as many articles as possible, and it is easier and quicker to conduct and report laboratory based studies. Field work, on the other hand, takes more time, and although it might well produce findings which are very useful, it is unlikely to produce as many publications and therefore will attract less *money*. As 'Deep Throat' says in *All the Presidents Men*, when the journalists are trying to unravel a political conspiracy, 'follow the money'.

Discourse Analysis

1 The resulting analyses can be insightful and challenging. Because discourse analysts often focus in great detail on very small sections of their data, their conclusions tend to be persuasive, and they

avoid the superficiality that some psychology suffers from. On the other hand, one is always left wondering how legitimate it is to generalise from their analyses, given the relatively small number of data sources that are typically used.

2   Attribution theory is concerned with the causes of human behaviour. Specifically, it examines the way in which people come to conclusions about the causes of their own behaviour and of the behaviour of others.

A Repertory Grid Study of Managers

1   To avoid the accusation of 'experimenter bias'. The authors ('experimenters') had expectations about what kinds of construct labels they would find in the grids of the new managers and in the grids of the experienced managers. These expectations might have affected the way they coded the construct labels. Having said this, they could have just made sure that when they were coding they did not know which grid each construct came from. This would have also prevented any bias from creeping in. (For a discussion of experimenter bias see Rosenthal & Fode, 1963, earlier in this chapter.)

2   We don't! This may not be too much of a problem, but the status of categorisation would have been much less in doubt if two independent coders had done the work, and if their respective classifications had then been compared. A high agreement in the assignments made by the two judges would have indicated that the final categorisations were sensible. This is how inter-coder reliability is assessed.

3   There were unequal numbers of new and experienced managers and, in any case, subjects did not necessarily generate an equal number of constructs each. This means, of course, that comparisons of the total numbers of construct types across the two groups would be meaningless.

GLOSSARY

ability tests Psychometric tests which are designed to measure what someone is already able to do, as opposed to what they might be able to learn in the future.

Acquired Immune Deficiency Syndrome (AIDS) AIDS is an infectious disease, most likely caused by a virus, that attacks the immune system making the host vulnerable to a variety of diseases that would be readily controlled by a healthy immune system.

action research A method of undertaking social research which acknowledges that the researcher's presence is likely to influence people's behaviour, and so incorporates the researcher's involvement as a direct and deliberate part of the research, with the researcher consciously acting as change agent.

adrenaline A hormone secreted by the adrenal glands, which causes increase in blood pressure, release of sugar by the liver and a number of other physiological responses to threat.

affective To do with feelings or emotions.

aggression A term used in several ways, but generally to describe negative or hostile behaviour or feelings towards others.

AI See *artificial intelligence*

alarm reaction A term used to describe the series of physiological responses brought about by the activation of the sympathetic division of the autonomic nervous system.

alpha coefficient (Cronbach's Alpha) A statistic which is used to give an estimate of reliability.

altruism Acting in the interests of other people and not of oneself.

amnesia The loss of memory, usually through physical causes.

analgesia Lack of sensitivity to pain.

anthropomorphism Attribution of human characteristics to animals.

anxiety hierarchy Constructed in the course of desensitisation, and comprising a rank ordered list of those stimuli which produce fear in a phobic person.

aphasia Literally speaking, an absence of speech.

arousal A general physiological state in which the sympathetic division of the autonomic nervous system is activated.

artificial intelligence (AI) Computer systems which are able to 'learn' and to produce the same kinds of outcomes as are produced by human thinking.

attachment The tendency of the young of many species to stay close to an adult, usually the mother.

attitude   A relatively stable opinion toward a person, object, or activity, containing a cognitive element (perceptions and beliefs) and an emotional element (positive or negative feelings).

attribution   The process of giving reasons for why things happen.

attribution theory   A social psychological theory which looks at how people understand the causes of their own, and other people's, behaviour.

authoritarian personality   A collection of characteristics found by Adorno to occur together, implying a rigid approach to moral and social issues.

autism   A condition of social withdrawal characterised by (i) impairment in reciprocal social interaction, (ii) impairment in verbal and non-verbal communication, and in imaginative activity, (iii) a restricted repertoire of activities and interests.

autonomic nervous system (ANS)   A network of nerve fibres running from the brain stem and spinal cord, which can activate the body for action, or set it into a quiescent state.

aversion therapy   A technique of behaviour therapy which involves associating unpleasant stimuli with things that are to be avoided.

Barnum Effect   Describes the fact that a carefully worded description of an individual's personality will often be uncritically accepted as valid if presented in sufficiently broad and general terms.

behaviour shaping   A process whereby novel behaviour can be produced through operant conditioning, by selectively reinforcing naturally occurring variations of learned responses.

behaviour therapy   The process of treating abnormal behaviour by looking only at the symptoms, and using conditioning techniques to modify them.

behaviourism   A reductionist school of thought which holds that the observation and description of overt behaviour is all that is needed to comprehend the human being, and that manipulation of stimulus–response contingencies is all that is needed to change human behaviour.

Bobo   Inflatable doll used by Bandura in studies on aggression.

body image   The way we imagine ourselves to look.

bystander intervention   The issue of when and under what circumstances passers-by or other uninvolved persons are likely to offer help to those who look as though they need it.

case history   A detailed clinical description of a person which characteristically forms the basis for some kind of therapeutic intervention.

case study   A detailed description of a particular individual or group under study or treatment.

categorisation   The first stage in the process of social identification, which involves grouping other people into social categories or sets. Research shows that such categorisation in itself, even if based on minimal criteria, can lead to a strong bias in favour of the in-group.

classical conditioning   A form of learning which involves the pairing of a neutral stimulus with a reflex.

cognition   Mental processes. Cognition includes the processes of perception, memory, thinking, reasoning, language, and some types of learning.

cognitive dissonance   The tension produced by cognitive imbalance – holding beliefs which directly contradict one another or contradict behaviour. The reduction of cognitive dissonance has been shown to be a factor in some forms of attitude change.

cognitive maps   Mental images about where things are. People develop cognitive maps as they get to know a town or an institution; rats develop one as they explore mazes.

cognitive science   A multidisciplinary approach to studying artificial intelligence and similar phenomena, bringing together psychologists, linguists, information scientists and others.

colonialism   Political oppression where one nation or culture dominates another one and, in particular, removes wealth from the dominated culture, believes it has a right of access into the dominated culture, and has a power base outside the dominated culture.

commissural tissue   Fibres that connect the two hemispheres of the brain.

compliance   The process of going along with other people – that is, conforming – but without accepting their views on a personal level.

computer simulation   The attempt to develop computer programmes which will replicate human processes such as skill learning or problem-solving.

concrete operational stage   Piaget's third main stage of cognitive development during which the child is able to use sophisticated mental operations, but in a limited way.

concurrent validity   A method for assessing whether a psychometric test is valid (that is, really measures what it is supposed to) by comparing it with some other measure which has been taken at the same time – that is, which is occurring concurrently.

conditioned response   A learned response which is produced to a conditioned stimulus.

conditioned stimulus   A stimulus which only brings about a response because it has been associated with an unconditioned stimulus.

conformity   The process of going along with other people – that is, acting in the same way that they do.

confounding variable   A variable which causes a change in the dependent variable; but which is not the independent variable of the study.

consciousness   The awareness of your own thoughts and feelings, and awareness of external stimuli.

conservation   According to Piaget, the ability to recognise that a quantity remains the same even if it changes its shape.

consonance   In the sense used in this book, this is the opposite of 'dissonance' (see *cognitive dissonance*).

construct validity   A method for assessing whether a psychometric test is valid (that is, really measures what it is supposed to) by seeing how it matches up with theoretical ideas about what it is supposed to be measuring.

constructive memory   The idea that in recalling an event we mentally reconstruct it from a series of cues.

control group   A group which is used for comparison with an experimental group.

cooperation   Acting together, in a coordinated way at work, leisure, or in social relationships, in the pursuit of shared goals, the enjoyment of the joint activity or simply furthering the relationship.

coping   The process of managing external or internal demands that are perceived as taxing or exceeding a person's resource.

correlation   A measure of how strongly two, or more, variables are related to each other.

correlation coefficient   A number between −1 and +1 which expresses how strong a correlation is. If this number is close to 0, there is no real connection between the two; if it is close to +1 there is a positive correlation − in other words, if one variable is large the other will also tend to be large; and if it is close to −1, there is a negative correlation − in other words, if one variable is large, the other will tend to be small.

cortex   The outermost layer of nerve tissue of the cerebral hemispheres.

cost-reward analysis   Cognitive judgement based on assessment of the relative rewards or costs of following a particular course of behaviour.

counterbalancing   A method of controlling against potentially confounding variables in experiments. Typically, counterbalancing is seen in action in repeated measures designs in an effort to control against order effects, and characteristically involves alternating the order in which subjects do the conditions of an experiment.

courtship   Behaviour preceding mating.

criterion validity   A method for assessing whether a psychometric test is valid (that is, really measures what it is supposed to) by comparing it with some other measure. If the other measure is assessed at roughly the same time as the original one, then the type of criterion validity being applied is concurrent validity; if it is taken much later, it is predictive validity.

cross cultural studies   Studies which examine psychological phenomonena in people from more than one cultural background.

cultural deprivation   A construct which has been used to explain educational failure among members of certain classes. Read the summary of Labov's work in Chapter 15.

deconstructionism   Originally a form of literary criticism, but more recently recognised for its value in philosophy. Developed by the French philosopher Jacques Derrida, it is a set of ideas which challenge our common-sense assumptions about the nature of language and its relationship to the world around us.

deductive approach   A research strategy in which theory is used to guide the collection of data which are then used to test propositions from that theory. See *inductive approach* for a description of an alternative strategy.

defence mechanisms   Protective strategies that the mind uses to defend itself against unwelcome or disturbing information.

defensible space   Clearly bounded or semi-private areas that appear to belong to someone.

deficit theory   A way of explaining educational failure among certain children by claiming that they, or their background, are somehow 'deficient'.

deindividuation   A state of awareness where a person develops a changed sense of personal identity which, in particular, leads to a reduced sense of personal agency (feeling that you are in control of your behaviour). The development of the state of deindividuation is often a response to conditions in the social environment.

demand characteristics   Those aspects of a psychological study (or other artificial situation) which exert an implicit pressure on people to act in ways that are expected of them.

denial   A coping strategy/Freudian defence mechanism where distressing facts are eliminated.

dependent variable   The thing which is measured in an experiment, and which changes, depending on the independent variable.

depersonalisation   A dissociative disorder where the individual often feels cut off or unsure of their identity.

desegregation   The political policy of mixing up peoples; in particular the policy in the USA in the 1960s of encouraging inter-racial mixing.

diabetes   Type I diabetes (also called, insulin dependent diabetes mellitus) involves a complete failure of the pancreas, and requires insulin replacement by injection. Type II diabetes (or non-insulin dependent diabetes) is far more common, and in this condition individuals retain some endogenous insulin and are able to maintain homeostatic glycemic control through diet, weight management and oral medication.

diary method   A way of studying what human beings do in everyday life by asking them to note down specific items of information at regular intervals, or on appropriate occasions.

diffusion of responsibility   The idea that people are less likely to intervene to help someone who seems to need it if there are others present, because they perceive responsibility as being shared between all present, and therefore see themselves as being less responsible personally.

discourse analysis   A method of studying human experience by analysing the things people say to one another, and how they express them, both symbolically and behaviourally.

discrimination   The behavioural expression of prejudice.

displacement   A cognitive alteration of reality that involves replacing the true object of your emotions with someone who is more innocent and less threatening.

displacement activity   Behaviour that is a substitute for the desired behaviour, for example, stroking the pet of someone you are attracted to.

dispositional attribution   When the cause of a particular behaviour is thought to have resulted from the person's own personality or characteristics, rather than from the demands of circumstances.

dissonance See *cognitive dissonance.*

double-blind control   A form of experimental control which aims to avoid self-fulfilling prophecies, by ensuring that neither the subjects nor the experimenter who carries out the study are aware of the experimental hypothesis.

Down's syndrome   A syndrome of behaviours and physical characteristics that is the result of having 47 rather than 46 chromosomes.

drapetomania   The tendency of Black slaves in America to run away from the slave owners: this entirely sensible behaviour was defined as a form of mental illness by the slave owners, and given this label.

DSM - IIIR   Published in 1987, it is the revised third edition of the Diagnostics and Statistical Manual of Mental Disorders developed by the American Psychiatric Association.

ecological validity   A way of assessing how valid a measure or test is (that is, whether it really measures what it is supposed to measure) which is concerned with whether the measure or test is really like its counterpart in the real, everyday world. In other words, whether it is truly realistic or not.

effect size   When psychologists detect significant differences in the performance of subjects in experimental conditions they talk about having 'got an effect'. The bigger the differences, the bigger the effect size.

egocentrism   The tendency to see things from your own personal perspective, to the exclusion of other possible perspectives.

ego-defence mechanisms   See *defence mechanisms.*

eidetic memory   'Photographic' memory – visual or acoustic memory which is so accurate as to be almost like a factual record.

elaborated language codes   Ways of using language characterised by extensive vocabulary, complex grammatical structure, and an attempt to make meaning verbally explicit.

electroencephalogram   A method of recording the electrical activity of the brain.

emasculation   Removing a man's sense of his masculinity.

empathic role taking   Putting yourself into someone else's shoes and seeing things from their perspective. The ability to do this depends upon having a sufficiently developed theory of mind.

empathy   In client-centred therapy, the accepting and clarifying of the client's expressed emotions.

encephalograph   Method for recording electrical activity in the brain.

epilepsy   A disorder of the brain characterised by excessive neural activity leading to mental and motor dysfunction.

equal status contact   One of the suggestions to reduce racism, is to encourage contact between peoples where they experience themselves as having equal status.

estrus   The portion of the estrous cycle when the female is sexually active.

ethics   A set of rules designed to distinguish between right and wrong.

ethnocentricity   Being unable to conceptualise or imagine ideas, social beliefs, or the world from any viewpoint other than that of one's own particular culture or social group. The belief that one's own ethnic group, nation, religion, scout troop or football team is superior to all others.

ethology   The study of behaviour in the natural environment.

eugenics   The political idea that the human race could be improved by eliminating 'undesirables' from the breeding stock, so that they cannot pass on their supposedly inferior genes. Some eugenicists advocate compulsory sterilisation, while others seem to prefer mass murder or genocide.

Eurocentric   The tendency to view Europe as *the* main culture in human societies, and to negatively compare all other cultures to Europe.

event recorder   A device used in observational research for recording the occurrence of (and if necessary the duration of) behaviours.

evolution   The development of bodily form and behaviour through the process of natural selection.

existential crisis   The realisation that you are alone in your experience of the world, and that the only meaning your life has is the meaning you choose to impose on it.

expectancy effect   A label to describe the way in which one person can effect the behaviour of another person simply by having expectations of that person. For example, it may be the case that having low expectations of a child in school can actually contribute to that child performing poorly.

experiment   A form of research in which variables are manipulated in order to discover cause and effect.

experimenter effects   Unwanted influences in a psychological study which are produced, consciously or unconsciously, by the person carrying out the study.

expert systems   Artificial intelligence systems designed to provide human experts with an extended information source, to aid them in making decisions.

external locus of control   The feeling or belief that events are caused by situations or by others, and cannot be influenced by oneself.

extinction (also extinguished)   The weakening of behavioural responses due to the absence of reinforcement (operant conditioning), or the absence of the unconditioned stimulus (classical conditioning).

extraversion   A general tendency towards outgoing, social behaviour.

Eysenck Personality Inventory   A psychometric scale for measuring neuroticism and extraversion.

face recognition unit   A hypothetical information-processing unit in the mind which is involved in identifying known people by their faces.

face validity   Whether a test or measure looks on the surface as though it probably measures what it is supposed to.

factor analysis   A method of statistical analysis which examines intercorrelations between data in order to identify major clusters of groupings, which might be related to a single common factor.

factorial design   A form of experimental design involving more than one independent variable.

false-feedback   Providing inaccurate biological feedback to someone; for example, suggesting that their heart rate is lower than it really is to convince them that their anxiety level is low.

feedback   Knowledge about the effectiveness of one's performance on a task or set of tasks. Feedback appears to be essential in most forms of learning, and is more effective if it is immediate.

feminist research   Mary Gergen (1988) suggested the following as the main themes of feminist research: (1) Recognising the interdependence of experimenter and subject; (2) Avoiding the decontextualisation of the subject or experimenter from their social or historical surroundings; (3) Recognising and revealing the nature of one's values within the research context; (4) Accepting that facts do not exist independently of their producer's linguistic codes; (5) Demystifying the role of the scientist and establishing an egalitarian relationship between science makers and science consumers.

field experiment   A study that follows the logic of an experiment, but is conducted in the outside world rather than the laboratory.

fieldwork   Research which is conducted outside the laboratory.

formal operational stage   Piaget's final stage of cognitive development where the child develops formal logic at around the age of 12.

frustration–aggression hypothesis The idea that frustrating circumstances or events, in which someone is prevented from reaching or achieving a desired goal, can produce aggression. Goals in this context do not need to be specific: for example, oppressive or impoverished social circumstances may frustrate a goal of leading a secure and comfortable life.

g The abbreviation for 'general intelligence': a kind of intelligence which is supposed to underpin all different types of mental operations, as opposed to more specific types of talents or aptitudes; also a spot.

GAS See *general adaptation syndrome.*

gedankenexperiment Thought experiment.

gender The inner sense of being either male or female.

general adaptation syndrome The process of physiological adaptation to long-term stress, resulting in lowered resistance to illness and other negative outcomes.

genetic Biological inheritance.

grooming Behaviour associated with cleaning the skin that has health, appearance and social functions; either of oneself or of others.

group In psychology, usually more than two individuals.

group dynamics The behaviour, feelings and cognitions of people within a group.

harem Literally, a domestic arrangement where a powerful man uses his influence and wealth to engage the exclusive sexual access to a number of women; commonly (and incorrectly) used to describe the social organisation of animals where a male mates with more than one female, who in turn, only mate with that male.

hassles Minor irritations.

helplessness See *learned helplessness.*

homeostasis A state of physiological balance or equilbrium in the body.

Human Immunodeficiency Virus (HIV) Human Immunodeficiency Virus is the virus that is believed to cause AIDS by attacking the immune system.

humanistic The humanistic approach to personality asserts that the most important feature of human beings is how they achieve their sense of self and how they actualise their potential.

hypnosis A temporary trance-like state that can be induced in healthy individuals.

iconic representation Coding information in the mind by means of sensory image, usually, though not always, visual ones.

identification As used in Freud's theory – the process by which someone internalises the characteristics, values, attitudes, mannerisms, etc. of another person.

identity The sense that you have of the sort of person you are.

ideology A set of overriding political or philosophical beliefs which govern the assumptions of a particular culture or society.

imitation Copying someone else's behaviour and specific actions.

implosion therapy A form of behaviour therapy based on 'overkill', in which the person is continually faced with the feared stimulus until their fear dies down.

incidental learning Used in cognitive psychology to describe tasks in which subjects are asked to remember material that they did not expect to be asked to remember.

independent measures (also **between subjects**, different subjects) An experimental design in which a different group of subjects perform each condition of the experiment.

independent-measures design   When a study involves comparing the scores from two or more separate groups of people.

independent variable   The conditions which an experimenter sets up, to cause an effect in an experiment. These vary systematically, so that the experimenter can draw conclusions about changes.

inductive approach   A research strategy in which theory is derived ('induced') from the data. See *deductive approach* for a description of an alternative strategy.

inference   Going beyond what we know to make an intelligent guess.

in-group   A group you define yourself as belonging to.

innate   Genetically pre-programmed.

instinct theories   The name given to the suggestion that the reasons why people do things or act in certain ways is because they are driven by some kind of inborn pressure, or 'instinct'.

institutionalisation   A pattern of experience and behaviours associated with people in institutional settings, in particular a lessened sense of personal agency.

intelligence   An inferred characteristic of an individual, usually defined as the ability to profit from experience, acquire knowledge, think abstractly, or adapt to changes in the environment.

Intelligence Quotient (IQ)   A numerical figure, believed by some to indicate the level of a person's intelligence, and by others to indicate how well that person performs on intelligence tests.

interaction effect   The result of at least two independent variables operating simultaneously on subjects' behaviour.

inter-coder reliability   A phrase which describes the extent to which two independent observers ('coders'/'raters') agree on the observations that they have made. Also known as inter-observer reliability and inter-rater reliability.

intergroup rivalry   Competition between different social groups, which can often lead to powerful hostility.

internal attribution   The judgement that a behaviour or act is caused by sources within the person – that is, their character, personality or intentions. This is also known as dispositional attribution.

internal consistency   If a test is internally consistent then the items in that test really are measuring the same thing (or same set of things). Note that this does not necessarily mean that they are measuring what they are meant to measure. In this respect, internal consistency has more to do with reliability than validity.

internal locus of control   The belief that important life events are largely caused by one's own efforts, abilities etc. as opposed to being caused by external circumstances.

interpersonal   Literally 'between persons', this term is used to describe actions or occurrences which involve at least two people affecting one another in some way.

intra-   As a prefix before any word, this means 'within'.

intuitive thought   Thought that predominantly uses the evidence from our senses.

jigsaw groups   Technique used by Aronson to encourage group cohesion and the acceptance of outsiders.

Kaposi's sarcoma   Disfiguring skin cancer found, most commonly, in around ten per cent of people who develop AIDS.

lateralisation of function   The distribution of some cognitive and motor functions to one hemisphere of the brain.

Law of Effect   The learning principle that actions which have a pleasant effect on the organism are likely to be repeated.

learned helplessness   The way that the experience of being forced into the role of passive victim in one situation can generalise to other situations, such that the person or animal makes no effort to help themselves in unpleasant situations even if such effort would be effective.

learning   A change in behaviour, or the potential for behaviour, that occurs as a result of environmental experience, but is not the result of such factors as fatigue, drugs or injury.

learnt reflex   The end result of classical conditioning.

levels of processing theory   The idea that what determines whether information is remembered, and for how long, is how deeply it is processed – that is, thought about and linked with other information.

libido   Freud's concept of internal motivational energy, commonly taken to mean the sex drive.

life events   Major events that happen to an individual such as marriage, pregnancy, unemployment, relegation.

Likert scale   Widely used in questionnaire studies and attitude surveys as the means by which subjects give 'ratings' in response to closed questions. The scale can be any size (often it is from 1–5 or 1–7), and each point on the scale is assigned a verbal designation. For example, on an attitude survey using a five-point Likert scale, a rating of one might represent 'strongly agree', a rating of five might equal 'strongly disagree', a rating of three might equal 'neither agree nor disagree', and so forth.

linguistic environment   A phrase used to describe the language that we hear and see around us.

living wills   A legal document that prevents medical staff from keeping an individual alive by extraordinary means (not allowed in the UK).

locus of control   Where control of what happens is perceived to come from. An internal locus of control means that the person sees it as coming from within themselves – so they are largely in control of what happens to them, or at least in a position to influence it. An external locus of control means that it is perceived as coming from sources outside of the person, and so is not something which the individual can influence.

longitudinal study   A study which monitors changes occurring over a period of time.

LTM   The common abbreviation for long-term memory.

matriline   A family tree based on the female line; that is, mothers, grandmothers, etc.

maturation   A pre-programmed growth process based on changes in underlying neural structures that are relatively unaffected by environmental conditions.

median   The middle score in a set.

medical model   The approach to understanding abnormal behaviour adopted by members of the medical profession, for example psychiatrists.

memory   The capacity to retain and retrieve information.

menarche   The onset of menstruation.

menstruation   See *menarche*.

microanalysis   A detailed analysis of observational data, usually using film/video material played back at slow speeds.

minimal group paradigm   An approach to the study of social identification which involves creating artificial groups in the social psychology laboratory on the basic of spurious or minimal characteristics (for example, tossing a coin), and then studying the in-group / out-group effects which result.

mnemonics   Strategies for helping people to remember information, usually involving cues such as rhyme or imagery.

monozygotic twin   A twin from the splitting of one fertilised ovum; commonly an identical twin.

moral development   The development of moral reasoning in children and adults concerning judgements of what is 'right' and what is 'wrong'.

moral reasoning   Using cognitive processes to make judgements about right and wrong.

motherese   A misleading label for the style of speech adults characteristically use when communicating with babies and very young children. It is misleading because all adults tend to use this style of speech, not just mothers. A more satisfactory label might be 'baby talk register'.

motion parallax   A visual depth cue. Objects and surfaces which are nearer to the viewer move more quickly within the field of vision than do objects and surfaces which are further away. Such differences in the relative movement of things within the visual field facilitate judgements of distance.

multiple personality   A dissociative disorder in which one or more personality exists in the same individual, and each personality is relatively integrated and stable.

natural experiments (also quasi-experiments)   Events in which variables change as a result of natural , political, social or economic circumstance, such that the outcome of these changes can then be studied.

nature–nurture debates   Fairly pointless theoretical debates, popular in the 1950s, concerning whether a given psychological ability was inherited or whether it was learned through experience.

negative reinforcement   Encouraging a certain kind of behaviour by the removal or avoidance of an unpleasant stimulus.

neonates   New-born animals.

neuroma   Nerve nodule which develops at a point where nerves have been cut.

neuromatrix   According to Melzack; network of neurons that responds to information from the senses and also generates a characteristic pattern of impulses that indicate the body is whole and is also your own.

neuroses   Mental disorders where the patient commonly suffers from anxiety but remains in touch with reality.

neutral stimulus   A stimulus that has no meaning for a person or animal before the onset of conditioning.

normative   Representing the norm; typical.

obedience   Complying to the demands of others, usually those in positions of authority.

observation   In its broadest sense this is the core of psychological research. It is not just 'observational studies' that are based on 'observing'. On the contrary, all empirical work is by definition grounded in the act of observation. Experimenters observe the behaviour of their subjects, interviewers observe the spoken responses of their subjects, discourse analysts observe the texts with which they are working, and so forth.

observational study A study which involves simply watching and recording what happens, rather than intervening and causing changes.

Oedipus complex According to Freud: the conflict between a boy's desire for his mother, and the fear of punishment by castration for that desire by his father.

olfaction The sense of smell.

operant conditioning The process of learning identified by B.F. Skinner, in which learning occurs as a result of positive or negative reinforcement of an animal or human being's action.

opinions Commonly used as a synonym for attitudes.

order effects A set of confounding variables which must be controlled against in experiments that use repeated measures designs. In the simplest case of a two-condition experiment, if all the subjects do condition A first, then condition B, and (for the sake of argument) perform better in condition B, a sceptic can argue that this is nothing to do with the experimenter's manipulation of the independent variable, but is simply due to the subjects having practised on condition A, and improved by the time they did condition B (a practice effect, which is one kind of order effect). Counterbalancing, controls against this confounding variable by alternating the order in which subjects do the conditions of an experiment.

orienting task This phrase is often used in connection with memory experiments. Orienting tasks are used in an attempt to get subjects to think about the stimulus materials in a certain way. In a word-list learning study, for example, some subjects might be oriented to think of the words in front of them as just collections of letters (perhaps by setting them the task of counting how many vowels there are) whilst other subjects are encouraged to think of the words in terms of their meanings (perhaps by getting them to fit the words together into sentences). Typically subjects' performance across orienting tasks is compared.

out-group A group you define yourself as *not* belonging to.

participant observation A method of study in which the investigator joins in the social process being observed.

pathology of power According to Zimbardo: the syndrome of oppressive behaviour that develops in people given the opportunity to exert personal power over another individual.

pattern density A visual depth cue. If you move away from a pattern such as a check, then the elements of the pattern get smaller as you move away and the pattern appears to get more dense.

pecking order A hierarchy first observed in chickens where the most dominant animal has preferential access to food, mating, videos etc.

peer group A group of people who are considered to be the equals of, or like, the person concerned.

people of colour A term used (mainly in the United States) to refer to people who are not White and European. It is used to include people from Asia, and Hispanics, as well as Black people.

perception The process by which the brain organises and interprets sensory information.

perceptual acuity Visual resolution or clarity.

person recognition   A key phrase used to label studies which look at the cognitive processes involved in recognising other people. Understanding how we are able to recognise others is a non-trivial task, as has been shown by early attempts to get computers to recognise people.

personal constructs   Individual ways of making sense of the world, which have been developed on the basis of experience. Personal construct theorists argue that getting to understand the personal constructs which someone applies to make sense of their experience is essential for effective psychotherapy, as well as for effective interaction in day to day living.

personal space   The physical distance which people like to maintain between themselves and others. This varies according to their relationship with and attitude to other people, and according to norms and contexts.

personality   A distinctive and relatively stable pattern of behaviours, thoughts, motives and emotions that characterise an individual.

personality type   A simple of classification of people into narrow stereotypes, for example extravert.

phantom limbs   The name given to the phenomenon experienced by amputees, of still feeling the limb as present and alive even though it has been surgically removed.

phenomenological   Concerned with the person's own perceived world and the phenomena which they experience, rather than with objective reality.

phobia   An anxiety disorder characterised by persistent fear out of proportion to the danger, a compelling desire to escape the situation, and a recognition that the fear is excessive.

phonemes   The basic units of sound in a language.

placebo effect   An inactive substance or fake treatment that produces a response in patients.

pluralistic ignorance   The tendency for people in a group to mislead each other about a situation; for example, an individual might define an emergency as a non-emergency because others are remaining calm and not taking action.

population   In the context of research methods in psychology this refers to the total set of potential observations from which a sample is drawn.

population norms   A set of scores for a particular population (for example, females aged 18–24) which establishes the normal range of scores for that population, on a particular psychometric test or measure. Tables of populations norms are used to judge whether an individual's test result is typical for their population group or not.

positive reinforcement   In operant conditioning, strengthening learned behaviour by direct reward when it occurs.

post-traumatic stress disorder   An anxiety disorder resulting from experience with a catastrophic event beyond the normal range of human suffering, and characterised by (a) numbness to the world, (b) reliving the trauma in dreams and memories, and (c) symptoms of anxiety.

predictive validity   A method of assessing whether a psychometric test is valid (that is, really measures what it is supposed to) by seeing how well it correlates with some other measure, which is assessed later, after the test has been taken.

prejudice   A fixed, pre-set attitude, usually negative and hostile, and usually applied to members of a particular social category.

pre-operational stage Piaget's second main stage of cognitive development where the child's ability to reason is limited by their difficulty in mentally manipulating symbols.

projective tests Psychometric tests which involve providing the person with ambiguous stimuli, and seeing what meanings they read into them. The idea is that this will illustrate the concerns of the unconscious mind.

pseudo experiment See *natural experiments.*

pseudo patient In Rosenhan's study, the name given to people who feigned mental ill health.

psychiatrist A person who trains as a doctor and then specialises in mental disorders (commonly with a beard and a European accent).

psychoanalysis Freud's theory of personality which describes how human behaviour is affected by unconscious thought and feelings.

psychodynamic Dealing with psychological forces that influence the mind and behaviour.

psychology The scientific study of experience and behaviour. Psychology draws together systematic studies of experience and behaviour using a wide range of methods, and focusing on many different angles and levels of experience.

psychometric tests Instruments which have been developed for measuring mental characteristics. Psychological tests have been developed to measure a wide range of things, including creativity, job attitudes and skills, brain damage, and, of course, 'intelligence'.

psychosis A mental state characterised by profound disturbances in reality testing, thought and emotion.

punishment According to behaviourist theory: anything that decreases the probability that a behaviour will recur in similar circumstances. More popularly: an aversive stimulus.

qualitative data Data which describe meaning and experience rather than providing numerical values for behaviour such as frequency counts.

quantitative data Data which focus on numbers and frequencies rather than on meaning or experience.

quasi-experiment See *natural experiments.*

race Commonly used to refer to groups of people such as White People or Black People etc. It implies a genetic component to the differences between these groups, but research shows that the term 'race' has no biological validity, and is best described as a political construct.

racism Using the pervasive power imbalance between races / people to oppress dominated peoples by devaluing their experience, behaviour and aspirations.

random assignment Allocating subjects to experimental conditions by using chance, such as a toss of a coin.

random sample A way of selecting a sample where every person from the defined population has an equal chance of being chosen.

rating scale See *Likert scale.*

rational-emotive therapy A form of psychotherapy which mixes rational argument with positive reward systems.

reactivity A term used to describe the way in which the behaviour of research subjects can be affected by some aspect of the research procedure. Most commonly it is used to describe the way in which the behaviour of someone who is being observed is affected by the knowledge that they are being observed.

reductionism   An approach to understanding behaviour which focuses on one single level of explanation and ignores others. The opposite of holism.

reflex   An automatic reaction to a stimulus; often inborn but can also be learned or modifed by experience.

reinforcement   Anything that increases the probability that a behaviour will recur in similar circumstances. The term is usually used of learned associations, acquired through operant or classical conditioning, but it may also be applied to other forms of learning.

reinforcement contingencies   The conditions under which positive or negative reinforcement are given.

reliability   The reliability of a psychological measuring device (such as a test or a scale) is the extent to which it gives consistent measurements. The greater the consistency of measurement, the greater the tool's reliability.

REM   Rapid eye movements during sleep.

repeated measures design (also **within-groups**)   An experimental design where each subject carries out each condition of the experiment.

repeated reproduction   A method used by Bartlett where the subject is asked to keep remembering the same event or drawing in order to investigate the systematic changes that people make in their memories.

repertory grid technique   A system for eliciting personal constructs and showing how individuals use them to interpret their experience.

repression   A coping strategy in which a person forces unwanted thoughts or feelings out of their conscious awareness into their unconscious.

restricted language codes   Ways of using language characterised by limited vocabulary, simple grammatical structures, and a heavy reliance on shared implicit meaning and paralinguistic cues.

role   A social part that one plays in society.

Rorschach test   A personality test made up of bilaterally symmetrical ink-blots. The test is designed to encourage the subject to project their unconscious fears and conflicts onto the ink-blots so that their description of what they see in the ink-blots should shine some light on their unconscious.

S–R learning   See *stimulus–response learning.*

sample   The group of subjects used in a study: the selection of people, animals, plants or objects drawn from a population for the purposes of studying that population.

schema   A mental framework or structure which encompasses memories, ideas, concepts and programmes for action which are pertinent to a particular topic.

schizophrenia   A mental disorder marked by some, or all of the following symptoms: delusions, hallucinations, incoherent word associations, inappropriate emotions, or lack of emotions.

scientific racism   The use of bogus scientific arguments to enhance the power of one group of people over another.

self-actualisation   The making real of one's abilities and talents: using them to the full.

self-concept   The idea or internal image that people have of what they themselves are like, including both evaluative and descriptive dimensions.

self-efficacy beliefs   The belief that one is capable of doing something effectively. Self-efficacy beliefs are closely connected with self-esteem, in that having a sense of being capable and potentially in control tends to increase confidence. But the concept is often thought to be more useful than the generalised concept of self-esteem, since people may often be confident about some abilities, or in some areas of their lives, but not in others.

self-esteem   The evaluative dimension of the self-concept, which is to do with how worthwhile and/or confident the person feels about themself.

self-fulfilling prophecy   The idea that expectations about a person or group can become true simply because they have been stated.

self-injurious behaviour   Behaviour which causes either physical or mental harm to the self. In extreme cases, self-injurious behaviour can become life threatening.

self-report   A number of popular research methods are based on self-report; for example, questionnaires, interviews, attitude scales and diary methods. These are methods which rely on research subjects' accounts of their own experiences and behaviour.

semantic   To do with meaning.

sensory deprivation   The cutting out of all incoming sensory information, or at least as much of it as possible.

sensory mode   The route by which information comes to the brain; for example, through vision, hearing, smell etc.

sensory-motor stage   The first of Piaget's stages of cognitive development where the infant learns to connect its sensations to its actions.

serial position curve   A technique in memory research which looks at the effect of the position of a word in a list on the probability of it being recalled.

serial reproduction   A method of examining the accuracy of memory by asking people to reproduce what they recall of a story, on several successive occasions.

set   In psychology, commonly refers to perceptual set which is a preparedness (or expectation) to see particular forms or patterns.

sex differences   A large body of psychological research exists which documents differences between females and males.

sexism   Using the pervasive power imbalance between men and women to oppress women by devaluing their experience, behaviour and aspirations.

shaped   Behaviour that has been moulded by the method of successive approximations.

shuttle box   Piece of equipment used by behaviourists to measure learning in animals, in which an animal commonly has to learn to jump from one side of the box to the other in order to avoid an electric shock.

sibling   Brothers and sisters.

sign stimuli   A simple sign provokes the response of a fixed action pattern.

simulation A method of investigation where the participants act out a particular scene or pattern of behaviours.

situational attribution   A reason for an act or behaviour which implies that it occurred as a result of the situation or circumstances that the person was in at the time.

social cognition   The way that we think about and interpret social information and social experience. In developmental psychology, the term refers to a theory of cognitive development which states that social interaction is the most important factor in a young child's cognitive development.

social-learning   See *Social Learning Theory*.

Social Learning Theory   The approach to understanding social behaviour which emphasises how people imitate action and model their behaviour on that of others.

social norms   Socially or culturally accepted standards of behaviour, which have become accepted as representing how people 'ought' to act and what is 'normal' (that is, appropriate) for a given situation.

Social Re-adjustment Rating Scale   Holmes and Rahe's attempt to quantify stressors by giving a stress value to a number of major life events.

social support   The perceived comfort, caring esteem or help which an individual receives from other people or groups of people.

sociolinguist   A person who specialises in studying sociological aspects of language.

somnambulist   A sleep walker.

spinal cord   The bundle of nerve fibres that runs up the spine to the brain. It is the pathway by which the brain sends and receives neural messages from the rest of the body.

split-half method   A system for judging how reliable a psychometric test is which involves splitting the test into two, and administering each half of the test to the same people, then comparing the results.

standard deviation   A measure of dispersion.

standardisation   (a) The process of making sure that the conditions of a psychological study or psychometric test are always identical; (b) the process of establishing how the results of a psychometric test will usually come out in a given population, by drawing up sets of population norms; and (c) the process of comparing a new psychometric test with older, more established measures of the same thing.

stimulus   An external environmental event to which an organism responds.

stimulus-response learning   The name given to the behaviourist approach to learning, which viewed it as a simple association between an external stimulus and the behavioural response, denying any cognitive or mental processing.

STM   The abbreviation used for short-term memory, or memory which lasts for only a few seconds.

stress experience   How we perceive the situation and the experiences we are having. The experience of stress is affected by our cognitive appraisal of the situation that we are in, so stress is not inevitable. We might easily see an event as exciting rather than stressful.

stress inoculation   The suggestion by Janis that people handle stress most effectively if they feel they are in control of their lives. To achieve this, he proposes 'stress inoculation' in which people: (1) are given information about what to expect, which is realistic but which still allows them to maintain optimism; (2) are encouraged to identify possible actions that can help them to survive and to find internal and external resources that allow them to take those actions; and (3) are helped to develop their own plan for responding to the situation.

stress response   Physiological changes, such as autonomic arousal, which occur as a result of stress.

stressors   Environmental changes that can induce a stress response.

structured observation   A method of recording behaviour where the behaviours are pre-categorised into a limited framework.

superordinate goal   A goal that over-rides existing goals.

surrogate   Substitute.

survey   A technique of collecting opinions from large numbers of people, generally involving the use of questionnaires.

symptom substitution   The situation where the treatment and removal of one symptom is immediately followed by the development of another symptom, because the cause of the disorder has not been dealt with.

systematic desensitisation   A classical conditioning technique for reducing fear and anxiety by replacing it with a calm response.

T-maze   A piece of equipment used by behaviourists to measure learning in animals, so called because it has one choice point for the animal and so resemble a T.

t-**test**   A statistical test that computes the likelihood of achieving a particular difference between the means of two sets of scores.

task-oriented leaders   Leaders who focus explicitly on the tasks which have to be done by the team, and who show little or no interest in interpersonal concerns within it, unlike relationship-oriented leaders.

taxonomy   A set of categories.

temperament   The stable aspects of the character of an individual, which are often regarded as biologically based, and as providing the basic dispositions which interact with the environment to develop personality.

territoriality   The name given to a set of behaviours which involve establishing and maintaining access to a particular area while refusing the same to potential competitors of one's own species.

territory   The space that is defended by a person or animal.

test-retest method   A system for judging how reliable a psychometric test or measure is, which involves administering the same test to the same people on two different occasions, and comparing the results.

thalamus   The sub-cortical structure in the brain which receives sensory information and relays it to the cerebral cortex.

theory of mind   The understanding we have that people, including themselves, have thoughts and beliefs about the world. Research suggests that autistic people lack a theory of mind.

therapy   The treatment of an individual by physical or psychological means.

trait   A specific facet of personality.

Turing test   In the Turing test a subject communicates via computer keyboard with two 'people' who are hidden from view; one of these people is a real person, and the other is a computer programme. If the subject cannot reliably identify which is the computer and which is the person, then the computer programme has passed the test and can be said to be able to think and understand.

Type A behaviour pattern   A pattern of behaviour characterised by (1) an intense, sustained drive to achieve your personal (and often poorly defined) goals, (2) a profound tendency and eagerness to compete in all situations, (3) a persistent desire for recognition and advancement, (4) continuous involvement in several activities at the same time that are constantly subject to deadlines, (5) habitual tendency to rush to finish activities, and (6) extraordinary mental and physical alertness.

Type B behaviour pattern A pattern of behaviour which is the opposite of Pattern A – characterised by the relative absence of drive, ambition, urgency, desire to compete, or involvement in deadlines.

uncertainty The feeling of uncertainty occurs when someone lacks a cognitive framework to understand their condition or situation, and when they cannot predict outcomes of their behaviour or condition.

unconditioned response A response which occurs automatically to a particular stimulus, and doesn't have to be learned.

unconditioned stimulus A stimulus which automatically, or reflexively, produces a response.

unconscious mind The part of our mind that is beyond our conscious awareness.

universal grammar The cognitive structures of language that are observed in all known human languages and which are therefore said to be universal.

uplifts Minor events that produce a raising of a person's mood.

validity The question of whether a psychometric test or psychological measure is really measuring what it is supposed to.

verbal deprivation hypothesis The idea that children who do not experience extended forms of language may suffer cognitive deficits as a consequence.

vicarious reinforcement A form of reinforcement said to occur when an individual observes someone else being rewarded for a particular behaviour.

wet nurse A woman who breast feeds another woman's child.

yoked control A yoked control experiences the same physical events as a member of the experimental condition, but whereas the experimental condition is able to influence these events, the yoked control is not.

REFERENCES

Adorno, T. W., Frenkel-Brunswik, G., Levinson, D. J. & Sanford, R. N. (1950). *The Authoritarian Personality.* New York: Harper.

Allport, G.W. (1958). *The Nature of Prejudice.* New York: Anchor.

Aronson, E. & Bridgeman, D. (1979). Jigsaw groups and the desegregated classroom: In pursuit of common goals. In E. Aronson (ed.), *Readings about the Social Animal,* 6th edn, pp. 329–40; originally in *Personality and Social Psychology Bulletin, 5,* 438–66.

Asch, S.E. (1955). Opinions and social pressure. *Scientific American, 193,* 31–35.

Atkinson, R.C. & Shiffrin, R.M. (1968). Human memory: A proposed system and its control processes. In K.W. Spence & J.T. Spence (eds), *The Psychology of Learning and Motivation,* Volume 2. London: Academic Press.

Austin, A.M.B. & Peery, J.C. (1983). Analysis of adult-neonate synchrony during speech and nonspeech. *Perceptual and Motor Skills, 57,* 455–59.

Baddeley, A.D. (1966). How does acoustic similarity influence short-term memory? *Quarterly Journal of Experimental Psychology, 20,* 249–64.

Bakeman, R. & Gottman, J.M. (1986). *Observing Interaction: An Introduction to Sequential Analysis.* Cambridge: Cambridge University Press.

Bales, R.F. (1955). How people interact in conferences. *Scientific American, 192,* 31–35.

Bandura, A., Ross, D. & Ross, S.A. (1961). Transmission of aggression through imitation of aggressive models. *Journal of Abnormal and Social Psychology, 63,* 575–82.

Bandura, A., Ross, D. & Ross, S.A. (1963). Imitation of film-mediated aggressive models. *Journal of Abnormal and Social Psychology, 66,* 3–11.

Baron-Cohen, S., Leslie, A.M. & Frith, U. (1985). Does the autistic child have a 'theory of mind'? *Cognition, 21,* 37–46.

Bartlett, F.C. (1932). *Remembering: A Study in Experimental and Social Psychology.* Cambridge: Cambridge University Press.

Baumrind, D. (1964). Some thoughts on the ethics of research: After reading Milgram's 'Behavioural Study of Obedience'. *American Psychologist, 19,* 421–23.

Becker, M.H. & Rosenstock, I.M. (1984). Compliance with medical advice. In A. Steptoe & A. Mathews (eds), *Health Care and Human Behaviour.* London: Academic Press.

Bem, S.L. (1974). The measurement of psychological androgyny. *Journal of Consulting and Clinical Psychology, 42,* 155–62.

Berne, E. (1968). *Games People Play: The Psychology of Human Relationships.* Harmondsworth: Penguin.

Bernstein, B. (1959). A public language: Some sociological implications of a linguistic form. *British Journal of Sociology, 10*, 311–26.

Bernstein, B. (1960). Language and social class. *British Journal of Sociology, 11*, 271–76.

Bettelheim, B.(1967). *Empty Fortress: Infantile Autism and the Birth of Self.* New York: Free Press.

Billings, A.G. & Moos, R.H. (1981). The role of coping responses and social resources in attenuating the stress of life events. *Journal of Behavioral Medicine, 4*, 139–57.

Boden, M.A. (1977). *Artificial Intelligence and Natural Man.* Brighton: Harvester Press.

Boden, M.A. (1979). *Piaget.* London: Fontana.

Bowlby, J. (1951). *Maternal Care and Mental Health.* Geneva: World Health Organisation.

Bowlby, J. (1965). *Child Care and the Growth of Love,* 2nd edn. London: Penguin.

Brown, C.A. & Detoy, C.J. (1990). A comparison of the personal constructs of management in new and experienced managers. In F. Fransella & L. Thomas (eds), *Experimenting with Personal Construct Psychology.* London: Routledge and Kegan Paul.

Brown, R. (1988). Intergroup Relations. In M. Hewstone, W. Stoebe, J. Codol & G. Stephenson (eds), *Introduction to Social Psychology: A European Perspective,* pp. 381–412. Oxford: Blackwell.

Cairns, E. & Wilson, R. (1984). The impact of political violence on mild psychiatric morbidity in Northern Ireland. *British Journal of Psychiatry, 145*, 631.

Calhoun, J.B. (1962). Population density and social pathology. *Scientific American, 206*, 139–48.

Cannon, W.B. (1929). *Bodily Changes in Pain, Hunger, Fear and Rage.* New York: Appleton.

Chomsky, N. (1957). *Syntactic Structures.* The Hague: Mouton.

Clark, K.B. & Clark, M.K. (1947). Racial identification and preference in negro children. In T. Newcomb & E. Hartley (eds), *Readings in Social Psychology.* New York: Holt.

Colman, A.M. (1987). *Facts, Fallacies and Frauds in Psychology.* London: Unwin Hyman.

Condon, W.S. & Ogston, W.D. (1966). Sound film analysis of normal and pathological behavior patterns. *Journal of Nervous and Mental Disease, 143*, 338–47.

Condon, W.S. & Brosin, H.W. (1969). Micro linguistic-kinesic events in schizophrenic behavior. In D.V.S. Sankar (ed.), *Schizophrenia: Current Concepts and Research.* Hicksville, N.Y.: PJD Publications.

Condon, W.S. & Sander, L.W. (1974). Neonate movement is synchronized with adult speech: Interactional participation and language acquisition. *Science, 183*, 99–101.

Conrad, R. (1964). Acoustic confusions in immediate memory. *British Journal of Psychology, 55*, 75–84.

Craik, F.I.M. & Lockhart, R.S. (1972). Levels of processing: A framework for memory research. *Journal of Verbal Learning and Verbal Behaviour, 11*, 671–84.

Dement, W. & Kleitman, N. (1957). The relation of eye movements during sleep to dream activity: An objective method for the study of dreaming. *Journal of Experimental Psychology, 53*, 339–46.

Dement, W. & Wolpert, E.A. (1958). The relation of eye movements, body motility, and external stimuli to dream content. *Journal of Experimental Psychology, 55*, 543–53.

Deregowski, J.B. (1972). Pictorial perception and culture. *Scientific American, 227*, 82–88.

Deutsch, M. *et al.* (eds) (1967). *The Disadvantaged Child.* New York: Basic Books.

Doms, M. & Avermaet, E. van (1981). The conformity effect: A timeless phenomenon? *Bulletin of the British Psychological Society, 34*, 383–85.

Donaldson, M. (1978). *Children's Minds*. London: Fontana.

Dweck, C.S. & Bush, E.S. (1976). Sex differences in learned helplessness: I. Differential debilitation with peer and adult evaluators. *Developmental Psychology, 12*, 147–56.

Dweck, C.S., Davidson, W., Nelson, S. & Enna, B. (1978). Sex differences in learned helplessness: II. The contingencies of evaluative feedback in the classroom and III. An experimental analysis. *Developmental Psychology, 14*, 268–76.

Ebbinghaus, H. (1913). *Memory*. New York: Teacher's College Press.

Edwards, J. (1979). *Language and Disadvantage*. London: Arnold.

Empson, J. (1989). *Sleep and Dreaming*. London: Faber and Faber

Fernald, A. (1985). Four-month-old infants prefer to listen to motherese. *Infant Behavior and Development, 8*, 181–95.

Festinger, L. (1957). *A Theory of Cognitive Dissonance*. Evanston Illinois: Row Peterson.

Festinger, L. & Carlsmith, J.M. (1959). Cognitive consequences of forced compliance. *Journal of Abnormal and Social Psychology, 58*, 203–10.

Fiedler, F.E. (1967). *A Theory of Leadership Effectiveness*. New York: McGraw-Hill.

Findley, M. & Cooper, H. (1981). Introductory psychology textbook citations: A comparison in five research areas. *Personality and Social Psychology Bulletin, 7*, 173–76.

Forer, B.R. (1949). The fallacy of personal validation: A classroom demonstration of gullibility. *Journal of Abnormal and Social Psychology, 44*, 118–21.

Fransella, F. & Thomas, L. (eds) (1988). *Experimenting with Personal Construct Theory*. London: Routledge & Kegan Paul.

Freud, S. (1909). Analysis of a phobia of a five-year-old boy. In *The Pelican Freud Library* (1977), *Vol 8, Case Histories 1*, pp. 169–306.

Friedman, M. & Rosenman, R.H. (1959). Association of specific overt behavior pattern with blood and cardiovascular findings. *Journal of American Medical Association, 169*, 1286–96.

Frith, U. (1989). *Autism: Explaining the Enigma*. Oxford: Basil Blackwell.

Furnham, A. & Varian, C. (1988). Predicting and accepting personality test scores. *Personality and Individual Differences, 9*, 735–48.

Gardner, R.A. & Gardner, B.T. (1969). Teaching sign language to a chimpanzee. *Science, 165*, 664–72.

Gatewood, J.B. & Rosenwein, R. (1981). Interactional synchrony: Genuine or spurious? A critique of recent research. *Journal of Nonverbal Behavior, 6*, 12–29.

Gibson, E.J. & Walk, R.D. (1960). The 'visual cliff'. *Scientific American, 202*, 64–71.

Gilligan, C. (1982). *In a Different Voice*. Cambridge MA: Harvard University Press.

Gilligan, C. & Attanucci, J. (1988). Two moral orientations: Gender differences and similarities. *Merill-Palmer Quarterly, 34*, 223–37.

Glenn, S.M. & Cunningham, C.C. (1983). What do babies listen to most? A developmental study of auditory preferences in nonhandicapped infants and infants with Down's Syndrome. *Developmental Psychology, 19*, 332–37.

Goldberg, E.L. & Comstock, G.W. (1980). Epidemiology of life events: Frequency in general populations. *American Journal of Epidemiology, 111*, 736–52.

Goodenough, D.R., Shapiro, A., Holden, M. & Steinschriber, L. (1959). Dreamers and non-dreamers. *Journal of Abnormal and Social Psychology, 59*, 295–302.

Gould, S.J. (1981). *The Mismeasure of Man*. Harmondsworth: Penguin.

Gould, S.J. (1982). A nation of morons. *New Scientist (6 May 1982)*, 349–52.

Gregory, R.L. (1973). The confounded eye. In R.L. Gregory & E.H. Gombrich (eds). *Illusion in Nature and Art*. London: Duckworth.

Gross, R. (1992). *Psychology: The Science of Mind and Behaviour*, 2nd edn. Sevenoaks: Hodder & Stoughton.

Guthrie, R. (1980). The psychology of Black Americans: An historical perspective. In R. Jones (1980). *Black Psychology*, 2nd edn. London: Harper Collins.

Handelsman, M.M. & McLain, J. (1988). The Barnum effect in couples: Effects of intimacy, involvement, and sex on acceptance of generalized personality feedback. *Journal of Clinical Psychology, 44*, 430–34.

Haney, C., Banks, W.C. & Zimbardo, P.G. (1973). A study of prisoners and guards in a simulated prison. *Naval Research Review, 30*, 4–17.

Happé, F. (1994). *Autism: An Introduction to Psychological Theory*. London: UCL Press.

Harlow, H.F. (1959). Love in infant monkeys. *Scientific American, 200*, 68–74.

Harlow, H.F. & Harlow, M.K. (1962). Social deprivation in monkeys. *Scientific American, 207*, 136–46.

Harris, B. (1979). Whatever happened to Little Albert? *American Psychologist, 34*, 151–60.

Hayes, K.J. (1950). Vocalisation and speech in chimpanzees. *American Psychologist, 5*, 275–76.

Hayes, N. (1994). *Foundations of Psychology*. London: Routledge.

Hess, E.H. (1958). 'Imprinting' in animals. *Scientific American, 198*, 81–90.

Hodges, J. & Tizard, B. (1989a). IQ and behavioural adjustment of ex-institutional adolescents. *Journal of Child Psychology and Psychiatry, 30*, 53–75.

Hodges, J. & Tizard, B. (1989b). Social and family relationships of ex-institutional adolescents. *Journal of Child Psychology and Psychiatry, 30*, 77–97.

Hofling, K.C., Brotzman, E., Dalrymple, S., Graves, N. & Pierce, C.M. (1966). An experimental study in the nurse–physician relationship. *Journal of Nervous and Mental Disorders, 143*, 171–80.

Hofstadter, R.D. & Dennett, D.C. (1981). *The Mind's I: Fantasies and Reflections on Self and Soul*. Brighton: Harvester Press.

Holmes, T.H. & Rahe, R.H. (1967). The social re-adjustment rating scale. *Journal of Psychosomatic Research, 11*, 213–18.

Howitt, D. (1991). *Concerning Psychology*. Milton Keynes: Open University Press.

Hraba, J. & Grant, G. (1970). Black is beautiful: A re-examination of racial preference and identification. *Journal of Personality and Social Psychology, 16*, 398–402.

Hudson, W. (1960). Pictorial depth perception in sub-cultural groups in Africa. *Journal of Social Psychology, 52*, 183–208.

Hyde, T.S. & Jenkins, J.J. (1973). Recall for words as a function of semantic, graphic and syntactic orienting tasks. *Journal of Verbal and Learning Behavior, 12*, 471–80.

James, W. (1890). *Principles of Psychology*. New York: Holt.

Janis, I.L. (1983). Stress inoculation in health care: Theory and research. In D. Meichenbaum & M.E. Jaremko (eds), *Stress Reduction and Prevention*, pp. 67–99. New York: Plenum.

Jones, E.E., Kanouse, D.E., Kelley, H.H., Nisbett, R.E., Valins, S. & Weiner, B. (eds) (1972). *Attribution: Perceiving the Causes of Behavior*. Morristown, New Jersey: General Learning Press.

Jones, R. (1993). *Black Psychology*, 3rd edn. Cobb & Hen.

Kamin, L. (1977). *The Science and Politics of IQ*. Harmondsworth: Penguin.

Kanner, A.D., Coynes, J.C., Schaefer, C. & Lazarus, R.S. (1981). Comparison of two modes of stress measurement: Daily hassles and uplifts versus major life events. *Journal of Behavioural Medicine, 4*, 1–39.

Kelley, H.H. (1967). Attribution theory in social psychology. *Nebraska Symposium on Motivation, 15*, 192–238.

Kellogg, W.N. & Kellogg, L.A. (1933). *The Ape and the Child*. New York: Whittlesey House.

Kelly, G. (1955). *The Psychology of Personal Constructs, Volume 1*. New York: Norton.

Kendon, A. (1970). Movement coordination in social interaction: Some examples described. *Acta Psychologica, 32*, 101–25.

Kitto, J. (1989). Gender reference terms: Separating the women from the girls. *British Journal of Social Psychology, 28*, 185–87.

Koff, E. (1983). Through the looking glass of menarche: What the adolescent girl sees. In S. Golub (ed.), *Menarche*, pp. 77–86. Lexington, Mass: D.C. Heath.

Kohlberg, L. (1968). The child as a moral philosopher. *Psychology Today, 2*, 25–30.

Kohlberg, L. (1969). The cognitive-developmental approach to socialization. In A. Goslin (ed.), *Handbook of Socialization Theory and Research*. Chicago: Rand McNally.

Koluchová, J. (1972). Severe deprivation in twins: A case study. *Journal of Child Psychology and Psychiatry, 13*, 107–14.

Kraepelin, E. (1913). *Psychiatry*. 8th edn. Leipzig: Thieme.

Kroll, N.E.A., Parks, T., Parkinson, S.R., Bieber, S.L. & Johnson, A.L. (1970). Short-term memory while shadowing. Recall of visually and aurally presented letters. *Journal of Experimental Psychology, 85*, 200–24.

Labov, W. (1969). The logic of nonstandard English. In P.P. Giglioli (ed.), *Language and Social Context*, pp. 179–215. Harmondsworth, England: Penguin, originally in *Georgetown Monographs on Language and Linguistics, 22*, 1–31.

Lakoff, R. (1975). *Language and Woman's Place*. New York: Harper and Row.

Landfield, A.W. (1971). *Personal Construct Systems in Psychotherapy*. Chicago: Rand McNally.

Lang, P.J. & Lazovik, A.D. (1963). Experimental desensitization of a phobia. *Journal of Abnormal and Social Psychology, 66*, 519–25.

Langer, E.J. & Rodin, J. (1976). The effects of choice and enhanced personal responsibility for the aged: A field experiment in an institutional setting. *Journal of Personality and Social Psychology, 34*, 191–98.

LaPiere, R.T. (1934). Attitudes vs. actions. *Social Forces, 13*, 230–37.

Latané, B. & Darley, J.M. (1970). *The Unresponsive Bystander: Why Does He Not Help?* New York: Appleton-Century-Crofts.

Lau, R.R. (1982). Origins of health locus of control beliefs. *Journal of Personality and Social Psychology, 42*, 322–34.

Lazarus, R. & Folkman, S. (1984). *Stress, Appraisal and Coping*. New York: Springer.

Lenneberg, E.H. (1967). *Biological Foundations of Language*. New York: John Wiley.

Leslie, A.M. & Frith, U. (1988). Autistic children's understanding of seeing, knowing and believing. *British Journal of Developmental Psychology, 4*, 315–24.

Lewin, K., Lippitt, R. & White, R. (1939). Patterns of aggressive behaviour in experimentally created 'social climates'. *Journal of Social Psychology, 10*, 271–99.

Loftus, E.F. & Palmer, J.C. (1974). Reconstruction of automobile destruction: An example of the interaction between language and memory. *Journal of Verbal Learning and Verbal Behavior, 13,* 585–89.

Lovaas, O.I. (1979). Contrasting illness and behavioural models for the treatment of autistic children: A historical perspective. *Journal of Autism and Developmental Disorders, 9,* 316–22.

Marshall, G.D. & Zimbardo, P.G. (1979). Affective consequences of inadequately explained physiological arousal. *Journal of Personality and Social Psychology, 37,* 970–88.

McDowall, J.J. (1978a). Microanalysis of filmed movement: The reliability of boundary detection by observers. *Environmental Psychology and Nonverbal Behavior, 3,* 77–88.

McDowall, J.J. (1978b). Interactional synchrony: A reappraisal. *Journal of Personality and Social Psychology, 36,* 963–75.

MacDermott, M. (1993). On cruelty, ethics and experimentation. *The Psychologist, 6,* 456–59.

McMasters, C. & Lee, C. (1991). Cognitive dissonance in tobacco smokers. *Addictive Behaviours, 16,* 349–53.

Melzack, R. (1992). Phantom limbs. *Scientific American, April,* 90–96.

Melzack, R. & Wall, P.D. (1985). *The Challenge of Pain.* Harmondsworth: Penguin.

Melzack, R., Wall, P.D. & Ty, T.C. (1982). Acute pain in an emergency clinic: Latency of onset and descriptor patterns. *Pain, 14,* 33–43.

Miles, R. (1988). *The Women's History of the World.* London: Paladin.

Milgram, S. (1963). Behavioral study of obedience. *Journal of Abnormal and Social Psychology, 67,* 371–78.

Miller, G.A. (1956). The magical number seven, plus or minus two: Some limits on our capacity for processing information. *Psychological Review, 63,* 81–97.

Miller, G.A. (1966). *Psychology: The Science of Mental Life.* Harmondsworth: Penguin.

Moscovici, S., Lage, E. & Naffrechoux, M. (1969). Influence of a consistent minority on the response of a majority in a color perception task. *Sociometry, 32,* 365–80.

Neisser, U. (1981). John Dean's memory: A case study. *Cognition, 9,* 1–22.

Nisbett, R.E., Caputo, C., Legant, P. & Marecek, J. (1973). Behaviour as seen by the actor and as seen by the observer. *Journal of Personality and Social Psychology, 27,* 154–64.

Nobles, W.W. (1976). Extended self: Rethinking the so-called Negro self-concept. *Journal of Black Psychology, 2.*

Nobles, W.W. & Goddard, L.L. (1984). Understanding the Black Family: A Guide for Scholarship and Research. California: Black Family Institute.

Orne, M.T. (1962). On the social psychology of the psychological experiment: With particular reference to demand characteristics and their implications. *American Psychologist, 17,* 776–83.

Orne, M.T. (1966). Hypnosis, motivation and compliance. *American Journal of Psychiatry, 122,* 721–26.

Orne, M.T. & Scheibe, K.E. (1964). The contribution of non-deprivation factors in the production of sensory deprivation effects: The psychology of the 'panic button'. *Journal of Abnormal and Social Psychology, 68,* 3–12.

Perls, F.S. (1969). *Gestalt Therapy Verbatim.* Utah: Real People Press.

Perrin, S. & Spencer, C. (1980). The Asch effect: A child of its time? *Bulletin of the British Psychological Society, 32,* 405–406.

Perrin, S. & Spencer, C. (1981). Independence or conformity in the Asch experiment as a reflection of cultural and situational factors. *British Journal of Social Psychology, 20*, 205–209.

Peterson, R.L. & Peterson, M.J. (1959). Short term retention of individual items. *Journal of Experimental Psychology, 58*, 193–98.

Piaget, J. (1932). *The Moral Judgement of the Child*. London: Routledge and Kegan Paul.

Piaget, J. (1952). *The Child's Concept of Number*. London: Routledge and Kegan Paul.

Piliavin, M., Rodin, J.A. & Piliavin, J. (1969). Good samaritanism: An underground phenomenon? *Journal of Personality and Social Psychology, 13*, 289–99.

Potter, J. & Edwards, D. (1990). Nigel Lawson's tent: Discourse analysis, attribution theory and the social psychology of fact. *European Journal of Social Psychology, 20*, 405–24.

Potter, J. & Wetherell, M. (1987). *Discourse and Social Psychology: Beyond Attitudes and Behaviour*. London: Sage.

Premack, D. & Woodruff, G. (1978). Does the chimpanzee have a theory of mind? *Behavioural and Brain Sciences, 4*, 515–26.

Ragland D.R. & Brand R.J. (1988). Type A behavior and mortality from coronary heart disease. *New England Journal of Medicine, 318*, 65–70.

Rawlins, R. (1979). Forty years of rhesus research. *New Scientist (12 April 1979)*, 108–10.

Rodin, J. & Langer, E.J. (1977). Long-term effects of a control relevant intervention with the institutionalized aged. *Journal of Personality and Social Psychology, 35*, 897–902.

Rogers, C. (1951). *Client-Centered Therapy*. New York: Houghton.

Rose, S., Kamin, L. & Lewontin, R.C. (1984). *Not in our Genes*. Harmondsworth: Penguin.

Rosenfeld, H.M. (1981). Whither interactional synchrony? In K. Bloom (ed.), *Prospective Issues in Infant research*. Hillsdale, New Jersey: Erlbaum and Associates.

Rosenhan, D.L. (1973). On being sane in insane places. *Science, 179*, 250–58.

Rosenthal, R. & Fode, K.L. (1963). The effect of experimenter bias on the performance of the albino rat. *Behavioral Science, 8*, 183–89.

Rosenthal, R. & Jacobson, L. (1966). Teachers' expectancies: Determinants of pupils' I.Q. gains. *Psychological Reports, 19*, 115–18.

Rotter, J.B. (1966). Generalised expectancies for internal vs external control of reinforcement. *Psychological Monographs 80* (1).

Rushton, J. (1990). Race differences, r/K theory and a reply to Flynn. *The Psychologist, 5*, 195–98.

Rymer, R. (1993). *Genie – Escape from a Silent Childhood*. London: Michael Joseph.

Sacks, O. (1986). *The Man Who Mistook his Wife for a Hat*. London: Picador.

Samuel, J. & Bryant, P. (1984). Asking only one question in the conversation experiment. *Journal of Child Psychology and Psychiatry, 25*, 315–18.

Sarafino, E. (1994). *Health Psychology: Biopsychosocial Interactions*, 2nd edn. New York: Wiley.

Scarr, S. (1981). *Race, Social Class and Individual Differences in IQ*. Hillsdale, New Jersey: Lawrence Erlbaum Associates.

Schachter, S. & Singer, J.E. (1962). Cognitive, social, and psychological determinants of emotional state. *Psychological Review, 69*, 379–99.

Searle, J.R. (1980). Minds, brains, and programs. *The Behavior and Brain Sciences, 3*, 417–57.

Sears, D.O. (1986). College sophomores in the laboratory: Influences of a narrow data base on psychology's view of human nature. *Journal of Personality and Social Psychology, 51,* 513–30.

Seaver, W.B. (1973). The effects of naturally induced teacher expectancies. *Journal of Personality and Social Psychology, 28,* 333–42.

Seligman, M.E.P. (1975). *Helplessness: On Depression, Development and Death.* San Francisco: Freeman.

Seligman, M.E.P. & Maier, S.F. (1967). Failure to escape traumatic shock. *Journal of Experimental Psychology, 74,* 1–9.

Sheridan, C. & King, R. (1972). Obedience to authority with an authentic victim. *Proceedings of the 80th Annual Convention, American Psychological Association, Part 1, 7,* 165–66.

Sherif, M. (1956). Experiments in group conflict. *Scientific American, 195,* 54–58.

Shulman, H.G. (1970). Encoding and retention of semantic and phonemic information in short-term memory. *Journal of Verbal Learning and Behavior, 9,* 499–508.

Shulman, H.G. (1972). Semantic confusion errors in short-term memory. *Journal of Verbal Learning and Behavior, 11,* 221–27.

Skinner, B.F. (1960) Pigeons in a pelican. *American Psychologist, 15,* 28–37.

Skinner, B.F. (1973). *Beyond Freedom and Dignity.* Harmondsworth: Penguin.

Skinner, B.F. (1974). *About Behaviorism.* Harmondsworth: Penguin.

Smith, M.L. & Glass, G.V. (1977). Meta-analysis of psychotherapy outcome studies. *American Psychologist, 32,* 752–60.

Snow, C.E. (1979). Conversations with children. In P. Barnes, J. Oates, J. Chapman, V. Lee & P. Czerniewska (eds). *Personality, Development and Learning: A Reader.* Milton Keynes: Open University/Hodder and Stoughton.

Snow, R.E. (1969). Unfinished pygmalion. *Contemporary Psychology, 14,* 197–99.

Sorce, J., Emde, R., Campos, J. & Klinnert, M. (1985). Maternal emotion signalling: Its effect on the visual cliff behaviour of 1-year-olds. *Developmental Psychology, 21,* 195–200.

Sperling, G. (1960). The information available in brief visual presentations. *Psychological Monographs, 74,* no. 498.

Sperry, R.W. (1968). Hemisphere deconnection and unity in conscious awareness. *American Psychologist, 23,* 723–33.

Tajfel, H. (1970). Experiments in intergroup discrimination. *Scientific American, 223,* 96–102.

Taylor, S. (1990). Health psychology: The science and the field. *American Psychologist, 45,* 40–45.

Terrace, H.S. (1979). How Nim Chimpsky changed my mind. *Psychology Today,* November, 65–76.

Thigpen, C.H. & Cleckley, H. (1954). A case of multiple personality. *Journal of Abnormal and Social Psychology, 49,* 135–51.

Thorndike, R.L. (1968). Review of 'Pygmalion in the Classroom'. *American Educational Research Journal, 5,* 708–11.

Tinbergen, N. (1952). The curious behavior of the stickleback. *Scientific American, 187,* 22–26.

Tinbergen, N. & Tinbergen, E. (1983). *'Autistic' Children: New Hope for a Cure.* London: Allen and Unwin.

Tizard, B. & Hodges, J. (1978). The effect of institutional rearing on the development of eight- year-old children. *Journal of Child Psychology and Psychiatry, 19,* 99–118.

Turing, A.M. (1950). Computing machinery and intelligence. *Mind, 59,* 433–60.

Ullman, L.P. & Krasner, L. (1965). *Case Studies in Behavior Modification.* London: Holt, Rinehart & Winston.

Valins, S. (1966). Cognitive effects of false heart-rate feedback. *Journal of Personality and Social Psychology, 4,* 400–8.

Watson, J.B. & Rayner, R. (1920). Conditioned emotional reactions. *Journal of Experimental Psychology, 3,* 1–14.

Weitz, R. (1989). Uncertainty and the lives of persons with AIDS. *Journal of Health and Social Behavior, 30,* 270–81.

Williams, J. (1987). *Psychology of Women: Behavior in a Biosocial Context,* 3rd edn. New York: Norton.

Wimmer, H. & Perner, J. (1983). Beliefs about beliefs: Representation and constraining function of wrong beliefs in young children's understanding of deception. *Cognition, 21,* 103–28.

Wolpe, J. (1958). *Psychotherapy by Reciprocal Inhibition.* Stanford, California: Stanford University Press.

Young, A.W., Hay, D.C. & Ellis, A.W. (1985). The faces that launched a thousand slips: Everyday difficulties and errors in recognizing people. *British Journal of Psychology, 76,* 495–523.

Zimbardo, P.G. (1973). On the ethics of intervention in human psychological research: With special reference to the Stanford Prison Experiment. *Cognition, 2,* 243–56.

INDEX

abnormality, 189–214
acoustic coding, 310–13
actor, 25, 26, 27, 30, 31
Adlerian psychotherapy, 198–200
adolescence, 150–5
Adorno, T.W., 57–59
adrenalin, 105
Afrocentrism, 184, 186
ageing, 381
aggression, 121, 246–52
AIDS related complex (ARC), 367
AIDS, 36, 367–72
Aitchison, 92
alcoholics anonymous, 51
Allport, G.W., 57
altruism, 15
American Sign Language (ASL), 90
amnesia, 202
anagrams, 147
androgyny, 157–63
anecdotal evidence, 329
animals in warfare, 80
anterior commissure, 96
anthropomorphism, 117, 121, 131, 220
Aronson, E, 65–8
arousal, 14, 103–9
Arsenal FC, 117
artefact (artifact), 31, 395–407
artificial intelligence (A.I.), 345–9
Asch, S, 5–10, 17, 416
asynchrony, 277
Atkinson, R.C., 310
attachment, 215, 217–32
Attanucci, J., 240–5
attentional system, 313

attitude change, 37–43
attitude survey, 35
attitudes and behaviour, 33–6
attitudes, 33–6, 69
attitudes, 415
attribution theory, 25–32
attributions, 25–32, 145, 419
Austin, A.M.B., 282
authoritarian personality, 57, 59
autism, 340–4
Avermaet, E. van, 8
avoidance, 368
awareness, 100

babbling stage, 91
backgrounding, 139
Baddeley, A.D., 312
Bales, R.F., 51–56
Bandura, A., 246–52
Banks, W.C., 45–50
Barnum effect, 164–9
Baron-Cohen, S., 340–4
Bartlett, F.C., 299–304, 305
baseline measures, 41
Baumrind, D., 22
Becker, M.H., 373
behaviour and attitudes, 33–6
behaviour modification, 198–200
behaviour therapy, 208–14
behaviourism, 246–52, 268–74
Bem, S.L., 157–63, 416
Bem Sex Role Inventory (BSRI),
    157–63
Bernstein, B., 289
Bettelheim, B., 340

498

between subjects design (see:
   independent measures design)
Billings, A.G., 360–6
Binet, A., 171
binomial test, 287
bio-psychology, 94–115
Black identity, 178–82, 183–8
bloomers, 409
Bobo doll, 246–52
Boden, M., 261, 345
bottom-up, 317
Bowlby, J., 215, 217–18, 253
brain stem, 94
Brand, R.J., 378
Bridgeman, D., 65–8
Brigham, C., 175
British Psychological Society (BPS), 170
Brosin, H.W., 277
Brown, C.A., 426–32
Brown vs Board of Education, 65
Bryant, P., 261–7
Bush, E.S., 143
bystanders, 11, 14

Cairns, E., 365
Calhoun, J.B., 129–34
cannibalism, 132
Cannon, W.B., 103
Caputo, C., 25–32
cardiovascular disease, 375–80
caregiver, 227
Carlsmith, J., 37–43
case study, 97, 202–7, 229–32
categorisation, 70, 191
central processor, 313
cerebral cortex, 94
Chelsea FC, 117
chi-square test, 243
child evidence, 259
Chinese room experiment, 345–9
Chomsky, N., 238, 275
chunking, 312
Civil Rights Movement, 178
Clark, K.B., 178
Clark, M.K., 178
classical conditioning, 77, 86, 268–74
Cleckley, H., 202–7

client-centred therapy, 198–200
coding, 28, 242
cognition(s), 37, 104
cognitive appraisal, 360
cognitive development, 261–7
cognitive dissonance, 37–43
Colman, A.M., 22
colonialism, 185, 329
commissural fibres, 96
communication, 89–93, 275–93
comparative psychology, 219–22
compliance, 17–23, 396
Comstock, G.W., 358
concentration span, 101
concrete operational stage, 261
concurrent validity (convergent validity,
   congruent validity), 161
conditioned response, 268–70
conditioned stimulus, 268–70
conditioned emotional response, 268–74
Condon, W.S., 277–83
confederates (experimenters' stooges), 6,
   8, 40, 105
conflict model of prejudice, 59
conflict (emotional), 254
conformity, 5–10
Conrad, R., 312
conservation, 262
construct validity, 160
constructive memory, 299–304
content analysis, 242, 428
coping, 84, 353–72
coping, focus of, 362–3
coping strategies, 360
coping, method of, 362–3
corpus callosum, 96
cortex, 94
cost-benefit assessment, 373
cost-reward analysis, 14
courtship, 123–7
Craik, F.I.M., 310–16
critical period, 223, 254
cross-cultural studies, 236, 238, 324–30
cultural diversity, 170–88

Darley, J.M., 11
Davidson, W., 143–9

deductive, 235
deficit theory, 289–93
demand characteristics, 72, 213, 263, 308, 395–401
Dement, W., 110–15
dependency, 49
depersonalisation, 193
deprivation, 229–32
depth cues, 321, 324–30
depth perception, 319–23
Deregowski, J.B., 324–30
desegregation, 65
Detoy, C.J., 426–32
diagnosis, 191–6
diary methods, 331–7, 377
diffusion of responsibility, 11, 14, 415
discourse analysis, 419–25
discourse, 329, 419–25
displacement activity, 127
dispositional attributions, 25, 28, 31
doll study, 178–82
dominance fighting, 131
Doms, M., 8
Donaldson, M., 261
double blind design, 406
Down's syndrome, 341–3
drapetomania, 184
dreams, 110–15, 256
drives, 128
DSM IV, 189
Duncan's multiple range test, 87
Dweck, C.S., 143–9

Ebbinghaus, H., 297, 299
ecological validity, 11, 22, 60, 299, 343
Edwards, J., 289
Edwards, D., 419–25
effect size, 198
effort after meaning, 303
ego-defence mechanisms, 363
egocentrism, 262, 416
elaborated linguistic codes, 289–90
electroencephalograph (EEG), 111, 205
ELIZA, 345, 348
Ellis, A.W., 331–7
emotional arousal, 103–9
emotional deprivation, 229–32

empathic role taking, 68
Empson, J., 110
Enna, B., 143–9
epilepsy, 96
episodic analgesia, 387
equal status contact, 67
ethics, 22, 49, 67, 82, 87, 237, 273, 322, 412
ethnocentrism, 57, 59, 63, 179, 238, 293, 328
ethology, 116–34
eugenics, 172, 183
Eurocentrism, 183
evaluation research, 65–8
Eve White, Eve Black, 202–7
event recorder, 53
evolution, 183
existential crisis, 192
expectancy effects, 402–7, 408–12
expectations, 195, 317, 402
experimenter bias (experimenter effects) 112, 402–7
eyewitness testimony, 305–9
Eysenck Personality Inventory (EPI), 164

face recognition, 331–7
factorial design, 286
factual discourse, 421
false feedback, 108
false belief, 341–3
family resemblances, 189
fear, 208–14, 268–74
femininity, 157–63
feminism, 139
Fernald, A., 284–8
Festinger, L., 37–43
Fiedler, F.E., 51
fight or flight syndrome, 105
film records, 278–281
First World War, 80, 172
fixed action pattern (FAP), 116
Flanagan's TOGA, 409
Fode, K.L., 402–7
Folkman, S., 360
Forer, B.R., 164–9
formal operational stage, 261
frame-by-frame microanalysis, 277–83
Freud, S., 59, 110, 254–60

Friedman, M., 375–80
Frith, U., 340–4
Fulham Bridge, 117
Furnham, A., 164

Gardner, R.A., 89–93
Gardner, B.T., 89–93
Gatewood, J.B., 282
gedanken experiment, 345–9
gender, 137–55, 240–1, 243, 251
generalisation, 91, 270
Genie, 231
gestalt psychotherapy, 198–200
Gibson, E.J., 319–23
Gilligan, C., 240–5
Glass, G.V., 197–202
Goddard, L.L., 186
Goffman, E., 45
Goldberg, E.L., 358
Goodenough, D.R., 114
Gould, S.J., 171–7, 183
Grant, G., 178–82
Gregory, R.L., 331
group behaviour, 51–6
group cohesion, 42
group conflict, 59–64
group dynamics, 55
group interactions, 51–6
group solidarity, 61
group structure, 60
Guthrie, R., 183

hallucinations, 391
Haney, C., 45–50
Hansard, 421
Harlow, H.F., 219–22
Harris, B., 273
hassles, 358
Hay, D.C., 331–7
Hayes, K.J., 89
health attitudes, 36
health behaviour, 373–92
health belief model, 373
health risks, 378
helping behaviour, 11–16
hemisphere deconnection, 96–102
hierarchies (dominance hierarchy), 116,

119, 121, 131
Hodges, J., 223–8
Hofling, K.C., 22
Holmes, T.H., 355–9, 360
Howitt, D., 15
Hraba, J., 178–82
Hudson, W., 324
hypnosis, 5, 9, 202, 398–9

identity, 49, 150, 154, 178–82
imitation, 90, 246–52
Immigration Restriction Act (1924), 175
implicit personality theory, 31
implosion therapy, 198–200
independent measures design (between subjects), 26, 39, 85, 209, 404
inductive, 235
ingroup, 70–1
initiation rights, 42
innate, 275, 319, 390
instinct, 123
institutionalisation, 87, 385
intelligence quotient (IQ), 171–7, 408–12
intelligence testing, 171–7
inter-observer reliability (inter-rater reliability, inter-coder reliability), 145, 242, 248
interaction effect, 27
interactional level of analysis, 282
interactional synchrony, 277–83
internal consistency (reliability), 159
interviews, 224, 242
intuition, 262
IQ test, 205

Jacobson, L., 408–12
James, W., 103
Janis, I.L., 370
jigsaw technique, 65–8
John Dean's memory, 308

Kamin, L., 172
Kanner, A.D., 358
Karposi's sarcoma, 368
Kellogg, L.A., 89
Kellogg, W.N., 89
Kelly, G.A., 426–32

Kendon, A., 277
King, Martin Luther, 178
King, R., 22
Kitto, J., 139–42
Kleitman, N., 110–15
Koff, E., 150–5
Kohlberg, L., 235–9, 240, 243–4
Koluchová, J., 229–32

labelling, 139–42, 402–7, 408–12
Labov, W., 289–93
Lage, E., 51
Lakoff, R., 139
Landfield, A.W., 428
Lang, C., 103
Lang, P.J., 208–14, 253
Langer, E.J., 381–6
language, 89–93, 100, 216, 275–93
language development (language
   acquisition) 275–93
language understanding, 345–9
LaPiere, R.T., 33–6, 373
Latané, B., 11
lateralisation of function, 96, 98
Lau, R.R., 385
law of effect, 79
Lawson, N., 421–23
Lazarus, R., 360
Lazovik, A.D., 208–14, 253
leadership, 51, 60
learned helplessness, 84–8
learning, 77–93, 251
learning: definition, 77
learnt helplessness, 49, 143–9
Lee, C., 42–3
Legant, P., 25–32
Lenneberg, G.H., 89
Leslie, A.M., 340–4
levels of processing, 310–16
Lewin, K., 51
libido, 256
life events, 355–9
lifestyle, 375
Likert scale, 26, 40, 158–9
limbic system, 94
linguistic codes, 289–90
linguistic environment, 275–93

Little Albert, 268–74
Little Hans, 254–60
Lockhart, R.S., 310–16
locus of control, 374, 381–6
Loftus, E.F., 305–9
long-term memory (LTM), 310–13
longitudinal study, 118, 223–8, 236
Lovaas, O.I., 340
lumf, 257, 259

MacDermott, M., 49
madness, 191–6
Maier, S.F., 84–8
Malcolm X, 178
male violence, 15
management, 428
managers, 428
Mann-Whitney U test, 212
Marecek, J., 25–32
Marshall, G.D., 108
masculinity, 157–63
massa intermedia, 96
maternal deprivation, 215
mating cycle, 126
matriline, 121
maze-bright (and maze-dull) rats, 402–7
McDowall, J.J., 282
McMasters, C., 42–3
McNemar matched samples test, 140
measuring personality, 156–69
Melzack, R., 387–92
memory, 101, 297–316
memory trace, 313
menarche, 150–5
mental health, 191–6
meta-analysis, 197–202
methodology, 393–432
microanalysis, 277–83
Milgram, S., 17–23, 45, 399, 416
Miller, G.A., 311
mind, 338–49
minimal group studies, 69–73
minority influence, 51
model, 13
monkey research, 219–22
Moos, R.H., 360–6
moral development, 215, 233–52

moral dilemmas, 236, 240–1
moral principle of care, 240–5
moral principle of justice, 240–5
moral reasoning, 233, 240–5
Moscovici, S., 51
motherese, 284–8
mothering, 217, 221
motion parallax, 321
motivation, 15, 37
multi-store model of memory, 310–13
multiple personality, 202–7

Naffrechoux, M., 51
nature-nurture, 231, 251, 275, 277–83, 319–23
negative reinforcement, 79
Neisser, U., 308
Nelson, S., 143–9
neonate, 277–83, 319–23
neuromas, 389
neuromatrix, 390
neurosignature, 390
neurosis, 258
neutral stimulus, 268–70
New York subway, 12
Nim Chimpsky, 92
Nisbett, R.E., 25–32, 416
Nobles, W.W., 183–8
non-standard English, 289–93
non-verbal responses, 100

obedience, 17–23
observation, 52, 61–3, 91, 107, 148, 193, 248, 277–83
observers, 12, 20, 26
Oedipus complex, 257
Ogston, W.D., 277
one-way mirror, 53, 286
operant techniques, 91, 284–8
operant conditioning, 78, 81
orienting tasks, 314
Orne, M.T., 22, 395–401
outgroup, 70–71, 72

pain, 387–92
Palmer, J.C., 305–9
pathological prisoner syndrome, 48
pattern density, 321

Pavlov, I., 268
pecking order, 123
Peery, J.C., 282
perception, 317–37
perceptual acuity, 81
Perner, J., 341
Perrin, S., 8
person perception, 331
person identity node, 336
personal identity, 49
personal validation, 165, 168
personal constructs, 426–32
personal construct theory (PCT, personal construct psychology, PCP), 426–32
personality, 156–69
perspective, 324
phantom limbs, 387–92
phenomenology, 100
phobias, 208–14, 254–60, 268–74
phonemes, 279
Piaget, J., 233, 235, 236, 253, 261–7
Piliavin, I.M., 11–16
Piliavin, J., 11–16
placebo, 105
pluralistic ignorance, 11
population density, 129–34
positive reinforcement, 79
Potter J., 419–25
power, 48
pre-operational stage, 261
prejudice, 33–6, 57–73
Premack, D., 340
prison simulation, 45–50
problem-solving, 53
processing capacity, 312
projective techniques, 150
psychiatry, 194–5
psychoanalysis, 208, 254–60
psychodynamic psychotherapy, 198–200
psychometrics, 20, 157, 164–9
psychotherapy, 197–202, 254–60
punishment, 79

qualitative data, 35, 290, 329, 371
qualitative methods, 419–25
qualitative research, 289–93
quantitative data, 35, 371

quasi-experiment, 97, 151, 198, 223, 242, 341, 383, 411
questionnaire, 29–30, 33, 34, 53, 224, 383

racial identification, 178–82
racial segregation, 65
racism, 58, 175
Ragland, D.R., 378
Rahe, R.H., 355–9, 360
rape, 15
rapid eye movements (REM), 110–15
rating scales, 248, 355–9
rational emotive therapy, 198–200
Rawlins, R., 118–22
Rayner, R., 268–74
reciprocal inhibition, 208
recognition units, 336
reductionism, 95, 293, 391
rehearsal effects, 314
reinforcement schedules, 81
relaxation, 210
reliability, 145, 157–61, 242, 248, 282
remembering, 299–304
repeated measures design (within subjects design), 28, 140, 285
repeated reproduction, 299
repertory grid, 426–32
response bias, 308
restricted linguistic codes, 289–90
reversibility, 262
reward, 37
rhesus monkey research, 118–22
rhetorical strategies, 424
Robber's Cave, 59–64
Rodin, J.A., 11–16, 381–6
roles, 44–6, 396
Rorschach ink blot, 205
Rosenfeld, H.M., 282
Rosenhan, D.L., 191–6
Rosenman, R.H., 375–80
Rosenstock, I.M., 373
Rosenthal, R., 402–7, 408–12
Rosenwein, R., 282
Ross, S.A., 246–52
Ross, D., 246–52
Rotter, J.B., 374, 381

Rushton, J., 58
Rymer, R., 232

Sacks, O., 231
Sally-Anne test, 340–4
SAM, 345
samples, 413–18
Samuel, J., 261–7
Sander, L.W., 277–83
Sarafino, E., 356
Sartre, J.P., 208
scales, 157–63
Scarr, S., 289
Schachter, S., 14, 103–9, 416
Scheibe, K.E., 399
schemas, 303
schizophrenia, 192, 202, 277
scientific racism, 175
scientific colonialism, 185
Searle, J.R., 345–9
Sears, D.O., 413–18
Seaver, W.B., 411
Second World War, 17, 80, 413
segregation, 178
self-assessment measures, 404
self-concept, 183–8, 415
self-esteem, 65, 67, 381
self-fulfilling prophecy, 292, 398, 408–12
self-injurious behaviour, 219
self-report measures, 106–7, 384
self-synchrony, 277
Seligman, M.E.P., 84–8
semantic coding, 311–13
semanticity, 92
sensation, 317
sensory cortex, 389
sensory deprivation, 399
sensory modality, 310–13
sensory motor stage, 261
sensory register, 310–13
sentence completion task, 153
serial position curve, 314
serial reproduction, 299
sexual differentiation, 152
sexuality, 254–60
Shakespeare, W., 45, 110
shaping, 79, 91

Sheridan, C., 22
Sherif, M., 59–64, 69
Shiffrin, R.M., 310
short-term memory (STM), 310–13
SHRDLU, 345
sibling similarity, 411
sign stimuli, 117, 127
Singer, J.E., 14, 103–9, 416
situational attributions, 25, 28, 31
Skinner, B.F., 79–83, 253, 275
sleep, 110–15
Smith, M.L., 197–202
smoking, 42–3, 378
snake avoidance test, 209, 211–12
Snow, C.E., 284, 288
Snow, R.E., 410
social cognition, 24–43, 340–4
Social Learning Theory, 246–52
social pressure, 3–23
social re-adjustment rating scale, 355–9,
    363
social resources, 363–4
social roles, 44–6, 396
social situation, 395
sociogram, 62
sociolinguist, 289
sociology, 289
somnambulism, 132
Sorce, J., 322
Spencer, C., 8
Sperling, G., 310
Sperry, R.W., 96–102
split-brains, 96–102
split-type drawings, 327–328
Spock, Mr., 82
stage theory, 235, 236
stereotypes, 251
stickleback, 123–8
stimulus–response (S–R)., 268
storage capacity, 312
stress, 353–72
stress experience, 361
stress inoculation, 370–1
stress response, 353
stressors, 353
structure dependence, 92
subject attrition, 224

subject matching, 224, 242
suggestibility, 5
superordinate goals, 63, 66
surrogacy, 219–22
surrogate mothers, 220
sympton substitution, 209, 258
systematic desensitisation, 198–200,
    208–14

t test, 211, 287, 405
Tajfel, H., 69–73
taxonomy, 54, 55
Taylor, S., 351
Terrace, H., 92
territory, 126, 129
test – retest reliability, 159
thalamus, 389
theory of mind, 68, 340–4
Thigpen, C.J., 202–7
Thorndike, E., 5, 79
Thorndike, R.L., 410
three-dimensional perception, 326
Tinbergen, E., 340
Tinbergen, N., 123–8, 340
Tizard, J., 223–8
top-down, 317
traits (trait descriptions), 30, 31, 164
transactional analysis (TA),
    198–200
trident illusion, 326
Turing, A.M., 347
Turing test, 347
turn-taking, 92
twins, 229–32
two-dimensional perception, 326
two-factor theory, 103–9
type A behaviour pattern, 374, 375–80
type B behaviour pattern, 374, 375–80
type C behaviour pattern, 376

uncertainty, 367–72
unconditioned response, 268–70
unconditioned stimulus, 268–70
unconscious, 254
uniforms, 46
universal grammar, 238
uplifts, 358

validity, 11, 22, 60, 157–61, 299, 343
Valins, S., 108
Varian, C., 164
verbal mental age, 341
video camera, 286
vigilance, 368
vignettes, 419
visual cliff, 319–23
visual field, 97–100
visual illusions, 318, 326, 331

Walk, R.D., 319–23
War of the Ghosts, 299
Washoe, 89–93
Watson, J.B., 77, 268–74, 351
Wechsler Intelligence Scale for Children
   (WISC), 230
Weitz, R., 367–72

Wetherell, M., 419
Where's Wally, 318
widdler, 255, 257
Williams, J., 135
Wilson, R., 365
Wimmer, H., 341
within subjects design (see: repeated
   measures design)
Wolpe, J., 208
Wolpert, E.A., 114
Woodruff, G., 340
World Health Organisation (WHO), 217

Yerkes, R., 172
yoked control, 84–5, 87
Young, A.W., 331–7

Zimbardo, P.G., 17, 45–50, 108